CORPORATE FINANCIAL
RISK MANAGEMENT

CORPORATE FINANCIAL RISK MANAGEMENT

Practical Techniques of Financial Engineering

DIANE B. WUNNICKE
DAVID R. WILSON
BROOKE WUNNICKE

John Wiley & Sons, Inc.

New York • Chichester • Brisbane • Toronto • Singapore

In recognition of the importance of preserving what has been written, it is a policy of John Wiley & Sons, Inc., to have books of enduring value published in the United States printed on acid-free paper, and we exert our best efforts to that end.

Copyright © 1992 by Diane B. Wunnicke and David R. Wilson.
Published by John Wiley & Sons, Inc.

All rights reserved. Published simultaneously in Canada.

Reproduction or translation of any part of this work beyond that permitted by Section 107 or 108 of the 1976 United States Copyright Act without the permission of the copyright owner is unlawful. Requests for permission or further information should be addressed to the Permissions Department, John Wiley & Sons, Inc.

This publication is designed to provide accurate and authoritative information in regard to the subject matter covered. It is sold with the understanding that the publisher is not engaged in rendering legal, accounting, or other professional services. If legal advice or other expert assistance is required, the services of a competent professional person should be sought. *From a Declaration of Principles jointly adopted by a Committee of the American Bar Association and a Committee of Publishers.*

Library of Congress Cataloging-in-Publication Data

Wunnicke, Diane B.
    Corporate financial risk management : practical techniques of financial engineering / by Diane B. Wunnicke, David R. Wilson, Brooke Wunnicke.
        p.   cm. — (Wiley finance editions)
    ISBN 0-471-52914-1
    1. Corporations—Finance. 2. Risk management. 3. Financial engineering. I. Wilson, David R., 1948–   . II. Wunnicke, Brooke. III. Title. IV. Series.
    HG4026.W86 1992   91-32397
    658.15—dc20   CIP

Printed in the United States of America

10 9 8 7 6 5 4 3 2 1

Printed and bound by Courier Companies, Inc.

To my parents,
David and Hellen Wilson,
and my wife and children,
Marcia, Emily, Seth, and Catie

D.R.W.

To Jimmie,
another book with our love

D.B.W.

B.W.

Foreword

In today's ever changing business climate, few areas present more interesting problems than that of corporate financial risk management. In this, their latest contribution to business and legal scholarship, Diane B. Wunnicke, David R. Wilson, and Brooke Wunnicke have combined accuracy with simplicity to produce an elucidating and highly relevant guide to problems we encounter in the increasingly complex corporate financial world around us. *Corporate Financial Risk Management: Practical Techniques of Financial Engineering* is a practical tool that will no doubt serve as an invaluable guide for anyone coming in contact with financial engineering products and their consequences, including bankers, corporate treasurers, regulators, accountants, auditors, and attorneys.

I can think of no persons more qualified than the authors to produce an accessible book on corporate financial risk management for experienced and inexperienced financial risk professionals alike. Diane B. Wunnicke is a corporate finance manager with over ten years' practical experience in various aspects of finance and treasury. David R. Wilson is vice-president of a large European bank, where he heads the corporate trading department. These distinguished individuals have joined Brooke Wunnicke, Esq., author, educator, practicing attorney, and cherished friend, in creating this scholarly text. I congratulate the authors and am grateful for their production of this necessary and stimulating book. It will serve as a useful reference for corporate executives, managers, and members of the legal profession.

SHERMAN G. FINESILVER
Chief Judge
United States District Court
District of Colorado

Preface

Are you reading this preface? Most people do not, and so this preface is short. The authors believe, however, that they should introduce themselves to readers and explain why they wrote this book.

Diane B. Wunnicke is a corporate finance manager with many years' practical experience in various aspects of finance and treasury, including handling the transactions for corporate financial risk management of commodity price, currency, and financial instruments.

David R. Wilson has many years' experience as a banker and trader in currencies and financial instruments. He daily assists corporate finance and treasury professionals with engineering and executing their corporate financial risk management transactions. He also prepares many presentations and teaches business students.

Brooke Wunnicke, Esq. is a practicing lawyer with many years' business law experience, including teaching and writing about complicated legal matters. This experience gives perspective to the broad legal framework and some current issues presented by the contracts for corporate financial risk management. Brooke is also our referee. Brooke Wunnicke and Diane B. Wunnicke are coauthors of *Standby Letters of Credit* (Wiley Law 1989, and Supps.).

David and Diane wrote this book because so many business friends—"corporates," bankers, and hedge brokers—said a book like this was needed and someone with "hands on" experience should write it. We thought that the legal dimension of financial engineering would be a desirable addition to the book, and so we "volunteered" Brooke because many corporate professionals use and understand *Standby Letters of Credit*.

We quickly learned why this book had not yet been written and are proud that we are, all three, still good friends. A clear and practical

ix

explanation of an inherently complex, broad, and diverse topic is not easy. Because the topic lends itself to at least three or four books, a big problem has been to define a useful scope for this book without misleading the reader with oversimplification.

We hope that you find this book a useful and practical guide with helpful suggestions, and a convenient reference.

DIANE B. WUNNICKE
DAVID R. WILSON
BROOKE WUNNICKE

Denver, Colorado
New York, New York
Denver, Colorado
March 1992

Acknowledgments

FROM DAVID R. WILSON:

This book was the product of the knowledge, experience, and advice of many professionals in financial markets today. Special thanks go to Ben Wells, David Barnhart, and Sybil Cannan, who reviewed the text and provided invaluable help and critiques. It was an imposition on friends who came through cheerfully and frankly. The book is the better for their efforts.

I would like to thank my colleagues with whom I work, for their ideas and support while the project developed. I also acknowledge Joe Spendley, who always looks at matters and events from different sides and often provides fresh perceptions.

Many friends and former colleagues have contributed thoughts and inspiration over the years. In no particular order, some of those professionals are: Jack and Elizabeth Bortz, Bob Hemstreet, Martin Yecies, Sal Constantino, Bill Orsini, Howard Adamski, Frank Pusateri, Harry Guardiola, Keith Mc-Cutcheon, Alan Ghazi, Noemi Camacho, Aurelio Areans, Bernard Graham, and Paul Bodin. I know that I have missed many friends' names who over the years have enhanced this effort through their influence on my career.

Most importantly, very special thanks to my best friend, Marcia, who always seemed to know when to ask how the book was going and when to tell me to go play golf. To Emily, Seth, and Catie, thank you for putting up with me while I worked on this project.

D.R.W.

FROM DIANE AND BROOKE WUNNICKE:

We have many grateful acknowledgements to those who have helped us with this book. To Honorable Sherman G. Finesilver: thank you for your consideration of our continuing efforts to present practical business issues in the context of law and for your generous foreword. Jerry Brown provided continuing inspiration to complete this book and important insights and perspective; Emma, thank you very much. We thank Harold Riley Roth (BA, MBA, JD, LLM in Taxation, and CPA) for reviewing the essential, but less than lively, chapter on accounting and tax highlights; Connie, thank you for sharing Hal's time and brightening our authors' lives with your basset hounds. We join with David in thanking Ben Wells for his thorough review and helpful comments. Thank you to Mary Davey for unflagging good humor with Diane's many telephone calls to David. Diane also appreciates the enthusiasm, illustrative vignettes, and advice from many business colleagues.

We also are grateful to our friends, both those previously acknowledged for sharing their expertise and those who provided their hospitality and loving support while we labored over this book.

D.B.W.
B.W.

From All the Authors:

Last but certainly not least, the authors appreciate John Wiley & Sons for undertaking to publish this book.

A special tribute from the authors to Maryan J. Malone of Publications Development Company of Texas, for her gracious guidance and constructive editing of the manuscript.

D.B.W.
D.R.W.
B.W.

Contents

13 Selected Developments in the Legal Arena   267

List of Tables and Figures

Tables

Figures

PART ONE
CONCEPTS AND ISSUES

1
Meet the Book

Zeal should not outrun discretion.
Look before you leap.

The Fables of Aesop (300 B.C.)

Does your business activity ever involve financial risk? Do commodity prices affect your cost of goods sold or the price or volume of your sales? Do changes in interest rates affect your interest expense or interest income on surplus cash? Do you ever have a foreign currency exposure? If you have none of these financial risks, ever, call us so we can all go into your line of business!

SHOULD YOU BUY THIS BOOK?

No, if you are looking for a book about the theories expounded for corporate financial risk management.
Yes, if you answered *yes* to the questions above.
Yes, if you provide professional services or counsel to businesses.
Yes, if the businesses you counsel would answer *yes* to the questions above.
Yes, if the following description of this book meets your objectives.

A SQUARE-ONE BOOK

To drive a car successfully, you do not need to understand the physics or engineering of the internal combustion engine, the transmission, or the

3

suspension system of the car. Understanding the machine's theoretical physics will not help you to avoid an unwanted meeting with an oncoming car or any other mobile or immobile object. You only need to know what the various knobs, buttons, pedals, levers, and wheels will do when you manipulate them. The best and most reliable drivers can drive any car, whether it's top-of-the-line in electronic gadgetry or rolling past 100,000 miles with all its old-style knobs, buttons, dials, and wheels still functioning. In your financial responsibilities, you should know how to "drive" any vehicle, new or old. This book will tell you how and will help you avoid unpleasant or even disastrous events.

This book is a square-one, practical guide for the financial engineering you will need to deal with problems of corporate financial risk management.

Many books and articles cover topics like options and debate the virtues of alternative pricing models for arriving at the "true value" of an option premium. This book takes the approach that the true value of anything is the amount a buyer will pay for it and a seller will take to part with it. Very little is written about what to do with an option "beast" after bringing it home to guard the corporate financial risk house. This book deals with the care and feeding of beasts, not their molecular physiology.

A single volume cannot be a comprehensive guide to all aspects of our topic. Our examples show over-the-counter contracts more than exchange-traded contracts—a result of book-length restrictions, not of preference. We selected the following basics of financial engineering for discussion:

- What are the basic tools of financial engineering and how are they bought and sold?
- How can the basic tools be combined for financial engineering?
- What is the problem, exactly defined?
- What are suitable tools to select, and when should they be selected?

The text is divided into three parts plus appendixes, including an important Functional Glossary.

- Part One, Concepts and Issues, defines and discusses *underlyings*— commodities, currencies, financial instruments/interest rates, and indexes; the basic tools, and derivatives and combinations of the basic tools; swaps; and the legal framework.
- Part Two, Business Studies, covers major categories of business activity—for example, importers, multinationals, repatriations, borrowers, and cash investors. Each Business Study has both good and bad examples and detailed cases, and offers discussion of related corporate finance risk management issues and strategies.
- Part Three, Making the Decision, includes practical considerations for defining and estimating risk, managing credit for contracts,

administration and internal controls, financial reporting and tax issues, and current legal issues.

The appendixes are important to using this book. Appendix A, the Functional Glossary, is a unique and comprehensive reference source for this area of finance. Throughout the book, all business terms introduced in italics are defined in the Functional Glossary. Appendix B provides reference sources—useful periodical articles, books dealing with the theories behind the tools for financial engineering, and addresses for obtaining reference materials from regulated exchanges and similar outlets. Appendix C is the International Swap Dealers Association (ISDA) Interest Rate and Currency Exchange Agreement; a complete exhibition of all financial engineering contracts forms would fill another book.

For different readers, the book is intended to serve different purposes. For the reader whose experience does not extend to all of futures contracts, forward contracts, options, swaps, and the myriad combinations of methods for managing corporate finance risks, the detailed case examples in the business studies can serve a "how to" purpose. Assorted types of companies, the financial risks they are trying to manage, and the applicable calculations are presented. The reader can select the business studies that appear to be most similar to a particular business problem, study the cases—with reference to the Functional Glossary—and then substitute the facts and figures of the reader's problem into the analysis and calculations shown. The cases are written in narrative form to provide practical nuts-and-bolts descriptions. Alternatives and evaluations are included because there is seldom only one "right way" for resolving a corporate financial risk management problem.

For the reader who is more experienced in using the types of contracts discussed, the business studies are intended to provide a convenient reference, to act as reminders, especially when training or making presentations to others, and to share the authors' ideas, garnered from their personal experiences.

For lawyers, regulators, central bankers, accountants, auditors, and anyone else coming in contact with the financial engineering products and their consequences, this can be both a general and specific sourcebook.

NEW NEEDS FOR NEW STRATEGIES

United States businesses compete in the U.S. market with both domestic and foreign companies; many U.S. businesses also compete in markets throughout the world. Foreign investment and ownership of U.S. companies brings the skills of foreign competitors to the U.S. market. The geographic dimension has been well summarized:

But it's not just Far Eastern cultures U.S. corporations should be studying. European companies . . . are demonstrating an admirable flexibility and adeptness at managing both business and financial risk. That threatens to deprive corporate America of precious margins and market share as it expands international sales. America's corporate culture will have to adapt quickly, bankers and businessmen agree . . . .[1]

As the global financial world shrinks because of almost instantaneous telecommunication, the volume and diversity of participants and contracts for financial risk management increase. For example, in 1990, Tokyo's Japanese bond futures contract, after trading for only 2 years, was already trading more in value than the Chicago Board of Trade's Treasury Bond futures contract.[2]

For a producer or consumer of raw commodities, controlling price risk has been an issue for many years. The classic, almost trite, example is the farmer who borrows money to plant wheat in the spring, not knowing what price will be received when the wheat is harvested nor what interest rates on the loan might do. The baker does not know in June what the price will be for holiday-season pastries. New strategies are continuously being devised and old techniques adapted to meet those needs.

In recent years, the problems of controlling interest rate risk and foreign exchange risk have also come to the fore. Stable interest rates were a "rule of the game" through the mid- to late 1960s. A ½ percent change in long-term interest rates over the course of a year was considered a major market event. The 1970s buried that pleasant assumption. The events of the 1980s taught both borrowers and investors a great deal about the impact of volatile interest rates—on their loans, their portfolios, and their professional careers.[3]

In 1973, financial professionals learned about a new area of corporate financial risk. That was the year when the major industrial countries finally abandoned pegging foreign exchange rates to some outside standard unit of measure such as the price of gold. Ever since, finance managers have been wrestling with the problems of measuring, controlling, and taking advantage of fluctuations in currency values.

---

[1] Laughlin, "Risk Management's Many Cultures," *Corporate Risk Management* (January/February 1990): 40.
[2] Hargreaves, *Financial Times* (London), March 2, 1990, sec. III, p. 1.
[3] Simpson, "Developments in the U.S. Financial System since the Mid-1970s," *Federal Reserve Bulletin,* 74 (January, 1988): 1–13. This short article is an excellent summary, with startling statistics, of the changes and volatilities in commodity prices, interest rates, and foreign exchange rates.

WHAT ABOUT FINANCIAL ENGINEERING?

"Fun! What a startling word. Engineering is fun, and similar to the creative arts in providing fulfillment."[4]

The tasks, however, may not be simple, and seldom can financial engineering be precise. The word "manage," in this book, has a very broad meaning: it describes any number of intentions ranging between the concept of controlling or eliminating to the concept of speculating that a market event will occur.

Given the breadth of topics addressed, a reader might well ask (as did some friends), "Why would anyone write this book?"

To manage and exploit market fluctuations, whole new finance professions have developed. Businesses now have available a full range of tools designed to help insure them against fluctuations in commodity prices, foreign exchange rates, and interest rate changes. The term "financial engineering" has been coined to describe a group of products, tools, services, techniques, and instruments developed to manage those risks. In many cases, the term is abused. Some people use it to imply that they have invented some startling new tool that is uniquely their own.

In fact, the new tools are often derivatives or new applications of very old financial instruments. The *currency swap,* for example, is a derivative of a parallel loan. "Financial engineers" sometimes combine two existing instruments and give the combination a new name. A "cylinder" is a combination of two options that is designed to avoid the expense of a premium. Financial engineering is truly an evolutionary process, not a revolutionary one.

There are many books and articles about volatility in markets, tracked in charts of prices jumping up and down. These issues and histories are not in the scope of this book. Brochures prepared for corporate financial risk managers will almost invariably include background about the price fluctuations of whatever is being recommended to be hedged. The reader is reminded to examine closely the scales on the charts, to see that the layout or graph scales do not exaggerate the price data fluctuations as part of the sales pitch for entering into a hedge contract.

The purpose of this book is to give the reader exposure to the basics of how financial engineering is done. Simple, and even simplistic, examples show how people use different financial instruments to hedge corporate financial risk in different situations. An important goal is to give the reader the foundation needed to be able to take apart a hedging tool in order to look at its parts. The authors hope the reader will obtain enough information to ask square-one questions when confronted with a cryptic chart and a wordy description of a "new" or "proprietary" product for corporate financial risk management.

[4] Florman, *The Existential Pleasures of Engineering* (1976), 95.

2
Foundations

The only dumb question is the question not asked.

An anonymous wise person

This chapter and Chapter 3 work together. This chapter explains the foundations—the basic contracts for corporate financial risk management and the markets for those contracts. Chapter 3 explains the derivatives of the foundations: options, swaps, and combinations of contractual tools. Chapters 2 and 3 combine to be a nontechnical reference for anyone involved with the management of corporate financial risks—corporate finance persons; those involved with operations, accounting, or legal activities; corporate officers and directors. These two chapters are not directed toward individuals who have significant experience in the highly sophisticated application of all these tools. Some parts of the two chapters may form a convenient reference for those preparing presentations about proposed corporate finance risk management strategies. Finance professionals, including bankers and *hedge* brokers, may find the chapters helpful in explaining to others what instruments are used under the general heading "financial engineering."

Chapters 2 and 3 are structured as follows:

- Chapter 2 introduces commodities, currencies, financial instruments, and newer indexes "underlying" the financial engineering described throughout the book. Figure 2.1 is a checklist for defining a specific underlying. The basic concepts and jargon for prices of commodities, foreign exchange, and financial instruments are explained. Cash, forward, and futures contracts are compared, settlement is discussed, and "basis" or "differential" is introduced.
- Chapter 3 introduces some of the derivative contracts that have been developed over many years. The oldest is the option contract. New

9

contracts are introduced and compared: cap and floor, collar, cylinder, range forward, tunnel, and participations. There is also an introduction to commodity and capital market swaps. (Definitions and comparisons of swaps are in Appendix A.) Combinations of futures contracts and exchange-traded options are introduced: synthetic options, spreads, straddles, and strangles.

Some cautions are given, to warn against backward quotations between markets, what is "better and smaller" or "worse and bigger" in foreign exchange rates, and other important caveats.

——— **Type of Underlying**   What are the name and standard unit of measure, for example: barrels of crude oil, pounds of pork bellies, dollars worth of Treasury Bills or borrowed funds, and number of Deutsche Marks?

——— **Quantity**   How much is the corporation *long* or *short* during the time period(s) of finance risk? Is the quantity evaluated for any adjustments, for example, royalties in kind on crude oil?

——— **Grade and Quality**   For a commodity, what is the exact quality and grade? For a currency, are there any applicable restrictions by its home country or elsewhere (e.g., domestic versus foreign lire)? For a financial instrument, is there a specific description (e.g., details of a bill, note, or bond, or, for borrowed funds, details of the credit agreement's rate-setting alternatives)? For an index, are the exact composition of the index and the frequency of its updated computation stated?

——— **Delivery, Time Period(s), Location(s), and Procedure(s)**   Are the details of timing (including timing for any instructions), location, and procedures for physical delivery or payments clearly stated? Are alternatives (if any) for the usual or planned deliveries or payments identified? Has "basis risk" been evaluated?

——— **Documentation**   Is the documentation required for evidencing ownership and transfer of title valid and complete? Are the documents showing corporate authority for the entity to enter into the contracts for financial risk management transactions, and the credentials of the individual(s) with authority to enter into contracts binding the corporation or other legal entity properly validated?

——— **Failure to Perform or Pay**   Are there any penalties for late or failing performance or payment and, if applicable, are there general credit assurance alternatives for transactions in the underlying? (Each market has its customs and traditions for "fails"—failures to make payment and take delivery at the time required by the contract.)

FIGURE 2.1   Checklist for defining an underlying.

THE UNDERLYINGS

In this book, the *underlyings* are commodities, currencies, financial instruments, and indexes. These underlyings are briefly categorized as follows:

- *Commodities* include raw materials, semimanufactured goods, and physical products in primary form. Metals, lumber, pork bellies, oranges, crude oil, and refined petroleum products are examples.
- *Currencies* are the legal tender of any country or the rate for exchanging a currency into another currency (foreign exchange).
- *Financial instruments* include short-term debt instruments traded in the *money market,* such as U.S. Treasury Bills, corporate commercial paper, and *Eurodollars;* middle- and long-term debt instruments traded in the *capital markets,* such as U.S. Treasury Notes, U.S. Treasury Bonds, and corporate bonds; and equities, the common stocks of corporations.
- *Indexes* are the computed averages of a group of prices or measurements, often expressed as a percentage of a base period index of 100. Contracts can be defined using indexes as underlyings. Some examples are: indexes of commodities prices (CRB Index), indexes of currencies, and indexes of financial instruments, such as the S&P 500 and similar indexes of selected equities' prices.

Most of the published financial quotations are sorted into the first three broad categories—commodities, currencies, and financial instruments sorted into government and corporate debt and equities. The index quotations are usually shown near the underlyings they measure or in a category called "index trading."

Quantity, quality, time, and cost are essential elements in any definition of an underlying. An understanding of the concept and exact nature or composition—including any logistics and time for delivery—of an underlying commodity, currency, financial instrument, or index is necessary before trying to trade it in any market, trying to design a suitable corporate financial risk management strategy, or hedging the underlying or one of its features through a *derivative* contract or swap.

Banks and brokers marketing corporate finance risk management products may dazzle with phrases like *basis, duration,* and *synthetics,* but the corporate financial risk manager who fully understands and documents the features of the underlying will not be confused (for very long, anyway) by fancy jargon. A friendly trader once commented, "It's easy to get sloppy about that," referring to the exact description of an underlying for a trade.

As shown in Figure 2.1, a checklist for defining any underlying can be created from the general categories of the same or a similar underlying's regulated futures contracts. If the underlying commodity, currency, financial instrument, or index has an exchange-traded futures contract, using the futures contract's specifications will make the checklist easier to prepare—even if dealing in futures contracts is not planned. Futures contract specifications precisely define an underlying and serve as a reminder of both common and unique features. Derivative contracts and many *swaps* involve prices for features of an underlying, so the checklist is useful preparation.

The items in Figure 2.1 form a broad structure for documenting all aspects of an underlying commodity, currency, financial instrument, or index before setting forth into the markets and selecting tools to use.

WHAT'S IN A PRICE?

The answer to that question comes in three steps:

1. Understanding the price quotations for a commodity, currency, or financial instrument;
2. Understanding whether and when a position is long or short;
3. Understanding both, in order to understand whether a price change is favorable or unfavorable.

These three steps and a clearly defined underlying are foundations of financial engineering that are sometimes lost in the excitement of exploring new strategies.

This section explains the quoted prices for commodities, in foreign exchange, for financial instruments, and for indexes. Some terminologies for quoting these prices—hereafter called "jargon"—for various price quotations are explained.

Commodity Prices

In the United States, each commodity seems to have its price quoted against a different unit of measure. Crude oil is priced by the barrel; diesel and motor gasoline, by the gallon. Precious metals are priced by the troy ounce, which is slightly heavier than the more common avoirdupois ounce. Base or industrial metals are priced by the pound or hundredweight. Lumber is priced by board feet; meat and poultry, by the pound; some grains by the bushel, others by the ton; mercury by the 76-pound flask; eggs by the dozen.

A consideration in commodity cash market pricing is the quantity for a "round lot" or "marketable amount." The terms are here synonymous. A marketable amount of gold may be 1,000 troy ounces. A round lot of silver may be 10,000 ounces. If a seller of gold has only 20 ounces, the price will be less than for a round lot.

In markets outside the United States, the measures may be the same as in the United States for some commodities and different for other commodities. A commodity producer or user trading in London or Tokyo or some other center should be certain to recheck the definition of the underlying in that market, including the basic unit of measure and round lot or marketable amount. Different terms may be used; for example, no. 2 heating oil in the United States is comparable to gas oil in the United Kingdom and Europe.

Favorable Versus Unfavorable Commodity Price Changes. The following coverage may seem oversimplified, but commodities provide a straightforward explanation of being long or short and comparing favorable and unfavorable price changes. This explanation is a convenient map for analyzing more complex transactions. The relationships are important to understanding more complex pricing relationships for positions in many financial instruments.

If you own a commodity that you need to sell, you are long the commodity or "have a long position" in the commodity. If you need to buy a commodity that you do not own, you are short the commodity or "have a short position" in the commodity. A farmer raising wheat is long wheat until it is sold in any or all of the cash, forward, or futures markets. A crude oil trader who sells to a refinery crude oil that the trader does not own is short crude oil until the trader purchases the crude oil for delivery under that short sale contract.

The timing for delivery is relevant to the long or short position. A refiner may purchase at a favorable price more oil for May delivery than can be both stored in tanks and refined, yet still be short oil for April ("long May, short April")—two underlying positions because of different delivery months.

If you are long a commodity that you intend to sell, you want the price to increase. The farmer wants the price of wheat to go up.

If you use a commodity, you are concerned about the margin between cost of goods sold and sales price for the goods. The oil refiner is concerned about the spread between the price of crude oil and prices of refined products—the "crack spread."

If you are short a commodity, you want the price to decrease. The crude oil trader who entered into a contract to sell oil to a refiner ("went short") wants to be able to buy the oil at a lower price than the sale contract price.

Foreign Exchange Prices

Foreign exchange is arguably the largest financial market in the world. A recent study, conducted by the Federal Reserve Bank of New York, The Bank of England, and the Bank of Japan, reported that, in 1988, average daily volume in New York and Tokyo approached USD 100 billion (100 billion U.S. Dollars) in each city and USD 200 billion in London. Volume worldwide, therefore, was probably in excess of USD 800 billion each and every business day of the year. With a USD 100 billion U.S. trade deficit, the full amount could be covered in just one day's trading in New York. The statistic implies that the vast majority of activity in the foreign exchange market comes from noncommercial flows. These include financial investment, capital investment, and portfolio allocation, as well as speculative flows.

The foreign exchange market is cloaked in a jargon all its own.

Currencies are usually quoted in terms of their exchange rate against the U.S. Dollar. Common practice is to quote most currencies in terms of units of currency per U.S. Dollar, in *European terms,* as shown in Table 2.1; the opposite is *American terms.*

Table 2.1 also introduces a methodology that will be used throughout this book in naming currencies. It uses *SWIFT* (Society for Worldwide Interbank Financial Telecommunications) codes to label currencies. SWIFT is an international bank payment system that uses a three-letter code to identify currencies; the code is made up of two letters from the country name and one letter from the currency name.

Using the quotations from the above table, one U.S. Dollar (USD) is worth, in European terms: 1.4430 Swiss Francs (CHF: Confederation Helvetica Francs); 1.6950 German Marks (DEM); 140.25 Japanese Yen (JPY); and 5.75 French Francs (FRF). In the jargon of the market: "Dollar Swiss" (USD/CHF) is 1.4430; "Dollar Mark" (USD/DEM) is 1.6950; "Dollar Yen" (USD/JPY) is 140.25; and "Dollar Paris" or "Dollar French" (USD/FRF) is 5.7500. The meaning of the verbal jargon is the opposite of what is being spoken. "Dollar Mark" refers to the number of marks per one dollar. This terminology is typical of exchange rates quoted in European terms, as well as most major cross rates.

Such jargon and European terms are typical of foreign exchange quotes in the interbank market, except for a handful of currencies that are routinely quoted in *American terms,* the value of one unit of currency in U.S. Dollars. These currencies are the Pound Sterling (GBP), the Australian Dollar (AUD), the New Zealand Dollar (NZD), and the European Currency Unit (XEU),

Table 2.1   Examples of Currency Quotations in European Terms

Currency Name	SWIFT Currency Code	Example of Exchange Rate in European Terms
Swiss Francs	CHF	1.4430
Deutsche Marks	DEM	1.6950
Japanese Yen	JPY	140.2500
French Francs	FRF	5.7500

Table 2.2   Examples of Cross Rate Bid and Ask Quotations

	DEM	GBP	JPY	CHF	FRF
DEM	—	0.3359/63	82.67/78	.8518/34	3.3853/17
GBP	2.9732/67	—	245.66/98	2.5257/96	10.0425/614
JPY	1.2080/96	0.4065/71	—	1.0277/99	4.0944/27
CHF	1.1717/40	0.3953/59	97.09/30	—	3.9786/27
FRF	0.2948/54	0.0994/96	24.37/42	0.2511/13	—

also known as the *ECU* (pronounced "ee-cue"): GBP 1 = USD 1.7510; AUD 1 = USD 0.7735; NZD 1 = USD 0.5875; XEU 1 = USD 1.2135.

A currency quoted directly against another, without quoting against the U.S. Dollar, is called a *cross rate*. With the increasing importance of the European and Japanese economies, cross rates have also escalated in importance. In an article aptly titled "Hot Cross Market," managers of foreign exchange trading departments reported that "corporate customers are making considerable use of the cross markets . . . . In the past, corporate customers called the bank and asked for a cross-price; with no ready-made market in that cross, they had to accept the components." The head of another trading department commented that "cross-rate trading now drives movements in the underlying currencies and not the reverse, as used to be the case . . . . Japanese foreign exchange traders are finding cross rates a particularly attractive way of simplifying the transfer of investment funds to Europe."[1] The most significant activity in cross rates is for those rates quoted against the German Mark, the Japanese Yen, the Swiss Franc, and the Pound Sterling.

Cross rates have their jargon, too, as illustrated by these examples of verbal cross rate quotations:

"Sterling Mark" (GBP/DEM) would be 2.9730, or Deutsche Marks 2.9730 per Pound Sterling;
"Mark Swiss" (DEM/CHF) would be .8520, or Swiss Francs 0.8520 per German Mark;
"Mark Yen" (DEM/JPY) would be 82.70 or Japanese Yen 82.70 per German Mark.

Again, the verbal jargon quotes rates backwards. For example, "Mark Yen" refers to the number of Japanese Yen per Deutsche Mark, not DEM/JPY, as in algebra. Table 2.2, an example from an on-line quotation system, illustrates the cross rate bid and ask quotations seen by a trader.

[1] Kotchan, "Hot Cross Market," *Euromoney* (May 1990):

Favorable Versus Unfavorable Foreign Exchange Rate Changes. In the United States, futures contracts for any currency are quoted in American terms even though the interbank market spot and forward rates are quoted in European terms, as above. A great deal of confusion can arise when trying to compare prices from one market to another.

Another source of confusion about foreign exchange rate changes arises from how to describe "what's going up and what's coming down" when one currency strengthens or weakens against another. This issue is a chronic virus for novices trying to manage the risks of foreign exchange; for experienced foreign exchange traders, it is a less frequent but no less troublesome "bug."

This book will usually use "appreciate" and "depreciate" to describe, respectively, favorable and unfavorable foreign exchange rate movements from the perspective of the hedger. Unfortunately, this is an exercise in tautology because as Currency 1 appreciates against Currency 2, Currency 2 depreciates against Currency 1.

If the U.S. Dollar appreciates against the German Mark, the Dollar commands more Marks per Dollar than previously. For example, if DEM/USD rises from 1.65000 to 1.7000, the U.S. Dollar has appreciated and the Mark has depreciated. During this appreciation, dealers would probably describe the Dollar as being "bid"—there are more buyers (bids) than sellers (offers) of Dollars at any given exchange rate.

If the Dollar subsequently depreciated to DEM/USD 1.6800 from DEM/USD 1.7000, dealers would probably describe the Mark as being "offered" during the depreciation. If the Dollar were "offered," there would be more sellers of Dollars (offers) than buyers (bids) of Dollars against Marks.

Don't lose patience with this issue because it is a reason to recheck your own logic and explanations to others. "If the number is bigger, is the U.S. Dollar worth more or less?" "What happens if the currency is Pounds Sterling?" "Which is the 'better' exchange rate of the two being quoted?" "Did that trader say, 'Dollar Mark is one-seventy-two fifty-six' and did I store the other trader's quote in register two or three of the calculator?"

Financial Instrument Prices

In this discussion, the financial instruments considered are debt instruments. The cash market pricing relationships of equity instruments is like commodities—long or short a stock; if long, hope the price goes up; if short, hope the price goes down. The debt instruments are notes and bonds issued in the *capital markets;* the commercial paper, certificates of deposit, Eurodollars, bankers' acceptances, and Treasury bills are issued in the *money markets.*

The basic concept for the pricing of debt financial instruments is this: there is an inverse relationship between the interest rates and the price of debt financial instruments. If interest rates rise, the price of the financial instrument will fall. If interest rates fall, the price of the financial instrument will rise. The adage that "gentlemen prefer bonds" arises from the fact that either the interest rate or the price of bonds is always getting stronger.

Two basic concepts need to be understood: *yield to maturity (YTM)* and *duration.*

When market participants talk about changes in interest rates, they are usually talking about YTM. In financial markets, YTM is the same as the internal rate of return on an investment, as the term is commonly used in finance texts. The interest rate for discounting, which makes the sum of all present values of future cash receipts equal to the amount invested, is the YTM.[2]

Duration should not be confused with the term length of a contract. Duration in finance is the weighted average life of all cash flows received from a fixed income security. Using a simple example, a USD 1,000 bond pays 10 percent at the end of each year and matures in 5 years. An investor will receive total cash flows of USD 1,500 by the time the bond matures: USD 100 per year in interest × 5 years + the USD 1,000 principal at maturity. The maturity of the bond is 5 years, but the duration is shorter because some of the cash (the annual interest payments) is received before the bond matures. In this case, duration is 4.3333 years.[3] The formula is the summation of each year's cash flow ÷ the total cash flow × the number of the year in which the cash flow is received.

If two bonds have the same maturity date, the bond with the higher coupon interest rate (say, 10 percent) will have a shorter duration than the bond with the lower coupon interest rate (say, 5 percent). The bond with the higher coupon pays, sooner, a greater percentage of the total cash to be received than the bond with the lower coupon. This concept is significant to many advanced portfolio hedging strategies.[4]

Duration will equal the maturity of a bond only in the case of a zero coupon bond—a bond with no coupon interest payments.

Prices, Interest Rates, and Yields. When investors and borrowers talk about interest rates rising and falling, they are generally talking about a change in the YTM of a financial instrument. Remembering the inverse relationship between price and yield is crucial to understanding the

---

[2] Any finance text will have detailed explanations of YTM calculation methods. This very simple explanation of YTM does not include such key issues as *reinvestment risk.* See Stigum, *The Money Markets* (1990).

[3] Duration = [(100/1,500) × 1 year] + [(100/1,500) × 2 years] + [(100/1,500) × 3 years]
    + [(100/1,500) × 4 years] + [(100/1,500) × 5 years], or

Duration = 0.0667 year + 0.1333 year + 0.2000 year + 0.2667 year + 3.6667 years = 4.333 years.

[4] For a detailed study of duration, see Platt, *Controlling Interest Rate Risk* (1986).

mechanics of futures contracts and derivative instruments that investors and borrowers use to manage interest rate risk.

For simplicity, consider a bond with an annual 8 percent coupon and 10 years to maturity. (*Eurobonds* typically have annual interest payments.) Bonds are often issued in face value of USD 1,000. Once a year, the bond will pay USD 80 interest. If bonds with similar risks and rating yield 8 percent, the bond will trade at "par," which means that the market price of the bond is the same as its face value, USD 1,000. If interest rates rise, then the yield on the bond must rise to attract investors. If an investor can buy a bond with a 9 percent coupon and a 10-year maturity with the same risk and rating, the 8 percent rate will not be attractive—unless its yield also rises. For the yield to rise, the financial instrument's purchase price must fall, as shown in Table 2.3.

Table 2.3 demonstrates the impact of changes in prevailing market interest rates on this bond's price. If interest rates rise for a comparable financial instrument, then the price of this 8 percent bond must fall, in order to make its yield competitive with the yield on bonds that have higher coupons. Similarly, if comparable financial instrument interest rates fall, investors will "bid up" the price of this bond for as long as its yield is higher than that on other bonds. Investors will "bid up" the price until its YTM falls to that of bonds with similar maturity, credit quality, and liquidity.

The inverse relationship between price and yield is a key concept for debt financial instruments. This concept follows through financial instrument futures contracts and options contracts on those futures. Debt financial instrument futures contracts and many options are quoted in terms of the price of the underlying, not the yield. When investors talk about a firmer or stronger bond market, they mean that bond prices are rising, and interest rates are falling. Rising bond prices mean lower interest rates. A weak or a falling bond market is synonymous with rising interest rates. Occasionally, traders will talk about "bonds falling out of bed." They mean that prices fell

Table 2.3 Bond Price Versus Yield ($1,000 Bond, 8 Percent Coupon, Annual Payment, 10-Year Maturity)

Yield to Maturity	Bond Value (USD)	Bond Price (USD)
6.00%	1,147.20	114.720
7.00	1,070.24	107.024
8.00	1,000.00	par
9.00	935.82	93.582
10.00	877.10	87.710

sharply and that yields rose sharply. Similarly, a "soaring market" refers to sharply rising prices and falling yields.

Remember: owning a debt financial instrument is to be *long* and to have the right to receive coupon interest payments and principal, if the instrument is held to maturity. Borrowing money is being *short,* because of the borrower's obligation to pay interest and principal.

Index Prices

An *index* is a computed average of a group of prices or measurements expressed as a percentage of a base period index of 100. Many indexes measure the relative value, over time, of various composites of data. Familiar examples of indexes for economic activity are the Consumer Price Index (CPI) and Producer Price Index (PPI).

Exchange-traded futures contracts and options have been derived from some indexes. The very actively traded Standard & Poor's 500 (S&P 500) stock index is a capitalization weighted index of 500 common stocks listed on the New York Stock Exchange. The Commodity Research Board (CRB) Futures Price Index, traded on the New York Futures Exchange (the "knife"), is a futures contract composed of the average of 27 different commodity futures contracts, from meats and grains to imported foodstuffs, lumber, energy, and precious metals. The exchanges continue imaginative development of new index contracts. (See Appendix B for sources of brochures.)

The price changes on index contracts are easy to see. If the index number goes up, it is increasing; if the index number goes down, it is decreasing.

CASH, FORWARD, AND FUTURES CONTRACTS, AND "BASIS"

Contracts for the purchase or sale of the underlying commodities, currencies, and financial instruments can be categorized, depending on the present or future time and terms for *settlement,* as follows: *cash, forward,* or *futures* contracts. This discussion begins with the end, settlement, because planning physical or cash settlement of a cash, forward, or futures contract is a critical consideration before entering into the transaction. The timing of settlement is also an important consideration to the price in any contract.

Settlement is payment of the amount due under a contract in exchange for what is to be delivered under the contract: receipt of the physical commodity; currency purchased in exchange for the currency sold; financial instrument; or cash for contracts that *cash settle,* which include commodity price swaps or other derivative contracts (see Chapter 3). Planning settlement means planning for the credit and performance exposure.

Basic Types of Settlement

Depending on the nature of the underlyings, purchase and sale contracts can settle. This is a list of the basic types of settlement:

1. Buying a physical commodity, taking physical delivery, and paying the seller.
2. Making payment in one currency and receiving payment in another currency—the physical exchange of the currencies settles a foreign exchange contract.
3. Buying and paying for a financial instrument and receiving one of the following documents evidencing its ownership:
   — a registered bond or stock certificate;
   — a custodian's receipt for safekeeping of the financial instrument;
   — a confirmation of having entered into the contract, for example, buying a forward or futures contract or placing a deposit with a bank.
4. Buying or selling an index contract at one value and subsequently selling or buying at another value for the index. This is *cash settling*— positive net cash flow for a profit and negative net cash flow for a loss.
5. Buying an option.
6. Making cash payments under a contract requiring periodic revaluation(s), for example, a *commodity price swap, interest rate swap, currency swap,* or other derivative contract.

Price, Time, and Delivery

This section briefly compares price basis and settlement terms for purchase and sale of cash, forward, and futures contracts.

- Cash or *spot* contracts have a price based on a contractually negotiated immediate or near-term delivery date, whichever is customary to the applicable business sector and underlying.
- Forward contracts have a price based on a contractually negotiated future delivery date, a date forward of the customary cash contract terms.
- Futures contracts have a price based on the open outcry trading on the floors of regulated exchanges for contracts with standardized future delivery dates and standardized requirements for physical delivery or cash settlement.

An example will help to clarify the comparison of cash, forward, and futures contracts. If you enter into a contract to buy a car standing on the car lot of the dealer, you are long the car in a cash transaction. When you take delivery and pay for the car, you have settled. If you sell your car for delivery to the buyer 3 months hence and you have not yet purchased your new car, you are short the car in a forward transaction; presumably, you hope to make money by buying your new car at a price lower than your sale price for your old one. If you order a car to be factory-built, you are long a car for forward delivery. You may be required to post *margin* in the form of a cash deposit. If a common type of car were traded on a commodities exchange and you bought a car by buying a futures contract to take delivery in a future month, you are long the contract for future delivery of the car. Suppose the price of the car underlying your futures contract goes up. If you want the profit instead of the car, you can sell the futures contract on the commodities exchange. If you do not sell the contract, at the futures expiration date the exchange will require your delivery instructions and payment arrangements for the car.

In any contract to exchange currencies, if you are long one currency, you are short the other currency. For example, if you are buying Deutsche Marks (DEM) against U.S. Dollars (USD) you are obligated to take delivery of DEM and obligated to deliver USD.

If you own a bond or certificate of deposit, you are long the interest income you will receive. If you are a borrower, you are short the interest you will pay.

If you purchase an index contract—usually as a futures contract—you are long and want the index number to increase. If you sell an index contract you do not own, you are short and want the index number to decrease until you have covered your short(s) with an offsetting purchase contract.

Beginners who are placing orders for cash, forward, or futures contracts should be certain to obtain and learn a written description of the types of orders—day versus *good till canceled, market, limit, stop, stop-limit,* and *spread.* When placing an order with a broker (or any trader), the type of order must be mutually stated and understood, in addition to "buy" (or "sell") and the contract month. One should never assume that a busy broker or trader will remember the exact details of what a naive "hedger" is trying to do.

In Chapter 4, the legal distinction between a forward contract and a futures contract is discussed in detail.

Cash Contracts

The cash contract contemplates earliest possible delivery. The quoted price may, however, be adjusted for any applicable delivery location differential or time required for delivery and the seller's payment for the delivery. "Where's the cash?" does not mean "Who has my billfold?" In the contract market, the phrase means "What is the relevant cash contract quotation?" The terms "cash" and "spot" have different meanings in different markets, even when referring to the same underlying. When referring to foreign exchange markets, futures traders talk about the cash market but bank traders talk about the spot market. Both are referring to the foreign exchange market, usually in relation to large transactions among banks and their large corporate and institutional clients. For the purposes of Chapters 2 and 3, cash and spot will be the same.

Cash markets for commodities, currencies, and financial instruments are dominated by two key groups: (1) traders and their employers, such as commodity trading houses, banks, and investment houses, whose business is to trade and make markets in their areas of expertise; and (2) producers and customers who need to make or take delivery of the underlying traded items.

Producers need to sell and deliver the commodities they produce. Processors and customers need to buy commodities and take delivery so that they can process or manufacture the products they sell. Importers, exporters, and international investors generate revenues and have obligations in one or more currencies. They may need to sell one currency and buy another. Entities needing to raise capital must issue and deliver financial instruments to investors who must deliver cash to the issuing entity and who hope for a return on their invested cash.

The key concept in a cash market is that each seller usually intends to deliver a commodity, currency, or financial instrument for cash. Each buyer intends to pay cash and accept delivery of a commodity, financial instrument, or currency.

Cash markets exist in a variety of forms; the best known is the stock market. Formal exchanges include the New York Stock Exchange, the American Stock Exchange, the Philadelphia Stock Exchange, and the Pacific Stock Exchange. In the United States and countries of similar economic development, the formal exchanges tend to be regulated by the government. Good information is available to the public about stock trading prices and the most recent price for a trade.

Over the counter (OTC) markets are markets outside of formal exchanges. In the United States, the OTC market for equities operates through the National Association of Securities Dealers (NASD) and the greatest volume of transactions is quoted through its automated quotation system, NASDAQ.

The cash or spot markets for commodities, currencies, and financial instruments (except equities and some corporate bonds) are nearly always OTC markets. The different markets are usually large trading rooms in which as many as several hundred traders are talking to other traders in other rooms by telephone, on-line computer communication systems, and telexes. A market may be as simple, however, as a one-to-one conversation.

Forward Contracts

Forward contracts enable some but not all commodities, currencies, and financial instruments to be traded for delivery at a later time than is allowed for cash contract delivery. The transactions are closed between buying and selling parties for the amounts and terms they mutually require. A forward contract usually implies and contemplates actual delivery of the currency, commodity, or financial instrument (the underlying) against payment by the buyer. The "take or make" obligation under a forward contract is not as easily closed as the delivery obligation under a futures contract. A futures contract can be covered ("offset") on the exchange, albeit with market risk of financial gain or loss. Eliminating the "take or make" delivery obligation of a forward contract requires negotiating liquidation of the contract with the counterparty. If the contract cannot be satisfactorily liquidated, a problem long or short position might be resolved through an offsetting contract with the counterparty, or elsewhere.

The difference between the cash price and forward or future price is driven in large part by the interest cost attributable to the time period between cash and forward or future settlement. (See this chapter's concluding section, on basis.)

Because of the extended time for settlement, the parties to forward contracts will usually review mutual credit in planning their contracts and may require payment or performance assurances such as a letter of credit. The first of many reminders: never forget about credit! Bear in mind the risk that one party may not be able to meet its obligations. For companies smaller than the Fortune 100, the requirements to obtain and maintain credit can become as big an issue for financial management as the financial risk being managed. (Credit issues are discussed in Chapter 11.)

The forward marketplace for a currency, commodity, or financial instrument is usually the same as its cash marketplace—commodity exchanges, dealers, and market makers for commodities; banks for cash, spot, and forward currency contracts; brokers for futures and options on futures contracts for currencies; banks, dealers, and some brokers for financial instruments.

Futures Contracts

Futures contracts are traded through futures exchanges, which are regulated marketplaces for trading futures and options on some of the futures contracts (traded options). Futures contracts for commodities developed as an alternative to cash and forward contracts. The futures markets offer efficient forward pricing, market liquidity, standardized terms and conditions, easy access for dealing, credit and delivery administration, and an alternative to the forward market for managing the seasonal gluts and shortages of commodities such as grains.

The access to U.S. regulated exchange marketplaces for commodity, currency, financial instrument, and index futures contracts is through brokerage firms or purchase of a seat on the exchange and direct trading on the floor. Some corporations buy a seat and employ floor traders, if the companies deal in large volumes of an underlying and the dealings are critical to their financial management and profitability.

The futures contracts on the exchanges are openly traded and regulated in all specifications: size of contract unit, trading hours, specific trading months, price quotations, minimum price fluctuation, maximum trading price change from prior day's close, standardized settlement procedures for contracts (whether by cash or physical delivery), and deliverable qualities. The exchange monitors the total volume and positions of contracts to maintain the integrity of the market. *Margin,* a minimum credit requirement per contract, is regulated by the exchange, subject to arrangements of the brokerage firms acting for the customers. Contrary to the forward market, most buyers and sellers of futures do not intend to take or make delivery. Like forward contracts, futures contracts can be used for either speculative investments or as hedging vehicles. Although more than 95 percent of all futures contracts are closed without taking or making delivery, the reader should not conclude that most transactions are speculative. Rather, many transactions are opened and closed by corporations busily managing their financial price risks.

What Is Basis?

Basis is the shorthand word for the difference between an underlying's cash or spot market price and the price in the forward or futures market for the same or most nearly comparable underlying. A synonym for basis is "differential." The difference in price is usually expressed by subtraction; the cash price is placed first in the formula:

Basis = Cash Price − Forward or Futures Price

A difference in quality, grade, or location, particularly of commodities, may be expressed as a ratio:

Basis = Cash Price ÷ Forward or Futures Price

Generally, however, basis is expressed with the subtraction formula giving another piece of jargon: "positive basis" if the cash price is more than the forward or futures price, or "negative basis" if the cash price is less than the forward or futures price.

The cash market underlying may not have an exact replica in the forward or futures market. The problem of underlyings not matching is particularly true for commodities—for example, different specifications and delivery locations for crude oil. A detailed description of the underlying will help identify differentials. Basis or differential is caused by inherent differences among each of the cash and forward and futures markets for any underlying.

Basis for commodities is driven by the interest cost for holding the commodity for the period of time between the cash and forward or futures market settlement dates plus any cost of storage, insurance, transportation, and delivery—"cost of carry." If basis is strengthening, the market reveals that the cash price is moving up faster than the forward or futures price. If basis is weakening, the market reveals that the cash price is moving down faster than the forward or futures price. (See Chapter 10 for examples.) The "cost of carry" for a forward or futures contract includes an assumption about future interest rates.

Basis for foreign exchange is the differential in interest rates between the two currencies. "A Deutsche Mark today looks the same as a Deutsche Mark tomorrow," but the difference between the interest rates on Deutsche Marks and U.S. Dollars will be the basis for the difference between the cash and a forward or futures price.

Basis for financial instruments is the positive or negative "interest carry"—the difference between the financial instrument's stated interest rate and the interest rates prevailing for comparable financial instruments. As an example, if borrowing at 6 percent for an 8 percent YTM U.S. Treasury Bond, the positive yield basis is 2 percent; conversely, if the borrowing rate moves to 10 percent, the negative yield basis is 2 percent.

Basis for index contracts is any difference between the index's contract price and the prices for the components of the index. In discussing the new Eurotrack 100 index contract on the London International Financial Futures Exchange (LIFFE), it was noted that "The contract could suffer from a lack of *liquidity,* partly because many of the underlying shares are not very actively traded. . . . The contract is expected to involve some basis risk, at least at the outset—that is, the contract price may not always accurately reflect the underlying share values."[5]

If the underlying is fully understood, the basis risk becomes intuitively obvious. Basis risk or opportunity should be identified when defining an underlying. Important to corporate financial risk management is the precise description of the basis for the situation at hand.

---

[5] "LIFFE Launches Euro-index Contract," *Financial Times* (London) February 28, 1991, p. 28.

3
Derivatives

A dog, used to eating eggs, saw an Oyster; and opening his mouth to its widest extent, swallowed it down with the utmost relish, supposing it to be an egg. Soon afterward suffering great pain in his stomach, he said, "I deserve all this torment, for my folly in thinking that everything round must be an egg."

The Fables of Aesop (300 B.C.)

OPTIONS

Relax, please; this section—and this book—will *not* discuss the singular or plural of option deltas, gammas, kappas, lambdas, rhos, thetas, or vegas, nor the volatilities and formulas hiding in computer models, nor will it debate which is the "best" option pricing model logic.

Options are, however, very valuable tools for corporate financial risk management. Understanding options is critical to understanding the newer tools available for financial engineering. This discussion of options is divided among three topics: options defined and described, a practical view of option pricing, and a comparison of exchange-traded and OTC options.

An option is a contract derived from an underlying cash, forward, or futures contract; hence, options are usually classified as one of the "derivatives." We introduce options as the "classic" derivative because options per se are not new and, in the "vanilla flavor" discussed here, options are straightforward.

Options Defined and Described

The textbook definition of an option contract goes as follows: a contract between two parties giving the option's holder the contractual right, but not the obligation, to buy from or sell to the option's *writer* a specifically defined commodity, currency, or financial instrument at a predetermined *strike price* on or before a specified *expiration* date. The commodity, currency, or financial instrument is referred to as the *underlying*. The option holder can buy and sell an option or, by *exercising* the option, can elect the option's right to buy or sell the underlying pursuant to the terms of the option. (We'll distinguish the holder from the option buyer, seller, and writer in the next section.) If the option has any remaining *time value* in addition to *intrinsic value,* and if the option holder has a *long* or *short* position in the underlying, the option holder will usually sell the option and cover the underlying position in the appropriate cash, spot, forward, or futures market.

The two classes of options are *call options* ("calls") and *put options* ("puts"). A call option gives the option holder the right to buy the underlying at the strike price from the option writer. A put option gives the option holder the right to sell the underlying at the strike price to the option writer. An option that can be exercised only on its expiration date is called a *European-style option.* An option that can be exercised at any time on or before the expiration date is called an *American-style option.* Later in the chapter, we shall discuss and define an *Asian option* and *lookback option.* Both terms refer to "whistles and bells" on the computation for an underlying's price for comparison to the option strike price—not to the timing for exercising the option.

An option buyer pays a *premium* for the rights of the option contract: the first buyer pays a premium to the option writer. The option buyer controls an unlimited potential that the underlying's price will move favorably, thus obtaining a form of insurance against loss. The option buyer's risk is limited to the amount of premium paid. In contrast, the option writer incurs unlimited risk for which the premium is intended to compensate.

For example, if an investor purchases 100 shares of stock at USD 90.00 per share and an American-style put option with an *expiration date* 6 months later for USD 4.00 per share (total price USD 400.00), the investor has spent USD 400.00 for 6 months of insurance. If the stock price declines below USD 90.00 per share, the investor's loss will not exceed USD 400.00 (excluding commissions). The writer of the option would incur unlimited risk if the stock price were to decline below USD 90.00 per share.

Option Writers, Holders, Buyers, and Sellers

We interrupt the definition and description of options to bring you the terms for the parties to option contracts. These terms are not to be used casually. Be careful to understand "the hat you're wearing." This book adopts the following terminology—in order of events, not alphabetically:

- *Writer* (a seller) is the party that incurs an obligation of contractual rights to the option holder, under an option contract.

- *Holder* is the party that holds the option contract to which the writer or issuer is obligated.
- *Buyer* is a purchaser of an option. A buyer is not always the same as a holder. For example, if a party is short an option, being a buyer by offsetting the option does not result in being a holder.
- *Seller* is a writer (or a holder) that sells an option. In this book, writer will be used to distinguish from a holder that becomes a seller.

Intrinsic Value

The cost of an option is its *premium.* A seemingly simple formula applies:

premium = intrinsic value + time value

Lurking in the weeds of time value is *volatility.*

Intrinsic value, a primary factor of very practical interest to the corporate financial risk management process, is the difference between the strike price and the current cash market for the underlying. The following examples compare the computation of intrinsic value for call and put options:

- If the strike price of a call is less than the current cash market price, the option will have intrinsic value equal to the difference between the call option's strike price and the current cash market price. In this situation, the call option holder can profit from exercising the call by purchasing the underlying from the writer at the strike price and selling it at a higher price in the cash market. This translates to buying cheaper through the call strike and selling higher in the cash market.
- If the strike price of a put is higher than the current cash market price, the option will have intrinsic value equal to the difference between the put option's strike price and the current cash market price. In this situation, the put option holder can profit from exercising the put by selling the underlying to the writer at the strike price and buying, at a lower price in the cash market, the underlying to cover that sale. This translates to selling higher through the put strike and buying lower in the cash market.

In the above two situations, each option is *in the money* because of the implicit profit opportunity.

An *at the money* option is an option (a put or a call) with a strike price equal to the current cash market price. An option that is *out of the money* is a call option with a strike price greater than the current cash market price of the underlying, or a put option with a strike price less than the cash market price of the underlying. When an option is out of the money, there is no implicit profit opportunity.

An option that is in the money will **always have a higher premium** than an otherwise identical option that is at the money or out of the money. By definition, the intrinsic value of an option must always be greater than or equal to zero. The concept of intrinsic value implies that a negative value is meaningless: if there is no profit potential at a point in time between the strike price and the cash market price, then the option has, at that time, no intrinsic value.

Option Pricing

A Fortune 100 company's corporate treasurer summarized a brutally practical view: "I don't care what the banks go through to price this stuff; I use competitive quotes. If one of them [the banks] makes a mistake to my advantage, that's their problem." This sounds like sharp dealing, but the "mistake" may be nothing more than a difference in quotations and the contract may be for exactly the terms intended for purchase or sale. A big difference in quotations often means a big and noticeable difference in contract terms.

The theory of option pricing is a subject of research and opinions. Some critics consider option pricing theory hocus pocus because of the mathematics of chaos and arguments about nonlinear relationships. Computer models are available to simulate option pricing, and many books and articles have been written on the subject. (Appendix B offers some pertinent references.) Some approaches can help to answer the often raised question: "How much should we pay?" As the Business Studies in Part Two will illustrate, there are better answers than "As little as possible."

Again, we advise the reader to relax and, remembering the versatility of options for corporate financial risk management, not be deterred by the seeming complication that the computed intrinsic value is not the only factor to determine an option's premium or, simply, where the money is.

The other factor in option premium pricing is the *time value,* the subject of the option pricing evaluation models. The time value or time premium of an option is the compensation, in addition to any intrinsic value, that the option writer receives through the premium, when writing the option. Remember that the option writer incurs unlimited liability when writing an option, if the cash market for the underlying moves against the writer. The time value is determined by the volatility in price fluctuation in the underlying's cash market, the length of time to expiration, the liquidity of the cash market, the political or other risks associated with delivery or pricing of the underlying, and the apprehensions of the writer and hopes of the holder. (Dissection and discussion of elaborate mathematical models are not in the scope of this book.)

In a recent example, as tensions built prior to the 1991 Persian Gulf War, the prices of crude oil option premiums on the New York Mercantile Exchange (NYMEX) fluctuated more sharply than the futures contracts. Intuitive logic indicates that the more volatile the cash market price fluctuation of the underlying, the more expensive the option premium attributable to time value will be. Because longer time periods increase the writer's exposure to unforeseen volatilities and general business risks, an option with a longer time to expiration will have a higher premium than an identical option with a shorter time to expiration. The longer the time to expiration, the greater the time risk to the option's writer.

The theories of option pricing may not render timely and practical answers for corporate financial risk management. It may be helpful to consider a price range for an option premium as being analogous to pricing insurance. For example, what percentage "insurance" premium does the corporate financial risk merit? Obtaining competitive quotations for OTC options or the advice of a broker when dealing in exchange-traded options can provide comparisons and helpful evaluations of timing and price for purchase and sale.

If an option has been identified as a suitable financial risk management tool, computer simulations for a "desirable" option premium will not cause the marketplace to make the option available at that premium. The authors have witnessed "financial engineers" missing a market that never looked back; they were waiting for option premiums to match some elegant computer model's output—"approved by management" as the exact target, or "bargain" price with "suitable" volatility.

Corporate financial risk management often does not have the exactitude that the appellation "financial engineering" might suggest.

Exchange-Traded Options

Option contracts against a wide variety of underlying futures contracts for commodities, currencies, financial instruments, and indexes are traded on regulated exchanges throughout the world. Exchange-traded options have two types of underlyings:

- An associated futures contract traded on the same exchange as the futures contract.
- An underlying that emulates but is not an actual futures contract and is therefore traded on a different exchange from the futures contract being emulated.

An exchange usually does not open trading on options on a futures contract at the same time that a new futures contract is first introduced for trading. Introducing a new exchange-traded option is usually deferred until trading volumes are more established in the underlying futures contract's spot and forward months.

The most recent trading prices for exchange-traded option contracts can be easily obtained by calling a stock or options broker or through computerized trading data bases. The exchange-traded option market has "transparency": the closing ask prices are cited in the financial press. Not all options are traded every day, so some blanks will appear in a newspaper listing. Some option premiums are, in part, a function of the underlying's price. Current quotations should be obtained. Don't rely on the prior day's newspaper prices as being indicative.

Like futures contracts, the exchange-traded options contracts are standardized for style (*American-style*), strike price increments, and expiration dates. Margin for credit is not required for purchasers of exchange-traded options, who pay the premium cash up-front, but is required for "naked" option writers—those who incur unlimited risk. A "covered" option writer has written an option against an existing and matching long or short position. Nonetheless, because the covered option writer has unlimited risk, margin is required. For example, suppose a writer purchases, on margin, 100 shares of IBM at 125 per share and writes (sells) one 125 call option at USD 5.00. If the stock trades at 120 or lower, the risk is unlimited.

If the underlying to an exchange-traded option is a commodity or index futures contract on that exchange and the futures contract does not *cash settle,* the option's expiration date is earlier than the futures contract's termination date. Because the option is a right to enter into a futures contract at the option's strike price, simultaneous expiration with the futures contract would not be feasible—unless the contract cash settles. Examples of contracts that cash settle are in the index futures and feeder cattle. Exchange-traded options styled around futures contracts on other exchanges may have simultaneous expiration.

Exchange-traded options, a tool of hedgers, can also be used to construct derivatives in *combinations* with futures contracts or other exchange-traded options. The volume in exchange-traded options and futures is from speculators, corporate hedgers, and the forward market's counterparties to corporations. These include banks that are hedging and speculating for their own accounts.

OTC Options

Over-the-Counter (OTC) options have their own attractions. Their most important feature is that, as with forward contracts, the buyer and writer can negotiate specific terms to meet the exact needs of one or both parties. For some situations, the OTC market is more useful than the market for exchange-traded options—for example, for customized options of large amounts related to foreign exchange and interest rates. Two characteristics of OTC options make them notably different from exchange-traded options:

1. Because each premium is negotiated, there is no good way to determine either a fair price for any option transaction or the price at which the last similar transaction took place. These options have no price "transparency."
2. The options buyer must be concerned with the creditworthiness of the option writer—the counterparty expected to perform according to the option's terms—whereas the exchange and brokerage firms manage counterparty credit on exchange-traded options through daily marked-to-market cash balancing.

An underlying has been defined as a commodity, currency, or financial instrument. Intrinsic value has been defined as the positive or zero (never negative) difference between the cash market price for the underlying minus the option's strike price. In other words, the intrinsic value can be zero or a positive number. If the cash market price is 100 and a call option strike is 100, the intrinsic value is zero. If the cash market price is 100 and a call option strike is 101, the option has no intrinsic value. If the cash market price is 100 and a call option strike is 99, the option has an intrinsic value of 1.

In computing the intrinsic value of an option, it is important to identify both the precise contract that is the underlying for the option and the market for that specific underlying—whether cash/spot, forward, or a futures contract. For example, an OTC option can be an option to enter into a spot foreign exchange contract or a forward foreign exchange contract. This careful identification can become more complicated (and more important) when financial engineers work merrily with more complex tools.

FINANCIAL ENGINEERING WITH OTC OPTIONS

OTC options and combinations of options can be crafted into all manner of tools for financial engineering. A London commentary observed: "As corporate executives overcome their long-standing wariness of the futures and options markets they are increasingly looking to derivatives as a way of improving turnover (sales) as well as hedging risk."[1] The article pointed out that, although companies had traditionally used derivatives to hedge currency risk, they are now increasingly looking at derivative contract opportunities as protection against changing interest rates and fluctuating commodity prices.

[1] "Europe's Wariness Eases." Corporate Survey Finance Section, *Financial Times* (London), June 18, 1990, sec. IV.

This section introduces and discusses the following OTC market, corporate financial risk management contracts: caps, calls, and ceilings; floors and puts; collars, tunnels, cylinders, and range forwards; participating forwards, and some other creatively "engineered" names on a list that seems endless.

Subsequent sections cover combinations of futures contracts and exchange-traded options contracts, forward rate agreements (FRAs), and swaps of all kinds.

The first caveat does not change: understand and write down the exact details of any proposed derivative contract—exactly what features of the underlying(s) are subject to the derivative contract, who pays whom how much, computed in what manner, and when.

The objectives of financial engineering with OTC options usually include one or more of the following.

1. Reduce or eliminate the exposure of a one-sided transaction. For example, a forward outright purchase or sale of any underlying locks in its price. To the extent of that contract, participation in any improvement in the underlying's price is thus eliminated—an opportunity loss. The outright forward sale of a specific commodity, currency, or financial instrument—left untouched by further financial engineering—eliminates any opportunity to sell all or part of that underlying at a higher price at a later date. Put another way, a forward outright purchase or sale fixes the purchase or sale price. If prices drop, the buyer cannot take advantage of a lower price but the seller is happy with the forward outright's higher price. If prices rise, the buyer is happy with the forward outright's lower price, but the seller cannot take advantage of the higher price.

2. Reduce or eliminate the cost of an option premium. There is still "no such thing as a free lunch": reducing the cost of an option premium requires a compromise to the benefit that the option's underlying may have an unlimited favorable price move. For example, sharing the profit potential of an option with the counterparty writer of the option will reduce the premium the writer charges. In other words, reducing the option writer's risk can reduce or eliminate the option premium while still providing a range of price protection.

3. Enable a counterparty's credit requirements to be met. A company may not be able to offer satisfactory credit for the continuing contingent liability of payments under a swap contract and may not have cash sufficient for the premium of an option, cap, or floor or credit sufficient for the contingent liability of one of the price range contracts.

What Is the Reference Price?

The word "price," for a level or range, refers to a commodity price, currency exchange rate (price), financial instrument interest rate or price, or index valuation. The *reference price* for the underlying to a derivative contract can be engineered in a variety of ways. This flexibility is one of the great advantages of OTC derivative products for corporate financial risk management. The derivative's price may be a specific cash, spot, forward, or futures contract price in a certain market. An "average price" option or contract—also known as an *Asian option*—has a reference price based on computing an average of the underlying's prices during each period, for *settlement* under the contract. A *lookback* option or contract has a final price computation based on "looking back" over the prices of the underlying and selecting the price(s) most favorable to the derivative's buyer during the contract term or during certain settlement periods of such term.

The reference price computation, the identification of the *notional amount(s)* to be hedged, the frequency of computation, the number of periods, and the frequency of potential cash settlement are the important variations to be engineered. The frequency of computation does not have to equal the frequency of potential cash settlement.

Kinds and Combinations of OTC Options

Financial engineering involving different kinds and combinations of OTC options is virtually limitless, with two big "ifs": if a counterparty can be found, and if credit is available for the exposure being incurred (unless the contract is fully prepaid). **Never** forget about credit. For companies smaller than the Fortune 100, the requirements to obtain and maintain credit for managing an otherwise nicely engineered financial risk management position can become a significantly larger financial management issue. (See Chapter 11 for more about these credit issues.)

Variations on the concept of options can be engineered to provide price protection with periodic settlement rather than settlement only at expiration. The reference price computation can be varied, as discussed above. The premium can be reduced or eliminated by combining types of options or reducing the otherwise unlimited contingent liability of the writer of the contract. Participating forward contracts anticipate forward delivery of the underlying, but the parties participate by sharing in favorable price or rate moves.

Three broad categories are useful "pigeonholes" for the financial engineer:

- A prepaid premium for buying one or more strike prices; call, cap, or ceiling, or puts and floors are examples;
- A reduced or zero premium for a range of unprotected price fluctuations between two strike prices—collars, tunnels, cylinders, and range forwards, for example;
- A commitment to forward purchase or sale—with a forward date delivery of the underlying, unlike the previous category—but adjusting the

forward price for participation in a percentage of favorable price move ("participating range forward").

Prepaid Premium for a Strike Price. As the name suggests, a *cap* or *ceiling* contract places a "lid" or top on the price of an underlying commodity, currency, or financial instrument. In exchange for the buyer's paying a premium, the writer of the cap or ceiling agrees to pay the buyer if, at periodic interim dates or at maturity, the reference price of the underlying is greater than the cap or ceiling strike price.

In present parlance, a cap usually refers to the underlying's reference price being compared for cash settlement to the option's strike on specific dates or at maturity. A ceiling usually refers to the underlying's reference price being a periodic average of the underlying's price, such periodic average being compared for cash settlement to the option's strike on specific dates or at maturity. Reference prices for a cap are usually periodic prices of the underlying; reference prices for a ceiling are usually an average of prices of the underlying—an Asian option or Asian cap. The important point is that specific proposed contract provisions should be reviewed. There are average price caps, and a name offers no assurance of the contract's contents.

The cap or ceiling is a form of call option. The holder of the cap owns the right periodically to call on the writer if the price of the underlying is greater than the cap or ceiling strike price. The important variations to be engineered are the method for computing the underlying's price (as discussed above) and the frequency and number of periods for cash settlement. Some brief examples will illustrate these variations.

- *Interest rate cap.* A borrower buys a 3-year, 10 percent, 3-month *LIBOR* interest rate cap with a declining *notional amount* based a loan's fixed quarterly amortization. Every 3 months, the loan's 3-month LIBOR interest rate is reset with the lending bank, and the borrower pays the bank interest on the loan for the preceding 3 months. On the same day, the 3-month LIBOR rate is compared to the cap's strike price. If the 3-month LIBOR rate is higher than 10 percent, the bank that wrote the cap (not necessarily the lending bank) sends a payment to the borrower. For example, if the notional amount were USD 1.5 Mio (million), if LIBOR were 12 percent at the beginning of a third or fourth calendar quarter, and if the cap were 10 percent, the bank that wrote the cap would pay the difference of 2 percent (12 percent minus 10 percent), computed as USD 1.5 Mio $\times$ .02 (2%) $\times$ 92/360. The holder of the cap continues to benefit from lower interest rates.

- *Commodity price ceiling.* At the beginning of January, a crude oil refiner buys a 2-year, USD 25.00 per barrel, reference average settle prices NYMEX second-month futures contract, semiannual settlement, for notional amount 5,000 barrels per calendar day. At the end of June (181 days), if the average of all the NYMEX reference prices is more than USD 25.00—say, USD 26.00—the writer of the ceiling or average price cap contract pays the refiner the $1.00-per-barrel difference: 181 days × USD 1.00 × 5,000 barrels.

The exposure protection of the 3-month LIBOR setting cap is as continuous for the borrower's rate-setting risk as the daily price of the crude oil ceiling is for a refiner's potentially daily crude oil price-change risk. The interest rate-setting risk arises on 1 day, every 3 months; the crude oil price-change risk can arise every business day. The derivative's reference price computation should be engineered to fit the underlying.

The *floor* contract places a floor or bottom on the price of an underlying commodity, currency, or financial instrument. In exchange for the buyer's paying a premium, the writer of the floor agrees to pay the buyer if, at contractually set interim dates or at maturity, the price of the commodity, currency, or financial instrument is less than the floor's strike price, the "level of the floor." The holder continues to benefit from appreciating price movements.

There are ceilings and floors, and there are caps; but there is no opposite to the cap, no shoes.

The floor is a derivative put option. The holder of the put owns the right periodically to "put it to" the writer if the price of the underlying is less than the floor's strike price. Like the caps and ceilings, the important variations to be engineered are the method for computing the underlying's price, as discussed above, and the frequency and number of periods for cash settlement. Parallels to the interest rate cap and commodity price ceiling would be a floating interest rate investor buying an interest rate floor or a crude oil producer buying a commodity price floor.

The caps or ceilings and floors are all variations on, respectively, call and put OTC option contracts. At the outset, the buyer pays a premium to the writer for the one-sided option contract; in exchange, the writer assumes unlimited potential liability.

Prepaid or Zero Premium for a Price Range. *Collar, cylinder, range forward,* and *tunnel* are names given to contracts that combine cap or ceiling and floor contracts. Party A buys a cap or ceiling, which Party B writes. Party A also writes a floor, which Party B buys, for the same underlying with different strike prices—the ceiling and floor have "room" in between. The reference price for the underlying moves up and down. On each settlement date, if the reference price is above the cap or ceiling, Party A is paid by Party B; if the reference price is below the floor, Party A pays Party B; if the reference price is between the ceiling and floor, no payments are made or received. The reference price may be an average of prices or a forward price at the contract's maturity (a forward range agreement). By comparison, most of the derivative contracts are referenced to average price. If the hedger wants protection against prices or rates rising, the hedger buys the call and writes the put; if the hedger wants protection against prices or rates falling, the hedger writes the call and buys the put.

The brochures for these products have charts, and the names may come from the drawings rather than vice versa. Depending on what image has the most clarity, the hedger has collared a neutral price range, contracted for a cylinder in which nothing happens, bought a forward range of price protection, or formed a tunnel in which to travel for free. An important purpose of these arrangements is to reduce or eliminate the cost of option premiums.

The size of the collar or cylinder or range forward or tunnel can be varied, depending on the premium Party A wants to pay (if any). The size of a zero-premium collar contract is constructed by determining the cap and floor strike prices for which premiums of the cap and floor are equal. Thus, the buyer of the cap is paying a premium equal to the premium to be received for writing the floor. A different size collar will require the payment of a premium for alterations.

The range protection contracts all involve the concept of eliminating or reducing the premium for a cap or ceiling and floor by giving up favorable price beyond a certain level and/or incurring a range of market risk in the price of the underlying.

Using the above example of the 3-month LIBOR cap, the borrower pays a premium for rate protection above 10 percent and enjoys 100 percent of the benefit if interest rates are below 10 percent. The premium could be eliminated or reduced with a collar contract, but the borrower, by writing a floor, will pay if rates drop below the floor's strike price of, say, 7 percent. Thus, the collar is three percentage points wide, 7 percent to 10 percent. The borrower will have set a LIBOR referenced rate range on the loan of not less than 7 percent nor more than 10 percent. The borrower will still be obligated to the lending bank for the entire interest payment, LIBOR, any reserve asset cost, and the lending bank's margin over LIBOR.

Participating Forward Contracts.   An important distinction of this group is that delivery of the underlying is contractually required. The contracts in this group are an elaboration of the basic forward purchase and sale contract discussed in Chapter 2.

A participating forward contract is the purchase or sale of an underlying for delivery at a forward date. The price, however, is adjusted so that the customer has a maximum purchase price or minimum sale price plus, importantly, the opportunity to participate, at a participating percentage rate, in a favorable price move. Assume a customer sells a commodity, currency, or financial instrument forward at a maximum purchase price; if the underlying price at the settlement date is higher than the contracted sale price, the customer is paid a percentage of the increase.

A variation is a forward contract with a "break" option. The customer purchases or sells a commodity, currency, or financial instrument forward at a maximum purchase price, with an option to benefit from a favorable price move. The premium cost is built into the forward price.

COMBINATIONS OF EXCHANGE-TRADED CONTRACTS

Some of the more picturesque names in financial engineering have developed in the world of combined futures contracts and traded options. *Combinations* are here defined as futures contracts and/or exchange-traded options combined into a position. Some exchanges and many hedge brokers have brochures about these combinations and synthetics. These publications briefly inventory many of the combinations, offer illustrative charts, and describe risk and profit potential profiles. Appendix B includes contact addresses for the exchanges.

This discussion has two purposes for corporate financial risk management: (1) to introduce the combinations more commonly used for corporate financial risk management; and (2) to alert readers to combinations that involve being "short" an option—the equivalent of "writing" an OTC option.

Many of the combinations—for example, the spreads—enable protection to be purchased for the lower cost of a straight option premium. Other positions—for example, the synthetic calls and puts—have been designed to provide opportunity from market fluctuations while retaining the unlimited favorable price move of a basic option.

Many books could be written on this topic, but we will move on and meet the combinations sometimes used by hedgers. Close relatives of these combinations are "black sheep," speculative positions.

Watch Out for "Short"

Some combinations involve writing an option—with its potentially unlimited liability that requires "engineering" to control. In the context of combinations of exchange-traded contracts, writing an option is usually described as being *short* an option—having a "short call" or a "short put."

If short an option as part of a combination, such as in a spread, be clear on how the other contract(s) to the combination protects the short option exposure.

Synthetic Long Options, Spreads, Straddles, and Strangles

Welcome to synthetic long calls and synthetic long puts; bull call spreads and bear put (not "barefoot") spreads; long straddles; and long strangles. The other combinations may give hedgers the "butterflies." One suspects that some combinations were first improvised in desperation, not engineered. Necessity is still the mother of invention.

Synthetic Long Options.   "Synthetic" is an artificial position created by combining a futures contract position and a traded option position. For example, a synthetic long put is a combination of a short futures position and a long call option position. Recent jargon uses synthetic to refer to emulating a derivative contract using exchange-traded contracts—for example, a "synthetic swap" using futures contracts.

The basic insurance when using an option contract is being long a call or long a put. The synthetic long call or long put is a combination of an option and futures position to imitate the long call or long put and provide some flexibility for price reversals or hedge management.

The synthetic of buying and holding a call option is being long a futures contract and buying a put option. The futures contract has unlimited profit potential if the futures price goes up. If the futures price goes down below the put option's strike price, the option offers unlimited profit potential to help offset the loss occurring on the futures contract. Typically, the strike price of the put is not identical to the entry price on the futures contract. Therefore, a loss gap exists if the price of the underlying stays lower than the futures' purchase price. The position can be modified by selling the put option—being long a futures contract—or by closing the futures position and holding the put.

Spreads.   Spreads can be very useful to the financial engineer. If traded option premiums are high because of high volatility, a spread may accomplish the hedger's objective at a lower premium. Two names to remember are "bull call spread" and "bear put spread." Spreads are useful to reduce the cost of call or put option premiums by giving up some potential favorable price move. The bull call spread is a long call option at a strike price lower than the strike price of the short call option. The protection is against a limited upward price movement—a somewhat bullish trend. Writing the call results in receiving some premium to offset the premium for buying the lower strike calls. The "bear put spread" is a long put option at a strike price higher than the strike price of the short put option.

Spreads require writing an option—being "short" either a call or a put. It is important to keep both legs of the position and not sell the long call or put.

Long Straddle or Volatility Straddle.   A long straddle is the combination of buying a put and call option at the same strike price. The cost of the position is the sum of the premiums. The position will profit if the market moves in either direction, and will realize particular gain from increased volatility. This position is a volatility hedge suitable for being in place in advance of

G7[2] or OPEC meetings, war, or other events certain to increase the volatility of an underlying with unknowable market direction.

Long Strangle.   A strangle is a cheaper straddle. A long strangle is a combination of buying a put option at a lower strike price and a call option at a higher strike price, when both strike prices are "away from the money." The option premiums are relatively inexpensive. The position will, however, profit if there is a large price move in either direction or a substantial increase in volatility.

FORWARD RATE AGREEMENTS

Forward rate agreements (FRAs) are useful *derivative, money market* contracts for the management of interest rate exposure. An FRA is an agreement between two parties for a notional loan or deposit in a certain amount, for a specified forward period of time, at a designated rate. An FRA is a short-term, single-period *interest rate swap.* The starting date for the FRA is rarely more than 12 months after the dealing date. FRAs are available for most *Eurocurrencies* and especially for *Eurodollars.* Banks are the primary market makers. Their *indication* quotes are available by telephone or, in some cases, on electronic quotation systems such as *Telerate.*

The jargon for FRA quotations is reminiscent of the lumber industry. A "one-by-four"—printed "1 × 4"—is a 3-month FRA beginning 1 month from the dealing date. A "2 × 8" is a 6-month FRA beginning 2 months from the dealing date. Generally, the market prefers that the FRA be effective on the first day of a month and be structured for money market term and size.

On the *spot* date or first day of the FRA's interest period, the *reference rate* for cash settlement is the then current spot market interest rate for the underlying—for example, a 3-month LIBOR. If the reference rate is higher than the FRA rate, the buyer pays the seller a settlement amount that is the net present value of the difference between the FRA rate and the reference rate computed on the notional amount. If the reference rate is lower than the FRA rate, the seller pays the buyer, using the same computation. The FRA buyer is "buying" the reference rate for a forward time period on the notional amount.

As an example, an investor would use an FRA to ensure receiving the FRA rate during a forward period of time. The investor would still receive the financial instrument's cash market or stated rate. By comparison, a borrower would use an FRA to ensure paying the FRA rate during a forward period of

[2] G7 is the collective label given to the world's seven largest industrial nations. Alphabetically, they are: Canada, France, Germany, Italy, Japan, the United Kingdom, and the United States.

time. The borrower would still pay the interest rate set for the loan (LIBOR, for example, plus the lender's markup and any reserve).

SWAPS

A *swap* is an exchange of two things of value. There are two broad categories of swap contracts: physical delivery swaps and derivative swaps. Physical delivery swaps are cash, spot, or forward market contracts between two parties for the physical exchange of an underlying(s). For example, a forward foreign exchange contract is a physical delivery swap. A derivative swap is a *derivative, capital markets* contract to exchange features of one or more underlying(s) for a certain period of time. For example, the parties to an interest rate swap contract use payments based on computed values for the types of interest rates being "swapped" but they do not exchange the notional principal amounts of the financial instruments. By comparison, *commodity swaps* require mutual physical delivery of the commodity(ies); the derivative *commodity price swaps* involve the exchange of payments related to the commodity(ies) price or other *basis,* but mutual physical delivery does not occur. Swaps are versatile and can be contractually engineered into all manner of corporate financial risk management tools.

A swap contract may involve more than one underlying—for example, swapping fixed and floating interest rates or an interest rate exposure with a currency or commodity price. Some types of swaps have a large number of open contracts, particularly interest rate swaps. Swap contracts can be closed by computing the present value of a contract and having one party appropriately pay off the other. Another alternative is to enter into a reversing trade. As further discussed in Chapter 4, a form of standard swap contract has been developed. A secondary market for trading swaps that are identical in contract documentation has been discussed. New futures contracts, designed around interest rate swaps as the underlying, have been developed.

There are all kinds of swaps. *Swaptions* (OTC options on some types of swaps) are available. This discussion has introduced the most common names. Many of the derivative swap contracts involve swapping "fixed to floating," a jargon referring to price computations and not to floating volumes.

A detailed listing of swaps terms appears in Appendix A.

4
Some Basic Legal Concepts

Life is made up of a series of judgments on insufficient data, and
if we waited to run down all our doubts, it would flow past us.

Judge Learned Hand

All the transactions discussed in this book are analogous to Hamlet's "play
within a play": they occur within a framework of law. Because the framework is still being built, some legal issues are not yet resolved; other legal
issues are judicially decided case-by-case; still others depend on the subjective decision of a party to the transaction; and new issues continue to arise as
financial engineering develops new kinds of transactions. In this book, the
discussions of "law" are limited to some arbitrarily selected legal issues that
are suitable for considering the contracts used in corporate financial risk
management.

What are some of the legal concepts and issues? Among them are at least
the following: Why is it important to know what is a contract? Why is the
difference between a forward contract and a futures contract of practical
importance? What is the legal connotation of fraud? If a legal dispute over a
contract results in litigation and the contracting parties are from different
states or countries, how is jurisdiction or choice of law determined? If a
judgment or arbitration award is expressed in the money of a foreign country, what date governs conversion of the judgment into U.S. Dollars—
breach-of-contract day, judgment day, or payment day? Answers that are
both definite and accurate are not possible, but the intent of the text is to
provide general guidance.

In the final chapter of the book, which is devoted to a brief review of
selected legal developments, the reader will find descriptions of such well-
known cases as *Franklin Savings,* with its detailed review of "hedge" accounting, and the internationally publicized *Hammersmith Council* case, which

held unenforceable an interest rate swap transaction because it was entered into for speculation rather than for interest rate risk management.

The quotation, on the copyright page of this book, from a *Declaration of Principles jointly adopted by a Committee of the American Bar Association and a Committee of Publishers* is particularly pertinent to the three "legal" chapters of this book:

> It [the book] is sold with the understanding that the publisher is not engaged in rendering legal, accounting, or other professional service. If legal advice or other expert assistance is required, the services of a competent professional person should be sought.

To ensure compliance with professional ethics, the lawyer co-author states that the same disclaimer of providing legal advice applies to the lawyer's contribution to this book.

Some caveats are in order. The reader should not rely on the legal portions of this book as a substitute for a competent lawyer's advice on a particular problem. Even a brief discussion of selected key legal concepts and issues reminds the lawyer co-author of the statement by the late Justice Harlan Fiske Stone of the U.S. Supreme Court: "Napoleon tried to do too much—and he did."

CONTRACT DEFINED

Every transaction discussed in this book involves a contract. A contract must be established, as a matter of law, for the transaction to be enforceable. The classic definition is: "A contract is a promise, or set of promises, for breach of which the law gives a remedy, or the performance of which the law in some way recognizes as a duty."[1] The definition makes plain that the obligation of a contracting party is based on that party's promise. In interpreting a contract, the courts emphasize its promissory nature.

Contracts are classified in several ways. This book is concerned only with informal contracts, which may be written or oral, express or implied in fact. Some currency and financial instruments contracts are written, but many others, although involving enormous amounts of currency, may be oral and equally binding. Informal contracts have four requirements for their formation: (1) parties that have a legal capacity to contract; (2) mutual agreement as to the contract's terms—"meeting of the minds"; (3) consideration; and (4) a lawful object.

---

[1] 1 Williston on Contracts § 1 (3d Ed. 1957), at 1; 1 (Lord) Williston on Contracts § 1 (4th Ed. 1990), at 2–3; Restatement (Second) of Contracts § 1 (1979).

To have the legal capacity to contract, an individual must be not a minor and not mentally impaired. For a corporation, the legal capacity to contract means that the corporation has the authority under its articles of incorporation to authorize the corporation's entering into the proposed contract and to designate individuals to act on behalf of the corporation in that regard. The requirement of corporate authority is particularly important with a forward contract, because of the requirement to deliver the underlying in a contract that may have a far longer term than would a cash contract. Of equal importance, the person entering into the contract on behalf of the corporation must have the corporately vested, documented authority to enter into the contract.

The mutual agreement requirement is exemplified by litigation in which a party seeks to rescind or cancel a contract because of mistake, namely "no meeting of the minds."

Consideration in contract law does not equate with money; for example, an act or a forbearance to act can be consideration. One party's promise given for the other party's promise, called a bilateral contract, is consideration. One party's promise given for the other party's performance of an act, called a unilateral contract, is also consideration; a common example is one party's promise to pay for a commodity in return for the other party's delivery of the commodity.

FORWARD CONTRACTS AND FUTURES CONTRACTS

In the United States, the Commodity Exchange Act[2] (the Act) established the Commodity Futures Trading Commission (CFTC) as the agency to regulate futures contracts on organized exchanges. The Act's exclusion of forward contracts from regulation by the CFTC is called the section 2(a)(1) exclusion.[3] Although the Act excludes forward contracts, the legal distinction between a forward and a future contract is sometimes blurred (see Chapter 13).

The Commodity Exchange Act expressly excluded from being a futures contract "any sale of any cash commodity for deferred shipment or delivery," namely, a cash forward contract.[4]

---

[2] 7 U.S.C.A. 1 *et seq.* (1980 and 1991 Cum. Supp.).

[3] 7 U.S.C.A. § 2 (1980 and 1991 Cum. Supp.); for excellent and detailed discussion of the history of the section 2(a)(1) forward contract exclusion from CFTC regulation, see Commodity Futures Trading Comm'n v. Co Petro Marketing Group, 680 F.2d 573, 577–78 (9th Cir. 1982), and 1978 Memorandum to the CFTC from its Office of the General Counsel, 44 Fed. Reg. 13,494, 13,498 (Mar. 12, 1979).

[4] 7 U.S.C.A. § 2(a)(1) (1980 and 1991 Cum. Supp.).

Forward Contracts

Forward contracts, by definition, are privately negotiated principal-to-principal contracts that are transacted over-the-counter.

Definitions of forward contracts usually include the criterion that physical delivery of the underlying is planned. Price or rate swap and derivative contracts require settlement by cash payments because the underlyings to these contracts are the prices or rates, not the commodity, currency, or financial instruments (the latter are not being physically delivered). The periodic cash payments are the physical delivery of the revalued prices or interest rates underlying the contract.

The CFTC recently issued its "Statutory Interpretation Concerning Forward Transactions under the Commodity Exchange Act,"[5] in which it quoted with approval the following description of a forward contract:

> First, the contract must be a binding agreement on both parties to the contract; one must agree to make delivery and the other to take delivery of the commodity. Second, because forward contracts are commercial merchandising transactions which result in delivery, the courts and the Commission have looked for evidence of the transactions' use in commerce. Thus, the courts and the Commission have examined whether the parties to the contracts are commercial entities that have the capacity to make or take delivery and whether delivery, in fact, routinely occurs under such contracts.[6]

In 1990, Congress amended the Bankruptcy Code to add a definition of "forward contract,"[7] which is discussed in the context of insolvency (see Chapter 13).

Futures Contracts

Futures contracts are standardized contracts "for the purchase or sale of a commodity for future delivery,"[8] which are traded on a regulated exchange. Futures contracts are sold at auction, sometimes called "outcry trading," on a regulated exchange, with the only open term in the transactions being the price. The CFTC has exclusive jurisdiction over futures contracts within its statutory jurisdiction and designates the contract markets for those contracts.

The Commodity Exchange Act requires that transactions in commodity futures contracts occur only on or subject to the rules of boards of trade that the CFTC has designated as contract markets.[9] The Act defines "board of

[5] 55 Fed. Reg. 39,188 (Sept. 25, 1990).
[6] *Id.* at 39,190–91.
[7] 11 U.S.C.A. § 101(24) (1979 and 1991 Supp. Pamphlet) (June 25, 1990, Pub. L. No. 101-311, Title I, § 101, Title II, § 201, 104 Stat. 267, 268).
[8] 7 U.S.C.A. § 2 (1980 and 1991 Cum. Supp.).
[9] 7 U.S.C.A. § 2(a) (1980 and 1991 Cum. Supp.).

trade" as any exchange or association of persons engaged in the business of buying or selling any commodity.[10] The Commission and the courts have consistently recognized, however, that the requirement for a futures contract to be executed on a designated contract market is what makes the contract legal, not what makes it a futures contract.[11]

Commodities

The Commodity Exchange Act (the Act) was substantially amended in 1974 to expand the meaning of "commodity" to include a broad spectrum of items that may be the subject of futures contracts. In addition to the agricultural commodities enumerated, the amendment added "all other goods and articles, . . . and all services, rights, and interests in which contracts for future delivery are presently or in the future dealt in."[12] Thus, since 1974, all types of commodities, both tangible and intangible, may be the subject of futures contracts.

In 1982, the CFTC's jurisdiction was limited when Congress granted the Securities and Exchange Commission (SEC) exclusive jurisdiction to regulate "any put, call, straddle, option, or privilege on any security . . . or any put, call, straddle, or option, or privilege entered into on a national securities exchange relating to . . . any instrument commonly known as a 'security.'"[13] Despite subsequent amendments to the Act, the CFTC retains exclusive jurisdiction over futures contracts involving financial instruments and options on those futures. Nonetheless, a jurisdictional gray area remains between the CFTC and the SEC, with respect to "hybrid instruments." This is addressed in Chapter 13.

In 1990, the CFTC issued its "Statutory Interpretation Concerning Forward Transactions,"[14] which specifies the features that it deems distinguish a forward from a futures transaction. These features are summarized as follows.

---

[10] 7 U.S.C.A. § 2 (1983) (1980 and 1991 Cum. Supp.).

[11] *In re* First Nat'l Monetary Corp. (1984–1986 Transfer Binder), Comm. Fut. L. Rep. (CCH) ¶ 22,698 at 30,975 (CFTC 1985); *In re* Stovall (1977–1980 Transfer Binder), Comm. Fut. L. Rep. (CCH) ¶ 20,941 at 23,776 (CFTC 1979); CFTC "Policy Statement Concerning Swap Transactions," 54 Fed. Reg. 30,694 at 30,695, n. 8 (July 21, 1989); CFTC Interpretive Statement, "The Regulation of Leverage Transactions and Other Off-Exchange Future Delivery Type Investments—Statutory Interpretation," 50 Fed. Reg. 11,656 (Mar. 25, 1985).

[12] 7 U.S.C. § 2 (1980 and 1991 Cum. Supp.).

[13] 15 U.S.C.A. §§ 77b(1), 78c(a)(10) (1981 and 1991 Cum. Supp.). At the same time, the Commodity Exchange Act was amended to provide that the FTC would have no jurisdiction to designate a board of trade as a contract market for any transaction specified in the amended SEC statute.

[14] 55 Fed. Reg. 39,188, 39,191 (Sept. 25, 1990).

1. Delivery of the underlying is the hallmark of a forward contract. To the contrary, the vast majority of futures contracts—even though they provide for delivery—are satisfied by either entering into an offsetting contract or selling the contract on the exchange—namely, no delivery. This is the primary distinguishing feature of forwards, in the view of the CFTC: "The Commission's emphasis on delivery as the feature distinguishing transactions within the scope of the section 2(a)(1) exclusion from futures contracts has its roots in the legislative history of the Act."[15] The CFTC has further stated that "Forwards also typically have been described by reference to the commercial nature of the counterparties which have the capacity to make or take delivery."[16]

2. A forward contract is entered into for commercial purposes related to the business of the party wanting to enter into the forward. The producer, processor, fabricator, refiner, or merchandiser may want to purchase or sell a commodity for deferred shipment or delivery as part of the conduct of its business. In contrast, "futures contracts are undertaken principally to assume or shift price risk without transferring the underlying commodity."[17]

3. A forward contract is privately and individually negotiated between two principals. A futures contract is an exchange-traded contract, with standardized provisions including: commodity units; margin requirements related to price movements; clearing organizations that guarantee counterparty performance; open and competitive trading on exchanges; and public dissemination of price.

4. A forward contract generally is not assignable without the consent of the contracting parties and does not provide for an exchange-style offset. A futures contract is fungible, because of its standardized form, and hence can be traded on an exchange.

5. With a forward contract, no clearinghouse, no settlement system, and—according to the CFTC—no variation margining is involved. All three of these features apply to a futures contract.

DISTINGUISHING FORWARDS AND FUTURES

Why is the distinction between a forward and a futures contract of any practical importance? A forward contract is not subject to CFTC regulation and its terms are flexible; a futures contract is subject to CFTC regulation and its contractual terms are not flexible, but it has liquidity. What are the advantages or disadvantages of each? This question is not subject to a ready answer. A forward contract is free from regulatory constraints and inherently

[15] *Id.*
[16] *Id.*
[17] *Id.*

involves individually negotiated terms. A futures contract offers the protection of regulated trading markets, regulations prohibiting manipulation or "cornering" of the underlyings traded and requiring disclosure of risk, and regulations proscribing fraud and requiring minimum financial standards. Some types of financial engineering contracts are traded only as forwards; others are traded only as futures contracts. In sum, the corporate financial engineer's decision in distinguishing a forward from a futures contract is both subjective and objective. Subjective: Is freedom from regulatory constraints vis-à-vis the regulatory protections desired? Objective: Where is the type of contract selected available, off-the-exchange or only on regulated exchanges?

Some courts have demarcated between the respective identifying features of a forward contract and a futures contract, as illustrated by the following examples. In *Breyer v. First National Bank Monetary Corp.*,[18] the court recognized that "standardization" is a distinguishing characteristic of a futures contract and that futures contracts have uniform delivery locations and dates even though many traders do not intend to take or make delivery. In *Commodities Futures Trading Commission v. Morgan, Harris & Scott, Ltd.*,[19] the court defined a commodity futures contract to be a contractual undertaking that is transferable to third parties, to buy or sell a fixed amount and grade of a certain commodity on some specified date. *Abrams v. Oppenheimer Government Securities, Inc.*[20] pointed out *inter alia* that the purchasers of forwards generally adopt a more long-term position, often actually taking delivery of the underlying commodity; in contrast, most futures contracts are entered into for speculation and "are discharged by entering into an offsetting contract."

In sum, the chief distinguishing aspect of a forward contract is its usual actual delivery of the underlying, and that of a futures contract is its standardized form. Nonetheless, the distinction between forward and futures contracts "is unclear from both an economics and a legal point of view."[21] Hence, when the distinction is not obvious, both the CFTC and the courts use an ad hoc approach to determine whether a transaction is a futures contract tradable only on a regulated exchange or an off-exchange forward contract. The criterion for the ad hoc determination is this: "The transaction must be viewed as a whole with a critical eye toward its underlying purpose."[22]

[18] 548 F. Supp. 955 (D.N.J. 1982).
[19] 484 F. Supp. 669 (S.D.N.Y. 1979).
[20] 737 F.2d 582 (7th Cir. 1984).
[21] First Nat'l Monetary Corp. v. Commodity Futures Trading Comm'n, 677 F.2d 522, 526 (6th Cir. 1982).
[22] Commodity Futures Trading Comm'n v. Co Petro Marketing Group, 680 F.2d 573, 581 (9th Cir. 1982), quoted with approval by the CFTC; "Policy Statement Concerning Swap Transactions," 54 Fed. Reg. 30,694 (July 21, 1989).

THE *TRANSNOR* CASE: WAS THE DISTINCTION BLURRED?

An apt statement is that "no bright-line definition or list of characterizing elements is determinative"[23] of whether a particular contract is one over which the CFTC has jurisdiction. The distinction between forward contracts and CFTC-regulated futures contracts was arguably blurred in the 1990 opinion rendered in *Transnor (Bermuda) Ltd. v. BP North American Petroleum.*[24] The opinion was a blockbuster in the Brent oil trading market and caused uncertainty that lessened liquidity in the U.S. forward markets.

In *Transnor,* plaintiff Transnor, a Bermuda corporation, was a small trader that purchased two cargoes of Brent oil in December 1985 at an average price of $24.50 per barrel, for delivery in Scotland in March 1986. Transnor refused to take delivery of the cargoes because their market value had declined after Transnor entered into the contracts. Transnor sued several multinational petroleum companies, including BP North America Petroleum, Conoco Inc., Shell Oil Company, and Exxon Corporation, alleging an antitrust conspiracy and commodities manipulation in violation of the Commodity Exchange Act.

The district court ruled that the two contracts involved, which were 15-day Brent contracts, were futures contracts within the meaning of the Commodity Exchange Act and hence were subject to CFTC jurisdiction. The court based its ruling on certain findings of fact, including the following:

- 15-day Brent contracts are "routinely settled by means other than delivery, most typically through the clearing techniques of offset and book-out." The customary use of offsetting and booking-out "strongly suggests" that physical delivery was not contemplated by the parties to the Brent contract.
- The Brent contracts have a "high degree of standardization" such as quantity, grade, delivery terms, currency of payment, and unit of measure—". . . bookout and other clearing techniques."

The *Transnor* opinion provoked immediate and adverse reaction from many oil companies, which predicted that the market's liquidity would be greatly restricted and that the exclusion of banks and financial institutions

---

[23] *Id.* at 581; statement quoted with approval in CFTC v. American Metal Exchange Corp., 693 F. Supp. 168, 192 (D.N.J. 1988).
[24] 738 F. Supp. 1472 (S.D.N.Y. 1990).

from off-exchange oil markets would significantly impair corporate ability to manage price risk.[25]

THE CFTC'S RESPONSE TO *TRANSNOR*

Within a few days after the *Transnor* ruling that the Brent 15-day market is a futures contract market, the CFTC began an examination of Brent trading. On September 25, 1990, the CFTC issued its "Statutory Interpretation Concerning Forward Transactions under the Commodity Exchange Act" ("the Statutory Interpretation").[26] The CFTC stated that it had recently received inquiries concerning the applicability of the section 2(a)(1) exclusion from CFTC regulation to 15-day Brent contracts, and noted that "these inquiries were triggered by an opinion and order" in *Transnor*. The Statutory Interpretation concluded that the 15-day Brent contracts, as described in the Interpretation, are within the scope of the statutory exclusion from regulation. The conclusion was not unequivocal, however; the CFTC noted: "This does not mean, however, that these transactions or persons who engage in them are wholly outside the reach of the Commodity Exchange Act for all purposes."[27]

The Statutory Interpretation is not limited to 15-day Brent contracts. It is a broad statement designed to provide guidelines for determining whether a particular commercial transaction is a forward contract exempt from regulation or a futures contract. The Statutory Interpretation does not, however, have the force and effect of a statute or a regulation. The CFTC declared:

> It is noteworthy that while such agreements may extinguish a party's delivery obligation, they are separate, individually negotiated, new agreements, there is no obligation or arrangement to enter into such agreements, they are not provided for by the terms of the contracts as initially entered into, and any party that is in a position in a distribution chain that provides for the opportunity to book-out with another party or parties in the chain is nevertheless entitled to require delivery of the commodity to be made through it, as required under the contracts.[28]

---

[25] *See, e.g.,* 68 Platt's Oilgram News, no. 80, Apr. 25, 1990, p. 1: "Meanwhile, the fallout from the court ruling [*Transnor*] appears to have created what one legal source with a Brent market participant described as a 'fear reaction.' The source linked lessened market liquidity in the U.S. to the ruling." *See also Financial Times* (London), Apr. 27, 1990, p. 42: "European traders said they would continue to trade with US partners with great caution until a final CFTC ruling was issued. One trader said that Brent market trading would probably continue to move out of the US, regardless of any CFTC action."

[26] 55 Fed. Reg. 39,188 (Sept. 25, 1990).

[27] *Id.* at 39,192, n. 16.

[28] *Id.* at 38,192.

Thus, the CFTC concluded that the prerequisite to a forward contract—the obligation of delivery—was met. Although the practice of bookout (payment of difference in lieu of delivery) extinguishes the delivery obligation, the CFTC views the bookout as a separate contract.

The CFTC's detailed analysis of a 15-day Brent contract both confirms that "no bright legal line" separates a futures from a forward contract and illustrates that an ad hoc determination is made by viewing the transaction "as a whole with a critical eye toward its underlying purpose."

SWAPS: LEGAL NATURE

Swap contracts are discussed in Chapter 3 and defined in Appendix A. The legal nature of a swap contract, excluding a swap for physical delivery of the underlying, is examined here, together with an overview of applicable law and contract forms. An old Latin legal phrase aptly describes the legal nature of a swap contract that does not involve physical delivery: *sui generis,* defined in *Black's Law Dictionary* as "Lat. Of its own kind or class; *i.e.,* the *only one* of its own kind; peculiar." Thus, a "no physical delivery" swap contract is analogous to a forward contract, but is not one. This type of swap contract is also analogous to a futures contract, because of its "lack of delivery" of the underlying. Such a swap contract is not a futures contract, as shown by the CFTC's definition of a swap:

> In general, a swap may be characterized as an agreement between two parties to exchange a series of cash flows measured by different interest rates, exchange rates, or prices with payments calculated by reference to a principal base (notional amount).[29]

The International Swap Dealers Association (ISDA) has pointed out that use of its suggested forms does not result in a "standardized" contract that is a hallmark of a futures contract. ISDA points out that, for example:

> the term, the effective date, the termination date, the interest rate option, the notional amount and the payment dates of Swap Market Transactions are not standardized. As a result, Swap Market Transactions are not standardized. As a result, Swap Market Transactions remain in most important respects individually tailored and negotiated commercial transactions.[30]

---

[29] 54 Fed. Reg. 30,694, 30,695 (July 21, 1989).
[30] Letter from ISDA to Office of the Secretariat, Commodity Futures Trading Association, Apr. 8, 1988, in response to Advance Notice of Proposed Rulemaking—Regulation of Hybrid and Related Instruments.

Swaps that do not involve physical delivery of the underlying have, therefore, a unique legal nature. Their uniqueness explains why swap transactions receive separate consideration in both statutes and regulations.

SWAPS: KEY STATUTES

Commodity Exchange Act

The Commodity Exchange Act does not expressly refer to swap contracts, and the regulatory determination of whether a swap transaction is subject to or exempt from CFTC regulation is based on section 2(a)(1)(A) of the Act.[31] That section grants the CFTC exclusive jurisdiction over "accounts, agreement [including any transaction which is of the character of . . . an 'option' . . .), and transactions involving contracts of sale of a commodity for future delivery traded or executed on a contract market . . . or any other board of trade, exchange, or market . . ."[32]

Financial Institutions Reform, Recovery and Enforcement Act of 1989 (FIRREA)

FIRREA,[33] a far-ranging statute relating to financial institutions, substantially changed the powers of the Federal Deposit Insurance Corporation (FDIC) as receiver or conservator for insolvent institutions and expanded its powers to include almost all banks as well as savings and loan institutions. FIRREA imposes substantial limitations, however, on the FDIC's powers over certain defined "qualified financial contracts,"[34] including swap agreements. A swap agreement is defined as follows:

(vi) *Swap agreement*

The term "swap agreement"—

(I) means any agreement, including the terms and conditions incorporated by reference in any such agreement, which is a rate swap agreement, basis swap, commodity swap, forward rate agreement, interest rate future, interest rate option purchased, forward foreign exchange agreement, rate cap agreement, rate floor agreement, rate collar agreement, currency swap agreement, cross-currency

---

[31] 7 U.S.C. § 2.
[32] *Id.*
[33] Pub. L. No. 101-73 (1989); for classification of the Act to the U.S. Code, see note under 12 U.S.C.A. § 1811, showing codification under various titles, *e.g.,* Federal Deposit Insurance Corporation, Commerce and Trade, Internal Revenue Code.
[34] 12 U.S.C.A. § 1821(e)(8)(D)(1) (1989 and 1991 Cum. Supp.) expressly including swap agreement under the term "qualified financial contract."

rate swap agreement, currency future, or currency option purchased or any other similar agreement, and

(II) includes any combination of such agreements and any option to enter into any such agreement.

(vii) *Treatment of master agreement as 1 swap agreement*

Any master agreement for any agreements described in clause (vi)(I) together with all supplements to such master agreement shall be treated as 1 swap agreement.

Bankruptcy Code

In 1990, Congress amended the Bankruptcy Code to add a definition of "swap agreement."[35] The definition is substantially similar to the definition in FIRREA except that the Bankruptcy Code definition does not include "interest rate future" and "currency future." A master agreement, with all supplements, is treated as one swap agreement.[36] The legal ramifications of a counterparty's bankruptcy are discussed in Chapter 13.

SWAPS: CFTC POLICY STATEMENT

In 1989, the CFTC issued a "Policy Statement Concerning Swap Transactions" ("the Statement").[37] The purpose of the Statement is to identify the swap transactions that will not be regulated as futures or commodity option transactions under the Commodity Exchange Act or related regulations. The CFTC expressly limited the Statement to swaps settled in cash, with foreign currencies considered as cash, and to options on swaps. In its safe harbor standards, the Statement makes no distinction for interest rate, currency, or commodity price swaps.

The CFTC, in setting forth its safe harbor standards, cautioned that neither the standards nor the presence or absence of additional elements is dispositive of whether a transaction is a futures contract.

The CFTC listed five requirements for swaps not to be subject to regulation as futures or commodity option transactions: individually tailored terms; absence of exchange-style offset; absence of clearing organization or margin system; undertaking the swap in conjunction with a line of business; and prohibition against marketing to the public.

The CFTC Policy Statement is just that, no more. It can be superseded by a federal statute and probably preempted by a state statute, and it has less

---

[35] Pub. L. No. 101-311, 104 Stat. 267 (1990), to be codified at 11 U.S.C. § 101(49)(A).
[36] *Id.*, to be codified as 11 U.S.C. § 101(49)(C).
[37] 54 Fed. Reg. 30,694 (July 21, 1989).

weight than a regulation or agency interpretation. Nonetheless, the CFTC's safe harbor standards, despite the criticisms they have provoked, give improved official guidance.

The reader's attention is also directed to the CFTC's "Regulation of Hybrid Instruments";[38] these are generally defined as instruments that combine the characteristics of commodity option contracts with debt, preferred equity, or depository interests.

ISDA MASTER SWAP AGREEMENT FORMS

The International Swap Dealers Association (ISDA), formed in 1985, is a worldwide association of swap dealers.

In 1985, ISDA published its Code of Standard Wording, Assumptions and Provisions for Swaps, which was expanded in the 1986 edition ("the ISDA Code"). The ISDA Code relates to U.S. Dollar *interest rate swaps.* The ISDA Code is not a contract, but it sets forth standard wording for such provisions as rate setting, calculation of fixed and floating amounts, and possible events of default. The ISDA Code offers alternatives for wording the provisions so that the parties may choose the appropriate wording for the individualized transaction being structured.

ISDA Master Agreements

ISDA has developed two forms of master agreements:

- The Interest Rate Swap Agreement is for U.S. Dollar-denominated interest rate swaps. It incorporates the ISDA Code and is governed by New York law.
- The Interest Rate and Currency Exchange Agreement is also an agreement for interest rate swaps but may be used, in addition, for interest rate swaps in any currency, *currency swaps,* and cross-currency interest rate swaps. The parties may elect to have New York law or English law apply. This agreement, sometimes called the "multicurrency form," does not incorporate the ISDA Code by reference, although its provisions are substantially the same as the pertinent ISDA Code provisions.

The two master agreement forms are complete contracts. They have no substantive differences, except minor ones required by the purposes of the multicurrency forms. Both have separate, supplementary documents ("the

---

[38] 54 Fed. Reg. 30,634 (July 21, 1989).

Schedules") that set forth the specific economic terms of the particular swap transaction. In May 1989, ISDA published two addenda to the Schedules, one for each of the master agreement forms. These addenda enable swap counterparties to include caps, collars, floors, and similar transactions under the agreements. In September 1989, in a commentary to the May 1989 addenda, ISDA analyzed the addenda, explained their use, and recommended that swap participants consult their lawyers before determining whether to have two separate master agreements, one for swaps and one for caps, collars, and floors. In addition to the printed master form and the appended Schedules, a confirmation of the swap transaction is also appended. All the documents together—the printed contract, the Schedules, and the confirmation—comprise a single swap contract.

The ISDA master agreement forms have been carefully developed by swap professionals, and use of the forms is greatly aided by ISDA's "User's Guide to the Standard Form Agreements" ("the User's Guide"). The forms have been designed to expedite swap transactions, and a special feature deserves emphasis: Users need only fill in certain identifying information in the printed text and then complete or make changes on the Schedule attached to each form. The User's Guide states: "Users of the form should employ the printed version and should not retype the main text of each form." The economic terms negotiated for the transaction are shown on the confirmation. This structuring provides desirable acceleration of a swap transaction, saving both lawyers' time and clients' money. ISDA facilitates use of the forms by this note on the copyright of the User's Guide: "ISDA consents to and encourages the use and photocopying of these forms for the preparation of swap agreements."

The CFTC "Policy Statement Concerning Swap Transactions" notes that formation of swaps pursuant to a master agreement between two counterparties that established some or all contract terms for swap transactions between the counterparties is not precluded by the requirement of individually tailored terms for safe harbor treatment.[39] Thus, the CFTC tacitly acknowledges that use of the ISDA master swap agreement forms does not result in characterizing the swap transaction as a futures contract.

As a practical note, some counterparty banks and other financial institutions have their own forms for swap agreements. If the reader encounters such a special form, a good way to check its provisions is to compare it with the ISDA master form agreement. If the only difference is that the confirmation is included—that is, the economic terms of the swap are made part of the agreement's text—this is not a problem, if the terms accurately reflect the swap negotiated. If the counterparty's own form differs from the ISDA form, however, in wording of the mechanical provisions or has added or deleted provisions, then the changes require scrutiny.

---

[39] 54 Fed. Reg. 30,694, 30,696, n. 17 (July 21, 1989).

The ISDA Interest Rate and Currency Exchange Agreement (1987) is reproduced as Appendix C.

1991 ISDA Definitions

The Definitions are intended for use with the ISDA agreements and in confirmations of transactions subject to the agreements. Appended as exhibits to the Definitions are sample forms for a letter agreement or telex of confirmation, and specific provisions to include in a confirmation of a rate swap or cross-currency rate swap agreement. This publication is a valuable reference.

As stated repeatedly in this book, understanding any proposed transaction before entering into a contractual obligation is essential. A sound decision to enter into a swap agreement cannot be made before becoming completely familiar with the ISDA standard form agreements, the User's Guide, the ISDA Code, and the Schedules.

NETTING OF SWAPS

The prescribed length for this book limits this section to an "inventory" of some important legal aspects of netting.

Netting of swaps has become an important legal issue because of uncertainty concerning its enforceability by courts and regulators. A 1990 amendment to the federal Bankruptcy Code (discussed in Chapter 13) has ameliorated uncertainty of enforcement in the bankruptcy setting.

Netting arises in two contexts: between the parties to the swap, and between and among banks. Netting between the parties to the swap is exemplified by the netting provision in each of ISDA's swap agreement forms. The User's Guide provides a simple description of the netting provision:

> Each form provides that payment due on the same date in the same currency under a given swap will be netted. Each agreement also enables the parties to elect that, when payment dates on two or more swaps coincide, the payments due under those swaps on the same day and in the same currency will be netted.[40]

Netting between and among financial institutions has also engendered considerable attention, but its discussion is not within the scope of this book.

The federal Bankruptcy Code, in a 1990 amendment, added a new provision that preserves a swap party's contractual right to terminate a swap agreement and offset any amounts owed under it, if the counterparty files bankruptcy or becomes insolvent or if a trustee is appointed for the party.

---

[40] Art. III.B.3.

THE LEGAL CONCEPT OF FRAUD

Fraud is a term that is as comprehensive as the means that the human mind can devise to gain advantage by false representations or concealment. The Anglo-American legal system has long imposed penal sanctions for criminal fraud and civil liability for fraudulent conduct. Fraud is accorded special treatment in law. For example, in a civil lawsuit, a claim for fraud must be pleaded "with particularity."[41] The burden of proving fraud is more onerous than for other civil claims. The evidentiary burden of proof in a civil suit is by a preponderance of the evidence ("over 50 percent"), except that the burden for proving a fraud claim is by clear and convincing evidence.

Fraud has various classifications; pertinent here are actual fraud, which requires an intent to deceive, and constructive fraud, which requires no ill intent but is conduct prohibited by law because it tends to deceive or to mislead others. The elements of actionable fraud, as they are most frequently stated by the courts, are:

1. Defendant made a material representation;
2. The representation was false;
3. Defendant knew that the representation when made was false, or made it recklessly, with knowledge of its untruth;
4. The representation was made with the intention that plaintiff should act on it;
5. Plaintiff acted in reasonable reliance on the representation;
6. As a result of the reliance, plaintiff sustained damages.

Realistically, when people have lost money, it is tempting to allege constructive fraud. Good faith in the transaction does not ensure against a claim of constructive fraud.

In sum, the elements of fraud are the representation, its falsity, scienter, deception, and injury. Scienter, which is Latin for "knowingly," now has common legal usage in fraud cases arising under the federal securities laws and the Commodity Exchange Act.

Law with respect to fraud involves innumerable areas of commercial activity. The legal concept of fraud is discussed here in the context of unauthorized futures trading. Section 4b of the Commodity Exchange Act renders it unlawful "to cheat or defraud" or "willfully to deceive" any person with respect to any contract, subject to the Act, that is in interstate commerce. Section 4b has been judicially construed to require that a person's acts be done with knowledge of their nature and character.[42] Mere negligence, mistake, or inadvertence does not meet Section 4b's scienter

---

[41] Rule 9(b), Federal Rules of Civil Procedure, adopted by many states.
[42] Commodity Futures Trading Comm'n v. Savage, 611 F.2d 270, 283 (9th Cir. 1979).

requirement.[43] "A willful violation" of the Commodity Exchange Act's Section 4b is fulfilled, however, by either "an intentional act or a careless disregard for the statutory requirement."[44]

Drexel Burnham Lambert Inc. v. Commodity Futures Trading Commission[45] is a good example of fraud considered in a client's suit against a brokerage firm for losses sustained in trades subject to the Commodity Exchange Act. The federal court of appeals for the District of Columbia held that mere negligence, mistake, or inadvertence failed to meet the Act's Section 4b scienter requirement. The court also held that the Section 4b language making it unlawful "to cheat or defraud" or "willingly to deceive" encompasses reckless conduct.

Messer v. E. F. Hutton & Co.[46] involved a suit by a client against a broker, alleging unauthorized trading in T-bond futures in violation of the Securities Exchange Act, the Commodity Exchange Act, and the Florida Securities Act. The court viewed the crucial issue to be whether Section 60(1)(A) had a scienter requirement and concluded that it did. The court then held in favor of the defendant broker, stating a reassuring rationale for honest traders who worry about unfounded fraud charges:

> A review of the record persuades us that no reasonable juror could have concluded that E. F. Hutton made the unauthorized trades with the requisite *scienter*. The record shows that E. F. Hutton made the unauthorized trades because the value of Messer's T-bond holdings was dropping precipitously and it wanted to protect the account. The record also shows that the trades were made without Messer's authorization because he was out of town and could not be reached at the time the decision had to be made. While opinions might differ on whether or not the decision to straddle the account was a good business decision, the expert testimony at trial established that straddling an investment is a common and accepted industry practice to protect an account against extreme losses. Far from supporting a finding that E. F. Hutton made the unauthorized trades with intent to defraud or reckless disregard for Messer's best interest, it appears that Hutton made a reasonable decision well within the bounds of accepted industry practice designed to protect the account.[47]

Although the trader was thus vindicated on appeal, the harsh reality is that the trader was sued, endured a jury trial with a verdict of fraud, and undertook an appeal—all entailing considerable worry and expense.

Two old Latin legal terms—malum in se and malum prohibitum—still provide a useful guide in the legal area of fraud. Malum in se means bad

---

[43] Drexel, Burnham Lambert Inc. v. Commodity Futures Trading Comm'n, 850 F.2d 742, 748 (D.C.Cir. 1988).
[44] Commodity Futures Trading Comm'n v. Savage, 611 F.2d at 283.
[45] 850 F.2d 742 (D.C.Cir. 1988).
[46] 847 F.2d 673 (11th Cir. 1988).
[47] *Id.* at 679.

and immoral in itself—for example, the wrongful killing of another person. Malum prohibitum means not inherently wrong, but wrong because prohibited by law. Malum prohibitum applies to the kind of fraud that is prohibited by the Commodity Exchange Act and by the federal securities laws. No one would disagree with those statutes' prohibition of dishonest and deceitful conduct. The problem arises in the administrative or judicial interpretation of those statutes: when does the trader's conduct constitute fraud within the meaning of the statutes? The best protections against violation are care in ensuring authorization to enter into the transactions and prudent and competent service to the client.

JURISDICTION AND CHOICE OF LAW

Jurisdiction, the authority of a court to hear and decide a case, is determined by federal or state constitutions or by statute. Because jurisdiction is a complex legal area, only a few basic rules are stated here, to avoid misleading the reader. Jurisdiction has two main categories: subject matter jurisdiction and personal jurisdiction. Each category is defined according to applicable state and federal constitutional provisions, statutes, and judicial precedents established by court opinions.

Subject matter jurisdiction can be determined by reference to the governing constitution (federal or state) or to statute. Federal district courts have jurisdiction in cases involving federal statutes, as well as cases based on diversity of citizenship of the parties, when the amount in controversy exceeds $50,000.[48]

Personal jurisdiction is determined according to the constitutional standard of due process. The United States Supreme Court set forth the standard for federal courts in the landmark case of *International Shoe Co. v. Washington.*[49] The Court held that the State of Washington Unemployment Compensation Act applied to a Delaware corporation that had its principal place of business in Missouri but maintained resident salespeople in Washington. The Court stated the following test for personal jurisdiction:

> [D]ue process requires only that in order to subject a defendant to a judgment in personam, if he be not present within the territory of the forum [place of litigation], he have certain minimum contacts with it such that the maintenance of the suit does not offend "traditional notions of fair play and substantial justice."[50]

[48] 28 U.S.C. § 1332(a).
[49] 326 U.S. 310 (1945).
[50] *Id.* at 316.

International Shoe recognized two other types of "forum-related" activity that would suffice to give personal jurisdiction:

> If a defendant's forum-related activities are "continuous" and "substantial," this can justify suit in that forum [place of litigation] against the defendant on causes of action arising from matters entirely distinct from those activities—so-called "general jurisdiction." Also, if a defendant's acts in the forum are not sufficient to support general jurisdiction, jurisdiction may still lie when the acts "because of their nature and quality and the circumstances of their commission" are deemed sufficient to subject the defendant to suit.[51]

Choice of law concerns which jurisdiction's law governs resolution of a lawsuit. For example, jurisdiction to hear and decide a case may be in Florida, but the judicial decision may be governed by New York law. Here is a brief description of "choice of law":

> An integral part of choice of law is the distinction between (1) *lex fori,* which is the law of the forum—that is, the law of the place where the legal relief is sought— and (2) *lex loci,* the law of the place where the right arose or the liability incurred that is the basis of the legal claim. *Lex fori* governs procedural and remedial matters . . . *lex loci contractus* . . . means the law of the place where the contract was executed, is to be performed, or by which the contract is to be governed.[52]

Business professionals are familiar with the contract clause stating that the contract shall be governed by the laws of a designated state. The law imposes limitations, however, on the contracting parties' right to agree on the governing law. Probably the modern prevailing view is that the law of the jurisdiction having the greatest interest in the litigation—sometimes referred to as the nexus to the litigation—will be applied. The federal courts, in a case in which jurisdiction is based on diversity of citizenship, will determine the choice of law according to the forum state's rule governing choice of law. For example, if a diversity case is in an Illinois federal district court, that court will apply Illinois law concerning choice of law to decide which jurisdiction's law will apply. In sum, choice of law is a misnomer: the contracting parties cannot choose, without legal restriction, which jurisdiction's law will govern their contract.

In recent years, the enforceability of the forum selection clause—the contract's provision stating what jurisdiction's laws shall govern—has been attacked in subsequent litigation arising under the contract. The courts have been divided on whether the forum selection clause is enforceable, but a recent opinion by the Seventh Circuit Court of Appeals upholds the validity of the party's contractual choice of law with an excellent discussion of its reason for

---

[51] Wunnicke and Wunnicke, *Standby Letters of Credit* (1989) at 250.
[52] *Id.* at 254.

doing so.[53] The courts are constrained by various rules for determining which state's or foreign country's law applies to a lawsuit.[54]

JUDGMENTS AND ARBITRATION AWARDS ON FOREIGN MONEY CLAIMS

This brief section is probably a source of editors' despair because it does not "fit" into any part of the book. Nonetheless, the subject is too pertinent and important to omit. When a claim sued on in the United States is expressed in money of a foreign country, in what money is a judgment or arbitration award on that claim expressed? When is the amount of the judgment or award converted into U.S. Dollars for payment by the debtor?

Courts in the United States have generally assumed that, when they enter judgments requiring payment of a sum of money, even though the claim was expressed in foreign money, the judgments must be denominated in U.S. Dollars. Three different rules have been applied for determining the conversion date for the foreign currency:

- Breach day rule—the date when the money should have been paid;
- Judgment day rule—the date when the judgment or arbitration award is entered;
- Payment day rule—the date when the judgment or award is paid.

The U.S. Dollar amount of the judgment can vary widely, depending on which rule is applied. For example, *Comptex v. Labow*[55] illustrated the different results from applying the three conversion rules:

Date	Exchange Value	Plaintiff's Award
Breach day	GBP = USD 2.20	USD 41,338.00
Judgment day	GBP = USD 1.50	USD 28,185.00
Payment day	GBP = USD 1.20	USD 22,552.00

Courts in the United States have generally followed either the breach day rule or the judgment day rule.[56] New York applies the breach day rule, and

---

[53] Northwestern Nat'l Insurance Co. v. Donovan, 916 F.2d 372 (7th Cir. 1991).

[54] See, for example, Restatement of the Law (Third) of the Foreign Relations Law of the United States (1987), § 8.22, providing that "a member state of the International Monetary Fund may not enforce exchange contracts involving the currency of another member state if such contracts are contrary to that state's exchange control regulations . . ."

[55] 783 F.2d 333 (2d Cir. 1986).

[56] See Restatement (Second) of Conflict of Laws § 144, which adopts the date of the award of judgment.

the award was USD 41,338 in *Comptex,* invoking the rationale that a debtor should not benefit from failure to make timely payment of a debt.[57] Many foreign countries, in determining when conversion should be made into their currency, follow the payment day rule.

The National Conference of Commissioners on Uniform State Laws, composed of lawyers from each of the states, has prepared and recommended for adoption by all the states a number of uniform laws, including the Uniform Commercial Code. In 1989, the Conference approved a Uniform Foreign-Money Claims Act; its Prefatory Note merits quotation:

> This Act facilitates uniform judicial determination of claims expressed in the money of foreign countries. It requires judgments and arbitration awards in these cases to be entered in the foreign money rather than in United States dollars. The debtor may pay the judgment in dollars on the basis of the rate of exchange prevailing at the time of payment.
>
> A Uniform Act governing foreign-money claims has become desirable because:
>
> These claims have increased greatly as a result of growth in international trade. Values of foreign moneys as compared to the United States dollar fluctuate more over shorter periods of time than was formerly the case.
>
> United States jurisdictions treat recoveries on foreign-money claims differently than most of our major trading partners. A lack of uniformity among the states in resolving foreign-money claims stimulates forum shopping and creates a lack of certainty in the law.[58]

Thus, the Uniform Foreign-Money Claims Act requires that judgments and arbitration awards in foreign money claim cases be entered in the money customarily used by the prevailing party. The Act adopts the payment day rule, followed by many countries with which the United States trades. In 1990, five states adopted this new Act: Colorado, Connecticut, Hawaii, Illinois, and Utah.

Admittedly, not all the pertinent basic concepts have been even mentioned, but this chapter is intended to provide the reader with a useful perspective of the legal framework within which financial engineering transactions operate.

---

[57] Newmont Mines Ltd. v. Adriatic Ins. Co., 609 F. Supp. 295, *aff'd* 784 F.2d 127 (2d Cir. 1986).
[58] Uniform Foreign-Money Claims Act (U.L.A.), Prefatory Note (1989).

PART TWO
BUSINESS STUDIES

5
Importers

Example is always more efficacious than precept.

Samuel Johnson, Rasselas (1735)

IMPORTERS MIRROR EXPORTERS

Importers and exporters of retail and wholesale goods share the problem of managing their exposure to changes in foreign currencies. For many businesses, the opportunities of multinational finance, as discussed in Chapter 7, are not available or suitable. The problems of importers and exporters are in mirror image.

For importers, if the domestic currency decreases in value relative to the required foreign currency:

1. The cost of imported goods for retail sales might increase because of a decreasing value of the currency the importer uses to purchase the goods;
2. A lower value of the importer's currency for purchasing goods may require an increase in the wholesale or retail price, thus causing the importer not to be competitive with others able to wholesale or retail at a lower domestic price;
3. If the full effect of the increased cost of goods sold cannot be passed through to the retail sales price, reduced profits or even losses may result for the importer.

For importers of commodities, an issue is the separation of currency risk from commodity price risk. (Exporters are discussed in Chapter 6.)

This chapter on importers details two case situations of foreign currency contracts arranged through the interbank market. Heatherstone China

Company, importing for the first time a line of table china to expand on its lines of domestic manufactures, buys a currency call option; the alternative of compensating forward foreign exchange contracts is discussed. Biped Shoe Company, regularly importing shoes from an Italian manufacturer to supplement its lines of domestically manufactured footwear, uses foreign exchange swaps; the company then decides to write its first currency option contract to hedge its foreign currency exposure—a "covered write."

INTERBANK FOREIGN EXCHANGE CONTRACTS

There are two main markets for hedging foreign currency exposure. One is the forward market, where companies buy and sell a currency which they will need or receive. The other is the options market, where they buy call or put options, giving the holder the right to buy or sell a currency at a set rate.[1]

A third, important market is the regulated exchanges for trading futures contracts and options.

The two case studies in this chapter dissect basic and very useful interbank contracts for managing foreign exchange risk and payment obligations: the forward contract, combinations of spot and forward contracts, the purchase of an option, and writing an option to hedge a foreign exchange exposure—a "covered write."

Some company treasurers prefer the forward market because they dislike paying option premiums or think options are too expensive. Others prefer the purchase of options because they are flexible and do not have to be exercised; the option buyer retains the benefit of favorable price move. By comparison, a forward contract, left untouched, sets the price for delivery. Some financial risk managers flatly avoid writing options: "'These things can go wrong. We tend to be risk-averse.'"[2] The Biped Shoe study details a company's financial engineering of a "covered write." Admittedly (and as discussed in the case), only an individual who has experience with options and a solid knowledge of the instrument should use the strategy of a covered write.

Both studies in this chapter demonstrate how easily an option can be misunderstood and how to avoid such a misunderstanding. The studies also give examples of the considerations in designing an option transaction. The traders did make recommendations to their clients. Were they the most suitable? Should another resolution have been considered? What corporate policies should have been in place?

---

[1] Tracy Corrigan, "Treasurers learn to hedge their bets," Capital Markets Section, *Financial Times* (London), March 28, 1991.
[2] *Id.*

As discussed in Chapter 1, no book of reasonable length can be comprehensive of the entire topic of financial engineering. New variations are continually being offered to corporate financial risk managers. The goal here is to provide a guide for financial engineering of some basic forward and option contracts for foreign exchange. We hope to help the reader develop the analytic skills needed to understand proposals of other option strategies that may be presented.

Positions opposite to an importer could be assumed by an exporter in a parallel business situation. These cases could be repeated, in mirror image, in Chapter 6.

HEATHERSTONE CHINA COMPANY

At issue in this study were currency call options and compensating forward foreign exchange contracts.

Business Risk Situation

Heatherstone China Company, a manufacturer of table china for restaurants, is located in a small midwestern town and has annual sales of about USD 150 million. To expand its product lines and begin selling to retailers, the company entered into a contract to import fine bone china from an English manufacturer. This was Heatherstone China's first international business contract.

The contract required Heatherstone China to pay the English company, in Pounds Sterling (GBP or "Sterling"), GBP 5 million, 90 days after shipment of the china. The first shipment date was expected to be in November, about 8 months after the contract's March execution date.

The English china contract posed this problem for Heatherstone China's treasurer: the Company had to pay a known amount of Sterling in about 1 year, but the exact payment date was not known. The treasurer thought a *forward outright contract* was unsuitable because a forward contract requires a specific delivery date. The treasurer recognized the volatility of foreign exchange markets. Heatherstone China had for years competed against Japanese exporters of tableware into the United States. The treasurer did not want the risk that Sterling might appreciate against the U.S. Dollar. An increase in Sterling versus the U.S. Dollar would increase the Company's cost for buying the Sterling to pay for the English china, thereby decreasing or precluding profits from the new product line.

Because the English contract was Heatherstone China's first foray into a foreign exchange transaction, the Company had no policy regarding this type of financial risk management. The treasurer decided the first task was to find competent advice. Although the Company's local bank is a branch of a large regional bank, neither is active in foreign exchange markets and the treasurer was advised that the needed help could not be provided. The treasurer then contacted the New York bank that handled part of the Company's banking business and was placed in contact with one of its foreign exchange advisers.

Bank's Analysis and Proposed Solution

The New York bank's foreign exchange adviser provided the following comments to Heatherstone China's treasurer. At the moment of their telephone conversation, Sterling was offered at USD 1.7985 per GBP for spot delivery ("spot cable"). Because Sterling interest rates were higher than USD interest rates, the Company could buy Sterling for delivery 1 year forward at USD/GBP 1.7335. Forward Sterling was trading, therefore, at a "discount" to spot Sterling of 6.50 cents or 650 points. This response failed to solve the treasurer's problem of how to manage around the still unknown date for actual delivery of the Sterling to the English Company.

In the adviser's opinion, Sterling would probably depreciate in the near future and thus would "later" cost less to purchase. High interest rates might continue to attract capital into the United Kingdom but bad "economic fundamentals," including a deteriorating trade balance, a rising inflation rate, and continuing weakness in the economy, could eventually force the market to shift its focus away from Sterling interest rates. The adviser believed that, although Sterling might continue to appreciate over the next few months, a year hence Sterling would be much lower than the current spot rate. The bank's adviser was confident, therefore, that the treasurer should wait before covering the Sterling exposure. Also, in several months, the treasurer could better predict when Heatherstone China would need to pay Sterling to the English company. Heatherstone's treasurer was anxious about the exposure, however, and felt that "we ought to do something."

The bank's adviser then recommended a Sterling *call option* and summarized the proposed contract: the treasurer could buy an at the money spot, *American-style* call option with an *expiration date* 1 year hence. The option would give Heatherstone China the right, but not the obligation, to enter into a *spot* foreign exchange contract to purchase Sterling against U.S. Dollars at the option's *strike price* at any time up to and on the expiration date. If Heatherstone China needed to make its Sterling payment earlier than presently planned, the Company could exercise the American-style call at any time up to or on the expiration date, by 10:00 A.M. local time of the bank writing the option. Before the option's expiration date, the treasurer would probably know the exact date when the Sterling payment would be required. If, on the expiration date, the market's spot exchange rate for Sterling versus U.S. Dollars was higher than the call option's strike price, Heatherstone China could first exercise the call, that is, exercise its right to enter into a spot foreign exchange contract for purchasing the Sterling at the call option's strike price and then, using a "foreign exchange swap," swap the Sterling forward to the Pounds Sterling delivery date for payment to the English company.

The bank's adviser mentioned that, if the payment date were earlier than the option's expiration date, an alternative available to the treasurer was to sell back the option and then enter into a suitable spot or forward contract. The treasurer could then recoup the remaining time value of the option. (The bank's adviser mentioned the "delta" concept, but the treasurer, whose eyes glazed at "delta," said that the company wanted something straightforward.)

An *at the money spot* call option would be cheaper than an *at the money forward* call option because of the difference in *strike prices*—USD/GBP 1.7985 "spot" versus USD/GBP 1.7335 "forward." Forward Sterling was cheaper than spot Sterling—650 points discount (1.7985 minus 1.7335). The premium for a call option with a strike price equal to the higher current spot rate (1.7985) would be less than the premium for a call option with a strike price equal to the lower exchange rate for delivery 1 year forward (1.7335). Worded another way (and all else being equal in the call options): selecting the call option with a strike price equal to the lower forward exchange rate will result in paying a higher premium. Conversely, selecting an option with a strike price equal to the higher and more expensive spot exchange rate will result in a lower premium. The option writer will want more premium money for the call option that has the lower strike price, because of its higher *intrinsic value.*

Exercising either option would result in the option holder's entering into a spot foreign exchange contract to purchase Sterling from the option writer at the strike price of the option.

An American-style call option would have a more expensive premium than the seemingly less flexible European-style call option because the American-style option can be exercised against the writer at any time. Although the European-style option can be exercised only at maturity, in theory it can be sold at any time; thus, in combination with a spot market transaction, the effect would be about the same as for the American-style option's flexible exercise date.

An American-style Sterling call option gives its holder the opportunity to profit from favorable foreign price fluctuations up to and including the expiration date of the option. Thus, the holder can take advantage of situations in which the current interbank exchange rate is greater than the strike price of the option. For example, an option holder owns a Sterling call option for GBP 5,000,000 with a strike price of USD/GBP 1.8000. If the interbank exchange rate for Sterling were USD/GBP 1.8050, the option holder could exercise or sell the option and pocket USD 25,000 in profit: buy the Sterling at, say, USD/GBP 1.8000, or USD 9,000,000, and sell the Sterling in the spot foreign exchange market at USD/GBP 1.8050, or USD 9,025,000.

There is a difference between "favorable price moves" for a speculator and a hedger like Heatherstone. The speculator holding the call option profits by an increase in the U.S. Dollar value of Sterling. By comparison, Heatherstone's overall position is improved by a decrease in the value of Sterling because it costs less to purchase the Sterling to pay for the imported china. The call option is insurance for Heatherstone in case the U.S. Dollar value of Sterling increases.

If the spot exchange rate is more favorable than the strike price of a currency option, the difference is a potential gain to the holder of the option. **The cost of the option has to be included to determine whether the purchaser has any profit.** In Heatherstone's case, that opportunity to profit is built into the price of an at the money forward call option (the more expensive option because it has 650 points of intrinsic value built into its price) versus an at the money spot call option. Comparative computations using simplified numbers show the difference between at the money forward and at the money spot options in an amount of GBP 1,000,000:

1. If the at the money forward call option has a strike price of USD/GBP 1.7300 and premium of USD 100,000, the *intrinsic value* is USD 70,000—the .0700 difference between the 1.8000 spot exchange rate and the 1.7300 call option strike price, multiplied by GBP 1,000,000. The remaining USD 30,000 assumed premium consists of *time value.*
2. The at the money spot call option has a strike price equal to the spot exchange rate of USD/GBP 1.8000 and an assumed premium of USD 40,000. The entire USD 40,000 premium consists of time value. The intrinsic value is zero because the strike price and spot exchange rate are equal.
3. If the at the money forward USD/GBP 1.73000 call option for a spot foreign exchange contract is exercised when the spot market is at USD/GBP 1.8000, the option holder could buy GBP 1,000,000 for USD 1,730,000 and sell the Sterling for USD 1,800,000, a gross profit of USD 70,000 minus the USD 100,000 premium, or a net loss of USD 30,000.
4. To break even in this at the money forward call option, a spot exchange rate of USD/GBP 1.8300 is required—buying the GBP 1,000,000 for USD 1,730,000 plus the USD 100,000 premium totals USD 1,830,000; when divided by GBP 1,000,000, the result is USD/GBP 1.8300. By comparison, the breakeven point in this at the money spot call option is USD/GBP 1.8040—buying the Sterling for USD 1,800,000 plus covering the USD 40,000 premium. (The cheaper the option, the further away the breakeven point; there is "no free lunch.")

By spending more for an *American-style option,* Heatherstone China purchased flexibility to exercise the option at any point in time up to or on the expiration date. A cheaper option premium would have been an at the money spot European-style call, because the option writer's exposure to the option's being exercised is only at its maturity. An alternative approach to Heatherstone's problem is discussed later in the study.

The bank's adviser summarized the bank's analysis:

> The risk of Sterling's appreciation against the U.S. Dollar could be managed at a known cost, the strike price of the option plus the cost of the option.
>
> Heatherstone China could still take advantage of any major depreciation of Sterling against the U.S. Dollar by purchasing the cheaper Sterling in the interbank market.
>
> Heatherstone China could exercise the option at any time up to or on the expiration date of the option. When exercising the option, the Company could purchase the Sterling at the option's contractual strike price.

Business Decision: Currency Call Options

For several years, the treasurer had been collecting and reading brochures about options. After deciding to use an option but still wanting a second opinion, the treasurer contacted an acquaintance who led the team of corporate finance specialists at another New York bank. The acquaintance thought an option "made sense" and arranged for one of that bank's options specialists to telephone the treasurer.

The options specialist quoted the cost of a 1-year Sterling call, American-style, with a strike price equal to the current spot rate, at approximately 6.25 percent of the U.S. Dollar value of the call. With a spot rate of USD/GBP 1.8000, the option would cost USD 562,500, computed as follows:

GBP 5,000,000 × USD/GBP 1.8000 × 6.25% = USD 562,500.00

Pounds Sterling payment to English Company multiplied by the amount of U.S. Dollars for each Pound Sterling equals U.S. Dollars 9,000,000 multiplied by 6.25 percent premium equals U.S. Dollars 562,500 option cost.

The treasurer calculated that Heatherstone China's maximum cost of Sterling—the "maximum exchange rate"—at a USD/GBP 1.8000 exchange rate plus the option cost of USD 562,500 would be USD/GBP 1.9125, computed as follows:

GBP 5,000,000 × USD/GBP 1.8000 = USD 9,000,000 + USD 562,500
= USD 9,562,500/GBP 5,000,000
= USD/GBP 1.9125, the maximum
exchange rate.

Pounds Sterling payment to English Company multiplied by the amount of U.S. Dollars for each Pound Sterling equals U.S. Dollars 9,000,000 plus the option cost of U.S. Dollars 562,500 equals a total U.S. Dollar cost to Heatherstone China of 9,562,500 for 5,000,000 Pounds Sterling. The total U.S. Dollar cost of 9,562,500 divided by the 5,000,000 Pounds Sterling purchased equals the maximum exchange rate of USD/GBP 1.9125.

If the treasurer had instead chosen an at the money forward, the cost would have been USD 823,412.50, computed as follows:

GBP 5,000,000 × USD/GBP 1.7335 = USD 8,667,500 × 9.5% premium
= USD 823,412.50 option cost

The maximum exchange rate would have decreased to USD/GBP 1.8982.

The treasurer reviewed Heatherstone China's profit plan for the line of English china: the maximum Sterling cost of USD/GBP 1.9125 would protect a sound profit margin on the import and sale of the English china. The call option capped (put a ceiling on) Heatherstone China's cost for the English china at USD 9,562,500, but Heatherstone China could take advantage of any depreciation in the Sterling exchange rate against the U.S. Dollar. For example, if Heatherstone China could purchase the GBP 5,000,000 at an exchange rate of USD/GBP 1.7800, the total cost for the Sterling would be USD 9,462,500 or an exchange rate of USD/GBP 1.8925, computed as:

GBP 5,000,000 × USD/GBP 1.7800 = USD 8,900,000
+ USD/GBP 1.8000 option cost of USD 562,500 = USD 9,462,500.

Doing the Trade: Apples to Oranges

The treasurer checked the option price with two banks, to obtain the cheaper *premium* (the price Heatherstone China would pay to the option writer). The treasurer enlisted the help of the cash manager and obtained two simultaneous quotations. Each bank was asked to quote the premium for an American-style call option for GBP 5,000,000 with a strike price equal to the current spot rate and an expiration date 1 year forward. After several minutes, Little Bank quoted the premium at 6.29 percent and Big Bank quoted it at 6.10 percent. The treasurer closed the transaction with Big Bank.

The details of the transaction were as follows. On the trade date of September 12, 1988, Heatherstone China purchased an American-style Sterling call option for GBP 5,000,000 with a strike price of USD 1.8025. The settlement date of the trade was September 14, 1988, and the expiration date of the option was September 14, 1989. Stated otherwise, Heatherstone China purchased from the option writer the right to enter into a spot foreign exchange contract for the purchase of GBP 5,000,000 at USD 1.8025 per Pound. Heatherstone China could exercise that right to purchase at spot at any time between the option purchase settlement date of September 14, 1988, and the option's expiration on September 14, 1989.

Heatherstone purchased an option for a *spot* foreign exchange contract. Option contracts for the right to enter into *forward* foreign exchange contracts are also written and purchased. The most usual OTC foreign exchange option, however, is for the right to enter into a spot foreign exchange contract. The market will assume this "vanilla flavor" unless a forward foreign exchange option is specifically requested.

If Heatherstone China exercised the option to purchase the Sterling for spot settlement on the option's September 14, 1989, expiration date, the spot settlement date for delivery of the U.S. Dollars to the bank and receipt by Heatherstone China—or such payee as it directed—of Sterling from the bank would be September 16, 1989, two business days later.

The option contract required Heatherstone China to pay for the option, by *wire transfer* of immediately available funds to Big Bank's main office in New York, the premium amount of USD 549,762.50, calculated below. All OTC option premiums must settle (be paid) in immediately available funds, not by check or bank draft, and usually on the spot date. The calculation used:

GBP 5,000,000 (amount of option) × USD/GBP 1.8025 (strike price)
× 6.10% (premium) = USD 549,762.50, Big Bank option cost

After the treasurer had closed the transaction with Big Bank, the cash manager pointed out that Little Bank, in calculating the option premium it quoted, had used a different strike price—USD/GBP 1.7975 instead of Big Bank's "winning" USD/GBP 1.8025.

Outcome of the Trade

The day after the treasurer paid for the call option, the company's controller called to ask about the proper accounting procedure for the option payment. How should Heatherstone China show the option on its books? What value should be shown for the option in preparing the quarterly and annual financial statements? To which department of the company should the premium expense be charged? Must the option be marked-to-market in each accounting period? If a gain or loss occurred, which department should accrue the income or expense? Finally, the controller asked about the exact procedure for exercising the option. The treasurer referred the controller to the company's independent auditors for answers as to procedure, and then called Big Bank regarding exercise of the option.

What Heatherstone Did Not Understand

Heatherstone China had purchased a financial instrument without completely understanding the following: the option's price; how to ask banks to quote the option price; how to use the option or exercise it after its purchase; the cost of financing the option position; the accounting for the transaction. Those aspects of the option transaction are discussed in the following sections. The treasurer had not consulted with the company's accountants about the financial reporting and tax implications of the proposed transaction.

Some financial reporting and tax considerations are discussed in Chapter 12.

Pricing

Option pricing is complex, and several pricing models and theories are used to determine the value of any option. Chapter 3 discusses option contracts, and Appendix B offers references on the theory of option pricing.

For a practical review of Heatherstone China's financial risk problem and option transaction, the following seven factors are relevant:

1. The *strike price*—the contractual exchange rate when the option is exercised;
2. The value of the *underlying*—the financial instrument or commodity against which the option is written (the underlying for the Heatherstone China option is the GBP 5,000,000);
3. The time to the *expiration date* of the option;
4. Interest rates:
    a. the cost of financing the option premium to be paid, either by borrowing the cash or reducing interest income by reducing the company's investable cash; or
    b. for a currency option, the difference in interest rates between the two currencies, which determines the difference between the spot and forward exchange rates;
5. Price volatility of the underlying;
6. Market liquidity for the underlying;
7. The style of option, American-style or European-style.

The Heatherstone treasurer made a mistake when taking the cheaper premium without knowing the strike prices for the options being quoted. The treasurer was comparing apples and oranges and did not know this precept of the option market:

If a call option premium is correctly quoted, an option with a lower strike price (option A) will always have a higher premium than one with a higher strike price (option B). Option A has a greater *intrinsic value* than option B; if both option A and option B are *out of the money,* option A is more likely to be exercised. Put another way, if option B's strike price is equal to the *spot* price and option A's strike price is *in the money,* option A has intrinsic value and is, therefore, more expensive.

As an illustration, if call option A's exercise price is 10 points below the market price and call option B's is 5 points above the market price, option A has 10 points of intrinsic value and option B has none. If the exercise prices of both call option A and call option B are higher than the cash market price, both are out of the money. Call option A is, however, more likely to be exercised than call option B because call option A's strike price is closer to the cash market price.

If the treasurer had closed the deal with Little Bank, Heatherstone China would have paid a smaller time premium but the total option premium would have been higher. Calculations are as follows:

> GBP 5,000,000 (amount of option) × USD/GBP 1.7975 (strike price)
> = USD 8,987,500 × 6.25% (premium)
> = USD 561,718.75, Little Bank's option cost

The USD 561,718.75 can be compared to Big Bank's option cost of USD 549,762.50 for a higher USD/GBP 1.8025 strike, USD 9,012,500, and lower 6.10 percent premium. The difference between the intrinsic values of the options is USD 25,000: USD 9,012,500 for Big Bank's 1.8025 option minus USD 8,987,500 for Little Bank's option.

The following is a tempting but incorrect effort to make Little Bank's apples equal to Big Bank's apples. Little Bank's option cost was USD 561,718.75. Subtracting the USD 25,000 difference in intrinsic values equals USD 536,718.75. Big Bank's option cost was USD 549,762.50. Big Bank's USD 549,762.50 was USD 10,043.75 more than Little Bank's USD 536,718.75, as adjusted. To conclude, however, that Little Bank's apple was a "better buy" to protect the GBP 5,000,000 may not be correct.

One option is an apple and the other option is an orange. The option can be "engineered" to the corporate financial risk situation. For example, a lower premium may sometimes be more important to a company than lowering the strike price and paying a higher premium. It is, however, very important to know an apple from an orange when taking quotations.

How to Do the Trade

By his method of asking for quotations, the treasurer betrayed his amateur status and set the trap to receive quotes for both apples and oranges in the option market. The banks should have been asked for an *indication* on spot Sterling. Professional market practice is to request an indication when one merely wants to know at what price a currency, financial instrument, or commodity is trading. Only when the caller wants to enter into a transaction during the telephone call should the caller ask for a price or rate.

Next, the treasurer should have specified to each bank all the details of the option to be purchased. For example, assuming that spot Sterling was currently USD 1.8000 per Pound Sterling, the treasurer should have asked the same question of both banks: "Where would the bank offer an American-style call option on Pounds Sterling 5 million with a strike price of U.S. Dollars 'one eighty' [USD/GBP 1.8000] and an expiration of September 14, 1989?" The style, call or put, currency, amount, strike, and expiration date should each be specified.

If the treasurer had asked that question of both banks, the quoted price could have been compared for two identical options: apples and apples.

Exercising or Selling the Option?

Options typically expire on a business day at 10:00 A.M. New York time or at the equivalent time in another contracting time zone—for example, 3:00 P.M. London time is equivalent to 10:00 A.M. New York time. The time should, however, be verified and not assumed, especially for customized, derivative contracts. Thus, if the counterparty bank is in a time zone different from that of the option holder, the holder must be aware of the local expiration time. For example, for a Los Angeles option holder, whose time zone is three hours earlier than a New York counterparty bank's, the option expires at 7:00 A.M. option holder's time. What does the option holder do? Set the alarm clock! This is not a facetious answer.

How is an option exercised? Usually, by telephone call. The option holder calls the option writer and informs the writer that the holder intends to exercise the option. During that conversation, the writer and holder should confirm the settlement details for each currency, the payment amounts, and the banking location details.

Warning! Even if an American-style option is in the money, exercise of that option before expiration almost never pays, for this reason: prior to its expiration, an option has *time value*. The rule has theoretical exceptions, but, for practical, everyday use, the rule should be considered iron-clad.

For Heatherstone China, two assumptions are made for the date of March 12, 1989: (1) the treasurer learned that he had to pay the GBP 5,000,000 on June 14, 1989, for the English china; (2) spot Sterling was trading at USD 1.8500 per pound. Heatherstone China would have been better off if it had bought Sterling at the strike price of its option, USD 1.8025, instead of the current spot rate of USD 1.8500. The savings would have been USD 237,500, as shown by this computation:

(GBP 5,000,000 × USD/GBP 1.8500) − (GBP 5,000,000
× USD/GBP 1.8025) = USD 237,500.

If, however, Heatherstone China were to exercise its option on March 14, three months before expiration, it would lose the remaining time value on the option. An option premium has two components, intrinsic value and time value. If the option is in the money, its intrinsic value is the difference between the cash market price and the option's strike price. If an option is out of the money, it has no intrinsic value. The intrinsic value of Heatherstone China's call option, as calculated above, is USD 237,500, but the option premium depends on other factors, including the time remaining before expiration. The option has value over and above its intrinsic value.

For example, at March 14, the option might have, in addition to its USD 237,500 intrinsic value, an additional time value of, say, USD 125,000. The USD 125,000 figure is only an example; the lengthy calculations of time value are not within the scope of this book. (Contact a bank or a broker who specializes in financial futures and options.) Suffice it to say that if Heatherstone China were to exercise its option 3 months early, it would throw away the option's time value.

The proper procedure would be as follows: purchase the required amount of Sterling at the spot rate in the foreign exchange market; sell the option back to the bank, liquidating the option. Both legs of the procedure can be tested with competitive pricing quotations. Following this two-step procedure, Heatherstone China would (1) receive the benefit from the difference between the strike price of the option and the current cash market price for Sterling, or USD 237,500, and (2) capture the time premium the market attributed as remaining on the option, for example, USD 125,000. The amount of the remaining time premium would offset part of the original premium paid for purchase of the option.

Financing the Option Premium

When Heatherstone China purchased the option, it incurred a cash expense of almost USD 550,000 for the option premium. If the company were in a net borrowing position, it would have to borrow an additional USD 550,000 to pay the premium. If the company borrowed at a prime rate of 10 percent, the company might attribute an additional USD 55,000 in interest expense for the year during which it owned the option—assuming the prime rate did not change during that period. If Heatherstone China were a net short-term investor, it would lose the use of and the interest income from the dollar amount paid for the premium. The amount of the implied expense should be included in a purchaser's calculation of the total option cost—financing cost plus premium.

An Alternative: Compensating Forward Foreign Exchange Contracts

Heatherstone China's treasurer may have used the wrong financial engineering "tool." Although the option premium was expensive, the treasurer recognized that a currency call option would enable the company to take advantage of favorable price moves in the underlying currency—for Heatherstone, a decrease in the U.S. Dollar cost of Pounds Sterling. The treasurer was especially attracted by the flexibility of the American-style call option: the Sterling could be purchased at some known, maximum exchange rate at any time up to or on the expiration date of the option. This seemed important because the treasurer did not know the exact payment date for the GBP 5,000,000 to the English china company. The bank emphasized that the American-style option to enter into a spot foreign exchange contract could be exercised at any time. Only two business days' notice for dealing at spot would be required to purchase the Pounds Sterling for the payment. The treasurer did not ask about selling the option and its remaining time value. The alternative transactions would be these: selling the option with its remaining time value back to the bank, and purchasing the Pounds Sterling for spot settlement. Either way, the treasurer could, in two business days, take delivery of the Pounds Sterling and pay them to the English china company.

The banks had advised the treasurer that, if it were profitable to exercise the option at its expiration, the company could do so even though it did not yet need to pay for the English china. The treasurer could *swap* the Sterling from the option's *value date* to the anticipated payment date for the English china. The value date in this case is when each party to the option had to pay to the counterparty the Pounds Sterling and offsetting U.S. Dollars. The bank's adviser had assumed that, when the value date arrived, Heatherstone's treasurer would probably know the exact payment date for the English china. Flexibility to control timing of the Sterling payments was crucial for Heatherstone.

The treasurer could have achieved the same flexibility in timing Heatherstone's payments—but greater advantage—by using a *forward foreign exchange contract*. Assume the treasurer had been certain that the earliest date for Heatherstone's Pounds Sterling payment to the English china company would be June 1989. On September 12, 1988, Sterling could have been purchased for delivery on June 14, 1989, the value date for this example of a 9-month *forward outright contract;* or, the treasurer could have selected any desired value date for delivery of the Pounds Sterling—for example, June 1, 1989.

With Heatherstone not required to make the Pounds Sterling payment until June 14, 1989, the treasurer could have swapped the Sterling either to (1) the exact payment date to the English china company, if that date were known, or (2), if not, one month forward, to July 14, 1989. This kind of transaction makes it possible to minimize cash flows. For example, if, for the value date of June 14 the treasurer had bought Pounds Sterling from Middle Bank, the treasurer might have sold the GBP 5,000,000 back to Middle Bank for value June 14 and bought it forward for value July 14. If Heatherstone did not need the Pounds Sterling before August 14, on July 12 (two business days before the July 14 date of the forward contract entered into on June 12) the treasurer could do a *foreign exchange swap:* sell the Sterling spot value date July 14 and purchase it for delivery at the next forward date, August 14. If one party does not want to take delivery, a maturing foreign exchange contract must be swapped to a new forward date. This transaction methodology is sometimes called "pushing the contract forward."

The swap on the rollover date, described in the above paragraph, should not be confused with an historic rate rollover, a transaction that is subject to abuse. Here is an example of an historic rate rollover: if Sterling were purchased 1 year forward at USD/GBP 1.8000 and 1 year later the Sterling spot rate were USD/GBP 1.6000 or USD/GBP 2.000, the "historic rate rollover" rate used would nonetheless be USD/GBP 1.8000—the rollover is not *marked-to-market*. All manner of abuses become possible: the recognition of gain or loss (or the day of cash reckoning) because of changed market price may be deferred. Some authorities frown on historic rate rollovers or prohibit them.

Under a *compensating forward foreign exchange contract,* Heatherstone China's spot sale for Pounds Sterling would offset the maturing forward contract. Hence, if the same bank was used, no Sterling payments would be made by either Heatherstone or its counterparty bank, because each offsetting contract would be for the same Sterling amount. A U.S. Dollar payment would be made to the extent that the spot exchange rate for Sterling differs from the exchange rate on the maturing forward contract. Hence, each contract would have a different U.S. dollar value, even though the Sterling amounts would be the same. One contract would have a higher dollar value than the other, and this would result in a net dollar amount due to one party from the other. The difference between the dollar amounts would be calculated, and one party would pay the other the dollar amount owed. The same result could be obtained by dealing the offsetting contract with a different bank.

Table 5.1 gives an example of cash transactions for a compensation agreement. For each alternative, assume that Heatherstone China had bought GBP 5,000,000 at a rate of USD/GBP 1.7400 for value June 14. The dollar value of the contract would be USD 8,700,000.

A *compensating forward foreign exchange contract* has several advantages and should be done whenever suitable. The most important advantages are that a compensating forward contract simplifies payments, reduces transaction costs of foreign exchange contracts, and reduces the credit exposure

Table 5.1   Cash Transactions for a Compensation Agreement

Exchange Rate for June 14	U.S. Dollar Value of GBP 5,000,000	Amount and Direction of U.S. Dollar Cash Flow from Compensation
1.7500	$8,750,000	Bank would pay Heatherstone China USD 50,000 resulting from the appreciation of Sterling against the U.S. Dollar
1.7300	$8,650,000	Heatherstone China would pay the bank USD 50,000 resulting from the depreciation of Sterling against the U.S. Dollar

of any *settlement risk* between the two parties. Settlement risk refers to the fact that, if there are substantial time zone differences between the countries of the currencies for a foreign exchange contract, one party must pay, for example, a European or Asian currency hours before it can be certain that it has received the equivalent U.S. Dollars.

BIPED SHOE COMPANY

Foreign exchange swaps and writing currency options to hedge exposure were at issue in this study.

Business Risk Situations

The Biped Shoe Company is a domestic corporation that sells its products to retailers. It manufactures most of its shoes, but has, for many years, imported part of its merchandise from an Italian shoe company. The Company earns a higher profit (22 percent) on sales of its imported goods than on sales of its own manufactured products (17 percent). It wants to protect its profit margin on the Italian imports.

The Italian shoe company has always shipped against commercial letters of credit payable in Italian Lira. As a result of this agreement to pay in Italian Lira, Biped Shoe Company has a substantial foreign exchange risk between the dates of placing its orders and the payment of the Italian company's invoices. The Company's "natural" position is short the Italian Lira, for this reason: because its operations do not generate Italian Lira, the Company needs to acquire Italian Lira for its customary three or four payments a year to the Italian company.

Foreign Exchange Swaps

Prior to adopting its 1990 strategy of writing currency options, early in each year Biped Shoe made a reasonable estimate of the Italian Lira amount that it would need for the coming year.

Biped Shoe's treasurer was aware that the foreign exchange market's prices were less competitive for odd amounts, small amounts, and odd dates. The treasurer was also aware that the market risk in using the foreign exchange swaps strategy is that an advantageous interest rate differential between currencies might reverse—for example, the interest rate differential between U.S. Dollars and Italian Lira. Fluctuation in the spot exchange rate is not the market risk of this strategy.

The Company would cover its short Italian Lira foreign exchange exposure with one or a combination of the following foreign exchange swap strategies.

1. Purchasing the amount of Lira estimated for each forecasted payment date and rolling to the actual payment date. When an invoice required payment, the Company would roll the exact payment amount to the actual payment date. Any Lira purchased in excess of the exact payment amount could be rolled forward to the next forecasted payment date or sold at spot. Conversely, if the estimated Lira purchased forward were less than the exact payment amount, the shortfall could be swapped from the forward contract for the next estimated payment date or purchased at spot.

2. Purchasing all the Lira estimated for the entire year for delivery on the last forecasted payment date and entering into swaps for the interim payment dates. When an invoice required payment, the Company executed a *foreign exchange swap:* it purchased on a spot basis the amount of Lira needed for the payment, and it sold the same amount forward for delivery on the same value date as the original forward contract.

As an example, on January 10, 1987, Biped Shoe's treasurer purchased Italian Lira (ITL) 25 billion against USD 17.17 million for delivery on January 10, 1988, at an exchange rate of ITL/USD 1456. On April 1, 1987, Biped Shoe's Purchasing Department notified the treasurer that the next payment due to the Italian company would be ITL 7.644 billion, on April 10, 1987. For April 10, 1987, the treasurer bought ITL 7.644 billion and sold the same amount forward for value on January 10, 1988—the *value date* of the original 1-year forward contract.

Biped Shoe executed a similar swap for each additional payment required on and before January 10, 1988. Each additional swap reduced the net amount of Lira that the Company would be obligated to receive on the January 10, 1988, value date. Thus, if the ITL 25 billion estimated amount became the exact amount needed during the period of the 1-year forward contract, then the net amount of Lira on the original contract's value date would be reduced to zero.

Hence, at the value date of January 10, 1988, the Company would have only a net dollar amount due to or from its counterparties to the Lira forward contracts. In practice, however, the zero Lira balance is unlikely to occur: accuracy "to the last Lire" is not a reasonable expectation. Instead, any net difference between the Lira on the 1-year forward contract and the Lira amounts swapped would also be settled on January 10, 1988.

3. Purchasing all the Lira estimated for the entire year for delivery on the first forecasted payment date and using a foreign exchange swap to roll over the unused Lira balance to the next projected Lira payment date. If the first payment to the Italian company was anticipated to be due in 3 months, the Company could enter into a 3-month forward contract. The Company could (1) make the payment required on or after the date of the forward contract's maturity, and (2) roll over, with a new forward contract, the balance of the projected Lira requirement to the next projected payment date.

An an example, on January 8, 1987, Biped Shoe purchased ITL 25 billion against USD 17.5 million for delivery on April 10, 1987, at an exchange rate of ITL/USD 1428.57. On April 1, the Purchasing Department informed the treasurer that the next payment to the Italian company would be ITL 7.644 billion, due on April 14, 1987. On April 8, 1987, Biped Shoe's treasurer:

- Rolled over for value April 10, 1987, and for delivery on July 10, 1987, ITL 17.356 billion (ITL 25.0 billion minus the payment of ITL 7.644 billion for April 14, 1987);
- Arranged to receive payment of the ITL 7.644 billion on April 10, 1987, and invested this amount for four days until the April 14, 1987, value date for the payment to the Italian company.

A new rollover date could be effected for each estimated invoice payment date to the Italian company. The example in Table 5.2 assumes a constant ITL 1428.57 forward exchange rate.

Table 5.2 can be used to test the effects of the following fluctuations. Fluctuation in the spot foreign exchange rate will have little effect on the total USD cost of the ITL requirements. Fluctuation in the spot foreign exchange rate has a somewhat greater effect on the present value of the total USD cash flow. This effect on the present value is attributable to the timing of USD cash flows with fluctuations in the ITL/USD spot exchange rate. The greatest risk is the potential for an unfavorable change in the relative interest rate differential between the two currencies. As discussed in *interest rate arbitrage,* a currency with a lower interest rate will trade at a premium to one with a higher interest rate in the forward foreign exchange market.

To test the risk of the foreign exchange swap strategy, assume that the spot exchange rate between the Italian Lira and the U.S. Dollar remains stable and

Table 5.2 Foreign Exchange Swap Worksheet—Example

Biped Shoe Company must pay a total of ITL 25 billion on four different future dates. Biped does not know the exact payment dates or the exact amount due on each payment date.

Biped estimates each date and the amount to be paid on each expected payment date on January 8, 1987.

Assumptions: Spot ITL/USD Rate: ITL 1420/USD
USD Interest Rate: 8.00%

Payment Number and Estimated Payment Date	Estimated ITL Payment (Billions)	Forward Foreign Exchange Rate	USD Equivalent	Present Value Factor	Present Value of Cash Flow
1. Apr. 10, 1987	7.644	1429	$ 5,349,195.24	0.980392	$ 5,244,309.06
2. July 10, 1987	4.955	1438	$ 3,445,758.00	0.961169	$ 3,311,955.01
3. Oct. 10, 1987	10.475	1447	$ 7,239,115.41	0.942322	$ 6,821,580.13
4. Dec. 10, 1987	1.926	1456	$ 1,322,802.20	0.923845	$ 1,222,064.76
Total USD Cash Flows			$17,356,870.85		
Total Present Value of USD Cash Flows					$16,599,908.97

that U.S. Dollar interest rates rise above Italian Lira interest rates. Assume that the interest rate differential in favor of the U.S. Dollar continues to increase, so that the difference between the spot and forward ITL/USD exchange rates changes from the modest U.S. Dollar premium on the initial trade date to an increasing U.S. Dollar discount. The total U.S. Dollar cash flow will increase sharply, and the present value of the cash flows will also increase.

To reiterate a very import point: the market risk in using the foreign exchange swaps strategy is not that there will be a fluctuation in the spot exchange rate. The market risk is that the interest rate differential between the currencies will change adversely over the time period of the hedge.

Currency Options and the Covered Write

Biped Shoe considered using currency options to hedge its Italian Lira exposure. The objective was to explore the potential advantages of options. After finding out that purchasing call options on the Italian Lira was expensive, the Company decided to make the costly premium inure to its benefit by *writing,* instead of purchasing, the options. (The Company's natural position was to be *short* the Italian Lira.) The Company wrote a *covered put,* a decision reached in the following manner:

- An estimate was made of the "worst case scenario" exchange rate for the purchase of Lira that would still maintain an acceptable return on

Biped Shoe's sales of the Italian shoes. The estimate was based on the following factors:

1. The known selling price of the Italian company's shoes to Biped Shoe;
2. The approximate retail selling price of the Italian shoes;
3. The anticipated gross profit margin on the imported shoes;
4. Estimated import duties, cost of transportation from the port to Biped Shoe's distribution center, and other related expenses.

The result was an estimated breakeven exchange rate of ITL 1196 per U.S. Dollar. The following is an example of how to compute a simplified breakeven exchange rate for a single item:

> If the Italian company charges Biped Shoe ITL 50,000 per item, and Biped Shoe's wholesale price for that item cannot exceed USD 51.00—including all cost factors and its desired 22 percent return on sales of imports—then Biped Shoe's USD import cost cannot exceed USD 41.80 (USD 51.00/1.22 percent);
>
> ITL 50,000/USD 41.80 equals ITL/USD 1196.

- After reviewing various currency hedging strategies, the Company ascertained that *writing* Lira puts, instead of hedging with a forward contract plus using swaps or rollovers, offered two advantages: the Company had an opportunity to take advantage of currency volatility, and, if the option holder exercised the option, the Company would be buying Lira that it needed. Thus, Biped Shoe's short Lira position would be covered. Because the Company was short the Lira, the strategy selected—writing Lira puts—was considered a *covered write.*

The covered write is a strategy that requires constant monitoring of an open position against the underlying's cash market. The covered write is used primarily by businesses wanting to hedge a cash flow, for example, an import or export transaction, an intercompany cash flow, or a similar cash flow from a third party. The covered write should be used with caution to hedge a balance sheet or currency translation exposure. This use of the covered write incurs unlimited cash flow risk to hedge what may be noncash items. If the option holder chooses to exercise the option, the balance sheet hedger pays cash to the option holder. The strategy can become a situation of using apples to hedge oranges.

Some experienced foreign exchange members write options when volatility in the foreign exchange market declines. When markets are quiet, the probability of options' being exercised is reduced and the writer's cost of repurchasing options, if the position is closed, will be relatively low. The writer's risk is that volatility may increase because of unforeseen events. The cost of closing the option position may then be greater than the premium earned plus the interest earned on the premium received.

Hedging Strategy and the Band of Protection

The procedure Biped Shoe developed for the hedging strategy of writing foreign currency options had the following steps:

- Estimate the foreign currency requirements.
- Decide contract details.
- Estimate interest income on premiums received.
- Estimate the "band of protection."

Estimate Foreign Currency Requirements.   The Company estimated the following payment dates and amounts to the Italian company:

March 31, 1990	ITL 4.828 billion
August 1, 1990	ITL 6.036 billion
November 15, 1990	ITL 13.277 billion

The Italian Lira to U.S. Dollar exchange rates for each date, based on indicative quotes from a bank, were the following:

Spot	ITL 1250.00/USD
March 31, 1990	ITL 1259.25/USD
August 1, 1990	ITL 1275.00/USD
November 15, 1990	ITL 1289.50/USD

Decide Contract Details.   One option contract could be written for each of the expected payment dates. If exercised, each option contract would become a spot foreign exchange contract subject to two business days for cash settlement. Thus, each option contract should expire two business days earlier than each payment date: March 29, 1990; July 30, 1990; and November 13, 1990. To preclude any possibility of a counterparty's exercising the option before its expiration date (when the Company would want the Lira), European-style put option contracts were selected; this type of option can only be exercised at maturity.

Banks were contacted for an *indication* of the premiums that a company would earn by entering into the transaction at the moment when the indicative

Table 5.3   European-Style Italian Lira Puts

Expiration Date: 1990	Strike Price	Currency Amount (Billions)	Estimated Premium (%)
March 29	1259.25	ITL 4.8	4.75
July 30	1275.00	ITL 6.0	7.00
November 13	1289.50	ITL 13.3	9.00

quotation is given (see Table 5.3). Obtaining indicative quotes helps avoid errors when actually dealing transactions, by providing a review of the proposed contract. Indicative quotations are also the source for market levels to compute estimates and plan strategies. Most counterparties will quote exchange rates and option premiums for odd amounts of currency. Some may provide better quotations for larger, marketable amounts and for an even amount of currency. The details of each option contract can then be summarized (see Table 5.3), including *type, style, expiration date, strike price, currency* amount and the estimated *premiums* for which the options can be written. The strike price of each option being considered by the Company is an *at the money forward* because the strike price is equal to the *forward outright exchange rate* for each option expiration date.

Estimate Interest Income on Premiums Received.   For each option it writes, Biped Shoe will receive a premium that could be invested. The investment's proceeds will partially offset the cost of Biped Shoe's purchasing the Lira to be paid to the Italian company. The Company can specify that the premium is to be paid to it in U.S. Dollars or Italian Lira. The interest income is assumed to be attributable to the option for the time between the date of the writer's receipt of the option premium and the date of the option's expiration. The amount realized is calculated as follows:

Estimated Dollar Value of the March 1990 Option Premium

ITL 4.8 billion (Bio)/ITL 1259.25/USD = USD 3,811,792.73

Currency amount divided by strike price equals USD equivalent of the currency amount.

Estimated Dollar Premium

USD 3,811,792.73 × 4.75% = USD 181,060.15

USD equivalent multiplied by option premium percentage equals USD premium to be received.

Estimated Interest Earned on the Premium

USD 181,060.15 × 8.00% × (78 Days/360 Days) = USD 3,138.38

USD premium multiplied by per-annum estimated interest income rate multiplied by (number of days from receipt of premium to expiration of option divided by 360 days in year because funds are assumed to be invested in the *Eurocurrency* market) equals USD interest income estimate.

Total Amount Earned from Writing the Option

USD 181,060.15 + USD 3,138.38 = USD 184,198.53

Sum of the estimated option premium plus the estimated interest income attributable to the option period.

Estimate the "Band of Protection."   A band of protection from writing each put option can be estimated. Estimated break-even exchange rates are calculated for each put option the Company writes.

Band of protection for the March 1990 option: The estimated band of protection from the strategy of writing a March 1990 ITL 1259.25 put option is ITL/USD 1201.20 to ITL/USD 1323.19. Calculations follow.

Bottom of band: If the U.S. Dollar at the option's maturity is equal to or less than the strike price of the option, then the option holder would not exercise the option. For example, using the contemplated March option, the exchange rate could be below ITL/USD 1201.20 before the Company would have to pay more for the Lira than it would pay if it bought the Lira at the forward foreign exchange rate—the ITL/USD 1259.25 strike price of the option.

Calculations: At the ITL 1259.25 strike price of the ITL 4.8 Bio March 1990 option, the U.S. Dollar cost would be USD 3,811,792.73; the Company would earn USD 184,198.53 from the premium and interest on the premium. The Company could, therefore, pay as much as USD 3,995,991.26 (USD 3,811,792.73 plus USD 184,198.53) for the ITL 4.8 Bio and still pay no more than if it had bought ITL 4.8 Bio at the forward outright rate of ITL/USD 1259.25. ITL 4.8 Bio divided by ITL/USD 1259.25 equals USD 3,811,972.73; ITL 4.8 Bio divided by USD 3,995,991.26 is equivalent to an exchange rate of ITL/USD 1201.20.

Top of band: If the U.S. Dollar strengthens so that the "Dollar Lira" are trading at an exchange rate equal to or greater than the put option strike price, the option holder would exercise the put. The Company would then be obligated to buy ITL 4.8 Bio at the strike price (1259.25) and pay the holder USD 3,811,792.73. The net cash flow to the Company would be USD 3,811,792.73 paid the holder minus the total of USD 184,1978.53 cash received from the option premium (USD 181,060.15) plus interest thereon (USD 3,138.38). If the Italian Lira to U.S. Dollar exchange rate did not exceed ITL/USD 1323.19, the strategy of writing the Lira put option would be better than purchasing the Lira on a forward outright basis at ITL/USD 1259.25.

Calculations: USD 3,811,792.73 minus USD 184,198.53 equals USD 3,627,594.20; ITL 4.8 Bio divided by USD 3,627,594.20 equals ITL/USD 1323.19.

Similar calculations can determine the band of protection for the other two options: for the July option, the band of protection would be ITL/USD 1173.49 to 1375.58; for the November option, the band of protection would be ITL/USD 1176.40 to 1426.66. The band of protection created by writing the November options is wider than that created by writing the July option, for two reasons. The option writer receives a larger premium because of the increased time value. The writer also earns more interest by investing, for a longer period of time, the premium received.

Expected Results of the Strategy

Biped Shoe's treasurer adopted two basic rules for managing the written put option positions:

1. Any additional gain that might have been obtained if the U.S. Dollar had appreciated—an opportunity to purchase the required Lira with fewer U.S. Dollars—would be treated as an *opportunity cost,* but the opportunity cost does not affect cash or earnings. The Company would not be able to realize any gain from a favorable market move relative to its put option positions.

2. Conversely, if the U.S. Dollar weakened to a point where the forward outright exchange rate for the particular payment date equaled the calculated band of protection exchange rate of any put option it had written, the Company would close the option position and buy the Lira on a forward outright basis. To close the option position, the Company would repurchase the put option from the bank to which the option had been written.

If the market did not move unfavorably outside the band of protection immediately after a put option had been written, two factors would work in the Company's favor. First, with the passage of time, the option's *time decay* would make it progressively cheaper to repurchase. Second, if the U.S. Dollar depreciated against the Lira, the value of the option would decrease as it moved further *out of the money.*

If the market moved outside the band of protection after a put option had been written, the most prudent decision would be to close the position by repurchasing the option. The assumption is that the hedger is "risk averse" with no desire to speculate. If the timing of the market's move outside the band of protection is closer to the option's expiration date, the option's time decay will have occurred; the option will have lost value and thus will be cheaper to buy back. If the U.S. Dollar has weakened, the put option may have become an out of the money option and, hence, cheaper. If the U.S. Dollar has become stronger and the option's expiration date is near, the writer gives up an opportunity to buy the Lira with fewer U.S. Dollars (an opportunity loss) but does not give up cash. The hedge concept here is this: if the market leaves the band of protection created by the hedge's contracts, the cash cost or opportunity loss will become ever greater by allowing the position to stay open. The advice, in plain terms, is "if it isn't working, get out!"

The Company's payment for repurchasing an option would have a cost of funds, which would be either its investment rate or borrowing rate. This cost of funds, calculated to the option's expiration date, may be considered an offset against the interest earned on the premium amount received when the option was written. The time period attributable to financing the repurchase premium would be shorter than the investment period for the premium the Company received when it wrote the option. The net amount of interest will probably be positive because the written option's premium income period will be longer than its repurchase premium expense period.

Biped Shoe's next consideration was the probability that the foreign exchange market might increase in *volatility* during the life of the options. In exchange for receiving the cash premium, the Company would limit its potential gain while assuming unlimited risk if the U.S. Dollar weakened. The rule "No one pays something for nothing" applies to the risk the option writer incurs in return for receiving the cash premium.

If the volatility of the underlying market increased, then the probability of the option writer's having a profitable position could decline drastically. The treasurer considered both probabilities: the U.S. Dollar's fluctuation, and the Lira's becoming more volatile against other currencies, including the U.S. Dollar. Thus, an estimate of the probability that the ITL/USD would trade outside of the band of protection could be made.

Doing the Trade

The treasurer called a bank and requested "good indications" or a "level" for forward outright Lira exchange rates and the three option expiration dates. When the treasurer found that the market had not changed while the treasurer had been completing the band-of-protection calculations, the treasurer asked for "firm" *bids* for the options that the Company wanted to write. An assistant called a second bank for simultaneous competitive bids. In requesting competitive bids, the Company gave the quoting banks the exact details for each option:

- European-style Lira put;
- Strike price for each option date;
- Expiration date for each option;
- Amount (in Lira) for which each option would be written.

Each bank was asked to provide the U.S. Dollar amount of the premium rather than quoting the premium as a percentage of the option amount. The simplicity of the cash premium quotations was considered helpful in avoiding mistakes as to which bank was quoting the better (higher) premiums for the options the Company wanted to write. (In general, if banks have a wide disparity in quotations or indicative quotations, requesting another quotation or indication may identify problems in communicating the option contract's terms or some other mistake.)

The treasurer closed the transactions with the "winning" bank and confirmed details with the trader on the telephone. The treasurer then arranged for Lira option premiums and invested these option premium funds to mature on the dates when the Company needed to make Lira payments to the Italian company. (An alternative would have been to take delivery into general corporate funds of U.S. Dollar option premium funds.)

"Unwinding" the Trade

A week after the transaction, the purchasing director advised the treasurer that the Italian company would not be able to ship shoes as planned because its main factory had been destroyed by fire. The Company would not, therefore, need to make any Lira payments. The Company now had a new risk to manage: if the U.S. Dollar appreciated sufficiently against the Lira, the put options obligated the Company to purchase Lira from the option holder. But the Company no longer needed any Lira. Because of changed business circumstances—the Italian company's factory fire—the put option contracts that were intended to hedge the original Italian Lira exposure were now exposing Biped Shoe to speculation: it faced both foreign exchange market risk and option premium risk for the amount it would have to pay to close the positions.

The treasurer chose to limit Biped Shoe's loss by repurchasing the options the Company had written. The treasurer requested indication quotations from the option holder bank. Because the U.S. Dollar had appreciated, Biped Shoe would incur a loss of about USD 150,000 in closing its option positions, including the interest expense on the premium it would pay to repurchase the options. (See Table 5.4.)

Table 5.4 Net Cost to Repurchase Options Written

Assumptions: USD Interest Rate: 8.00%
Repurchase Trade Date: January 2, 1990

| | Payment Number | | | Totals/ |
	One	Two	Three	Net Cost
Payment date	Mar. 31, 1990	Aug. 1, 1990	Nov. 15, 1990	
Option expiration date	Mar. 29, 1990	July 29, 1990	Nov. 13, 1990	
Option amount (ITL Bio)	4.8	6.0	13.3	
Strike price (ITL/USD)	1259.25	1275.00	1289.50	
Premium Earned (%)	4.83%	7.10%	9.12%	
Income from options written:				
Premium earned (USD)	184,109.59	334,117.65	940,643.66	
Interest income (USD)	3,600.37	15,666.41	66,263.12	
Income Earned (USD)	187,709.96	349,784.06	1,006,906.78	
Total income earned (USD)				1,544,400.80
Expense to unwind the trade:				
Premium paid (%)	5.31%	7.81%	10.03%	
Premium paid (USD)	(202,520.55)	(367,529.41)	(1,034,708.03)	
Interest expense (USD)	(3,645.37)	(16,661.33)	(71,279.89)	
Expense (USD)	(206,165.92)	(384,190.74)	(1,105,987.92)	
Total Expense (USD)				(1,696,344.58)
Net cost to repurchase options written (USD)				(151,943.78)

Evaluation

The foreign exchange hedge position became an open liability when the Italian factory burned down.

The first problem was what to do with the options—and when? Because of changing conditions in the foreign exchange markets, closing the option positions would cost a substantial sum of money; however, the cost of closing might go still higher. The cost of repurchasing the options might be reduced by waiting for a more favorable market opportunity, but Biped Shoe was not in the business of running speculative foreign exchange positions. The treasurer decided, therefore, to "bite the bullet" and accept a known cost to close out the options. The treasurer resisted the temptation to delay closing, to speculate by hoping for a lower closing premium price. Hoping that a market will turn favorable is "speculation" and can lead to despair.

The next problem was how to deal with the closing of the options: Should competitive bank quotations be obtained for premiums to repurchase the options? The treasurer elected for simplicity and closed the contracts with the original counterparty. If the treasurer had done otherwise, the Company would have had six open option contracts—the three originally written and three purchased elsewhere. By closing the original three options, the treasurer prevented the problem of managing open option contracts and eliminated the need to monitor the foreign exchange market to see whether any options would be exercised. If any of its written options had been exercised, the Company would need to exercise the corresponding option it had purchased from another bank. The treasurer avoided the potential problems and expenses of cash settlements in both Lira and U.S. Dollars, including third-party *lifting charges*. By obtaining competitive quotations for the option premiums, the treasurer determined that the original counterparty offered a fair market price.

Another consideration is whether the Company's use of options was technically correct. Many option traders are concerned about *delta hedging* when they write options. (*Delta* is discussed later in the book.)

In the authors' opinion, the treasurer's use of the contracts was suitable for Biped Shoe's payment requirements. Although not a perfect hedge, the option position was reasonable and logical. If the treasurer had adopted delta hedging, the treasurer would have written options for twice the amount of the Company's exposure. Given Biped Shoe's relatively infrequent involvement in foreign exchange and only occasional foreign currency payments, a larger position would not have been prudent.

6
Exporters

Drive thy business; let not that drive thee.

Benjamin Franklin, Poor Richard's Almanack (1733)

ALTERNATIVES FOR EXPORTERS

The exporter's risk from fluctuations in foreign currency exchange rates mirrors the importer's risks discussed in Chapter 5. For the exporter, if the domestic currency increases in value relative to the foreign currency, these are the possibilities:

1. The domestic currency income from export sales might decrease because of decreasing value of the foreign currency receipts;
2. A higher value of the exporter's currency for cost of goods sold may cause the exporter not to price competitively to others able to sell at a lower price in the same foreign location; or
3. If the full effect of the increased cost of goods sold cannot be passed through to the sales price, reduced profits or even losses may result.

In April 1991, the U.S. Dollar rally prompted *Barron's* to review the effects on major U.S. corporations:

> For some companies, the impact of changing currency relationships is easy to quantify. . . [at one company] . . . every 1% drop in the value of the dollar boosts profits . . . by two cents a share; a 1% rise shaves two cents. "It's wonderful when the trend is in our favor . . . and its terrible when it's the other way."[1]

[1] Eric J. Savitz, "The Buck Hits Here," *Barron's,* April 22, 1991, p. 14.

A spokesperson from another company noted that 60 percent of the company's revenues are from outside the United States:

> He adds that there isn't much the company can do to blunt the impact of shifting currency markets: "We can change our pricing structure, but there's only so much you can do with that. You have to be competitive."[2]

Another view stated:

> [the company] uses options trading and forward selling of currencies to try to minimize the effects of the rising dollar . . . but hedging isn't a cure-all. "There's no question, if the dollar stays where it is now, or if it continues to rise, we'll be worse off as a result."[3]

Chapter 5 detailed some basic arrangements suitable to importers' foreign exchange exposures. In this chapter, practical techniques more suitable to exporters are discussed. Often, the importers' arrangements are mirrored for exporters. The chapter includes a review of exchange-traded currency contracts, which are sometimes suitable for importers or exporters.

Exporters typically need to price and sell in the currency of the foreign country and to convert all or part of the sales receipts into the exporter's domestic currency—in these discussions, U.S. Dollars. Some business sectors are able, by tradition, to quote and be paid in a particular currency. For example, crude oil traditionally trades worldwide in U.S. Dollars; exporters of crude oil, therefore, often ask that suppliers of equipment and services quote to them in U.S. Dollars. For most exporters, the issue of foreign exchange rate risk is inescapable; they may employ some of the following practical techniques.

A foreign currency bank account may be useful, if the exporter regularly has both receipts and disbursements in a particular currency; the account may also improve control of cash. The frequency of currency exchange transactions can be reduced by holding the currency until needed for the next disbursement. This alternative reduces exchange rate risk by retaining the currency until needed rather than selling upon receipt and buying when needed for disbursements. This alternative is probably not suitable if the receipts are not foreseeably needed for future disbursements.

A *foreign exchange swap* may be suitable. In the detailed study of Biped Shoe in Chapter 5, three strategies for foreign exchange swaps were detailed. All three strategies were for an importer's purchase of a currency. In contrast, the exporter might sell the surplus currency at spot and simultaneously repurchase for forward value. If the currency is not received in the amount and at

---

[2] *Id.* at 15.
[3] *Id.*

the time expected, the deficit can be covered by purchasing at spot and simultaneously selling forward. Table 5.1 can easily be modified to the exporter's situation.

An opportunity for *interest rate arbitrage* may tempt the exporter to sell at spot the expected currency receipt and deposit the funds for interest income, or to reduce a loan in the domestic currency.

Foreign currency loans can be arranged and the funds used for either working capital or general corporate purposes.

Currency options, either in the interbank market or exchange-traded, may be suitable. The study in this chapter describes the use of currency options to protect a tender or contract bid price. The currency option protects against an unfavorable price move without a forward contract's commitment for delivery.

Some exporters use factoring to eliminate foreign exchange risk. The factor, for a fee, coordinates the exporter's foreign currency invoicing and collection. The factor guarantees the exporter's exchange rate for the foreign currency invoices when and as the invoices, stated in the domestic currency, are received from the exporter. This arrangement is different from export trade financing through a "forfait"—the nonrecourse sale of a receivable at a discount to a forfait house, which will usually require a bank's guarantee of the foreign customer's credit.

If the exporter trades with many countries, an analysis of receipts may identify a rather predictable mix of currency receipts. An ECU or U.S. Dollar Index futures contract may be suitable for hedging a "basket" of currencies. The weightings of the index contracts can be modified, or a tailor-made hedging "basket" can be created, thus minimizing basis risk. A careful data analysis is first required, as suggested in the following study.

SUPERDATA COMPANY

Exchange-traded foreign currency contracts were common in this software design firm, which had customers on three continents.

Business Risk Situation

SuperData Company is an innovative designer of application software for personal computers (PCs). Its best selling product is a "user friendly" data base system for home and office PCs. Users can build files for name and address lists, labels, collectibles, and similar types of small and medium-size inventories. The software has been sold in PC software retail stores and through magazine advertisements in the United States, Europe, the United Kingdom, and Japan. To the extent possible, SuperData minimizes its foreign inventory by arranging shipments to foreign retailers or end users as orders are received.

SuperData's marketing vice president and treasurer—and its client retailers—have sometimes been shocked at the rapid changes in the value of the U.S. Dollar. The treasurer recently told the marketing vice president that SuperData's export price would need to increase because the U.S. Dollar was increasing in relative value. Six months later, the U.S. Dollar was declining again. Meanwhile, the marketing vice president insisted that a stable price announced in each country and through magazine advertisements was crucial to expanding sales. The marketing department finally persuaded the treasurer that the company might be losing both gross sales and net income because of the effects of erratically fluctuating foreign exchange rates on its foreign currency pricing.

The treasurer called the foreign exchange department of the company's bank. The bank arranged for a foreign exchange adviser to explain the forward and options contracts that could help the company. The foreign exchange adviser suggested that the treasurer provide forecasts of foreign currency receipts so that the advice could be directed toward the company's specific situation.

The treasurer also contacted a financial futures and options broker referred by the marketing vice president. The treasurer explained that the Company's goals over a year or two were to stabilize its sales prices somewhat and to maintain or improve the difference between the sales prices it could charge and its U.S. Dollar revenue from the foreign sales. The broker mentioned the brokerage firm's many years' experience in helping farmers and ranchers hedge in the grain and cattle commodity markets and its more recent expertise in assisting with management of interest rate and foreign exchange risks. The brokerage company has a direct line, through its Chicago office, to the trading floor of the International Monetary Market (IMM) division of the Chicago Mercantile Exchange (CME) and can also deal on the Philadelphia Exchange. The broker identified the IMM's foreign currency futures contracts and the IMM's and Philadelphia Exchange's foreign currency option contracts that might be suitable for SuperData's foreign exchange risk management. The broker mailed brochures (prepared by the exchanges) describing IMM's foreign exchange contracts and FINEX's U.S. Dollar Index. The brochures gave specific examples of how to use currency futures and options contracts to hedge an exporter's currency exchange risk.

Futures Contracts

The broker explained that SuperData was "long the cash" each time it contracted to sell exports with payment due in a foreign currency. One way to hedge the *long* position was to sell (going *short*) foreign currency futures contracts that would go down in value if the U.S. Dollar went up. The general concept of an exporter's going short by selling foreign currency futures contracts to protect against unfavorable exchange rate movements is described as follows. The profits on the short futures contracts as the price went down would help offset the lower amount of U.S. Dollars received at spot or forward—the amount of U.S. Dollars Superdata received from the foreign exchange department of its bank—when SuperData purchased U.S. Dollars with the foreign currencies it received from the sale of exported goods. Conversely, if the U.S. Dollar decreased in value, the money lost on the foreign currency short futures contracts would be offset by Superdata's receiving more U.S. Dollars on spot or forward sale of foreign currencies received from the sale of its exports.

The broker then explained that, on the U.S. regulated exchanges—the IMM and the Philadelphia Exchange—the price of the "commodity," or the foreign currency in *American terms,* determines the decision of whether to buy or sell the futures contract or whether to select put or call options for purchase. For example, if the treasurer sold a Pounds Sterling futures contract at USD/GBP 1.8060 and the price went down to USD/GBP 1.7500, SuperData would make U.S. Dollar money. The change in rate from USD/GBP 1.8060 to USD/GBP 1.7500 shows that the Pounds Sterling rate is weaker relative to the U.S. Dollar—the U.S. Dollar has strengthened—and that selling the foreign currency would generate fewer U.S. Dollars. For example, shorting one GBP 62,500 futures contract at USD/GBP $1.8060 \times$ GBP $62,500 =$ USD 112,875, and covering the short at USD/GBP $1.7500 \times$ GBP $62,500 =$ USD 109,375, a profit of USD 3,500 per contract.

The IMM trades futures contracts for the next three calendar quarterly cycles for the Japanese Yen, Deutsche Mark, British Pound, Canadian Dollar, Swiss Franc, and Australian Dollar. The U.S. Dollar equivalent of the foreign currency contract sizes can be computed as follows: DEM 125,000 contract size is equivalent to USD 75,850 if USD/DEM 0.6068 is the rate of exchange, computed as DEM $125,000 \times$ USD/DEM 0.6068. The GBP 62,500 contract size is about USD 113,500 at a USD/GBP 1.8155 rate of exchange, computed as GBP $62,500 \times$ USD/GBP 1.8155. The JPY 12.5 million was about USD 85,000, computed as JPY 12.5 million $\times$ .006773. The quoted prices for the JPY futures contract will require the addition of two zeroes for computations if noted in the newspaper as "12.5 million yen; $ per yen (.00)." For example, .7618 equals .007618 and the conversion would be .007618 times JPY 12,500,000 equals USD 95,225.

The broker pointed out that no maximum daily limit applies to the amount that currency futures contracts can fluctuate in a day's trading. For example, if SuperData sold a DEC90 DEM futures contracts at USD/DEM .6650 (the reciprocal European-style quotation would be DEM/USD 1.5038, 1.000/.6650) and the DEM went up to the contract's previous lifetime high of USD/DEM .6821 (DEM/USD 1.4661), for each DEC90 contract SuperData sold at the USD/DEM .6821 level, it could lose USD

2,137.50: USD/DEM .6821 – .6650 = USD/DEM .0171 × DEM 125,000 per contract = USD 2,137.50. Continuing the example, if the DEM fell and the U.S. Dollar increased in value to the contract "low" of USD/DEM .5754 and SuperData "covered its short" contracts at that level, it could make USD 11,200.00: .6650 – .5754 = USD/DEM .0896 × DEM 125,000 per contract = USD 11,200.

There is one important requirement: SuperData would have to provide the brokerage firm with the initial cash margin to open the futures contracts and, if the futures contracts position continued to potentially lose money, more cash for maintenance margin as required by the exchange and the firm. SuperData could enter a *stop loss* order, but that order could be filled at less than its stop level if the market "went past" the stop. Hence, Super-Data could not, in advance, ensure the exact amount of any loss. SuperData would also pay the broker's commission charges on the transactions.

The treasurer added together the current approximate U.S. Dollar amounts for a DEM, a GBP, and a JPY futures contract. For DEM 125,000, each 1-cent increase or decrease in the value of the U.S. Dollar resulted in a futures contract change of USD 1,250 (DEM 125,000 × .01). The comparable GBP 62,500 change was USD 625 [GBP 62,500 × .01], and the comparable JPY change, USD 1,250 [JPY 12.5 million × .0001]. The treasurer, remembering no daily limit on the futures contract price fluctuation, was concerned that, if the foreign currencies were declining in value, SuperData might not always have enough cash for the margin calls and might have to close the futures positions intended to hedge its foreign currency requirements.

The treasurer was puzzled about how to select the futures contracts the Company would sell. SuperData expected foreign currency receipts in months for which there were no futures contracts. The payment months and the futures contract months were not always the same. SuperData had never developed a detailed cash flow forecast by currency of receipt dates and estimated amounts.

Exchange-Traded Foreign Currency Options

Responding to the concern about margin calls, the broker suggested that SuperData consider foreign currency puts—options that would increase in value relative to the foreign currency if the U.S. Dollar "went up" (appreciated in value). The treasurer computed an IMM option premium: an IMM 6650 Deutsche Mark call option settling in January 1991 at "1.18 cents per mark" would be equivalent to USD 1,475.00 (1.18 × .01 (to convert to decimal dollars) × 125,000).

The treasurer inquired about the Philadelphia Exchange's ("Philly") option quotations. The Philadelphia Exchange options are half the underlying size of the IMM options; also, the options settle for cash because their underlying is not a futures contract as for IMM options. The trading hours on the IMM for foreign currency futures and options contracts are 7:20 A.M. to about 1:20 P.M. Chicago time—the contracts close about two minutes apart, starting at 1:16 P.M. The Philadelphia Exchange's foreign currency options trading hours are virtually 24-hour days. The broker pointed out that, although the IMM might offer more liquidity because more contracts were traded, the extended market hours of the Philadelphia Exchange might be useful, especially with its interface with the interbank markets in the Far East and Europe.

Foreign Currency Index Contract

SuperData's treasurer asked about the U.S. Dollar Index (USDX) futures and options contracts. USDX contracts are not heavily traded, in comparison to the IMM currency contracts, but the broker pointed out that Super-Data would not be "hitting the market" with a huge number of contracts to buy or sell. The volume of SuperData's orders would not cause the option prices to move significantly up or down. If the treasurer were concerned about maintaining margin for futures contracts, options on the U.S. Dollar Index contracts might be an alternative.

SuperData had software sales in every country represented in the index: Germany, Japan, France, the United Kingdom, Canada, Italy, the Netherlands, Belgium, Sweden, and Switzerland. The FINEX U.S. Dollar Index increases in value as the U.S. Dollar increases relative to the overall value of the Index's weighting for its currencies. Each point in the Index is worth USD 500; at 90.26, the Index is USD 45,130 (USD 500 × 90.26), and if, during the trading day, the Index moves up to 91.26, the Index is USD 45,630 (USD 500 × 91.26). Effective with the September 1992 contract, the index multiplier is being doubled to USD 1,000.

The multicurrency index futures contract or options may be convenient for managing some types of multicurrency exposure. The USDX contract is typically less volatile than the individual currency contracts. Orders can be placed for an average of the opening and closing prices for any trading day (an "average price order"), thus avoiding buying on the trading day's high or selling on its low. Futures contracts orders can be placed contingent on the spot USDX price, an advantage for participants in the cash market. Index contracts are introduced in Chapter 2. The USDX and ECU futures contract are discussed and compared in Chapter 7.

Cash Flow Analysis

SuperData's treasurer decided to accept the recommendations of the bank's foreign exchange adviser and the broker. SuperData needed to do some homework to evaluate whether any interbank or exchange-traded contracts might help the problems it had only vaguely measured. These were the steps recommended in the evaluation:

1. Prepare a matrix of the U.S. Dollar volume of export sales by country and by calendar quarter. This matrix could be compared to the composition of the ECU and USDX contracts for mix of currency "basis risk." Also or alternatively, the data would enable identification of specific currency exchange rates of the greatest corporate financial risk to the company.

2. Try to identify how much of the recent years' fluctuations in SuperData's export revenues is attributable to changes in the quality and volume of products it exported and its competition and how much to a decrease in U.S. Dollar price of the same software. In an effort to improve its sales volume, SuperData had been adding low-cost, simplified software products to its line.

3. Develop a U.S. Dollar cash flow forecast with at least quarterly time periods. The forecast would be supported by forecasts prepared in the same format as the foreign currency forecasts. With the ability to forecast different exchange rates and with space on the page for simulating hedging transactions, a cash plan document would be available. The "model logic" could be tested against the prior year's transactions. By recording actual transactions, the documents would become a comparison of actual to planned results and also a continuously rolling cash flow forecast.

4. Develop, with the assistance of both the foreign exchange adviser and the broker, hypothetical hedges using potentially suitable interbank and exchange-traded contracts. The cash flow effects of "what if" currency fluctuations could be simulated. These simulations could include examining the problem that the receipts could not be aligned with the expiration dates of exchange-traded futures and options contracts. Initial and maintenance margin requirements could also be simulated. By using the bank's foreign exchange swap contracts, the forward and option contracts could be compared. Mixing interbank and exchange-traded contracts seemed a long way from not using any hedging contracts, but the treasurer recognized the possibility.

5. Explore the alternative of not converting the foreign currencies to U.S. Dollars immediately upon receipt. SuperData could take delivery of the foreign currencies and place funds in short-term foreign currency investments with a bank. SuperData could then plan more optimum dates for U.S. Dollars conversions; its cash flow forecast would help plan the timing and amounts of U.S. Dollars needed for corporate cash flow. The bank's foreign exchange adviser pointed out that this was the speculative alternative.

SuperData, a midsized exporter of personal computer software, has a multicurrency cash receipts problem but is doing more planning and research than Heatherstone China Company (studied in Chapter 5) did for its first foreign exchange transaction of about USD 9 million.

LIMBER TIMBER COMPANY

Look-back pricing was a key issue for a lumber exporter in its dealings with a Japanese trading company. The Limber Timber Company, located in the Pacific Northwest, was a middle-market company with sales of approximately USD 40 million. It sold construction lumber primarily to building supply companies located in western states. The Company had timber rights to high-quality Douglas fir stands in the Pacific Northwest.

The Company had recently been approached by a Japanese trading company, Takemake Trading Ltd. The high quality of the harvested timber, together with the overall quality of the lumber produced by Limber Timber's two mills, would be highly prized by Japanese woodworkers. Takemake was interested in a 1-year contract that would be renewable for a 5-year term if the agreement proved acceptable to both parties after the first year. Estimated first-year sales under the contract were the equivalent of 1 million board feet of lumber, increasing thereafter by 2 million board feet per year.

Pricing would be "basis" the CME lumber futures contract at the time when each order was placed. The proposal was attractive to Limber Timber for three reasons:

- Renewal of the contract would provide stable growth.
- The contract could reduce some of the cyclical fluctuations in Limber Timber's business.
- Renewal of the contract would mean that Takemake would help Limber Timber, with favorable terms, to upgrade its mills using Japanese machinery.

One wrinkle in the deal made Limber Timber's management uncomfortable. Takemake wanted to make payment in Japanese Yen. With no experience in international trade or finance, Limber Timber had no idea what to do with Yen payments. Its management knew that foreign exchange markets were volatile and that accepting the Yen revenues could be a significant risk.

The Company's bank was regional and had a limited presence in the foreign exchange market. The bank admitted that it was not able to provide any significant assistance or advice on the issue. Takemake Trading, having had much experience in foreign exchange, proposed the following solution. Payments to Limber Timber could be made in U.S. Dollars, but the contract would be priced in Yen. The companies would share the foreign exchange risk for each transaction. Takemake explained briefly that the U.S. Dollar price of each contract would be set at the time each order was placed. Payment would be made under the usual terms of an export documentary letter of credit. The exchange rate to be applied to each order would be based on the following formula:

140 JPY/USD − ((140 − Spot rate JPY/USD)/2)

When an order was placed, the following steps would occur. Takemake would issue a documentary commercial letter of credit for the Yen amount of the contract. Limber Timber would receive payment under the terms of the letter of credit. Takemake's paying bank would convert the Yen amount of the letter of credit into U.S. Dollars and pay Limber Timber the U.S. Dollar proceeds.

Takemake provided the following example and explanation. The Yen was currently trading at about 130 Yen per U.S. Dollar. If Takemake placed an order with a dollar value of USD 500,000.00, the value of the contract would be converted to Yen at a rate of JPY 135.00 per dollar. Using the above formula, the result would be:

140 − [(140 − 130)/2] = 140 − (10/2) = 135.00

The Yen value of the contract would be JPY 67,500,000 (USD 500,000 × JPY/USD 135). Takemake said that, if Limber Timber shipped the order immediately and made proper presentment under the letter of credit—including the required shipping documents—to the U.S. branch of Takemake's bank, the company could expect to receive payment in less than a week. The exporter's foreign exchange exposure would then be relatively short—about 1 week from the time the order was received until the time the product was shipped. Several issues were not, however, addressed in Takemake's presentation.

The first problem was the impact of any delay between the receipt of an order in Yen and the time it was shipped. Delays could occur because of the time required to obtain and prepare the conforming documents required for payment under the letter of credit. Mailing the documents to the U.S. branch of Takemake's bank required at least 1 day. The bank might take 3 full business days to approve or deny payment of the presentment under the letter of credit. Thus, the foreign exchange transaction converting the Yen to U.S. Dollars might not be executed by the bank until the morning of the fourth business day. Even processing the shipping documents might consume more time than the week indicated. The 1 week of foreign exchange exposure also assumed that Limber Timber could schedule its production immediately to fill and ship Takemake's orders. Given the volatility of the foreign exchange markets, Limber Timber might end up receiving significantly fewer U.S. Dollars than it anticipated.

A second issue not addressed in Takemake's scenario was the mechanism for converting the Yen order amount into U.S. Dollars. The bank issuing and paying under the letter of credit had discretion for the conversion transaction. It could apply any exchange rate that it saw fit. The exchange rate did not have to be competitive (much less favorable) to Limber Timber.

A fundamental issue in this sort of contract is selection of the reference rate for pricing the transaction. For the proposed contract, Takemake suggested a rate near the current spot exchange rate between the U.S. Dollar and the Yen—140 Yen per Dollar. Table 6.1 shows examples of the effect.

Because the reference exchange rate was close to the current spot rate, Limber Timber ran a significant risk if the U.S. Dollar appreciated against the Japanese Yen. It would receive fewer Yen than if the contract were converted into Yen at the spot rate.

Table 6.2 shows that, as the dollar appreciates, Limber Timber's Yen revenues fall significantly below the amount of Yen that would be received by converting the order to Yen at the current spot rate.

A look-back pricing arrangement is not necessarily a bad business practice for an exporter or importer. An exporter wants to have a reference rate as high as possible relative to the current spot rate, to maximize Yen revenues and as compensation for incurring risk. An importer wants to set as low a reference rate as possible, to minimize the cost of imported goods or components. Setting a reference rate under such an agreement requires thought as to both the expected direction of exchange rates and the impact of changes in exchange rates on expected revenues or costs. Finally, the

Table 6.1 Look-Back Formula Exchange Rates

Spot Exchange Rate	Reference Rates for Calculating Exchange Rates				
	120	140	160	180	200
130	125	135	145	155	165
140	130	140	150	160	170
150	135	145	155	165	175
160	140	150	160	170	180
170	145	155	165	175	185
180	150	160	170	180	190
190	155	165	175	185	195
200	160	170	180	190	200
210	165	175	185	195	205
220	170	180	190	200	210

Look-back formula: Reference rate − ((Reference rate − Spot rate)/2)

Table 6.2   Look-Back Yen Value Table—Example

Spot Exchange Rate	JPY Value at Current Spot	Yen Value of a USD $.5 Million Order at Each Spot Rate, Based on the Reference Rate (Millions)				
		120	140	160	180	200
130	65.0	62.5	67.5	72.5	77.5	82.5
140	70.0	65.0	70.0	75.0	80.0	85.0
150	75.0	67.5	72.5	77.5	82.5	87.5
160	80.0	70.0	75.0	80.0	85.0	90.0
170	85.0	72.5	77.5	82.5	87.5	92.5
180	90.0	75.0	80.0	85.0	90.0	95.0
190	95.0	77.5	82.5	87.5	92.5	97.5
200	100.0	80.0	85.0	90.0	95.0	100.0
210	105.0	82.5	87.5	92.5	97.5	102.5
220	110.0	85.0	90.0	95.0	100.0	105.0

reader should remember that a look-back agreement shares foreign exchange risk between importer and exporter. It does not eliminate market exposure.

UPSON DOWNS ELEVATOR COMPANY (A DIVISION OF BIG MACHINE CORPORATION)

The interbank currency options available to a multinational conglomerate were the subject of interest in this study.

Business Risk Situation

Big Machine Corporation ("the Company") is a multinational manufacturing conglomerate with USD 20 billion in assets. The Company has four operating groups, each of which has individual operating units and subsidiaries that have, subject to compliance with the parent company's objectives, considerable authority in long-term planning and product development. The parent company has centralized financial management: all cash management, treasury functions, and financing or investment decisions are handled by the treasury department at corporate headquarters. This centralized management enables senior management to oversee budgets as well as to perceive and address financial problems before they become critical.

Machine One is one of the parent company's four groups. Machine One's main operating division is Upson Downs Elevator Company (Upson Downs). In 1988, Machine One notified the parent company's treasury department that Upson Downs was considering bidding on a contract for a major government-sponsored project in the Côte d'Ivoire, known before 1986 as the Ivory Coast. The project would include two or possibly three hotel–resort complexes, a major international business center, and apartment buildings for foreign executives. Machine One's primary competition for the contract would be a Japanese company. The Japanese company usually priced its bids in either Yen or U.S. Dollars, and offered financing concessions that Machine One had difficulty matching.

Equipment Components and Contract

Two primary considerations were reviewed: the source for manufacturing components, and the currency for the contract bid.

Machine One informed the treasury department that Upson Downs's bid specifications would require components from a Canadian company. The Canadian components would cost either USD 8.5 million or CAD (Canadian Dollars) 10.54 million. A check of the Reuters screen showed that the Canadian Dollar was trading at CAD 1.2550 per U.S. Dollar. Hence, if the company contracted in Canadian Dollars for the components, Upson Downs could save about USD 100,000, based on this computation:

USD 8,500,000 – (CAD 10,540,000/1.2550)
= USD 8,500,000 – USD 8,398,406.37 = USD 101,593.63

Upson Downs considered the Canadian company's pricing for its components to be high. The high price was attributable to the strengthening of the Canadian Dollar for the previous 3 years as a result of Japanese investors' purchasing of Canadian Dollar bonds.

The Company contemplated pricing its bid for the contract in French Francs. The C.F.A. Franc, the currency of the Côte d'Ivoire, was then "pegged" to the French Franc at the rate of 50 C.F.A. Francs to 1 French Franc. The Company's bid in French Francs might offer these advantages:

- The Côte d'Ivoire government might be attracted to a bid in French Francs because the contract would then—by reason of the "pegged rate"—be denominated in a proxy for its own currency.
- Bidding in French Francs would provide some protection to the Company from any change in the status of the C.F.A. Franc.
- The Company might be able to obtain a slightly higher contract price because of the reduced risk for the Côte d'Ivoire government with a French Franc contract versus a contract priced in either Yen or U.S. Dollars.
- The Company could then estimate the U.S. Dollar cost to Machine One of the proposed contract, using both Canadian Dollar and U.S. Dollar costs for the Canadian components.

Hedging Analysis

If the Company sold French Francs as soon as it decided to bid but then was not awarded the contract, or if the contract's execution were delayed, the Company might be short French Francs. If the Company won the bid but the U.S. Dollar strengthened after the contract was signed, then the U.S. Dollar value of Machine One's revenues would be much less than planned. A similar problem would arise with a Canadian Dollar position.

The treasury department made the following analysis of the hedging situation.

The Company would do nothing if it anticipated that the U.S. Dollar might weaken against the French Franc and strengthen against the Canadian Dollar. Under that hypothesis, more U.S. Dollars would be needed to buy French Francs, but Canadian Dollars could be bought more cheaply. Some corporations, including Machine One, have a policy that permits leaving a foreign exchange position unhedged if a favorable currency market is anticipated. Such a policy requires identification of the foreign exposure, both as to amount and *transaction exposure*. This policy assumes that transaction exposure, as distinguished from *translation exposure,* occurs when an obligation by (or to) the corporation is incurred. A U.S. Dollar value—based on the current forward foreign exchange rate at the time the obligation is incurred—is assigned to the transaction.

Selling French Francs forward and buying Canadian Dollars forward was not a sound course because the Company, not knowing whether it would be the successful bidder, had no assurance that it would either be receiving the French Francs or needing the Canadian Dollars. The treasury department considered using options: a French Franc *put* and a Canadian Dollar *call*. Stated in transactional terms, the Company could:

1. Purchase an out of the money French Franc put with a strike price lower (for example, FRF/USD 6.6000) than the current 6-month forward foreign exchange rate (for example, FRF/USD 6.2725) for the underlying currency, the French Franc;
2. Purchase a Canadian Dollar call with a strike price of higher value (for example, CAD/USD 1.1550, a lower number) than the Canadian Dollar's 6-month forward foreign exchange rate (for example, CAD/USD 1.1600).

Six months was a reasonable estimate of the maximum time between submission of the bid and signing of the final contract if the bid were accepted. Options would allow the Company to lock-in exchange rates throughout the bid-and-contract period, without incurring unlimited risk by "running" an exposed position caused either by entering into forward foreign exchange contracts or by doing nothing. The cost of the options could be kept to a minimum by choosing an *out of the money* option, rather than an *at the money* option.

After the Côte d'Ivoire government had informally indicated its approval of a bid with French Franc pricing, the bid was prepared in final form. The total value of the proposed contract would be USD 29.75 million. At the then current exchange rate of French Francs (FRF) 6.25 per U.S. dollar, the French Franc value of the contract would be nearly FRF 186 million (USD 29.75 × FRF/USD 6.25 = FRF 185,937,500).

Intercompany Netting?

Upson Downs asked the Canadian company to price its components in Canadian Dollars because it would be about USD 100,000 cheaper (see the earlier computation formula). Foreign investors and speculators were deemed likely to continue buying and investing in Canadian Dollars because of the high yields. Hence, the Canadian Dollar would probably continue to strengthen. Machine One's treasury staff looked at the Company's other operations for possible sources of Canadian Dollars. These sources might be a natural offset to Upson Downs's obligation to pay the Canadian supplier.

Machine Two, another of the parent company's four groups, was scheduled to receive from its Canadian subsidiary a royalty payment of nearly CAD 13 million. This royalty payment had not been hedged. The due date and amount of the royalty payment almost matched the payment schedule to the Canadian supplier—if the Côte d'Ivoire contract were closed. The cost of hedging with options could be reduced by offset of the two amounts: the royalty payment to Machine Two, and Machine One's Upson Downs's payment to the Canadian supplier. However, the reduction of option cost by offset was subject to several contingencies.

Machine Two's receipt of payment from its Canadian subsidiary might be delayed, or Machine One's payment to the Canadian supplier might be earlier than expected. If either of those contingencies occurred, the Company would have to finance the purchase of Canadian Dollars through short-term borrowing, which could be expensive.

An adverse tax ruling was possible. The Company's treasury department was aware that Revenue Canada could rule that transferring the Machine Two subsidiary's payment to Upson Downs, a subsidiary of Machine One, was a dividend rather than a royalty payment. In the event of such a ruling, the payment would be subject to a 15 percent Canadian withholding tax. The Company's tax department gave advice on how to structure the transaction so that the treasury department could use the Company's available Canadian Dollars.

The contingent risks of timing and tax associated with using Machine Two's Canadian Dollars could be managed. The treasury department decided, therefore, to use the Company's available Canadian Dollars. The currency transaction exposure to Upson Downs's Canadian supplier was thus eliminated, and hedging with a Canadian Dollar call option was unnecessary.

The Option Transaction

The option transaction involved the following steps.

1. An estimate was made of the break-even exchange rate, including the estimated profit margin, and was determined to be FRF 6.9600 per U.S. Dollar.
2. The term of the option was considered, and a 6-month put option was chosen because 6 months was a reasonable time frame for submitting the bid and then negotiating a contract.
3. The cost of an *at the money forward* put was estimated. The 6-month forward outright rate for the French Franc against the U.S. Dollar was FRF 6.2725. An at the money forward put was estimated to cost about 5.1 percent of the total value of the total contract bid; an additional expense was the financing of the cost of the premium—either interest on a loan or loss of interest income on funds paid for the premium. A put with a strike price of FRF 6.60 per U.S. Dollar, however, would cost less—approximately 3.5 percent premium plus the financing cost. The strike price of FRF/USD 6.60 was selected because 1.035 (1 + the 3.5 percent premium, or 103.5 percent) × FRF/USD 6.6 = FRF/USD 6.8, which still provided leeway for contingencies, in comparison to the break-even exchange rate of FRF/USD 6.9600. The lower-cost put was also feasible because Machine One had some flexibility in its pricing. The 3.5 percent option premium still allowed reasonable profit and flexibility in pricing relative to exchange rate fluctuation.
4. A *European-style put option,* exercisable only on its expiration date, was chosen because the Company did not intend to exercise the option.
5. If contract negotiations moved more quickly than anticipated, the Company could sell the option back to the bank from which it had been purchased and thereby reduce the cost of the option's premium.

After the decision was made, the Company called one of the banks with which it dealt and asked for a good *indication* of the bank's offer for a European-style French Franc put with a strike price of FRF 6.6000 per Dollar, expiring on October 15, 1988, for FRF 195 million. After several moments, the bank's trader offered to sell the put at a premium of 3.98 percent. That indication was substantially higher than seemed appropriate to the Company in view of the *implied volatility.* The trader attributed the expensive indication to an anticipated decline in liquidity and a corresponding increase in volatility because of a holiday later that week. The trader suggested that the Company leave the bank an open order to sell the put to the Company on its stated terms, including the 3.45 percent premium that the Company wanted to pay. The Company declined placing an open order because option pricing is too complex to be done on an open-order basis. For example, in this case:

1. Implied volatility might change in the Company's favor, thereby reducing the cost of the option;
2. U.S. Dollar or French Franc interest rates might change, with resulting change in the cost of the premium;
3. The U.S. Dollar might weaken sharply against the French Franc, thus reducing the cost of the put. If that happened, the Company might want to change the strike price for the put.

The treasury department estimated 3.75 percent as the highest premium that the Company should pay. Three banks were called for prices on the option described above, namely: European-style French Franc put with strike price of FRF 6.6000 per U.S. Dollar, expiring October 15, 1988, on FRF 195 million. A quote of 3.69 percent was obtained, and the Company bought the put.

Evaluation

The treasury department acted prudently in the following respects:

1. Defining clearly the exposure that needed to be hedged;
2. Estimating a break-even exchange rate;
3. Looking for a natural offset in the Company's other operations;
4. Considering other possible consequences of the proposed hedging transaction.

The first two steps, definition of the exposure to be hedged and estimation of the break-even exchange rate, provided information that allowed flexibility in engineering the hedge. The third step, looking for a potential offset, disclosed a Canadian Dollar flow generated elsewhere in the Company. Using this offset eliminated extra costs in hedging multiple exposures in the same currency—with a bonus of simplicity. Finally, looking at other consequences of the proposed transaction led to consideration of possibly adverse tax results.

7
Multinationals

Things done without example, in their issue, are to be feared.
Shakespeare, Henry VIII

MULTINATIONALS ARE DIFFERENT

The corporate financial risk management of multinational business organizations is broadly discussed in a variety of monthly business magazines. Although the exact proprietary details of their financial engineering may not be disclosed, sharing the concepts involved is useful. The most sophisticated multinational, multicurrency companies use both simple and complex financial engineering; their problems and opportunities are different from those of many less diverse or smaller companies, but their approach to and experience in solving foreign risk problems provide useful ideas.

For example, FMC Corporation's foreign exchange manager's job is described as "making the U.S. dollar invisible." FMC describes supporting its marketing by pricing in local currencies and then hedging the resulting risks. To build and hold market share, FMC promises up to several years of stable, long-term pricing supported by "strategic hedging." Once contracts are "on the books," the company uses the portfolio approach—netting out receivables and payables by currency and deciding when to hedge imbalances.[1] The concept of netting in a multicurrency environment is an approach reminiscent of netting for single-currency cash and credit management.

Another frequently used concept is to manage all foreign currency exposures, as well as borrowing and investments, through a centralized treasury. Imperial Chemicals Industries (ICI), one of the U.K.'s largest manufacturers,

---

[1] "The FMC Goal: Making Cash Flow King," *Corporate Risk Management* (Mar./Apr. 1990), pp. 19–23.

sells about half of its production abroad. ICI has centralized all its currency transactions in a company called ICI Finance. ICI Finance monthly assigns a forward currency rate to all foreign currency positions of its businesses and then takes over managing the actual receipts and disbursements and hedging in the forward market. ICI comments that currency swaps should be only part of the borrowing portfolio: "'If you get into a position where they are bigger than the underlying borrowing position, then one doesn't know what they are doing,'" says the finance director, reiterating FMC's edict of selling to the customer in the local currency.[2]

The advantages of a centralized treasury are reiterated by The Gillette Company; 70 percent of its total sales come from abroad, primarily from Europe. The company concluded that a policy of waiting for "purchasing power parity" to provide a natural hedge created too long a wait, and market share suffered in the interim. Some advantages of the centralized treasury are summarized here. Global funding needs are centralized so that inter-company loans, dividends, and capital contributions place the right currency where needed at the right time. The company uses a reinvoicing center and netting; hedging costs are minimized. The company generally does not hedge transaction exposures among countries in the European Monetary System (EMS) and tries to have the same price on its products in each European country. No speculation is allowed, but the company closely manages open currency positions by monitoring and by using stop-loss targets.[3]

Arco Chemical regularly deals with long-term foreign economic risks because of its projects and its terms of contracts. The company reported recently that it had, on occasion, embedded an option or sharing of unfavorable exchange rate change in long-term contracts. Arco's treasurer pointed out that the tools for managing residual foreign exchange risk are not financial instruments. The company is trying to integrate foreign exchange considerations into the planning for site selection and product sourcing.[4] The report included a succinct example of how the difference between a company's productivity and the national productivity affects a company's cost advantage. Only if change in the company's productivity is higher than change in the national productivity will the company have a positive cost advantage.

Black & Decker's treasury group acts as a consultant to the company's departments on topics such as purchasing materials, manufacture, and inventory management, and tries to provide an "early warning system" to managers on the location of new facilities. Many of the company's products can be manufactured in more than one place. The company can therefore try for

[2] Kibazo, "We sell to the customer in his own currency," *Financial Times* (London), May 14, 1990, sec. VI (special foreign exchange section).
[3] "Gillette: Smoothing Close Shaves in Finance," *Corporate Risk Management* (Jan. 1991), pp. 18–21.
[4] "A planning role for forex experts," *Corporate Finance, Risk & Arbitrage* (Apr. 1990), p. 11.

strategic allocation of its foreign exchange risk by shifting capacity utilization. The company also uses forward contracts and options to hedge transaction exposure, but reports that it manages income translation exposure primarily through pricing strategies.[5]

Duracell suggests five steps to foreign currency financial risk management:

1. Arrange manufacturing and distribution to eliminate cross-border flows;
2. Net intercompany cash flows to avoid interbank currency transactions—an action that is estimated to eliminate 50 percent of otherwise required transactions;
3. Employ foreign exchange rate sharing agreements with suppliers;
4. Try to exploit or create natural hedges;
5. Use financial transactions through third parties, to reduce or eliminate risk.

"The first four are free but also the dog work," the assistant treasurer comments. "Operational hedges are often less expensive. . . . Only when we have exhausted them will we go into the market to hedge."[6]

With large, centralized treasury departments, it was perhaps inevitable that some companies would see opportunities to imitate the activities of the interbank foreign exchange market. An emerging activity among large corporations is arranging foreign currency transactions among each other. "All these corporations have one feature that distinguishes them from banks: their long-term outlook." The corporations are reportedly looking to counterparties hedging long-term exposure.[7] The banks are, however, a long way from down and out because of the depth and liquidity of the interbank market and their ability to arrange long-term transactions with mismatched risk. Despite recent problems in the banking industry, many banks still offer a counterparty credit advantage.

EXOTIC IDEAS

Exotic and minor currencies are here defined as currencies that, compared to heavily traded currencies, are (1) less frequently traded, (2) less liquid or even illiquid, (3) generally restricted to the home market, and/or (4) subject to government regulations and restrictions that may change frequently. These currencies are usually associated with countries that have less industrial and

---

[5] "Managing Corporate Risk," *Euromoney* (May 1990), p. 139.
[6] "Why Duracell Is Charged Up in a Long-Life LBO," *Corporate Risk Management* (October 1990), p. 20.
[7] "Forex Funding Free of Banks," *Euromoney* (May 1989), pp. 24–25.

commercial development than Europe, the United Kingdom, Canada, Japan, and the United States. More recently industrialized countries may create illiquid currencies because of currency import and export controls, or limits on the amounts that can be traded in a business day; examples are the New Taiwan Dollar and the South Korean Won. The financial instruments to hedge currency exposures are not generally available for many currencies in Africa, Asia, and Latin America. Since 1990, the countries of Eastern Europe present another region of exotic currency problems for commercial venturers; the banking and currency rules have not yet been written, let alone rewritten.

The solutions range from negotiating foreign exchange rate agreements, described later in this Chapter, to old-fashioned barter. For example, Pepsico had a 10-year barter agreement with the USSR to receive vodka in exchange for Pepsi-Cola. Barter agreements can "get out of balance" if the original equation of market demand changes. A speaker at a 1990 Moscow conference pointed out that every time the Americans were annoyed at the then USSR's foreign policy, USA demand for their vodka went down while the Soviet's demand for Pepsi stayed stable. Consequently, U.S. Dollar receipts became less than anticipated for the volume of Pepsi being bartered.

Some countries try to manage their currencies against a basket of main trading partners. If the currency basket formula is known, a broad hedge can be arranged, albeit with probable *basis* risk. For example, the Thai baht might be hedged with 80 percent U.S. Dollars and the balance in a mix of Deutsche Marks and Japanese Yen, according to the head of foreign exchange at Standard Chartered Bank in Bangkok.[8]

Some currencies seem to have defeated experienced multinational hedgers. The director of worldwide foreign exchange for General Motors has warned: "'There is no efficient hedging market for the Korean won.'" The currency has a litany of problems. There are restrictions in the Korean capital markets. The offshore market has premiums of 15 to 20 percent for forward contracts above spot rate of exchange. The basis studies have not identified a basket of actively traded currencies for a hedge. A company could lose money on the Won and also on the hedge.[9] This comment has been echoed by an expert at Bank of America, who adds Taiwan to the list.[10]

A company about to purchase exotic currency for a capital investment in the "exotic's" country might investigate whether there is U.S. Dollar-denominated or other hard currency-denominated government paper available for purchase at a discount. The notes or bonds may be discounted because investors are concerned about sovereign risk. However, the government may be willing to redeem the paper at face value for conversion into the local currency.

---

[8] "Exotic Forex Problem," *Corporate Finance* (Apr. 1989), p. 24.
[9] *Id.*
[10] "Running a Race with New Risks," *Corporate Risk Management* (Mar./Apr. 1990), p. 43.

There are no simple answers, but research is the first important step. A commercial bank representative for the country is a good contact. A major international bank, the International Chamber of Commerce, and the International Monetary Fund are all sources for reliable information. Excellent suggestions may come from the local office staff of international banks and accounting firms doing business in the country. Legal counsel in the country can be contacted through law firms arranging business deals in the locale. The country's central bank may have recommendations. Many Third World countries have regulations and guidelines, and special exemptions for good projects can sometimes be arranged. Last but not least, noncompetitors doing business in the country may best "know the ropes."

EC, EMS, ERM, AND ECU

The business articles about Western Europe's economic integration in 1992 buzz with four abbreviations:

EC	European Community
EMS	European Monetary System
ERM	Exchange Rate Mechanism
ECU	European Currency Unit

The ERM links the exchange rates of the participating European currencies.

Developments in the European business community are obviously relevant to multinational companies with operations in some or all of the countries. Less obviously, perhaps, a company with a U.S. Dollar exposure to a single ERM member currency will eventually become very interested in the machinery underlying these abbreviations. In recent years, companies have diversified their purchasing and tried to create competitive cost advantage by "foreign sourcing" with contracts in Asia—China, Thailand, Malaysia, and the Philippines—as well as in Latin America. In the new era of Europe 1992, companies are moving some foreign sourcing into lower production-cost countries such as Greece and Portugal, or quota countries such as Italy and France.[11] The scope and prescribed size of this book do not permit detailed analyses and examples, but an introduction to the four abbreviations is in order here.

The European Community (EC) is an amalgam of three preexisting European member country industrial and commercial communities. The 1965 Treaty of Brussels created a single council for policy decisions, a commission for administration, a court of justice, and a parliament. By 1978, the financing for the EC was not by contribution but was instead an imposed

[11] *Id.*

share of import duties and VAT revenues from the member countries. The purpose of the EC is to integrate the economies of the member European countries into a supranational economy. Objectives have included elimination of national tariffs, and common policy for external trade and agriculture. In 1985, the member states committed to completing this internal market by 1992.

This single European market intends to eliminate exchange controls and withholding taxes. Cash management will be liberalized. The elimination of withholding taxes will facilitate pan-European cash, investment, and borrowing transactions. European commercial banking systems will facilitate money movements. Intercompany netting can be done daily or weekly, instead of monthly. "Companies that have never had cash pools—central collections of money—will establish them."[12]

The European Monetary System (EMS) was created by the EC and began operating in the 1980s. Its first purpose was to stabilize the currencies of the EC member countries. Another objective was to create a common monetary unit, the European Currency Unit (ECU). The weighting of each country's currency in the ECU was according to its share in the EC output. The European Currency Unit (ECU) is a basket of the 12 currencies for the 12 member countries of the European Community (EC). It is a currency, however, and should be not confused with the Exchange Rate Mechanism (ERM) parity grid for exchange rates for 10 of the EC individual countries' currencies. The currencies of the United Kingdom, Portugal, and Greece are included in the ECU. In October 1990, the United Kingdom joined the ERM, but Greece and Portugal are not ERM members. The currencies of 12 countries are in the ECU, but 10 of those countries participate in the Exchange Rate Mechanism (ERM). The ECU components, the method for computing the U.S. Dollar value for an ECU with each component currency, and the relative weightings (expressed as percentages) are shown in Table 7.1.

The ERM provides that each ERM member country should maintain the exchange rate of its currency within a 75 percent margin from central parity, the currency's "divergence indicator." The divergence indicator is not the same as the ERM's "bands"—ERM's regulation of spread between the currencies. The governments of currencies in the ERM's narrow 2.25 percent band agree that their currencies may only spread from each other by plus or minus 2.25 percent. The 6 percent wide band allows a wider spread and is intended as a transitional, entry band. Italy joined in the wide band and is now in the narrow band. Spain and the newly joined U.K. are the two currencies in the wide band.

A simple example of the interrelationship of the divergence indicator and the width of the bands is as follows. Consider the DEM/GBP exchange rate.

---

[12] "Cash Sans Frontiers," *Corporate Finance* (Aug. 1989), pp. 21–25.

Table 7.1   Composition of the European Currency Unit,
Based on Rates as of May 20, 1991

Currency	Component of ECU	USD Foreign Exchange Rate (American Terms)	USD Value of ECU Component	Weight in ECU (Percentage)	USD Foreign Exchange Rate (European Terms)
BEF	3.301000	$0.028376	$0.093668	7.8539%	35.2410
LUX	0.130000	0.028376	0.003689	0.3093	35.2410
DAK	0.197600	0.152765	0.030186	2.5311	6.5460
DEM	0.624200	0.583431	0.364177	30.5356	1.7140
GRD	1.440000	0.005332	0.007678	0.6438	187.55
ESB	6.885000	0.009425	0.064892	5.4410	106.10
FRF	1.332000	0.171939	0.229023	19.2032	5.8160
IEP	0.008552	0.639264	0.005467	0.4584	1.5643
ITL	151.800000	0.000780	0.118363	9.9245	1282.05
NLG	0.219800	0.517598	0.113768	9.5393	1.9320
PTE	1.393000	0.006695	0.009326	0.7820	149.37
GBP	0.087840	1.734900	0.152394	12.7779	1.7349
Dollar value of 1 European Currency Unit			$1.192631	100.0000	

If the Deutsche Mark is 4 percent stronger than its 2.95 central rate, the Pound Sterling could only depreciate 2 percent from the Deutsche Mark and the other ERM currencies.

The actual relationship is somewhat more complex, as shown in the ERM grid in Table 7.2.

The ERM grid shows the central rates and the upper and lower bands for each member currency quoted against the others. Each column shows the number of units of currency against the number of units specified in the left-hand column. The number in the middle of each box is the central (or official) rate. The top (smaller) number is the lower band. The bottom (larger) number is the upper band. The upper and lower bands show the maximum range of fluctuation in value in the exchange rates permitted under the ERM.

Two examples might clarify how to read the grid. The first row shows the value of BEF 100 against the currencies of the other members of the ERM. The central rate for the Belgian Franc against the Danish Kroner is DAK 18.49380 per BEF 100 (DAK 0.18943 per 1 Franc). The lower band (top number) for the Belgian Franc is DAK 18.08310. That is the smallest amount of Kroner that BEF 100 could command in the foreign exchange market and still be within the ERM grid. That number is the Franc's lower band against the Kroner.

Similarly, BEF could be worth as many as DAK 18.91430 in the foreign exchange market and still be within the ERM grid. That is the Franc's upper band (bottom number). The lower band is one currency's minimum value against a second. The upper band is its maximum value. This is a discussion

Table 7.2 ERM Grid, Effective October 8, 1990

	BELGIUM	DENMARK	FRANCE	IRELAND	ITALY	NETHERLANDS	GERMANY	SPAIN	ENGLAND
100 BELGIAN FRANCS		18.08310	15.89900	1.76950	3546.90000	5.34105	4.74000	296.80200	1.54790
		18.49380	16.26080	1.80981	3627.64000	5.46286	4.84837	315.14300	1.64352
		18.91430	16.63100	1.85100	3710.20000	5.58700	4.95900	334.61900	1.74510
1 DANISH KRONER	5.28700		0.85970	0.09568	191.79000	0.28883	0.25630	16.04900	0.08370
	5.40723		0.87926	0.09786	196.15400	0.29539	0.26216	17.04050	0.08887
	5.53000		0.89925	0.10009	200.62000	0.30210	0.26810	18.09400	0.09436
1 FRENCH FRANC	6.01295	1.11200		0.10883	218.18000	0.32848	0.29150	18.25300	0.09519
	6.14977	1.13732		0.11130	223.09100	0.33595	0.29816	19.38060	0.10107
	6.28970	1.16320		0.11383	228.17000	0.34360	0.30495	20.58200	0.10732
1 IRISH PUNT	54.02500	9.99130	8.78500		1959.84000	2.95100	2.61900	163.99700	0.85526
	55.25450	10.21860	8.98480		2004.43000	3.01848	2.67894	174.13100	0.90812
	56.51150	10.45110	9.18900		2050.03000	3.08700	2.74000	184.89200	0.96424
1,000 ITALIAN LIRE	26.95300	4.98500	4.38300	0.51025		1.47250	1.30650	81.82000	0.42669
	27.56610	5.09803	4.48247	0.49890		1.50590	1.33651	86.87260	0.45306
	28.19300	5.21400	4.58450	0.48780		1.54000	1.36700	92.24000	0.48105
1 DUTCH GUILDER	17.89850	3.31020	2.91040	0.32394	649.28000		0.86780	54.33100	0.28334
	18.30540	3.38537	2.97661	0.33129	664.05300		0.88753	57.68830	0.30086
	18.72150	3.46240	3.04440	0.33887	679.12000		0.90770	61.25300	0.31945
1 DEUTSCH MARK	20.16550	3.73000	3.27920	0.36496	731.57000	1.10168		61.21700	0.31928
	20.62550	3.81443	3.35386	0.37328	748.21700	1.12673		65.00000	0.33898
	21.09500	3.90160	3.43050	0.38183	765.40000	1.15235		69.01700	0.35997
100 SPANISH PESETAS	29.88500	5.52600	4.85950	0.54086	1084.10000	1.63250	1.44900		0.49116
	31.73160	5.86637	5.15981	0.57428	1151.11000	1.73345	1.53847		0.52151
	33.69300	6.23100	5.47850	0.60977	1222.30000	1.84050	1.63300		0.55374
1 ENGLISH POUND	57.30350	10.59760	9.31800	1.03710	2078.79000	3.13050	2.77300	180.59000	
	60.84510	11.25260	9.89389	1.10116	2207.25000	3.32389	2.95000	191.75000	
	64.60500	11.94790	10.50550	1.16920	2343.62000	3.52950	3.13200	203.60000	

in tautology. If currency one is at its upper band against currency two, currency two is at its lower band against currency one.

A second example is the value of 1 Deutsche Mark (seventh row in the left-hand column) versus the French Franc (third country column). The central rate for the French Franc against the Deutsche Mark is FRF 3.35386 per DEM. The Deutsche Mark's lower band (top number) against the French Franc is FRF 3.27920. Its upper band (bottom number) is FRF 3.43050.

The combination of the bands and the divergence indicator quickly complicates seemingly straightforward computations. The bands change to 6.17 percent upside and 5.83 percent downside. The divergence indicator is calculated after considering the weight of each currency based on the central rate. The composition of the ERM is readily displayed with an example of one day's quotations from the financial press. A typical format is shown in Table 7.3.

The computation of a currency's relative "ECU central rate" goes as follows, using Pounds Sterling (GBP) and Deutsche Marks (DEM) in the example. The Pound Sterling is "pegged" to the DEM at 2.95: DEM/ECU 2.05586 divided by GBP/ECU .696904 or, using Table 7.2, GBP 1.00/DEM .33898 = 2.95. The "currency amounts against ECU" are that day's closing exchange rates for each currency in relation to the ECU. The "percent change from central rate" is, for example,

GBP/ECU .695209 − .696904 or .001695 ÷ .696904 or −2.4%

The "percent spread versus the weakest currency" clearly shows that the Spanish Peseta is pushing the 6 percent top (actually 6.17 percent) of the wide band when compared to the weakest currency, the Pounds Sterling,

Table 7.3 Example of EMS Daily Quotations
Using Quotations from January 31, 1992

	Spread from Weakest Currency	ECU Central Rate	Currency/ ECU	Currency Percent Change from ECU Central Rate	Divergence
Pounds Sterling	0.00%	0.696904	0.710208	1.91%	66
Danish Krona	0.90	7.84195	7.92002	1.00	44
French Franc	0.94	6.89509	6.96159	0.96	43
Italian Lira	2.05	1538.24	1536.08	−0.14	−6
Irish Punt	2.06	0.767417	0.766305	−0.14	−6
Deutsche Mark	2.51	2.05586	2.04385	−0.58	−26
Dutch Guilder	2.60	2.31643	2.30086	−0.67	−30
Belgian Franc	2.68	42.4032	42.0848	−0.75	−33
Spanish Peseta	5.95	133.631	128.540	−3.81	−66

Currencies are listed in order by their spread from the weakest currency.

set at zero for the spread scale. The ECU is quoted in *American terms;* the currency amounts against the ECU show that the Peseta is stronger than its ECU central rate and the French Franc is weaker than its ECU central rate.

When the divergence indicator warns that a currency is starting to move toward breaching the bands of the ERM, its government, working with the other member countries, can act to strengthen or weaken the currency. The government can intervene in the usual currency markets by using its central bank reserves to sell (weaken) or buy (strengthen) the currency. The other alternative is to decrease or increase interest rates for the currency, thus repelling or attracting investors and causing the currency to be sold (weakened) or bought (strengthened). Occasionally, the ERM is realigned, thus changing the relative central rates.

As governments work to maintain their currencies within the constraints of the ERM, the effect is intended to be stabilization among the currencies in the group. An erroneous conclusion is that the effect of the ERM is stabilization of any member currency's exchange rate against the U.S. Dollar or other non-European currency such as the Japanese Yen or Canadian Dollar.

ECU VERSUS USDX

The *ECU* (European Currency Unit) is a monetary unit. It could be considered a "derivative" currency—derived from the composite of the member countries' currencies. The ECU is quoted in American terms.

The U.S. Dollar Index (USDX)—with futures and exchange-traded options contracts on the Financial Instrument Exchange (FINEX)—parallels the Federal Reserve Board's trade-weighted geometric average of 10 currencies against the U.S. Dollar. USDX is an index, not a monetary unit, and it is quoted in European terms. The ECU is traded in the interbank spot and forward market. Both ECU and USDX futures and options contracts are traded on the FINEX.

The currency composition of the ECU changes as the relative values of the currencies change in the ERM. The ECU weights, as computed and shown in Table 7.4, can be compared to the U.S. Dollar Index.

ECU interbank and exchange-traded contracts are particularly useful to companies doing business in ECUs or with ECU-denominated debt instruments in their investment portfolios. Multinational corporations with a broad exposure to European currencies may find the ECU a useful hedging tool. The USDX does not include all the EC member currencies, but nearly 25 percent of the USDX includes two major non-European currencies, the Japanese Yen and the Canadian Dollar. The USDX is quoted in European terms; the ECU is quoted in *American terms.* Because of their inverse or

Table 7.4 Comparison of ECU Percentages
and USDX Weights as of May 20, 1991

Currency	ECU Percentages (12 Currencies)	USDX Weight (10 Currencies)
German Mark (DEM)	30.5356%	.208
French Franc (FRF)	19.2032	.131
British Pound (GBP)	12.7779	.119
Italian Lira (ITL)	9.9245	.090
Dutch Guilder (NLG)	9.5393	.083
Belgian Franc (BEF)	7.8539	.064
Luxembourg Franc (LUX)	0.3093	n.i.
Danish Krone (DAK)	2.5311	n.i.
Greek Drachma (GRD)	0.6438	n.i.
Irish Pound (IEP)	0.4584	n.i.
Spanish Peseta (ESB)	5.4410	n.i.
Portuguese Escudo (PTE)	0.7820	n.i.
Japanese Yen (JPY)	n.i.	.136
Canadian Dollar (CAD)	n.i.	.091
Swedish Krona (SEK)	n.i.	.042
Swiss Franc (CHF)	n.i.	.036
Total	100.0000	1.000

n.i. = not included.

reciprocal pricing relationship, the USDX and ECU futures contracts movements are inversely related: when the U.S. Dollar value goes up, the USDX rises and the ECU declines; when the U.S. Dollar value goes down, the USDX declines and the ECU rises. The relative difference between the movements of the two futures contracts is almost entirely attributable to the U.S. Dollar's movements against the Japanese Yen and the Canadian Dollar.[13]

The ECU and USDX may be suitable and convenient for hedging multicurrency exposures without having to arrange contracts for each major currency. Significant "basis" risk between the composition of the USDX or ECU and the mix of currencies being hedged can sometimes be minimized. The currencies most likely to create significant basis risk may well be major currencies with both interbank and exchange-traded contracts available. We acknowledge the observation of a trader: "More corporates have 'stuffed' using the ECU than have benefited by it—their mistake?" A manager should be careful in the analyses of a company's basket of currencies vis-à-vis the ECU weighting.

[13] Financial Instrument Exchange (FINEX), *USDX, U.S. Dollar Index Futures and Options* (1989), p. 12.

With good understanding and documentation of the underlying's cash market multicurrency exposure (see Chapter 2) and comparison to the ECU or USDX, the financial engineer can compute possible hedge combinations to minimize undesirable basis risk. Consider some examples. An offsetting position could be arranged to strip or adjust the weighting of one or more currencies, for example, Japanese Yen, Deutsche Marks, or Canadian Dollars in the USDX. The ECU could be "stripped" of its British Pound percentage—by an offsetting GBP position—if a company does business throughout continental Europe but not in England. If the Deutsche Mark's percentage in the ECU is far larger than the Deutsche Mark component of the European cash flow to be hedged, a suitable portion of offsetting futures contracts or a forward contract could be used to "engineer" a customized "quasi-ECU" or "cross-rate USDX." The sequence in the following example isolates Pounds Sterling from the USDX:

Compute the value of the USDX, for example, $90.00 \times$ USD 500 per index point = USD 45,000.

Compute the U.S. Dollar value of the component currency; the GBP percentage in the USDX is 11.9 percent (.119) $\times$ USD 45,000 = USD 5,355.

The Pounds Sterling could be "stripped" from the index by buying or selling USD 5,355 worth of Pounds Sterling.

The transaction to "strip" a currency will be opposite of the USDX position. If long the USDX, sell to strip; if short the USDX, buy to strip.

One or more currencies in an index can be reweighted or stripped using a similar methodology.

Detailed examples of changing index weights, USDX and ECU spread, and USDX or ECU cross-rate transactions will not fit in this book. The reader is recommended to the FINEX for some well-done pamphlets with good ideas and computed examples (see Appendix B for the address). The financial engineering opportunities are interesting to consider.

CENTIPEDE COMPANY

This study is a lesson in how NOT to do a currency swap.

Centipede was a billion-dollar U.S. corporation with a hundred "legs." The Company manufactured mechanical and electronic control devices for use in industry, and high-ticket consumer products such as golf clubs. It manufactured primarily in the United States and had a subassembly facility in Singapore. Its extensive marketing operations included most Western European countries. To comply with expected guidelines for the European Community (EC), Centipede was building a major manufacturing plant in Strasbourg, France.

The Company was only 15 years old. A pioneer in its field, it had some of the most sophisticated technology in the world. Its international operations were relatively new. It has recently hired a new chief financial officer (CFO) who had been previously employed by a major regional U.S. bank.

In mid-1989, the CFO had arranged a financing package for the European operations: a USD 30 million facility, through a small consortium of banks, with a 3-year maturity and a ½ percent spread over *LIBOR*. USD 7 million would be used to finance construction of the French plant. Work would begin in the fall of 1989, and the plant would be complete in late 1991. USD 23 million was to be divided among the European subsidiaries and used for working capital. The USD 23 million working capital portion of the loan was to be divided as shown in Table 7.5.

Although the subsidiaries all earned revenues in the respective currencies of the countries in which they operated, the intercompany loans were denominated in U.S. Dollars. The interest rate on each loan from the parent to the subsidiaries was booked at 3-month LIBOR plus 1 percent. Thus, Centipede booked a ½ percent spread on each loan to the subsidiaries, less bank fees and other transaction costs.

Shortly after the bank facility was signed but before the proceeds had been divided among the various European subsidiaries, the CFO became worried about two factors: U.S. interest rates were rising, and the U.S. Dollar had strengthened from DEM/USD 1.8300 to DEM/USD 1.9500.

One of Centipede's bankers presented the CFO with the possibility of entering into a *currency swap*. Centipede would lend the bank the USD 30 million proceeds from the term loan. The bank would lend Centipede the equivalent amount in Deutsche Marks. The bank would pay Centipede 3-month LIBOR on the USD 30 million. Centipede could pay the bank either 3-month LIBOR or a fixed interest rate in Deutsche Marks. At

Table 7.5 Division of Loan for Working Capital

Country	U.S. Dollars (Millions)	Percent of USD 23 Million
France	3.0	13.04%
Germany	5.0	21.74
Sweden	1.5	6.52
Norway	2.5	10.87
United Kingdom	5.0	21.74
Netherlands	3.0	13.04
Italy	1.0	4.35
Belgium	0.5	2.17
Spain	1.5	6.52

the time the transaction was proposed, 3-month U.S. Dollar LIBOR was quoted at 8.75 percent, 3-month Deutsche Mark LIBOR was quoted at 6.625 percent, and 3-year fixed rate Deutsche Marks were 8 percent for a company of Centipede's credit rating.

According to the banker, this transaction would have several advantages for Centipede:

1. Centipede could lock-in a lower interest cost by swapping into Deutsche Marks.
2. Centipede could lend the proceeds of the Deutsche Mark currency swap to its subsidiaries instead of U.S. Dollar. The Deutsche Mark loan would reduce the foreign exchange risk because the currencies in which the individual subsidiaries earned their revenues were generally more closely linked to the Deutsche Mark than they were to the U.S. Dollar.
3. The currency swap would not involve any additional foreign exchange exposure for the parent company because the funds to repay the swap would come from the maturity of the intercompany loans to the subsidiaries.

Centipede eventually entered into a currency swap, but the CFO proceeded to bungle the transaction.

Instead of converting the intercompany loans into Deutsche Marks as the banker had proposed, Centipede's CFO sold the Deutsche Marks and bought USD 30 million at an exchange rate of DEM 1.9500 per USD. The CFO reasoned that, because Centipede was a U.S. Dollar-based company, the intercompany loans should stay in USD. The CFO was still expecting to profit from the interest differential between the U.S. Dollar and the Deutsche Mark that had existed at the time when Centipede had entered into the currency swap. (The problem discussed in the next paragraph—the interest rate differential's disappearance—had not yet occurred.)

The situation deteriorated because of the CFO's next step. The CFO entered into a floating Deutsche Mark swap by swapping the USD 30 million against DEM 58.5 million based on 3-month Deutsche Mark LIBOR. The CFO could have swapped for 3-year Deutsche Marks at a fixed interest rate of 8 percent. With the spread on the bank loan, the total interest cost would have been $8^{1}/_{2}$ percent. Over the course of the swap, German interest rates rose sharply to the point where they were quoted at $8^{1}/_{2}$ percent. U.S. Dollar interest rates fell during the same period to $8^{1}/_{16}$ percent. The CFO incorrectly guessed the market directions of interest rates in the respective countries.

The malign result of this conversion of Deutsche Marks to U.S. Dollars was that the U.S. Dollar fell against the Deutsche Mark from DEM 1.9500 in late summer, when the CFO did the transaction, to DEM 1.7000 by the end of the year. That difference resulted in a year-end translation loss of over USD 4.4 million for Centipede, computed as follows:

DEM 58.5 million/DEM 1.9500 = USD 30 million
−DEM 58.5 million/DEM 1.7000 = USD 34.4 million.

The translation loss was USD 4.4 million.

The CFO, realizing that there might be a potentially serious problem, proceeded to perform the coup de grace. Intending to create a hedge for the Deutsche Marks that had been sold, the CFO entered into a new foreign exchange contract. The CFO bought USD 30 million worth of Deutsche Marks at DEM 1.70 per dollar (DEM 51 million) and sold ECU at USD 1.2150 per XEU (XEU 24,691,358.02). Both were pushed forward for 6 months.

The CFO had made a bad decision, for several reasons. First, there was a Deutsche Mark difference of DEM 7.5 million between the amount originally swapped and the amount purchased: DEM 1.9500 − DEM 1.7000 = .25 × USD 30 million. Further, the CFO created a new foreign currency exposure while attempting to alleviate the old one. Making matters even worse, because of the markets' fears of inflation resulting from German reunification in 1990, the Deutsche Mark weakened against the ECU, thus adding to the CFO's losses as the dollar eroded in value against the European currencies in general!

The following summary lists the effects of the CFO's decisions and actions. It is not possible to specify the final cost of these transactions because none of the transactions had settled in this study. The new risks created can be enumerated.

1. The decision to use the currency swap would have been a reasonable one if the subsidiary loans had also been converted from U.S. Dollars to Deutsche Marks. Instead, the CFO created a new exposure on Centipede's books. The decision to accept a floating rather than fixed Deutsche Mark interest rate was a judgment call that, in hindsight, was wrong. Events of enormous historical import were on the horizon but no one foresaw, when the CFO made the decision, that the events would push German interest rates much higher in the coming months and years.

2. The conversion of the Deutsche Mark proceeds of the currency swap into U.S. Dollars was the result of muddle-headed thinking. By keeping the subsidiary loans in U.S. Dollars, the CFO created a USD 30 million foreign exchange exposure on Centipede's books. The final cost or gain of this transaction would depend on the final exchange rate when the transaction was unwound.

3. The forward sale of Deutsche Marks and the purchase of ECUs was another poorly thought out attempt to match the subsidiaries' cash flows to the Deutsche Mark exposure created by the loan, the swap, and previous foreign exchange transactions. The CFO incurred an additional risk that the ECU would depreciate against the Deutsche Mark. Furthermore, the Deutsche Mark equivalent of this transaction did not match the Deutsche Mark amount of the original swap.

PETUNIA PERSONAL PRODUCTS COMPANY

This company was selected for study because its experience illustrates the use of the *participating forward*.

The Company's Foreign Currency Exposure Policy

Petunia Personal Products Company ("the Company") is a large manufacturer and marketer of consumer products, including toothpaste, soaps, laundry detergents, personal hygiene products, and baby care products. The Company sells its products either directly or under license in nearly every country, and has manufacturing operations in almost 80 countries. Its global sales revenues from all products are nearly USD 3 billion annually, with 45 percent derived from sources outside the United States. Revenues in currencies other than U.S. Dollars annually total about USD 1 billion.

The Company's foreign currency exposure is managed by a staff of three people: the assistant treasurer for international operations and two finance managers (collectively, "the treasury"). The Company's foreign currency exposure policy, adopted in the 1970s, remains based on two assumptions. First, the Company could determine with reasonable accuracy its anticipated cash flows for 3 years in advance. Although the Company's market share for individual products might change, its diversity of products and its marketing skill remedied a decline in one product's sales, usually, by increased sales of its other products. Second, the Company could not project or hedge foreign exchange rate fluctuations 3 years in advance:

- Hedging all exposures for a time as long as 3 years was not economical;
- Hedging costs for some currencies were too high;
- Some transactions and cash flows would offset other cash flows.

To handle the routine payments, the treasury had established a *netting system,* operated by the Company's subsidiary, Petunia Finance S.A. Petunia Finance is headquartered in Western Europe and manages all payments, short-term financing, and investment transactions for the European operations as well as the Company's transactions with other subsidiaries, affiliates, and licensees outside the United States. Petunia Finance is also responsible for handling all royalty, licensing, and dividend payments between and among the European subsidiaries and the parent Company.

This arrangement has resulted in substantial cash flows from one currency to another but has failed to address the need for appropriate hedging of foreign exchange exposures over a multiyear horizon. The treasury had historically taken an aggressive approach to managing foreign exchange rate exposure. Thus, if the treasury perceived a trend developing in one currency against another, the practice had been to buy the currency that was expected to appreciate, then use any profit generated to offset other exposures that could not be easily managed, such as those for a longer term. This policy, which had allowed the treasury to enter into speculative trades in order to profit from volatility in foreign exchange markets, operated under three rules:

1. Total speculative positions outstanding could not exceed USD 50 million;
2. Each position had to be revalued at the close of each day, using the current market exchange rate for the position;
3. Each position would be liquidated if there were an adverse move in market exchange rates equal to 2 percent of the previous day's revaluation rate.

This policy was established to limit the effect of adverse foreign exchange market movements.

To maintain an independent accounting, as well as to control all foreign exchange positions and trades, the Company's controller prepared and maintained a separate summary of foreign exchange positions and outstanding contracts. The controller also confirmed all foreign exchange transactions with individual counterparties.

Business Risk Situation and Analysis

After the October 1987 stock market crash, the treasury anticipated a sharp fall by the U.S. Dollar in the foreign exchange market. On October 20, the treasury decided to establish a foreign exchange position by selling U.S. Dollars 25 million and buying Deutsche Marks for delivery 3 months forward at an exchange rate of DEM 1.7675. The value date of the contract was January 22, 1988. The U.S. Dollar fell steadily over the next several months, declining to USD 1.6350 by December 15. The effect of the USD 1.6350 level was that the Company would need fewer Deutsche Marks to make its January 22 delivery and hence had made a profit. At this juncture, the treasury made an analysis as to whether the Company should take the profit on the position by closing it.

The treasury considered the following issues pertinent to managing its profitable position. There was a possibility that the U.S. Dollar would fall further against the Deutsche Mark by December 31, thus increasing its profit. Around year-end, however, foreign exchange markets usually become thin because fewer banks trade for their own account. As a result, foreign exchange markets have an historical year-end tendency to become volatile. Most open positions of traders and speculators were identical to the Company's position: short U.S. Dollars against major currencies. Hence, if these positions were liquidated, traders would buy U.S. Dollars and thereby push up sharply the value of the U.S. Dollar.

By December 15, the Company had a profit of approximately USD 2 million in its position, shown by the following calculation:

USD 25,000,000 × DEM/USD 1.7675 = DEM 44,187,500
DEM 44,187,500/DEM/USD 1.6350 = USD 27,025,994
USD 27,025,994 − USD 25,000,000 = USD   2,025,994

A simple decision was made: obey the adage "No one ever lost money taking a profit." If the U.S. Dollar were traded up sharply on position *squaring,* the Company could lose much of the profit that it had gained. Although profit taking or squaring positions before year-end was not a certainty, a sound course was to seek protection of the profit that the Company had already gained in its forward contract position.

The treasury analyzed the following three alternatives for locking-in the profit that the Company had gained on its outstanding October forward contract.

At the Money Forward Put Option

The recent volatility of the foreign exchange market would result in an expensive premium for this type of option. Nonetheless, the treasury called a senior corporate trader at one of the Company's main banks and requested an *indication* on an *American-style* Deutsche Mark *put* with a *strike price* of DEM 1.6300 and an *expiration date* of January 20, 1988.

The terms of the requested indication were based on the following considerations. With a January 20 expiration date for the option, the settlement date for the option, if exercised, would be January 22, 1988—the same *value date* as the October forward contract. If the Company decided to exercise the new put, it could deliver the Deutsche Marks that it had purchased under its outstanding forward contract because the strike price of DEM 1.6300 was approximately equal to the forward outright rate to January 22 of DEM/USD of 1.6350. The treasury was, in effect, requesting a strike price equal to the *at the money forward* rate. By setting the exact strike price, the treasury could control a variable of the option premium.

As anticipated, the indicated option premium for a strike price equal to the at the money forward rate was expensive: 3.23 percent, which computed to a cost of more than USD 875,000 for a 6-week option, as follows:

At-the-Money Forward Option Premium

DEM 44,187,500/DEM/USD 1.6300 = USD 27,108,895.71
USD 27,108,895.71 × 3.23% = USD 875,617.33,

The option premium was USD 875,617.33.

Out of the Money Put Option

A put option with a strike price of DEM/USD 1.6800 would protect approximately 60 percent of the Company's profit under its outstanding forward contract, less the option premium, as shown by the following computation:

Percentage of Profit Protected

DEM/USD 1.7675 (exchange rate for the outstanding forward contract)
– DEM/USD 1.6300 (put strike price) = DEM/USD 0.1375;

DEM/USD 1.7675 – 1.6800 (out of the money put strike price) = 0.0875
0.0875/.1375 = 63.6% (percentage of profit protected).

The treasury then asked for an indication for another put with identical terms except with a strike price of DEM/USD 1.6800. The indication given was a *premium* of 2.05 percent or USD 539,192.71, computed as follows:

Out-of-the-Money Put Option Premium

DEM 44,187,500/DEM/USD 1.6800 = USD 26,302,083.33
USD 26,302,083.33 × 2.05% = USD 539,192.71

Participating Forward

The bank explained that the participating forward is so named because the counterparty to the transaction participates in any favorable price move while still being guaranteed a minimum forward exchange rate at some future date. The participation rate is the percentage of the favorable move that the Company retains. The Company could select either a participation rate or a foreign exchange strike price for the participating forward contract.

Specifically, the Company could buy an *out of the money put* with a strike price of USD/DEM 1.6800, and write an *in the money call* with the same strike price of DEM/USD 1.6800, each with the same premium. The DEM/USD 1.6800 put option's strike price would be higher (bigger number, higher USD value) than the current exchange rate of around DEM/USD 1.6350. Under the terms of the proposed put option, the Company would not sell the *underlying* Deutsche Marks at an exchange rate higher than the strike price of DEM/USD 1.6800. Hence, the put would have only time value—a value that would decrease as time passed toward the put's expiration.

The call option written, however, would have primarily intrinsic value, for the same reason that the put option would have only time value: the call option's strike price would be the same as the put option's strike price and would be higher than the current DEM/USD 1.6350 exchange rate. Because the call would have intrinsic value, it could be written against a much smaller amount of Deutsche Marks than the Deutsche Mark amount of the put option. By writing the call, the Company would not have to pay up front any put option premium.

The following computation illustrates how broadly to approximate the amount of Deutsche Marks needed to equal the call premium which will, in turn, offset the put option premium (see the computation for the out of the money put option premium). In the following computation, DEM (the algebraic "unknown") refers to the estimated Deutsche Mark amount needed to equal the premium for the participating forward. This computation results in a quick and broad approximation but not an indication or close estimate because the time value is not a factor.

Approximating the Amount of DEM Required for Call

USD 539,193 (put option premium of 2.05 percent computed as shown in the previous computation) = (DEM/1.63 – DEM/1.68);
$$(1.68 \times 1.63) \times 539{,}193 = (DEM/1.63) - (DEM/1.68)$$
$$2.7384 \times 539{,}193 = 1.68DEM - 1.63DEM$$
$$1{,}476{,}526 = .05DEM$$
$$1{,}476{,}526/.05 = DEM$$
$$29{,}530{,}522 = DEM$$

According to the bank's trader, DEM 29,530,522 was a high estimate of the Deutsche Mark amount needed to equal the USD 539,193 premium. The trader indicated that DEM 21,500,000 would probably be closer to the amount of Deutsche Marks needed to enter into a participating forward with a strike price of DEM 1.6800 per U.S. Dollar. This lower estimate was based on the fact that volatility was then relatively high and the option had, therefore, a relatively high time value.

The participating forward constructed with the Company's buying a DEM 44.2 million put option and writing a DEM 21.5 million call option would result in the Company's participating in about 50 percent (21.5/44.2) of the incremental profit if, at expiration, the Deutsche Mark to U.S. Dollar exchange rate was below the strike price of DEM/USD 1.6800.

Mechanics of the Participating Forward

The treasury asked the following questions about the mechanics of trade in a participating forward, and received the answers shown.

1. Would the Company need to pay any up-front costs to enter into a participating forward?

No. The premium on the Deutsche Mark put would be offset by the premium on the call that the Company wrote. Hence, neither counterparty would pay any premium to the other.

2. Could either option be exercised before its expiration?

No. In this case, each option would be a *European-style* option, which is exercisable only on the expiration date. This type of option was suitable for the Company's proposed transaction because its purpose was to protect a cash flow that would occur on a known date. If the date when the cash flow needed protection was uncertain, then the best strategy would be to pick an early expiration for both options. If either the put or the call were to be exercised, the currency amount to be delivered could be managed through a *foreign exchange swap* from the settlement date of the exercised option to the actual date of the cash flow being protected. In practice, the bank would be unlikely to exercise the option prior to expiration because it would lose any remaining time value.

3. What would happen on the expiration date?

If the "Dollar Mark" (exchange rate of Deutsche Mark per Dollar) were trading below DEM 1.6800 per Dollar, the counterparty-bank would exercise the DEM 21.5 million call option—namely, purchase the underlying currency, the Deutsche Marks. The Company would then deliver to the bank the amount of Deutsche Marks against which it had written the DEM 21.5 million call option and receive U.S. Dollars in an amount determined by the DEM/USD 1.6800 strike price. The DEM 44.2 million put option with DEM/USD 1.6800 strike price would expire worthless. The Company could sell the balance of the Deutsche Marks that it owned at the current spot exchange rate. For example, if, at expiration, DEM/USD exchange rate were DEM/USD 1.6500, then the company would deliver to the bank DEM 21.5 million and receive USD 12.798 million at a strike price of DEM/USD 1.6800. The Company would sell the balance of DEM 22.7 million at DEM/USD 1.6500, current spot exchange rate, for USD 13.758 million, and the Company's weighted average exchange rate to close its profitable position would be DEM/USD 1.6644. The Company's profit of USD 1,548,606 can be computed:

USD 25,000,000 × DEM/USD 1.7675 = DEM 44,187,500
DEM 44,187,500/DEM/USD 1.6644 = USD 26,548,606
USD 26,548,606 − USD 25,000,000 = USD 1,548,606

If, on the expiration date, the Dollar Mark were trading higher than DEM 1.6800 per U.S. Dollar, the Company would exercise the DEM/USD 1.6800 put option, deliver the put option's DEM 44,187,500 to the bank, and receive the U.S. Dollar equivalent. The call option would not be exercised, being worthless—a DEM/USD 1.6800 call gives the holder the right to buy Deutsche Marks at USD .5952 per DEM (1.0000/1.6800), but if the current spot market is at DEM/USD 1.7000, the call holder can buy DEM less expensively at USD .5882 per DEM (1.000/1.7000). For example, if, at expiration, the exchange rate were DEM/USD 1.7000, the Company would exercise the DEM/USD 1.6800 put option and receive USD 26,302,083 for a profit of USD 1,302,083, computed as above.

4. May the participating forward transaction be liquidated before *expiration* of the options?

Yes. The liquidation would be simple. Each counterparty would sell back to the other the option that it owned, thereby liquidating the option obligation of each to the other. A net premium would probably be due, however, to one party or the other.

If, on the date of liquidation, the participating forward's DEM/USD 1.6800 strike price were higher than the current exchange rate (e.g., 1.6300), then the call option that the Company had written would be worth more because of intrinsic value than the time value of the put option that it had purchased. The Company would then have to pay to the bank the difference between the two premiums. For example, assume that, at the date of liquidation, the exchange rate is DEM/USD 1.6300 and the put option time value is USD 200,000. (The hypothetical liquidation is well prior to the expiration date.) Then:

DEM 21.5 million/DEM/USD 1.6300 = USD 13.190 million and
DEM 21.5 million/DEM/USD 1.6800 = USD 12.798 million
subtracting the intrinsic value = USD .392 million
less the put option, time value = USD (.200 million)
Company pays bank = USD .192 million

If, conversely, on the date of liquidation, the participating forward's DEM/USD 1.6800 strike price were lower than the current exchange rate (current exchange rate is a bigger number than 1.6800), then the Company's put option would have a higher premium than the bank's call option. The bank would have to pay the difference in premiums to the Company.

If, on the date of liquidation, the DEM/USD exchange rate is equal to the participating forward's strike price, the bank would owe the Company the difference between the premiums because the amount of the put is larger than the amount of the call.

Early liquidation of a participating forward will have a cash flow effect that cannot be forecasted or controlled before entering into the contract.

Reasons for Rejecting the Three Alternatives

The treasury rejected the first two alternatives—an at the money forward put and an out of the money put—because their respective premiums of more than USD 875,000 and USD 539,000 were deemed prohibitively expensive. The treasury also rejected the third alternative, a participating forward, based on the following analysis.

Writing the call option to cover the premium for the put option was merely hiding the real cost of the put. The Company would actually have an unlimited exposure under the call and relatively little control over the final cost of the transaction. Moreover, the Company would be losing a substantial part of its already obtained profit, as the following analysis illustrates.

The Company was currently *long* DEM 44,187,500. By entering into a participating forward, the Company could lock-in a maximum profit on DEM 21.5 million by writing the call option. In exchange, however, the Company would have an unlimited profit potential on the remaining DEM 22.7 million.

The Decision and Its Evaluation

The treasury decided not to use an option to protect its profit position. Instead, it decided to use the following strategy: take the profit on one-half the position, selling DEM 22.1 million one month outright at DEM 1.6300 per U.S. Dollar, and keep the other half of the position. If the U.S. Dollar rose to DEM/USD 1.6800, the Company would sell the other half. If the U.S. Dollar continued to fall, the Company would keep that half of the position until its original forward contract matured the next month, on January 20. At that time, a new decision would be made on whether to keep the remaining portion of the Deutsche Mark position or to liquidate it.

The treasury probably had taken a sensible approach to protecting the Company's profit in a speculative foreign exchange transaction because the following factors had been considered in making the decision.

1. The Company's problem had been defined: a speculative position in which the Company had a long position of approximately DEM 44 million.
2. The Company's goal was defined: to protect the profit that had accrued, because of favorable moves in the foreign exchange market, on the Company's position under its outstanding forward contract.
3. The probable impact of various likely market moves on the Company's position was appraised—for example, the U.S. Dollar's rising or falling in value against the Deutsche Mark.
4. The alternative strategies, and their respective costs, for protecting the Company's position were investigated.
5. The treasury made sure that it understood how a move in the underlying foreign exchange market would impact the strategies that it had considered.
6. The treasury's decision was both informed and consistent with the analyses that had been made.

The final decision, although based on "objective information" obtained, was "subjective." Although the treasury chose to forego an opportunity for protection, which an option strategy might have provided, it determined that the costs vis-à-vis the potential benefits did not warrant the possible expense.

The strategic decision made had virtually the same result as the participating forward considered and rejected. The strategy adopted entailed no cost or sacrifice of profit to the Company. The Company liquidated half its position at an exchange rate of DEM 1.6300 per U.S. Dollar versus the strike price of the call (DEM/USD 1.6800) that it would have written in the participating forward. Thus, the Company gained an extra profit as shown by the following calculation:

DEM 21,500,000/DEM/USD 1.6800 = USD 12,797,619.05
DEM 21,500,000/DEM/USD 1.6300 = USD 13,190,184.05

Additional profit:

USD 13,190,184.05 − USD 12,797,619.05 = USD 392,565.00

Hence, the Company's selected strategy could realize nearly USD 400,000 more in profit than by using the alternative of the participating forward.

Finally, the treasury set a stop loss review level at DEM 1.6800 per U.S. Dollar. If the U.S. Dollar traded at DEM/USD 1.6800, the Company could consider selling its remaining Deutsche Marks at the prevailing market. The

Company would thus liquidate its remaining position and thereby protect part of its profit accrued on its forward contract. The risk in placing a stop loss order is that if the rate briefly trades above the stop and then falls again, the company would be "stopped out" and would not be able to profit from renewed depreciation of the U.S. Dollar against the Deutsche Mark. A stop loss order is a relatively rigid strategy. By comparison, an option would offer flexibility and protection in this situation. The flexibility could be purchased with an option premium or by sharing a portion of the profits on the position. The stop loss order is cheap but, if strictly adhered to, sacrifices flexibility.

The strategy selected has the same impact as purchasing an out of the money Deutsche Mark put with a strike price of DEM 1.6800 per U.S. Dollar: in the worst case, the Company would have sold its Deutsche Marks and bought U.S. Dollars at an exchange rate of DEM 1.6800. By setting a stop loss review level of DEM/USD 1.6800, the treasury could assure nearly the same result—without having to pay a premium of nearly USD 500,000 for those results. The only potential cost to the Company in the stop loss review level is any additional time required for monitoring the position. This was an unlikely additional cost because financial prudence already required close monitoring of the Company's sizable and speculative foreign exchange position.

Uses of Participating Forward and Comment
About Option Products

A participating forward should be used only when a cash flow exposure is clearly defined. The basic reason for using a participating forward is to avoid an option premium cost at the outset of the transaction. The expiration and exercise of the options underlying the transaction or the early liquidation of the transaction may have a negative cash flow impact. A participating forward is not a transaction suitable for every balance sheet or translation hedge.

One of the basic features of options is that they permit the combination of writing and buying puts and calls in different ways to accomplish different objectives. Purveyors of options are constantly offering different and sometimes new combinations with strategies to avoid or lower the initial cost of the premium(s). (See the discussions in Chapter 3.)

CORNUCOPIA CONSUMER PRODUCTS INC.

This study of a multinational engaged in selling consumer goods explores the Euronote market.

Business Risk Situation

Cornucopia Consumer Products Inc. ("Cornucopia," "the Company") is a giant, multinational consumer products company with headquarters in New York. Cornucopia's various divisions and subsidiaries sell leading consumer products. Over the years, Cornucopia has followed the same basic strategy: it rarely attempts to establish new brands of products; instead, it prefers to acquire established but stagnant brand names or companies and build them up with its own capital and marketing methods. Most of the Company's acquisitions have become "cash cows" after 5 years. The Company maintains sophisticated finance operations.

In 1979, as part of a plan to continue its strong but stable growth, the Company expected to become a net borrower. As a result of the anticipated net borrowing position, the Company explored different methods of raising capital. Its long-term debt was rated single A by major debt rating agencies, and its commercial paper was rated A1 and P1 by Standard & Poor's and Moody's respectively. The long-term rating reflected primarily the level of leverage that the company chose to keep, rather than its level of profitability or capability of generating cash flow. Cornucopia's management also thought that increasing the leverage could offer protection against hostile takeover attempts.

The same year, 1979, the Company faced serious problems of financial risk planning for several of its divisions. Its cosmetic company's success in Europe had far exceeded corporate expectations. In Germany alone, the cosmetic company had generated net cash flows of nearly DEM 350 million per year. The problem was that the U.S. Dollar stood at DEM 1.7800, near its then historic low. If the U.S. Dollar were to strengthen sharply, the Company would lose a substantial amount of U.S. Dollars when repatriating the cash flows to the parent company in the United States.

The Company's stagnant soft drink subsidiary was, however, struggling to survive. Although it was not losing money, its market share continued to sag because of strong competition from other leading brands.

In the United States, interest rates were rising and inflation appeared to be escaping control. As inflation increased, the Company's interest rate expenses from its commercial paper borrowings would also increase. The Company's commercial paper dealer had informed the Company's treasury department that short-term interest rates might climb to 11 percent or 12 percent in the coming months. The Company anticipated that it would require huge medium-term borrowings over the next 2 or 3 years to finance major capital projects. In the prior year, the Company had acquired a large United States beer company and needed to invest nearly USD 900 million to modernize and increase the brewery's capacity. The treasury department estimated that the Company could borrow that sum in a series of note issues for the 5 to 10 years that the notes would be outstanding. The inherent risk was that the present cost of about 11 percent on medium-term, fixed-rate debt would continue to climb in the future.

Alternatives

In September 1979, after analysis of the various finance issues, the treasury staff could document the following considerations and conclusions.

1. With respect to the Deutsche Marks that the cosmetic division generated, the Company could sell a portion of the current year's cash flows in the forward foreign exchange market. The more serious problem was that the cosmetic division's foreign cash flows were expected to grow, and no sound way to hedge the longer-term exposure was apparent. Because the foreign exchange market's liquidity for periods beyond 1 year was too small, covering the projected cash flows was not a realistic hope.

2. Cornucopia's management had thought, during the years of declining sales, that the soft drink division's fundamental problem was its marketing department. The treasury department thought the products were too sweet for contemporary consumer tastes. If the division's prospects did not improve within 6 months, the treasury department's recommendation would be to divest or to liquidate the division.

3. The rising interest rates for U.S. Dollar commercial paper were a major problem. Rates for the Company's paper were currently running around 9 to 9½ percent for maturities of 1 to 3 months. The alternatives were either to reduce the Company's capital investment program, already approved by the board of directors, or to borrow medium-term. The latter alternative—issuing medium-term notes of 11 percent or 12 percent for the next 7 to 10 years—was financially unattractive. Because the recently acquired brewery would soon need to raise USD 100 million to pay for the initial construction phase of new and modernized facilities, a prompt decision was required as to the best financing method.

The treasury department considered the following methods. The Company could issue Deutsche Mark or Swiss Franc bonds. The rate for 7-year Deutsche Mark corporate bonds was 7 percent; for Swiss Franc bonds, it was only 4½ percent. A treasury staff member recalled that, in the late 1960s, shortly before the U.S. Dollar was devalued, many United States corporations had used the strategy of issuing foreign currency bonds and had incurred a disastrous result with the devaluation. As the U.S. Dollar had weakened, these companies' interest costs had skyrocketed: they used cheaper and cheaper dollars to buy the foreign currencies to pay the interest. Cornucopia was different; it had surplus Deutsche Marks being generated from operations of the German cosmetics division.

Cornucopia's treasury staff decided on the following strategy:

1. As soon as possible, the Company could issue DEM 150 million in
    Euronotes with a 7-year maturity and a coupon of about 7 percent.
    The cost over the life of the notes, including the underwriting fees,
    would be about 7.20 percent.
2. The Company could sell the proceeds of the Euronote issue in the
    foreign exchange market for U.S. Dollars and use that sum to fund
    the first phase of the brewery's construction project.
3. The cosmetic division generated DEM 350 million a year in Deutsche
    Mark cash flows. These DEM cash flows would both service the con-
    tinuing issuance of Deutsche Mark notes and serve as a hedge against
    future foreign exchange rate fluctuations. Cornucopia could continue
    issuing more Euronotes as required for the brewery's capital expendi-
    tures program. The Euronotes could be in Deutsche Marks, in the
    lower-interest-rate Swiss Francs, or in both. The Swiss Franc often
    fluctuated, although not invariably, approximately in line with the
    Deutsche Mark against the U.S. Dollar. If the Company obtained a
    favorable ruling from its accountants, it could issue the Swiss Franc
    bonds and declare them to be a hedge against its cosmetic division's
    Deutsche Mark exposure.

The treasury department prepared a formal proposal for the Cornucopia
management's approval. A Deutsche Mark Euronote issue in the amount of
DEM 150 million would be underwritten from the London office of the
Company's lead investment banking firm. After the issue's authorization by
the Company's board of directors, the issuance could probably be effected
within a week. Cash flows from the cosmetic division's German operation
would be used to service the Euronotes. The Company would then sell the
proceeds of the issue in the foreign exchange market for U.S. Dollars;
the Dollars would then be used to finance the projected capital expenditures
of the brewery.

Approval was also obtained to issue a continuing series of Deutsche
Mark and Swiss Franc Euronotes over the next 2 years, to meet the Company's borrowing needs. Total financing needs for the next 3 years were
projected to be USD 2 billion for both new money and refinancing of
maturing debt. Based on current exchange rates, that amount would repre-
sent total borrowings of DEM 3.6 billion if all loans were issued in
Deutsche Marks. For the current year, the cosmetic division was to generate
DEM 350 million in cash flows. Cash flows were projected to grow 15
percent per year in Germany for the next 10 years because of changing
demographics, the increasing wealth of the German population, and the
increasing number of German women entering the labor force and using

more cosmetics. Hence, the cash flows were projected to be more than enough to meet the servicing of the Deutsche Mark debt.

The proposed strategy for the Company's borrowing needs would protect the value of the cosmetic division's Deutsche Mark cash flows against any strengthening of the U.S. Dollar in the foreign exchange markets by the devaluation of any debt outstanding. By borrowing in Deutsche Marks, any depreciation in the value of the Deutsche Mark would reduce both the U.S. Dollar value of the outstanding bonds and the anticipated value of bonds.

Issuing Euronotes

A *Euronote* is a medium-term debt instrument—its original maturity is about 1½ to 10 years—usually intended for the international investment community. Because the tenor of most *Eurobonds* rarely exceeds 10 years, the terms Euronotes and Eurobonds are often used interchangeably. Euronotes are denominated in the currency of a country other than the one where the note is issued; for example, a U.S. Dollar note or a Deutsche Mark note will be issued out of and payable in London. Euronotes offer at least two advantages for issuers: the issuer can gain access to a wider group of investors than is obtainable from borrowing in a domestic market, and, because the Euronote market is almost unregulated, issuing procedures are comparatively fast and simple. A Euronote issue can be completed for a well-known borrower on only 1 or 2 days' notice after suitable documentation has been prepared between the Company and the underwriter.

Attempting to Tune a Hedge

Cornucopia eventually issued a total of DEM 2 billion and CHF (Swiss Franc) 500 million in Euronotes. The average interest rate was 6.75 percent on the Deutsche Mark issues and 4.75 percent on the Swiss Franc issues. From 1979 to 1985, the U.S. Dollar strengthened against the Deutsche Mark from DEM 1.7800 to nearly DEM 3.50; against the Swiss Franc, the U.S. Dollar strengthened from CHF 1.6500 to about CHF 2.9000. During the same period (1979 to 1985), interest rates in the United States rose to a high of 18 percent in 1981 for medium-term corporate bonds.

The strategy that Cornucopia's treasury adopted had been successful—but the Company did not leave it alone. In summer 1982, when the Company had issued the last of the Euronotes to finance the brewery's construction project, the Deutsche Mark stood at DEM 2.2500 against the U.S. Dollar. Cornucopia's executive management predicted that the U.S. Dollar would not strengthen further, and directed its treasury department to "hedge the hedge." The treasury bought German bonds with the same maturity as the Company's earliest maturing Euronote. The strategy of purchasing Deutsche Mark bonds was to match the assets to the Deutsche Mark Euronote liability.

The bonds would also provide a stream of Deutsche Mark income to service the Deutsche Mark Euronotes debt. If the U.S. Dollar depreciated, the Deutsche Mark Euronotes would appreciate in value. Cornucopia would increase the asset side of its Deutsche Mark exposure and hope that the U.S. Dollar would fall against the Deutsche Mark. The "hedged hedge" was that the Deutsche Mark bonds would appreciate in U.S. Dollar terms if the U.S. Dollar were to fall in value against the Deutsche Mark.

This hedge strategy did not work: the U.S. Dollar strengthened to DEM 2.4000 before the Company sold its bonds at a loss in U.S. Dollar terms. This failed "hedged hedge" has an important moral: avoid the almost inevitable temptation to tinker with a finance hedge, especially when a strategy works as well as the one that Cornucopia had put into effect. Individuals involved are tempted to believe that they can accurately predict future directions and trends in financial markets—usually with the same adverse result as occurred here.

A few words of advice: if the financial engineering is working and is doing what it was supposed to do, do not throw a monkey wrench ("spanner") in the works without an excellent reason. For example, if the Company had sold its cosmetic division or its brewery, it would have had a compelling reason to consider hedging the Deutsche Mark and Swiss Franc bonds (or Euronotes). A change in opinion about trends in financial markets is not an appropriate reason to change a hedge that is working properly.

8

Repatriations

> There is no sphere of human thought in which it is easier to show superficial cleverness and the appearance of superior wisdom than in discussing questions of currency and exchange.
>
> *Winston Churchill*

MONEY FROM FOREIGN OPERATIONS

This chapter discusses arrangements for the repatriation of cash from foreign operations. Examples of these repatriations are dividends from foreign subsidiaries or affiliates, foreign sourced royalties, and licensing fees earned abroad. The problems of arranging a medium-term repatriation of large amounts of a somewhat exotic foreign currency are also discussed. The examples for these cases are repatriations into U.S. Dollars.

The U.S. parent company may control the timing for a single, very large repatriation payment. The planning and transactions may be managed by a treasury staff at the company's headquarters, working closely with the company's domestic and foreign tax advisers. Managing the timing of any single repatriation payment is typically different from managing, for example, the variables in an exporter's stream of receipts in foreign currencies or the complexities of multinational streams of receipts and disbursements.

The initial work with the tax advisers and perhaps with local legal counsel and bankers should determine the feasibility of the transaction. It is fine to assert that a company should not start doing business in a country without a plan for repatriation of profits, but governments and regulations change; the initial plan may be a long way from the final reality. The following excerpt from an interoffice memo documents what can happen to the cash flow from a marginally profitable activity:

> In response to our inquiry, [legal counsel in the foreign country] has replied that there is at present no legal means of converting the excess [currency] to U.S.

Dollars for repatriation. He noted, however, that pending legislation in [the country] may result in some relaxation of the current restrictions.

Based on our cash flow projection, it would appear that the government has solved our excess cash problem for us by imposing a significant increase in corporate income tax. Projected tax installments are double what we paid last year. While 1990 was a better year than 1989 for our sales, it was not that much better! Assuming the new tax rates are permanent, there probably won't be any excess funds to worry about by the time our 1991 taxes are paid next year.

Assuming that the transaction is legal and feasible and that the tax aspects have been arranged, planning the transaction should define a time frame: for example, during the third quarter of the year or by the end of December or end of the fiscal year. If the U.S. Dollars are needed for specific corporate purposes, the timing may be less flexible. The economic fundamentals that would affect the foreign exchange rate within the time frame should be considered. The alternatives for managing the foreign exchange risk should be documented. The important review by the company's U.S. and foreign tax advisers should include the alternatives being considered by the company's financial risk management. Documents of corporate authority may be required (for example, if declaring a dividend).

So much for the "shoulds." The Jolly Jeans study sets forth the alternatives and problems in managing and dealing with the foreign exchange risk of a repatriation by a dividend of Pounds Sterling to U.S. Dollars during 1990 and early 1991. The Phi Pharmaceutical Company study describes hedging intercompany cash flows; the derivative range forward contract is disassembled into its component parts with suggestions about dealing the transactions. In the chapter's final study, the Tau Tire and Rubber Company solved its problem because its bank was able to find a multinational company with a somewhat offsetting position. This study provides insight into both repatriations and a multinational's financing of capital expenditures in somewhat exotic currencies.

JOLLY JEANS U.K. LIMITED

This study involves the management of foreign exchange risk for a dividend from a foreign subsidiary to its U.S. parent.

Business Risk Situation

Jolly Jeans ("the Company") is a U.S. holding company. Through its foreign subsidiaries, Jolly Jeans sells its American designed and manufactured jeans worldwide; a prominent red, white, and blue label states that the jeans are

"Made in the USA." Very little of the Company's production is sold in the United States, and almost all payments are received in local currency. Periodically, profits from foreign subsidiaries must be repatriated into U.S. Dollars to fund the general and administrative overhead of Jolly Jeans's worldwide headquarters in New York. Jolly Jeans U.K. Limited (Jolly Ltd.) is the English subsidiary. Jolly Ltd. sells only in the United Kingdom, and its receipts are all in Pounds Sterling. Its Pounds Sterling expenditures are quite limited and consist of maintaining a small representative office in London, to coordinate advertising. Jolly Ltd.'s substantial cash surplus is held as Sterling time deposits with banks in the United Kingdom. (See Chapter 9 regarding *forward rate agreements.*) Jolly Jeans has centralized its treasury management with a three-person staff at the Company's headquarters in New York.

The 1990 annual budget for Jolly Jeans had identified USD 3 million per month as the approximate amount of U.S. Dollars needed for the next 1 to 2 years of domestic expenditures. The then current U.S. Dollar balances of USD 17 million were sufficient for about the next 6 months. The Company decided that Jolly Ltd. should declare and pay a dividend of GBP 25 million to the U.S. parent, Jolly Jeans. Jolly Jeans also checked with its tax advisers in its efforts to maximize the advanced corporation tax (ACT) refund because of the U.K. ACT on dividends and the joint U.K./U.S. tax treaty. The logistics and amount of an ACT refund are not in the scope of this generalized study.

The date for declaring and paying the dividend could be established as part of the management of the foreign exchange rate risk. In recent months, the exchange rate of Pounds Sterling to U.S. Dollars (*cable*) had ranged from USD/GBP 1.7000 to 1.9000. (Cable is quoted in *American terms.*) The 20-cent range, computed against the planned GBP 25 million, was USD 5 million. An exchange rate of USD/GBP would result in covering almost 2 months' home office expenditures. Jolly Jeans management was keenly aware of Sterling's sometimes abrupt exchange rate fluctuations.

Jolly Ltd. had GBP 50 million in time deposits maturing over the next few months. The time deposits had been placed when Sterling interest rates had peaked around 15 percent; the interest rates were still about 14.50 to 14.75 percent. U.S. Dollar interest rates were about 8 percent. The negative interest income effect per million Pounds Sterling, upon conversion to U.S. Dollars, could be estimated as follows:

Sell GBP 1 million at USD/GBP 1.7000.
USD 1.7 million invested at 8 percent = 1 year's U.S. Dollar interest income of USD 136,000.
By comparison, GBP 1 million could be invested at 14.50 percent to yield 1 year's Sterling interest income of GBP 145,000.

The USD/GBP spot exchange rate was about 1.7000; the forward points were – 949 so the forward outright exchange rate was 1.7000 – .0949 or 1.6015.[1]

Jolly Jeans was very much more concerned, however, about unfavorable Sterling to U.S. Dollar exchange rate fluctuation. The president and chief financial officer vividly remembered when Sterling had traded at USD/GBP 1.04.

Forecasts and the European Monetary System

Jolly Jeans contacted foreign exchange advisers at banks where it did business. The following discussion is a composite of their comments.

Interest rates in the United Kingdom were not likely to rise higher than the prevailing 14 to 15 percent. Any easing in Sterling interest rates might cause the currency's exchange rate to weaken against U.S. Dollars, other major European currencies, and the Japanese Yen. The foreign exchange market was disposed to forecast bad economic fundamentals in the United Kingdom—high inflation, poor balance of trade, and recession.

The big unknown, however, during the third quarter and early fourth quarter of 1990 was whether the United Kingdom would enter the "grid" of the Exchange Rate Mechanism (ERM) of the European Monetary System (EMS). Many commercial interests in the U.K. were pressuring politicians, arguing that the United Kingdom would be left outside of the "new Europe" if it failed to join. Improved Sterling exchange rate stability might help U.K. exporters. Arguments raged daily in the financial press.

If Sterling entered the ERM, its exchange rate would be tied to the Deutsche Mark at DEM/GBP 2.95. The ERM has two bands for a currency's fluctuation against the "central rate": a narrow band of 2.25 percent and a wide band of 6.00 percent. If Sterling entered in the EMS's narrow band, its maximum exchange rate fluctuation against the central rate would be about 5.50 percent, 2.25 percent above or below. If Sterling entered in the EMS's wide band, its maximum exchange rate fluctuation against the Deutsche Mark would be about 12 percent, 6 percent above or below. (Chapter 7 gives a detailed discussion of the EMR and EMS and of the calculation of exact tolerances for fluctuation.) In this context, the first "big if" was whether Sterling would enter the ERM. If "yes," the second "big if" was whether it would enter in the wide (6 percent) band or narrow (2.25 percent) band. The wide band is intended as a transitional band to the narrow. The Italian Lire had entered in the wide band and recently converted to the narrow band. The Spanish Peseta had entered and was still in the wide band (the only currency then in that band).

---

[1] Please see appendix to Chapter 9, pages 195–196.

The cross rate of Sterling to Deutsche Mark, which was watched closely, was DM/GBP 2.9000. If Sterling entered the EMS 6 percent wide band at that exchange rate, its cross rate could fluctuate between approximately DM/GBP 2.7260 and 3.0740:

$$2.9000 \times 1.06 = 3.0740$$
$$(1 - .06) = .9400$$
$$2.9000 \times .9400 = 2.7260$$

If "Dollar Mark" stayed stable at the then rate of DEM/USD 1.6650 and Sterling were in the EMS wide band, cable could fluctuate in the range of USD/GBP 1.6330 to USD/GBP 1.8506 (USD .2176 or 22 cents):

$$\text{DEM/GBP } 2.7260 \div \text{DEM/GBP } 1.6650 = \text{USD/GBP } 1.6372$$
$$\text{DEM/GBP } 3.0813 \div \text{DEM/GBP } 1.6650 = \text{USD/GBP } 1.8462$$

The 22 cents times GBP 25 million was the same USD 5 million foreign exchange risk range that the company had estimated "on the back of an envelope."

Advisers pointed out that, if Sterling joined the EMS, a very important part of the equation for a Pounds Sterling/U.S. Dollar exchange rate forecast was the U.S. Dollar/Deutsche Mark exchange rate forecast. During 1990, foreign exchange traders expected the U.S. Dollar to be lower against the Deutsche Mark after the December 1989 union between West and East Germany. Some "German traders" expected Dollar Mark to trade as low as DEM/USD 1.4000. If Dollar Mark traded as low as DEM 1.4000 and Sterling entered the EMS, cable could trade higher than USD/GBP 2.000:

$$\text{DEM/GBP } 3.08125 \div \text{DEM/USD } 1.4000 = \text{USD/GBP } 2.2009$$

Jolly Jeans's president, the chief financial officer, and the treasury staff were excited by the prospect of converting GBP at anywhere near USD 2. The difference between converting GBP 25 million at USD/GBP 1.7000 (USD 42.5 million) and converting it at USD/GBP 2.0000 (USD 50 million) was USD 7.5 million, a considerable amount in absolute terms and additional 2½ months' home office overhead.

Alternatives for Conversion

The treasury staff reviewed suggestions from banks' foreign exchange advisers and outlined five alternatives for the chief financial officer and president. Descriptions of these alternative strategies follow. The computations required to compare alternatives 2, 3, and 4 conclude this section.

1. Speculate on the Pounds Sterling/U.S. Dollar exchange rate. This strategy consists of "lying in the weeds" and waiting for a favorable moment to convert Sterling, either at spot or at forward, depending on the maturity of the time deposits and the cost of *breakage*. The treasury staff requested authorization for most and least favorable target exchange rates for one or more blocks of the GBP 25 million; for example, most favorable USD/GBP 2.0000 and least favorable USD/GBP 1.8500.

2. Purchase one or more put options on Sterling. Other suitable derivatives listed were *range forward, covered write,* or *spread* strategy. The Sterling put option would "offer flexibility and potential to benefit from Sterling's appreciation." If the put option strike price were USD/GBP 1.7500 and Sterling strengthened to USD/GBP 2.000, the Company could benefit from the strong cash market price for conversion of the Sterling to U.S. Dollars. If the put option strike price were USD/GBP 1.7500 and Sterling weakened to USD/GBP 1.6000, the Company could benefit from the profit on the put option to offset the lower amount of the U.S. Dollar for cash market conversion of the Sterling.

The wide interest rate differential between Sterling and U.S. Dollars would also plague the cost of this strategy by increasing the option premium. Again, because of the wide interest rate differential, the range that could be obtained on a range forward would be narrower than the Company might desire. The high premium cost could be paid to the Company if it were willing to contract for a covered write; see the Biped Shoe study in Chapter 5.

One foreign exchange adviser pointed out that the derivatives, which were complex and expensive, required consistent monitoring of the foreign exchange market. Unwinding some positions can also be difficult.

3. Conclude the forward outright sale of some or all of the GBP 25 million to the date(s) of maturing Sterling time deposits. The advantages are: simplicity of the transaction, absence of monitoring, and the ability to unwind the transaction easily if needed. The transaction could be unwound by repurchasing the Sterling for the same *value date* as the original forward sale.

The disadvantage was that, because of the interest rate differential between Pounds Sterling at about 14.50 percent and U.S. Dollars at about 8.00 percent, the strategy could cost almost 1 U.S. cent (USD .01) per month forward.

4. Borrow Sterling, sell the proceeds at spot, and repay the loan when the time deposit(s) matures. This strategy would succeed with only certain relative interest rates, as discussed below.

The Company called Bank B, one of the banks holding a Jolly Ltd. GBP 10 million time deposit, and inquired about the interest rate the bank would charge for a loan fully secured by the time deposit it was holding. Bank B was willing to charge Sterling *LIBOR* but still would be required to add a markup for administration and for satisfaction of the new risk-based capital adequacy rules; it could not put a loan on its books "for free." Bank B's trader disagreed with the foreign exchange adviser who had recommended the loan alternative. Bank B's trader said that selling forward would be a better strategy than borrowing to sell at spot, because the interest rate differential in a forward rate would be less than the interest rate differential available through a loan.

5. Break GBP 25 million into time deposit(s), sell the Sterling at spot, and invest the U.S. Dollars to the same date as the maturity of the time deposit(s). This alternative results in the Sterling being immediately available, as does the second alternative—selling Sterling at spot and borrowing Sterling until the Sterling time deposit(s) matures to repay the loan.

Examples using numerical computations will allow a comparison of alternatives 3, 4, and 5. Assume GBP 10 million invested at 14.375 percent maturing October 31. Assume today's date is August 26, the spot date is August 28, with 64 days to October 31; spot rate is USD/GBP 1.9450.

Alternative 3: Sell forward to October 31

USD (19,450,000) = GBP 10 million, spot rate USD/GBP 1.9450
                     forward points   (.0210)

USD 19,240,000   = GBP 10 million, spot rate USD/GBP 1.9240

USD (210,000) amount forfeited if sold forward versus spot

GBP (107,969) USD 210,000 at USD/GBP 1.9450
GBP   252,055 interest on GBP 10 million at 14.375 percent for 64/365

GBP   144,086 net gain selling forward and not borrowing

Alternative 4: Borrow GBP 10 million, secured by time deposit to October 31 maturity, sell GBP 10 million at spot

Assume borrowing Sterling LIBOR 15 percent plus 3/16 percent quoted by bank; assume investing in U.S. Dollars at 8 3/16 percent.

GBP (266,301) GBP 10 million at 15.1875 percent (15 percent LIBOR plus 3/16) for 64/365
GBP   252,055 interest on GBP 10 million time deposit at 14.375 percent for 64/365
GBP   145,555 USD 283,105 interest on USD 19.450 million at 8.1875 percent for 64/360; converted to USD at spot rate USD/GBP 1.9450

GBP   131,309 net gain borrowing and selling at spot

Alternative 5: Break GBP 10 million into time deposits, sell GBP at spot, invest USD to October 31

If Sterling LIBOR at 15 percent, assume LIBID at 1/8 less or 14.875 percent.

GBP (	8,767)	GBP 10 million at 14.875 percent vs. time deposit rate of 14.375 percent for 64/365
GBP	145,555	USD 283,105 interest on USD 19.450 million at 8.1875 percent for 64/360; converted to USD at spot rate USD/GBP 1.9450
GBP	136,788	net gain breaking time deposit and spot sale

The difference among the alternatives with these interest rates and foreign exchange rates is negligible. The method of comparative review can, however, disclose opportunities under certain market conditions. Some traders and experienced professionals may abbreviate the computations, but the method shown above is one way to compute the comparison.

Outcome

There is rarely only one "right way" to manage a corporate financial risk situation. Jolly Jeans had a small corporate staff. The treasury person responsible for dealing the repatriation transaction and communicating with banks had direct access at any time to the treasurer and president. The Company decided that it was equipped to monitor and, more importantly, respond timely to the relevant economic situation in the United Kingdom and to Sterling and U.S. Dollar foreign exchange conditions. Two of the Company's foreign exchange advisory banks were asked to call with any dramatic market news. The pressure was increasing daily for the United Kingdom to enter the EMS, and the USD/GBP 2.0000 exchange rate might be achieved without the contractual commitments of alternatives 2, 3, and 4.

The United Kingdom entered the EMS on October 8, 1990. Jolly Jeans's treasurer decided that USD/GBP 1.9900 was the number and ordered the treasury staff to place an order to sell GBP 25 million at that rate with a bank. The bank's foreign exchange adviser commented: "If cable hits one-ninety-nine, it goes to two." He recommended that the company split the order between 2.0000 and just below 1.9800, to be sure and "get a fill on part of this and come out about the same."

The treasurer remained oblivious to the daily advices of traders and staff, and Jolly's president decided not to interfere. Sterling went to 1.9400, then "bounced back." The treasurer changed directions. The company canceled the order to sell at 1.9900. The company sold the 25 million at 1.9500 and 1.9700 levels. Sterling then shot past 1.9800 and sailed over 2.0000 before settling back to the USD/GBP 1.8000 range by mid-March, 1991.

PHI PHARMACEUTICAL COMPANY, INC.

How to use—and not use—the range forward to hedge intercompany cash flows is illustrated in this study.

Business Risk Situation

Phi Pharmaceutical Company, Inc., the parent company ("the Company"), is a multinational manufacturer and distributor of ethical pharmaceutical products. Its average annual sales are USD 8 billion. The Company and its subsidiaries have manufacturing operations in 22 countries and sell their products in more than 75 countries. European operations are managed from the Rotterdam (The Netherlands) office. The Company has structured its Rotterdam operations to minimize the tax impact on cash flows repatriated to the parent company's home office in New Jersey. Each subsidiary makes various types of payments to the Company—primarily licensing fees, royalties, and dividends. The components of the subsidiaries' payments vary, depending on the laws and regulations of the subsidiaries' respective countries. The subsidiaries make their payments, in the domestic currency of each remitting subsidiary's country, to a Dutch holding company, Phi Pharmaceutical International N.V.

The company has centralized foreign exchange risk management with a risk staff of five people in its New Jersey headquarters. The risk staff had earlier adopted a policy guideline of not entering into any overtly speculative positions and had, in past years, consistently rejected use of options to hedge foreign exchange risk because of premiums deemed costly or the high risk of proposed option strategies.

In January 1990, the risk staff considered a *range forward* to hedge the foreign exchange risk attributable to a particular situation. The Company was anticipating that a royalty payment from Germany, from Phi Pharmaceutical Company Gmbh (Gmbh denotes a limited liability company), was imminent. The royalty payment of approximately DEM 50 million was due near the end of June 1990. At February 1, 1990, although the U.S. Dollar was under pressure in the foreign exchange markets, it was not then depreciating and was relatively stable. Because of rising German interest rates and the then current political situation in Europe, most traders expected the Deutsche Mark to strengthen. A range forward contract appeared a desirable hedging method for obtaining some profit from any Deutsche Mark appreciation, with a limited downside risk—and no up-front cost.

Proposed Transaction

The Company's expected date for the royalty payment from its German subsidiary was June 30, 1990. On February 1, 1990, when the risk staff asked its bank for an indication of the exchange rate for its proposed transaction, the Deutsche Mark was trading at approximately DEM/USD 1.6750 for delivery on the *spot date*. The bank proposed to guarantee that, on the spot value date of June 28, 1990, the royalty payment to the Company would be within the exchange rate range of DEM/USD 1.7180 to DEM/USD 1.6380. The bank stated three possible scenarios for the proposed transaction:

1. If the U.S. Dollar strengthened to a level higher than DEM/USD 1.7180, the bank would convert the Deutsche Marks to U.S. Dollars at 1.7180—the Company's "worst case" situation. At the worst rate of DEM/USD 1.7180 for DEM 50 million, the Company would receive USD 29,103,609.
2. If the U.S. Dollar weakened, the best rate that the Company would receive would be 1.6380, even though the U.S. Dollar might then be trading lower than that exchange rate. At the best rate of DEM/USD 1.6380 for DEM 50 million, the Company would receive USD 30,525,030.
3. If at the time the option expired, the U.S. Dollar was trading within the range forward's contractually locked-in exchange rates—between DEM/USD 1.7180 and DEM/USD 1.6380—the bank would convert the Deutsche Marks to U.S. Dollars at the exchange rate prevailing on June 28, 1990. Between the rates of DEM/USD 1.7180 and DEM/USD 1.6380 for DEM 50 million, the Company would receive an amount ranging between USD 29,103,609 and USD 30,525,030.

The risk staff asked the bank whether it would be possible to change one side or the other of the range forward's exchange rate limits. The bank explained that, because of the way the proposed transaction was structured, if one "leg" of the range were adjusted, the other "leg" would be adjusted by the same amount. For example, using a worst-case exchange rate of DEM/USD 1.7000, the best case for Phi Pharmaceutical would be DEM/USD 1.6560—an adjustment of .0440 to each leg of the range. Similarly, if the Company wanted to lower the best-case exchange rate, then the worst case exchange rate would have to be raised by the same number of *pips*. Stated otherwise, any increase in potential gain had to be offset by an identical increase in risk of a worse-than-anticipated exchange rate. In sum, the range forward would allow a fixed limit of potential gain against a known and limited amount of risk, with no up-front cost payable on entering into the transaction.

The bank proposed to structure the transaction so that Phi Pharmaceutical would be obligated to deliver Deutsche Marks to the bank. The exchange rate would be set at 10:00 A.M. New York time on June 28, 1990. If the U.S. Dollar was then trading outside either limit of the exchange rate range for the transaction, the limit exchange rate would apply. Thus, if on the June 28 trade date, the U.S. Dollar was trading between the two limits of the range—DEM/USD 1.6380 and DEM/USD 1.7180—then the exchange rate applied would be the bank's 10:00 A.M. offered exchange rate for selling U.S. Dollars and buying Deutsche Marks for spot delivery. The risk staff decided to enter into the range forward contract.

The Transaction and Outcome

When the risk staff called during the afternoon of February 1, 1990, to enter into the transaction, the U.S. Dollar had, since the staff's morning call, weakened against the Deutsche Mark, with a resulting change in the contract. The spot exchange rate was DEM 1.6715, and the forward outright rate to June 30, 1990 was DEM/USD 1.6745. Using the same proposal made that morning, except for the changed range in exchange rate, the Company agreed to sell the Deutsche Marks against a range forward contract using the exchange rates of DEM/USD 1.6345 and DEM/USD 1.7145. This represented a change in the range of .0035 or 35 pips since the bank's morning quote of DEM/USD 1.6380 and DEM/USD 1.7180.

On June 28, 1990, at 8:30 A.M., the risk staff members saw on their *Telerate* screen that the U.S. Dollar was quoted at 1.6450 against the Deutsche Mark. A few minutes later, the bank called to notify that an exchange rate of 1.6465 would be applied to the transaction. The DEM/USD 1.6465 rate was 15 pips higher than the 1.6450 shown on the Telerate screen. At DEM/USD 1.6465, the Company would receive nearly USD 28,000 less than anticipated, computed as follows:

$$(DEM\ 50,000,000/DEM/USD\ 1.6450) - (DEM\ 50,000,000/DEM/USD$$
$$1.6465) = USD\ 30,367,446 - USD\ 30,395,136 = USD\ 27,690.00.$$

The risk staff questioned the difference between the execution price and the price shown on the Telerate screen. The bank responded that the rates banks post to Telerate and comparable services are only indicated market levels, not dealing prices. The Company had agreed to accept the bank's exchange rate on the transaction if that exchange rate were between the stated limits of the range forward contract. The risk staff usually competitively priced foreign exchange rates and was, therefore, concerned about the bank's explanation because the market was quiet on June 28. The risk staff's experience had been that, in a quiet market, the screen rates were sound indications of "real" market prices. The risk staff's problem was that it had no way to confirm fairness of the price.

What the Company Did Not Understand

A range forward is a pair of *out of the money* options. An out of the money option is one that is not profitable to exercise. An out of the money-call option has a strike price greater than the current market price of the underlying commodity or security. An example is a Deutsche Mark put option with a strike price of DEM/USD 1.8000 when the interbank exchange rate is DEM/USD 1.6500. The option holder would not exercise the put at DEM/USD 1.8000 if the holder could sell the Deutsche Marks at DEM/USD 1.6500.

The Company's range forward contract was actually the purchase of an out of the money Deutsche Mark put option and the writing of an out of the money Deutsche Mark call option. Because the premium paid for purchasing the put would be offset by the premium received from writing the call, the net upfront cash outlay would be zero. The bank had "bundled" two separate instruments into a single contract. As a consequence of the two bundled contracts, the risk staff would have difficulty in obtaining competitive quotes either for the composite or for either leg of the contract. The bank had not only structured two option transactions but had arranged that, if the Deutsche Mark/U.S. Dollar exchange rate remained between the two locked-in exchange rates, the bank had the sole contractual right to convert the Company's Deutsche Marks to U.S. Dollars on an "at best" basis. This contractual right allowed the bank to obtain, at its discretion, an additional spread because the conversion transaction could not be competitively traded.

What Could Have Been Done

An alternative way to enter into a range forward is to contract separately each leg of the transaction. Before entering into a range forward, the risk staff could have done the following:

1. Determined the approximate forward outright rate for the anticipated forward date. In this case, the risk staff should have assumed a rate of DEM/USD 1.6750—the rate at which the Deutsche Mark was trading on February 1, 1990, for delivery on June 30, 1990.
2. Selected either the target stop-loss level or the target gain. After deciding the maximum potential loss in value of the Deutsche Mark that the Company was willing to sustain, the risk staff might have decided on a target stop-loss of DEM/USD 1.7150. That decision would have required purchasing a Deutsche Mark put.
3. Chosen either an American- or European-style option. An American-style option is one that can be exercised at any time up to and including its expiration date. It offers greater flexibility to the option holder than a European-style option, which can be exercised only on its expiration date.

How to Do the Transaction: Two Alternatives

A competitive transaction for a range forward can be completed using either of two methods:

Method 1: Contract, but not simultaneously, each leg of the range forward;
Method 2: Contract simultaneously each leg of the range forward.

These two methods are described using the data from this case.

Method 1.   The first step is to purchase the put option. Competitive quotes should be obtained for a European-style, Deutsche Mark put with a strike price of DEM/USD 1.7150 on DEM 50 million and an expiration date of June 30, 1990. The request for quotes should always specify whether the Company is purchasing a European-style or an American-style option.

Because a range forward is intended, the European-style option will probably be the better choice. If the U.S. Dollar declined suddenly and sharply, the Company would want to avoid a required delivery of Deutsche Marks several months before the anticipated receipt of Deutsche Marks from its German subsidiary.

After obtaining competitive quotes, the Company would purchase the option with the lower premium. The premium, assuming 4 percent, is calculated as follows:

DEM 50,000,000 / DEM/USD 1.7150 × 4% (.04) = USD 29,154,518.95
× 4% (.04) = USD 1,166,180.76 = premium for the put option.

The next step is to write the call option. Competitive bids should be obtained for the offsetting call option that needs to be written. In this case, the Company should write an out of the money European-style Deutsche Mark call. The purchase price that the Company receives for the call should be about the same amount that the Company must pay for purchasing the put—USD 1,166,180.76. Hence, the bid inquiry should be: "At what strike will the bank buy the call option and pay a premium of USD 1.166 million?"

If Bank A bids a strike price of DEM/USD 1.6355 and Bank B bids a strike price of DEM/USD 1.6345, the Company should "do the deal" with Bank B. The reason is that the Company will be seeking the lower strike price because the lower strike price improves the potential for appreciation of its Deutsche Marks. The comparison is computed as follows:

Bank A: DEM/USD 1.6355 × USD 1.166 million = DEM 1,906,993
Bank B: DEM/USD 1.6345 × USD 1.166 million = DEM 1,905,827

The lower amount of DEM improves the potential for appreciation.

To summarize Method 1: Write a European-style, out of the money Deutsche Mark call option on DEM 50 million that will earn a premium of USD 1.166 million, which is the cost of the European-style out of the money Deutsche Mark put option that the Company purchases.

The option that is written **must** be the same style as the option that is purchased—in this case, a European-style option. Otherwise, the exposures under the transaction will not match.

When both the put and call options have been executed, the Company will have locked-in the exchange rate range within which it will exchange its Deutsche Marks for U.S. Dollars. The outcomes are the same as those computed in the scenarios earlier, with an important exception: now the Company would have the flexibility to deal at competitive exchange rates if, at the expiration date of the European-style options, the Deutsche Mark/U.S. Dollar exchange rate were trading within the range of the options' two strike prices.

Method 1 is very time-consuming for use in volatile foreign exchange markets. The value of an option to be purchased or written will change as the exchange rate changes for any *underlying* currency—in this case, the Deutsche Mark exchange rate to U.S. Dollars. Hence, volatile market conditions may render it impossible to purchase and write options with the strike prices desired for a range forward that will also result in offsetting cash premiums to be paid and received.

Method 2. The better method is to purchase and write both options at the same time. The risk staff would follow the three steps listed earlier under "What Could Have Been Done." Next, assuming DEM/USD 1.7150 was selected as the stop-loss level, the risk staff would call one or more banks to obtain quotations for dealing the following transaction.

The Company would buy a European-style out of the money Deutsche Mark put option with a strike price of DEM/USD 1.7150 on DEM 50 million and would write an offsetting out of the money Deutsche Mark call option.

The inquiry to the bank would be: "At what strike price for the call option will your bank purchase the call and write the put?" The obvious and proper objective is the lowest possible strike price.

A more complex transaction is not easy to deal competitively, but unbundling the range forward can be advantageous if unwinding may be required.

Unwinding the Transaction

Unwinding an "unbundled" range forward is straightforward compared to unwinding a "bundled" contract. With "unbundled" contracts, the Company would sell the put option back to the bank from which it had purchased that option; the Company would then purchase the call option from the bank with which it had been written. Whether a net loss or a net gain would result would depend on whether the U.S. Dollar had strengthened or weakened.

The Company can keep one leg of the transaction and close one leg. For example, the Company might be able to purchase the call, thus closing the downside leg of the range forward. At the same time, the Company could keep the put option if it expected the U.S. Dollar to appreciate further against the Deutsche Mark.

Awareness of the impact of time decay on the value of option premiums is always important. A significant part of an option's premium is determined by the length of time from the option's transaction date to its expiration date. All other terms, conditions, and *intrinsic value* being equal, an option with a longer time until expiration will have a higher premium (because of *time value*) than an option with a shorter time to expiration. The time value will decrease as time passes toward the option's expiration date; this decreasing value is called *time decay.*

Summary: Uses for a Range Forward

The range forward is typically used as a hedge against a specific transaction, to protect the value of a cash flow. An "unbundled" range forward is generally not suitable to hedge a balance sheet exposure or *translation exposure* because a negative cash flow will probably result if the holder exercises the written option. (See the discussion of the "covered write" with Biped Shoe, Chapter 5.) If a company uses a range forward to hedge the foreign currency equity in a subsidiary, the exercise of the option written as part of "unbundled" range forward contracts would result in the purchase and sale of foreign currency at a loss to the company.

The typical scenario for use of the range forward is to hedge against unfavorable exchange rate change for a foreign currency payable or receivable. In another scenario, a currency is at the extreme of an expected range. The user of the range forward expects a favorable price move, does not want to pay the high premium to buy the appropriate option, and is willing to limit potential gain as a trade-off for limiting potential loss.

TAU TIRE AND RUBBER COMPANY

This study illustrates a foreign exchange rate agreement and the hedging of medium-term risk in exotic currencies.

Business Risk Situation

Tau Tire and Rubber Company ("Tau Tire") had owned a rubber plantation in Malaysia for many years. The government of Malaysia, however, was encouraging foreign multinational corporations that had large land holdings or that were engaged in extractive industries to sell their interests to local investors. Tau Tire received from a wealthy Malaysian, Singh, an offer that included government-backed financing for Singh's purchase of the plantation.

Singh offered a purchase price of 80 million Malaysian Ringgits (MYR) or nearly USD 30 million, based on current exchange rates. Singh's offer included the agreement of Bank Negara Malaysia, the central bank of Malaysia, to convert the Ringgits into U.S. Dollars after the transaction had closed. The exchange rate that would be applied to the transaction would be the current rate for the U.S. Dollar against the Ringgit on the day of the currency conversion.

Singh's offer, which was reasonably fair and suitably financed, was made in July 1990. With the negotiations still in progress, and looking toward the government approvals required to proceed with the transaction, a closing date for the transaction was probably 18 to 24 months hence, or between January and July of 1992.

A primary obstacle to entering into the sale was the foreign exchange risk in the transaction. The Malaysian government officials would not begin their review of the transaction until after the sales agreement had been executed, which was expected to occur at least 18 months hence. Although the Bank Negara would guarantee to do the conversion from Ringgits into U.S. Dollars, it would convert only at the exchange rate on the day when the conversion took place.

Alternatives

When Tau Tire contacted its bank for advice, the bank's foreign exchange advisery set forth three basic alternatives for the management of the financial risk involved in conversion of the Ringgits:

1. **Sell Ringgits and swap forward.** Tau Tire could sell Ringgits 6 months outright and continue swapping the Ringgits until it received the final payment from Singh. This was not a practical solution to the foreign exchange risk exposure, for several reasons. The size of the transaction (MYR 80 million) relative to the foreign exchange market was too large. The market did not have sufficient depth to cover a capital transaction this large for a long-term exposure in Malaysian Ringgits. Malaysian regulations might change, making a rollover transaction more difficult or even impossible.
2. **Borrow Ringgits and sell for U.S. Dollars in spot markets.** Tau Tire could try to borrow Ringgits and sell them for U.S. Dollars in the spot foreign exchange market. This strategy was also flawed. Fixed-rate financing could not be obtained "in size" in Ringgits. A foreign company might not even be able to borrow that large an amount of Ringgits to finance a foreign exchange transaction. Tau Tire advised that it did not want to incur additional debt.
3. **Arrange an offsetting transaction with another company.** Tau Tire's bank could attempt to locate another U.S. company that had an

offsetting transaction in Malaysia. An important role of banks is that each bank has a portfolio of customers with different needs and, for each customer, the bank has information that is not otherwise available. The identity of the offsetting counterparty company would typically not be disclosed to Tau Tire. The bank would manage the price negotiations and assume the counterparty credit risks—and retain a profit for itself.

Credit risk would be an important consideration in any proposed transaction—for all parties. Both Tau Tire and major U.S. banks had suffered significant financial losses.

Tau Tire's bank had been working with Chi Computer Corporation ("Chi Computer"), a U.S. corporation that planned to build a plant in Malaysia to supply components for its computers. The Malaysian government was financing the construction of the plant, which was underway and on schedule. When the plant was finished, Chi Computer would then pay the Malaysian government in Ringgits for the cost of building the plant. The total cost of the plant was contracted to be MYR 68 million, or about USD 25 million at the current exchange rate of MYR 2.72 per U.S. Dollar.

Chi Computer's payment to the Malaysian government was due in 20 months, in March 1992, and the computer company was concerned that the Ringgit might appreciate against the U.S. Dollar during that interval. Many foreign companies were investing in Malaysia both to build products for export and to meet the growing domestic market. With large investment flows into Malaysia and a sharp growth in its exports, the Ringgit could appreciate. The Ringgit was allowed to float, with the Bank Negara periodically altering the direction of the float. No *medium-term* forward market existed for the Ringgit, and Chi Computer did not want to tie up cash, which it needed elsewhere, by buying and investing Ringgits.

Tau Tire and Chi Computer both had a Ringgit exchange rate risk: Tau Tire wanted to repatriate MYR 80 million in 18 to 24 months; Chi Computer needed to make a MYR 68 million payment in 20 months. Although the two transactions differed in the amounts and the timing of the payments, nonetheless the bank thought that using one company's exposure to offset the other company's exposure might be feasible.

The first suggestion from the bank to each company was simple: the bank would predetermine an exchange rate for Tau Tire's payment of MYR 68 million and receipt of the dollar equivalent; the bank would then clear the trades between Tau Tire and Chi Computer. This proposal was rejected for three reasons:

1. Tau Tire had no assurance of receiving its Ringgit payment by the date when Chi Computer needed to make its payment;

2. The proposed "offset" would leave Tau Tire with an exposure of MYR 12 million or USD 5 million;
3. Tau Tire's agreement with the Malaysian government required that Tau Tire do the conversion from Ringgits to U.S. Dollars with the Bank Negara.

Foreign Exchange Rate Agreement

The next offset proposal considered was a *foreign exchange rate agreement* (FERA). With this type of agreement, the bank would in effect stand between Tau Tire and Chi Computer with an exchange rate guarantee to each company. The bank would guarantee to each company a predetermined exchange rate between the Malaysian Ringgit and the U.S. Dollar. For example, the bank could guarantee Tau Tire that the sale of its Ringgits would be at an exchange rate of MYR 2.75 per U.S. Dollar. The bank could also guarantee Chi Computer that the company would buy Malaysian Ringgits at an exchange rate of MYR 2.70 per U.S. Dollar.

Under the bank's initial FERA proposal to Tau Tire, the bank would guarantee that Tau Tire would sell its Ringgits at a rate of MYR 2.75 per U.S. Dollar. If, on the FERA's expiration date, the exchange rate were more than MYR 2.75 per U.S. Dollar, the bank would pay Tau Tire the Dollar difference. If, on the FERA's expiration date, the exchange rate were lower than MYR 2.75 per U.S. Dollar, then Tau Tire would pay the bank the U.S. Dollar difference between the market exchange rate and MYR 2.75 per Dollar. For example, MYR 80 million would be worth USD 29,090,909.09 at an exchange rate of MYR 2.75 per dollar. Under a foreign exchange rate agreement, if the exchange rate on the maturity of the FERA were MYR 2.80 per U.S. Dollar, then the bank would pay Tau Tire USD 519,480.52, calculated as follows:

$$\text{MYR } 80,000,000/\text{MYR}/\text{USD } 2.7500 = \text{USD } 29,090,909.09$$
$$\text{MYR } 80,000,000/\text{MYR}/\text{USD } 2.8000 = \text{USD } 28,571,428.57$$
$$\text{USD } 29,090,909.09 - \text{USD } 28,571,428.57 = \text{USD } 519,480.52$$

If the Ringgit/U.S. Dollar exchange rate were trading at 2.770 on the expiration of the FERA, Tau Tire would owe the Bank USD 538,720.54, calculated as follows:

$$\text{MYR } 80,000,000/\text{MYR}/\text{USD } 2.70 = \text{USD } 29,629,629.63$$

$$\text{USD } 29,629,629.63 - \text{USD } 29,090,909.09 \text{ (MYR } 80,000,000/\text{MYR}/\text{USD } 2.7500) = \text{USD } 538,720.54$$

In making its initial FERA proposal to the "offset" company, Chi Computer, the bank indicated a similar foreign exchange rate agreement. The bank proposed a FERA with a rate of MYR 2.65 per U.S. Dollar. If the Ringgit appreciated in value to less than 2.65 per U.S. Dollar at the FERA's maturity, the bank would pay Chi Computer the U.S. Dollar difference between the value of the Ringgits. If the Ringgit weakened in value, that is, if it were trading at the FERA's expiration for more than MYR 2.65 per U.S. Dollar, then Chi Computer would pay the bank the U.S. Dollar difference between the market value of the Ringgit and the FERA contract rate.

How the Bank Analyzed and Structured the FERA Proposals

Structuring the foreign exchange rate agreements with Tau Tire and with Chi Computer presented three basic problems for the bank:

1. Credit risks with each company;
2. A need for special knowledge of each company's timing requirements;
3. An imaginative solution to the imperfect offset of the transactions that would still allow the bank to earn a profit on the transactions.

Credit Risk. An advantage for the bank in using a foreign exchange rate agreement was that the credit risk of the transaction was smaller than the *notational amount.* In this example, the actual amount of risk incurred by each party to the transaction would be less than the notional amount (MYR 80 million) for Tau Tire. The risk would be the U.S. Dollar difference between the spot market rate at maturity and the contract rate of the FERA. For example, if a FERA has a notional amount of USD 30 million, the credit risk for the bank would be that Tau Tire would not pay the USD 538,000 due the bank if the Ringgit were trading at MYR 2.70 per U.S. Dollar on the FERA's expiration date. If the exchange rate were substantially different from the FERA rate, the credit risk could be in millions, not thousands. Because of Tau Tire's recent financial difficulties, its potential nonpayment was an important consideration for the bank. Chi Computer was a prime credit, however, and hence the bank believed that the credit issue would not be a problem in structuring a FERA. The bank's policy was that the deemed credit risk on an FERA should not exceed 5 percent of the transaction's notional amount.

With respect to determining the notional amount of the FERA, three alternatives were available:

1. Tau Tire could enter into a FERA for MYR 68 million—MYR 12 million less than it needed to hedge;
2. Chi Computer could enter into an FERA for MYR 80 million, MYR 12 million more than it needed to hedge;
3. The bank could enter into a separate transaction with each company for the amount that each wanted to hedge, and the bank would

assume the risk of the difference between the two amounts, somehow adjusting for the imperfect offset.

Timing.   The timing difference of the two companies' respective hedging needs was complicated. Chi Computer knew almost the exact due date of its payment to the Malaysian government; Tau Tire could only estimate the timing of the cash flow that it needed to hedge. Tau Tire might not want to enter into a hedging arrangement if it could not make an accurate estimate of the timing of the cash flow to be hedged.

Under the bank's proposed FERA for Chi Computer, if the Ringgit were to appreciate at the FERA's maturity to less than MYR 2.60 per U.S. Dollar, the bank would pay Chi Computer the U.S. Dollar difference between the two Ringgit rates. If the Ringgit were to weaken and to trade at more than MYR 2.60 per U.S. Dollar, then Chi Computer would pay the bank the U.S. Dollar difference between the market value of the Ringgit and the FERA contract rate. Thus, unless the Ringgit were trading at exactly MYR 2.60 per U.S. Dollar at the FERA's maturity, either Chi Computer or the bank would have a contractual obligation to make a U.S. Dollar payment to the other. The FERA would be somewhat like a double-bladed forward foreign exchange contract. Neither party would be able to profit from a favorable market-move in the MYR/USD exchange rate. For Chi Computer, a Ringgit becoming weaker in value to the Dollar would have been a favorable price move because it needed to buy Ringgits for its capital expenditures. However, Chi Computer would pay the bank if the exchange rate were more than MYR/USD 2.60. By giving up an otherwise favorable price move, Chi Computer hedged through the FERA against the MYR/USD exchange rate being less than MYR/USD 2.60—a stronger Ringgit requiring more U.S. Dollars for the capital expenditures. While the FERA was in effect, Chi Computer and the bank would be locked into the rate of MYR 2.60 per U.S. Dollar.

Adjusting for the Imperfect Offset.   Tau Tire had estimated that after fees and expenses, it would net MYR 75 million from the sale price of MYR 80 million. The purchaser, Singh, had obtained a guarantee from the Malaysian Minister of Finance that all the necessary approvals would be consummated so that the transaction was ready to close in March 1992, and the sales agreement would so provide. Chi Computer was receptive to a FERA for more than the MYR 68 million because, in addition to construction capital, its Malaysian subsidiary would need startup working capital. Chi Computer estimated its total need would be MYR 71 million, with January 2, 1991, as the payment date for plant construction.

The bank wanted to earn as large a profit on the transaction as was reasonably possible. If, however, neither Tau Tire nor Chi Computer were willing to be flexible about the timing of its own transaction, the bank might incur a significant risk of an unfavorable exchange rate fluctuation in the Ringgit between the maturity of one FERA and the maturity of the other. Similarly, if the amount of one FERA were different from the amount of the other FERA, then the bank would incur the risk of an unfavorable exchange rate movement.

Before the bank could make its formal FERA proposals to Tau Tire and Chi Computer, it needed to select a *reference rate* that would determine the value of the Ringgit against the U.S. Dollar on the maturity date of each FERA. The reference rate selected had to be fair to, and independently verifiable by, the two companies. The Ringgit, as is true for other "exotic" currencies, is not a deeply traded currency. Obtaining an accurate value of the Ringgit at a specific future time is, therefore, difficult. Bank Negara Malaysia does not have a formal fixing; *Reuters* and *Telerate* do not post independent rates; and the posted rates of other banks could not be feasibly verified. Another source for value of a foreign currency is the rate from the International Monetary Fund (IMF) monthly periodical, *International Financial Statistics,* but that rate was not scheduled to be published until about 6 weeks after each FERA had matured. Thus, for a FERA maturing on March 31, 1992, the bank could not obtain the IMF's rate until about the middle of May, at the earliest.

The bank decided to call three Malaysian banks that actively traded the Ringgit, using either the telex or the *Reuters Direct Dealing System* at a date and time to be specified in the foreign exchange rate agreement. The bank would take the average of the midpoints between the bid and offer of the three quotations to determine the then current market exchange rate for the Ringgit against the U.S. Dollar. Both Reuters and the telex would produce a "hard copy" of the quote, showing the date and time of the call, as well as the name of the quoting bank. Thus, the selected reference rate could be easily documented for the purpose of settling each FERA.

Bank's Second FERA Proposals

Although resolution of the pricing issue was still pending, the bank made a second tentative proposal to each company. The proposal to Tau Tire was based on Chi Computer's indicated needs and was directed toward determining both Tau Tire's continuing interest and its flexibility of position. The proposed FERA for Tau Tire would have a notional amount of MYR 71 million (Chi Computer's indicated interest), a contract rate of MYR 2.75 per U.S. Dollar, and a maturity date of January 2, 1992 (Chi Computer's indicated payment date). The proposed FERA for Chi Computer would be for MYR 75 million (Tau Tire's amount), a contract rate of MYR 2.60 per U.S. Dollar, and a maturity date of March 31, 1992 (Tau Tire's anticipated date for settling the sale of its rubber plantation).

For the bank, the second round of proposals was important because it enabled the bank to:

1. Retain room for negotiation with each company;
2. Determine the flexibility, if any, in each company's position;
3. Make substantial adjustments in the pricing of the transaction for either company or both, depending on flexibility, and still earn a reasonable profit on the transaction;
4. Assure that each company understood the proposed FERA, with its integral commitments.

For the companies, the second round of proposals was equally important: the bank would make sure that the companies fully comprehended how the FERA worked and the finality of obligations under an executed FERA—no flexibility and no extending or shortening of the contract's term. After the transaction closed, each company would be contractually bound with the bank to make or receive a U.S. Dollar cash payment, depending on the MYR/USD exchange rate applicable to the two FERAs. Tau Tire and Chi Computer would each make or receive a U.S. Dollar cash settlement with the bank, two business days after the contract's maturity date, for the amount equal to the difference between the U.S. Dollar value of the notional amount and the value determined by the reference rate.

The Final Proposals: Negotiation and Acceptance

The bank's discussions with Tau Tire and Chi Computer are described separately here.

Negotiation with Tau Tire.   Although Tau Tire had indicated an interest in the bank's first two proposals, the company was concerned about the difference in timing and the amount of the other company's required hedge, for two reasons:

1. Tau Tire wanted flexibility as to the maturity of any hedge, because of its uncertainty as to the exact timing—or even the occurrence—of the Ringgit payment to the company;
2. Tau Tire required a hedge of the full MYR 80 million.

In discussing the company's concerns with its finance personnel, the bank found only a vague understanding of the transaction. To provide a detailed explanation of the FERA's mechanics, the bank prepared a written and verbal presentation.

First, Tau Tire and the bank would agree to set a U.S. Dollar value on the MYR 75 million to be hedged. This value would be based on a reference exchange rate of MYR 2.75 per dollar.

Second, no Ringgit payment would be due at the FERA's maturity. Instead, pursuant to its sales agreement with Singh, Tau Tire would sell Bank Negara the Ringgit proceeds—received in Ringgits—from the sale of the rubber plantation. Bank Negara would then pay Tau Tire the sale proceeds in equivalent U.S. Dollar value and remit in accordance with the company's instructions at that time.

Third, the FERA between Tau Tire and the bank would be a separate, "stand alone" agreement. The FERA would appear on Tau Tire's books as a hedge of the Ringgit proceeds from the sale of the plantation. The contract for settlement of the FERA with the bank was to be completely independent of settlement of the foreign exchange transaction with Bank Negara.

Finally, the bank presented an analysis of the cash flows, using different exchange rates, to show how Tau Tire and the bank would settle the FERA contract at maturity. A U.S. Dollar payment would be made, equal to the difference in value between the Ringgit contract rate and the Ringgit market exchange rate at the FERA's maturity.

Pricing and maturity of the transaction were troublesome issues. Tau Tire acknowledged that investment capital was flowing into Malaysia, but feared that some political or financial shock might send capital fleeing from the country, as happened in Venezuela during the early 1980s. The company considered the bank's indication of MYR/USD 2.75 expensive for an 18-month forward exchange rate, for this reason: the indication did not seem consistent with the fact that, out of 6 months, the U.S. Dollar traded at a 150-point discount against the Ringgit, which should have implied an even deeper discount for a longer maturity. The bank responded that the proposed settlement date was 18 months rather than 6 months in the future. More importantly, Ringgits had no forward market and no real capital market beyond 6 months. The pricing issue remained unresolved.

The timing issue also remained unresolved. Tau Tire could not designate an exact payment date because it depended on two dates that could not be precisely predicted: the date of the Malaysian government's approval of the proposed sale by Tau Tire to Singh, and the subsequent date of consummating the sale. Tau Tire anticipated that approval and sale would occur about the end of March 1992, but was aware that these events might occur earlier or later. Flexibility in the hedge was, therefore, critical.

The bank suggested the following strategic steps to accomplish Tau Tire's hedging objective:

1. Select a maturity date of January 2, 1992, for the FERA. By January 2, 1992, Tau Tire would probably know the settlement date for the sale,

and consummation of the sale would be unlikely to occur before that date.

2. In early January 1992, Tau Tire could sell an amount of Malaysian Ringgits forward from the transaction to the date of the payment (2 or 3 months thereafter). The bank currently traded spot and forward Ringgits out of its Singapore, London, and New York offices, and, hence, could handle the January forward transaction for Tau Tire.

3. On the *value date* of the two forward foreign exchange contracts, Tau Tire would buy the Ringgits back from the bank and the then current spot exchange rate and compensate the Ringgit amounts by payment in U.S. Dollars. Thus, neither Tau Tire nor the bank would make any payments in Ringgits. Instead, the U.S. Dollar difference between the two contracts would be netted, and either Tau Tire or the bank would pay, to the other, the U.S. Dollar difference between the two contracts. This proposed strategy would, in effect, be similar to the FERA transaction.

The proposed strategy had the inherent risk of a change in foreign market conditions or in Malaysian regulations that would make such an offsetting transaction difficult. Nonetheless, the strategy was the best available for Tau Tire because its need for flexibility limited its hedging opportunities.

Negotiation with Chi Computer.   Chi Computer was aware of the potential advantages that it could derive from the ability to "make" the FERA at any of the bank's foreign branches. Involvement of any Malaysian entity, such as a local subsidiary, and of Malaysian governmental intervention could thereby be avoided. Payment of Malaysian Ringgits by one FERA party to the other could also be avoided. Further, the transaction might be structured so as to avoid any tax implication for Chi Computer. The FERA could be arranged with Chi Computer's off-shore finance subsidiary, if the bank had established a foreign exchange line with the subsidiary, perhaps with Chi Computer's guarantee of the subsidiary's credit.

The bank had learned during its prior negotiations with Chi Computer that the company was interested in a FERA and understood the nature of the proposed transaction because it had previously used interest rate forward rate agreements. Chi Computer was flexible as to the FERA's amount because of its probable working capital needs in Malaysia, and agreed to a FERA amount of MYR 75 million.

Exchange rate and timing still posed problems. At the time of the negotiations, the spot foreign exchange rate for the Ringgit was MYR/USD 2.7200 and the 6-month forward rate was MYR/USD 2.7050. The company's position was that the 6-month forward rate implied an 18-month forward rate of MYR/USD 2.6750. This position was based on a simplistic but not necessarily correct logic: the difference between a spot contract and a 6-month forward was − 0.0150 Ringgit per U.S. Dollar; hence, the difference for three times as long (18 months) should be three times the difference between the spot and the 6-month rate, or − 0.045 Ringgit per U.S. Dollar. The bank responded that this logic was not realistic, because foreign exchange points could not be arbitrarily extrapolated from forward points for a shorter period, especially for a period longer than 1 year.

The bank offered Chi Computer some leeway in pricing the FERA, but cautioned that the pricing would be affected by several factors, including the anticipated risk that the Ringgit would appreciate in value against the U.S. Dollar. The bank knew, too, that the pricing would be affected by how closely it could match the Chi Computer and Tau Tire transactions.

The timing issue was crucial for Chi Computer: its payment in Ringgits was due January 2, 1992, and the company would have to buy Ringgits for settlement on that date. Although the ideal maturity date for Chi Computer's FERA would be December 30, 1991, the company would delay maturity until January 2, 1992, but would be unwilling to delay until March 1992.

The Bank's Final Proposal. Based on its negotiations with the two companies, the bank structured the following final proposal, believing it would be acceptable to both companies. Each FERA would be in the amount of MYR 75 million, with a maturity date of January 2, 1991. The pricing offered to Tau Tire was a guaranteed exchange rate of MYR/USD 2.75; the offering to Chi Computer was MYR/USD 2.65. Both companies accepted their respective proposals, and the bank could look forward to a profit on the maturity of the two FERAs of USD 420,000.

Commentary

This business study has illustrated several practical aspects of hedging. Both Tau Tire and Chi Computer solved difficult hedging problems in a country with relatively thin and immature financial markets. They solved their problems by going outside their organizations to consult with the bank's experts in hedging financial risks. "Networking" can be crucial in the type of risk situation that the two companies faced.

The bank booked a substantial profit, earned by the skill of its employees and substantial time spent in solving the risk problems of Tau Tire and Chi Computer. The bank's personnel had also spent considerable time in "educating" the two companies to make certain that each fully understood the proposed risk-hedging transaction. Finally, the bank had contacts and information to which neither company had access.

In addition to accommodating the stated business purposes, the FERAs have some conveniences for each company. There is no up-front cash flow, and no fee or premium must be paid. The FERA contracts can be entered into with the bank outside of the foreign country. Any changes in local regulations—as may more frequently happen in lesser or newly developing countries—will have minimal impact on the FERA agreements. Cash settlements can be made outside the country in U.S. Dollars, regardless of each company's underlying transactions within the country.

Some words of practical advice are in order. When a company is considering whether to enter into a new transaction, such as a FERA, its finance personnel should not hesitate to ask apparently naïve questions. For example: What are the cash flows that result from the transaction? What are the market risks? What are the credit risks? Are there any local regulations that might impact the transaction? Are there accounting or tax implications? For Tau Tire and Chi Computer, the last two questions would probably need in-house answers. Outside bankers cannot be expected to understand each individual entity's tax situation or accounting policy. They should know, however, the basic flexibility and features of the proposed transaction and be able to explain the fundamental impacts of the transaction.

Before entering for the first time into a transaction such as a FERA, a company's finance personnel should be certain to comprehend fully: (1) the mechanics of the transaction; (2) each term and condition in the agreement; and (3) the documentation of the transaction incorporated into the agreement, either directly or by reference. Once the FERA has been contracted, the FERA cash settlements will occur regardless of whether the *underlying* contracts and transactions occur. Each FERA is an independent contract. Further, each company should ask what would happen if for any reason it needed to unwind its FERA contract.

In this case study, no provision was made for the bank's unwinding the transactions with either Tau Tire or Chi Computer. Each party was bound to its agreement with the bank, even though neither company might ever complete the underlying transaction. Unwinding a customized contract such as these FERAs could be very costly and perhaps virtually impossible. Each FERA is specialized and specific to a company's requirements. If either Tau Tire or Chi Computer had wanted to "unwind" the transaction, the bank would have had to search for suitable replacement company(ies) with needs of timing and amount that matched the original FERA. The more specific and unique the hedge, the less flexibility is possible in making future adjustments.

9
Borrowers and Cash Investors

When 'tis fair, be sure you take your coat with you.

Ben Franklin, Poor Richard's Almanack (1734)

CASH AND INTEREST

The discussions in this chapter are from the perspective of borrowers and investors of cash, especially corporate cash managers who invest cash in money market instruments. Because borrowers often have investable cash, the borrower and investor may be the same person.

This chapter does not include issues of investment portfolio management; it is not a chapter about hedging a portfolio. It does provide details of basic techniques for interest rate risk management that are often only broadly described: interest rate arbitrage; forward rate agreements; interest rate swaps for a borrower; a comparison of swaps, caps, floors, and collars; an inventive cash investor experiment with interest rate swap engineering; and the effects of an executive exchange rate forecast. There is not enough room in this book for detailed examples of the new Chicago Board of Trade (CBOT) swap futures contracts or of building a swap using futures contracts. The authors hope, however, that the situations and details given will offer practical reference for both basic and more complicated projects of financial engineering to manage interest rate risk. The products for managing interest rate risk are widely used and of diverse design.

The warnings for this topic are to remember "basis" and considerations of credit and liquidity.

INTEREST RATE ARBITRAGE

Interest rate arbitrage is one of the oldest strategies in international financial markets. The difference between the spot exchange rate and the forward exchange rate is determined by the difference between the interest rates of the two currencies for the time period in question. Theoretically, the spot, forward, and money market interest rates align so that there is no advantage to be gained by investing or borrowing in another currency while being fully hedged against currency exchange rate risk. Frequently, however, the forward foreign exchange rate for a currency moves out of alignment with the spot foreign exchange market and money market interest rates.

The forward foreign exchange rate between two currencies is in part a function of the interest rate differentials for the currencies. If the forward foreign exchange rate between two currencies is properly aligned with the interest rate differential, there is no short-term advantage to investing in either currency. If, however, the forward foreign exchange rate is not aligned with the interest rate differential, an opportunity arises to profit by arbitrage. The result of this financial engineering is sometimes called "covered interest rate arbitrage" or "hedged [name of currency] money market instruments." The money markets are rather efficient, so these opportunities are not always available. A bank's money market or foreign exchange desk may monitor the market for its own book or, sometimes, for an interested corporate client.

The opportunity can work to the advantage of either a borrower or a short-term cash investor. For example, a borrower may have the opportunity to swap a borrowing to a foreign currency, enter into a forward contract to convert back to the domestic currency on the maturity of the interest period, and thus repay in the domestic currency—and save a few points of interest rate. This can work both ways: for example, a European corporation might issue U.S. Dollar commercial paper. Conversely, a short-term cash investor may gain a few points of interest rate. The windows of interest rate arbitrage often open and close quickly during the trading day. In the hasty enthusiasm to pick up basis points, however, reviewing the credit of the foreign government or instrument in which the foreign currency will be invested should not be forgotten. The foreign exchange risk may be hedged, but the underlying instrument's credit risk should not be ignored.

The following example provides ¼ percent improvement in the investment of overnight U.S. Dollars. A corporation had USD 5 million available for overnight investment; the best overnight *Eurodollar* rate from a creditworthy bank was 8.75 percent. The bank mentioned that, at that time of the morning, it could arrange an overnight investment to yield 9 percent through a fully hedged swap into Canadian Treasury Bills. The overnight foreign exchange rate was temporarily not aligned with the relevant overnight U.S. Dollar and Canadian Dollar (CAD) interest rates.

The company sold on March 15 USD 5 million at an overnight spot rate of CAD/USD 1.22982 for CAD 6,149,100. (Spot for Canadian Dollar/U.S.

Dollar foreign exchange transactions executed in North America is 1 business day instead of the usual 2 business days.) Under a repurchase agreement with the bank, on March 15 the company purchased Government of Canada Treasury Bills and agreed to resell them to the bank on the next business day, March 16, at CAD 6,150,537.25. The company also agreed to sell CAD 6,150,537.25 at CAD/USD 1.2298 for delivery on March 16. The overall return on the transactions was 9 percent. The detailed computations are:

CAD 6,150,537.25/CAD/USD 1.2298 = USD 5,001,250.00 received on March 16 versus USD 5,000,000 invested on March 15:

USD 1,250 × (360/1)/USD 5,000,000 = 9 percent

The components of the return are the Canadian investment yield and the amount earned on the U.S. Dollar/Canadian Dollar swap. Traders sometimes refer to these USD/CAD or CAD/USD swaps as "northbound" and "southbound." The problem is to determine whether the trader is referring to the "spot" or "forward" leg of the swap; because traders may not be consistent in using the terms, this terminology haunts the Canadian/U.S. Dollar swap market. Traders should confirm exactly which currency is being sold at spot and which currency is being purchased forward—without using a compass.

The return on the Canadian Dollar repurchase agreement is:

CAD 6,150,537.25 March 16 maturity − CAD 6,149,100 invested = CAD 1,437.25

CAD 1,437.25 × 360/1/CAD 6,149,100 = 8.4144 percent

To enable comparison with the 8.75 percent U.S. Dollar Eurodollar (360 basis) yield, the Canadian Dollar yield is here computed on a 360 basis. The market quotations for Canadian Dollar investments are usually 365 basis, except for Eurocanadian money market investments. Applicable withholding tax should be considered.

For the return on the foreign exchange swap, these are the calculations:

Purchase CAD/USD 1.22982 on March 15 and sell CAD/USD 1.2298 on March 16 for a gain of "two pips" on the day; again, on the 360 basis, .00002/1.2298 × 360/1 = .5855 percent[1]

The total return was 8.4144 percent +.5855 percent = 9 percent, all on 360 basis for comparison to the Eurodollar market. These computations can be done on a 365 basis, to keep apples with apples.

Interest rate arbitrage creates opportunities to improve cash investment yields and lower borrowing costs.

---

[1] This formula is detailed in an appendix at the end of this chapter.

FORWARD RATE AGREEMENTS

Forward rate agreements (FRAs) are handy financial engineering tools for both cash investors and borrowers. Forward interest rate agreements would be a more descriptive name. FRAs are derivative contracts because the principal amount on which interest is computed is a *notional amount*. FRAs are agreements to fix a future period's interest rate, the "strike rate," on a notional principal amount. FRAs can be arranged in most major currencies, and are usually done with the start date not more than 12 months from the dealing date.

In the FRA contract and market, the "buyer" buys an FRA rate and thus is protected by the "seller" if interest rates rise above the FRA rate for the FRA contract period. The "seller" sells the FRA rate and thus is protected by the "buyer" if interest rates fall below the FRA rate for the FRA contract period. For cash investors, "selling" an FRA protects against declining interest rates in one or more future time periods. For borrowers, "buying" an FRA protects against rising rates in one or more future time periods. FRAs are particularly suited for fixing the interest rate on near-term *Eurocurrency* LIBOR-based time deposits or loans. An investor might want to deal the interest rate for one or more blocks of notional cash at both spot and forward periods. A borrower could fix the rates for the coming year's quarterly or semiannual floating rate loan balance. Borrowers with long-term, fixed rate, amortizing loans may identify temporary windows of positive interest rate margin. If cash is being internally escrowed toward the next one or two installments, FRAs could lock-in the positive margin.

Quotations for FRAs sound vaguely like a lumberyard. For example, a 6-month FRA starting 1 month hence would be a "1 by 7" (1×7); a 3-month FRA starting 2 months hence would be a "2 by 5" (2×5). Setting up a quotation form can avoid confusion about dates. A suggestion for staying organized when taking FRA quotations is given in Table 9.1. In this example, an investor is "selling" 6-month interest rates starting 2 business days later, at *spot* and/or periods starting 1 and 2 months later.

The FRA cash settlement is computed on the spot date for the start of the FRA contract period. Using the example in Table 9.1, assume the contract is for a 1×7 8 $^1/_{16}$ percent starting November 26; the spot date is assumed to be November 24. On November 24, if 6-month U.S. Dollar LIBOR rates are higher than 8 $^1/_{16}$ percent, the seller/investor would pay the buyer/borrower. If 6-month U.S. Dollar rates are lower than 8 $^1/_{16}$ percent, the buyer/borrower would pay the seller/investor.

The settlement is computed as paid on the first day of the contract period and is therefore discounted to present value. The party receiving payment is assumed to invest the settlement amount at the settlement rate. The following formula and computed example form a handy reference unit:

Formula: [(Settlement rate – FRA rate) × Days in FRA contract period × notional amount] ÷ [360 (see note below) × 100] + (Settlement rate × Days in FRA contract period) = Settlement amount. If the settlement rate is higher than the FRA rate (a plus number), the seller/investor pays the buyer/borrower. If the settlement rate is lower than the FRA rate (a minus number), the buyer/borrower pays the seller/investor.

Computed example: Assume USD 1 million, LIBOR for settlement date, which is start date of FRA contract, is $8\frac{1}{2}$ percent, FRA rate is $8\frac{1}{16}$ percent, 181 days in FRA contract period, 360 basis:

[(8.5 − 8.0625) × 181 × USD 1,000,000]/(360 × 100) + (8.5 × 181)
= .4375 × 181 × 1,000,000/36,000 + 1,538.50
= 79,187,500/37,538.50
= USD 2,109.50 settlement amount seller pays buyer.

Note: The basis will usually be 360 for a *Eurocurrency* FRA, including *Eurodollars,* and 365 for a domestic currency, subject to market custom.

Because of the market bid/ask spread between LIBID and LIBOR, the exact FRA contract rate may not be obtained when investing the FRA cash settlement amount. Using the above example, assume the investor sells a

Table 9.1   FRA Quotation Worksheet

Notional amount: USD 1 million

Quote date: October 24

Time: 8:15 A.M.

Spot date: October 26 (2 business days later)

Sell to fix 6-month time deposit interest rate [or label "Buy," if fixing borrowing period interest rate]

Fixing reference: Discuss with quoting banks. In this example, the reference is "6-month U.S. Dollar LIBOR Telerate screen number, rounded to 5 decimal places."

Period	Bank A (percent)	Bank B (percent)	Bank C (percent)
Spot October 26 to April 26	8	$7\frac{15}{16}$	8
1 × 7 November 26 to May 26	$8\frac{1}{16}$	8	8.05
2 × 8 December 26 to June 26	$8\frac{1}{8}$	$8\frac{1}{16}$	$8\frac{1}{8}$

USD 1 million, 1×7, $8\,{}^1\!/_{16}$ percent strike rate FRA and, on the fixing date, 6-month LIBID/LIBOR is $8\,{}^1\!/_4$ to $8\,{}^1\!/_2$ percent. The seller/investor pays the buyer/borrower USD 2,109.50. If the buyer/borrower is matching a borrowing over the same time period as the FRA, the borrow rate is $8\,{}^1\!/_2$ percent LIBOR but the FRA proceeds are invested at LIBID $8\,{}^1\!/_4$ percent toward payment of interest at the end of the LIBOR interest period.

FRAs are especially useful for protecting short-term, Eurocurrency interest rate risk over specific future blocks of time. The concept of the imputed yield curve suggests that the market's view of future interest rates is, on any given day, the best predictor of those rates. Put another way, on any day, the market forecasts what 6-month U.S. Dollar LIBOR will be 3 months from now. An FRA is an opportunity to contract for that market forecast without entering into futures contracts or buying options.

TRYST INNS, INC.

This study untangles some of the complicated aspects of interest rate swaps and swaptions.

Business Risk Situation

Tryst Inns, Inc. is a regional motel chain with units located on major interstate highways near large cities along the Boston-to-Washington corridor. In early 1990, the company committed to a major expansion into the southeastern United States—10 new motels, each costing an average of USD 5 million, over a 3-year period.

The company's concern was the selection of the best method for financing the expansion. The company's owners rejected a public debt issue because they did not want to release financial data to the public. A second alternative was a private placement. Two insurance companies were willing to lend the company the required USD 50 million as a private placement. They would provide fixed rate financing, but each wanted semiannual amortizing principal with a maturity of 7 years and a required yield of 12.5 percent. The company's president and chief financial officer (CFO) were aware that other companies with balance sheets comparable to Tryst's had recently issued 7-year debt at 10.5 percent. Was the company's name going to cost 2 percent?

The company's lead bank offered to arrange a syndicated, floating rate facility based on either *Eurodollars* or *prime rate*. The bank offered alternative financing arrangements: (1) a *spread* of 1 percent over the Eurodollar offered rate for 1-, 2-, 3-, or 6-month interest periods; or (2) the bank's prime lending rate. The term of the loan would be 10 years, with a "bullet" repayment of all the principal at maturity. Prepayments in minimum increments of USD 10 million were permitted after the fourth year, with cancellation of commitment for any amounts prepaid. This translated to the company's being able to repay but not reborrow after the fourth year. The company could draw down the funds as needed during the first 2½ years of the loan.

The company's president and CFO evaluated the two offers and decided that the bank's offer was more advantageous, for the following reasons:

- The company could borrow the money as needed, rather than draw down the full amount at closing as required by the two insurance companies; borrowing costs would be substantially reduced.
- *Eurodollar* interest rates currently ranged from 8 to 8.5 percent for maturities out to 1 year, which meant the interest rate on the loan would be lower than the insurance companies' fixed rate of 12.5 percent—If U.S. interest rates did not rise significantly.
- The insurance companies required an up-front fee of 1 percent of the principal of the loan. The bank's charge was a commitment fee of ½ percent on closing and ⅜ percent annually on the unused portion of the commitment. The fee for the insurance companies would be USD 500,000 in advance; the bank's proposal would cost only USD 250,000 at the closing.

According to the chief financial officer's estimated construction schedules, the company would need USD 20 million at the beginning of the first year of the facility, USD 20 million after 18 months, and USD 10 million after 30 months, in the middle of the third year. Thus, total fees to the bank were estimated to be USD 400,000, and they would be over the first 2½ years of the loan.

Although the bank loan looked attractive, it had *floating rate* interest. If interest rates rose, the company might incur more interest expense over the life of the bank loan than it would by accepting the insurance companies' fixed rate proposal.

The CFO discussed with the bank the company's concern about the floating interest rate. The bank responded that an interest rate *swap* would remove the floating interest rate risk by locking-in the company's interest cost at the time when the swap was contracted. An advantage of a swap was that the company could negotiate the best possible financing arrangement on a bank loan and then, through one or more interest rate swap agreements, separately lock-in one or more fixed interest rates for one or more time periods, when and if the company chose during the life of the loan. An interest rate swap would involve no additional expense or fees when the company entered into the loan agreement.

The banker and the bank's swap trader met with the company's president and CFO to explain the mechanics of an interest rate swap. The swap trader stated that the swap was a highly flexible tool with many variations on the "plain vanilla" flavor; the bank could customize a swap to meet the company's specifications. The trader's bank used the standard International Swap Dealers Association (ISDA) Interest Rate and Currency Exchange Agreement ("the standard agreement"). The trader gave the company a reference copy along with a copy of ISDA's 1991 Definitions, and recommended that anyone involved with over-the-counter (OTC) contracts for financial engineering of commodities prices, currencies, or interest rates should have a desk copy. (See Appendix B for ISDA's address and Appendix C for a copy of Standard Agreement and some relevant pages.)

Mechanics of an Interest Rate Swap

The swap trader then provided the following detailed explanation of the mechanics of a basic interest rate swap with 6-month settlement periods.

The bank and the company would agree to net out a difference between two interest rates every 6 months. One interest rate would be a floating rate equal to a predetermined 6-month LIBOR rate. The other interest rate would be a fixed rate determined at the time when the bank and the company entered into the swap contract. Assume these details:

Notional amount	USD 50 million
Fixed rate	10.00 percent
Floating rate	6-month LIBOR
Term	10 years

At the first settlement date for the interest rate swap, the bank would calculate the amount of interest payable on USD 50 million for 6 months at each interest rate—the fixed rate and the 6-month LIBOR floating rate. The cash settlements under the interest rate swap are not related to the company's regular floating interest rate payments for the committed loans, as explained later in this study. The interest rate swap agreement and the credit agreement are two separate agreements. The amount payable under the interest rate swap by either the bank or the company would be determined as:

- If the amount payable at the 6-month LIBOR rate was more than the amount payable at 10 percent for the period, the bank would pay the company the difference between the two amounts.
- If the amount payable at the 6-month LIBOR rate was less than the amount payable at 10 percent for the period, the company would pay the bank the difference between the two amounts.

The interest rate swap proposed to Tryst would use the U.S. Treasury Bond method to calculate the amount of money due at fixed rate, and the money market method to calculate the amount of interest due at LIBOR. The swap trader offered to explain the LIBOR date and rate arrangements after giving examples of the calculation methods.

Determining the Fixed Rate Amount (U.S. Treasury Bond Method). The fixed rate calculation would be the fixed contract rate divided by two, to determine the semiannual interest rate. For example, using a fixed rate of 10 percent, the fixed rate for calculation would be 5 percent.

The amount of 6-month interest due on the notional amount would be: USD 2.5 million = USD 50 million × 5 percent.

Determining the Floating Interest Amount (Money Market Method). The calculation for the floating rate side of the interest rate swap would be different. In this example, the notional amount would be multiplied by the 6-month LIBOR rate multiplied by the actual number of days in the period, divided by 360 days:

$$\$I = \$A \times (L \times N/360)$$

where: $\$I$ = USD floating rate swap interest amount due;
$\$A$ = notional amount of swap;
L = 6-month LIBOR rate;
N = actual number of days in interest period.

Assuming a notional amount of USD 50 million, a LIBOR rate of $8\frac{3}{8}$ percent (.08375) for the 6-month period, and an actual number of 182 days, the floating rate interest calculation would be:

USD 2,117,013.89 = USD 50,000,000 × (.08375 × 182/360).

Thus, under the proposed interest rate swap agreement, if the fixed rate were 10 percent and the floating reference interest rate for the 6-month interest period were $8\frac{3}{8}$ percent, the company would pay the bank USD 382,986.11: the difference between the fixed rate amount of USD 2,500,000 and the floating rate amount of USD 2,117,013.89.

If 6-month LIBOR were 10.5 percent, the payment flow would be different under the swap:

USD 2,654,166.67 = USD 50,000,000 × (.105 × 182/360)

The bank would then pay the company USD 154,166.67: the difference between the floating rate amount of USD 2,654,166.66 and the fixed rate amount of USD 2,500,000.

To recapitulate for this example: the dollar amounts at the fixed rate of the interest rate swap and at 6-month LIBOR would be calculated at each payment date, and the difference between the two would be calculated. If the amount due at 6-month LIBOR is higher than the amount due at the fixed rate, the bank would pay the company the difference. If the amount due at 6-month LIBOR is less than the amount due at the fixed rate, the company would pay the bank the difference.

Fixing the Interest Expense

The bank's swap trader next explained how the proposed interest rate swap would enable the company to be protected under the proposed loan agreement's floating rate interest. The loan agreement being negotiated with the bank would allow the company to borrow USD 50 million for 10 years with interest rate periods of 1-, 2-, 3-, or 6-month LIBOR, plus 1 percent. Since January 1, 1991, *reserves* have no longer been required for U.S. Dollar loans, whether booked in the United States or abroad. Loans in some other countries, for example, loans in Pounds Sterling in the United Kingdom, may have a variable reserve cost in addition to the bank's margin. The reserve cost varies over time and from country to country, but is typically less than $1/4$ percent. At its most recent phase in the United States, the reserve was 3 percent of the stated interest rate; for example, if LIBOR was 8 percent, the reserve was .24 percent. The 6-month interest period is assumed to be 182 actual days; the LIBOR rate, referencing *Eurodollars,* is 360 basis.

For example, if at the beginning of any interest rate period the company elected 6-month LIBOR and the rate was $8^3/8$ percent, the company's interest expense for the period would be calculated at 1 percent more for an "all-in" total of $9^3/8$ percent. The dollar amount of interest would be USD 2,369,792 (USD 50 million × (.09375 × 182/360).

If 6-month LIBOR were $10^1/2$ percent, the company's interest expense for the period would be calculated at $11^1/2$ percent, and the amount of interest would be USD 2,906,944 = (USD 50 million × .1150 × 182/360). Regardless of whether an interest rate swap agreement is in place, the company is responsible for paying the interest due under the credit facility: the margin over the LIBOR cost of the loan—here, 1 percent over LIBOR (plus any applicable reserve cost).

The interest rate swap would protect the company from the risk of increasing the floating interest rates. The company could fix the LIBOR interest rate—before margin and reserve—for each 6-month period. As previously stated, if the amount due at 6-month LIBOR were more than the amount due at the fixed rate, the bank would pay the company the difference. The bank's payment would offset the floating LIBOR interest rate cost under the credit facility. However, the company would pay the bank if the floating LIBOR interest rate were less than the fixed reference rate of the swap. It is important to understand the swap's opportunity cost: the company gives up the benefit of any favorable, lower floating interest rates. In sum, if the fixed rate side of the interest rate swap were 10 percent, the company's interest cost would be locked-in at 11 percent—the fixed rate of the swap plus the 1 percent spread that it paid over LIBOR.

Example 1.   If LIBOR were $10^1/2$ percent:

- The company would pay the bank USD 2,906,944.44 under the loan agreement (USD 50 million × (.1150 all-in × 182/360); but

- The bank would pay the company USD 154,167 (the difference in amount between the 10½ percent LIBOR rate, USD 2,654,167, and the fixed 10 percent contract rate, USD 2,500,000) under the interest rate swap agreement. The company's net LIBOR interest cost, therefore, would be USD 2,752,777 (USD 2,906,944 – USD 154,167).

On "actual days to actual days" basis (182 days/365-day year), this is an all-in rate of 11.04 percent (USD 2,752,777/USD 50 million × 365/182): the 10 percent swap fixed interest rate plus 1 percent margin. For this purpose, the yield computation is converted from the 360 Eurodollar basis to the fixed interest rate side of the swap's 365 basis. The yield "doesn't pass the smell test," in finance jargon, if done on 360 basis—always an important criterion.

The bank would owe the payment of USD 154,167 to the company because the amount due under the swap's LIBOR rate was more than the amount due under the swap's 10 percent fixed rate. In determining the amount due under the credit agreement with the same 10½ percent 6-month LIBOR rate, 11½ percent is used to calculate the amount that the company owes the bank; however, 10½ percent is used to determine the bank's swap agreement payment to the company. The reason (and a reminder) is that the company remains responsible for the 1 percent spread (plus any applicable reserve costs) over the life of the loan.

Example 2. If LIBOR were 8⅜ percent:

- The company would pay the bank USD 2,369,792 = USD 50 million × (.9375 × 182/360) under the loan agreement; and
- The company would pay the bank USD 382,986 under the interest rate swap agreement (USD 2,117,014 = USD 50 million × .08375 × 182/360) – USD 2,500,000, the bank's 10 percent fixed rate payment to the company.

The company has given up the potential advantage from lower, floating interest rates: it pays USD 2.5 million for the interest period instead of about USD 2.1 million.

In sum, the interest rate swap would enable the company to take advantage of the bank loan's up-front costs, which are lower than those of the insurance companies' loan, and to eliminate the bank loan's floating interest rate risk. Moreover, entering into the swap agreement would not require the company to pay any additional fees. It is important to remember, however, that a swap will require the company to pay the bank if floating interest rates are lower than the swap rate. An interest rate swap is not the same as an interest rate cap or floor.

Synchronizing Loan and Swap Dates and Rates

The trader's examples seemed very straightforward and the interest period dates and floating LIBOR rates were all assumed to be synchronized.

(If either or both floating rates and interest period dates between the loan and swap are not synchronized, the old problem of "basis risk" again emerges.)

The CFO asked whether the LIBOR under the swap agreement would be the same LIBOR as under the loan agreement. Who would set the swap agreement's floating LIBOR? The swap trader suggested that LIBOR under the swap agreement could be established by the bank as a "reference bank" because it had a London branch. If the interest period dates were the same, the swap rate could be matched to the loan's LIBOR setting. Alternatives were one of the LIBOR options, such as the Reuters Screen LIBO or ISDA page, or the Telerate BBA (British Bankers Association) LIBOR. Tryst Inns was not a subscriber to market-dealing information services. The CFO thought that arranging both the interest rate swap's floating LIBOR rate and the loan's LIBOR settings through the same bank had the virtue of simplicity. The 11:00 A.M. LIBOR could be checked in the financial press.

The CFO then asked: "If the company chose under its loan agreement to elect a 1-month LIBOR interest period instead of 6-month LIBOR, what would happen under the swap agreement?" The swap trader responded: "The swap's interest amounts are always calculated based on the rates agreed in the swap contract. If the swap contract called for 6-month LIBOR, then the interest calculations under that contract would always be based on 6-month LIBOR."

The trader commented: "There's more than one way to get dates out of sync, and it can drive you nuts."

There are two ways in which an interest rate swap's reset dates can become "out of sync" with interest periods for an underlying loan: (1) deliberate setting of loan interest periods at lengths different from the swap's interest periods; and (2) accidents (of wording, so that the swap documentation does not match the rate-setting provisions of the underlying credit facility) or errors in loan administration.

For example, under the proposed loan agreement, Tryst could choose, on each interest rate reset date, any of 1-, 2-, 3-, or 6-month interest periods. If the company were protecting the floating interest rate exposure with a 6-month interest rate swap contract, choosing a loan reset of other than 6 months would create two risks. First, if the company chose a loan interest period different from the 6 months of the swap's interest periods, then the interest rate swap could lose some or much of its hedge value if interest rates oscillated in the interim between the two dates (basis risk, again). Second, the company might not be able to resynchronize the maturity dates of the reset periods to the reset dates on the interest rate swap.

An example will demonstrate the potential problems. Assume that the company's loan interest period *rollover* date and interest rate swap reset date are on March 31. The company selects a 1-month rollover of its bank loan

Table 9.2 LIBOR Yield Curve Example

Rollover Period (Months)	LIBOR Rate (Percent)
1	8¹/₈%
2	8¹/₄
3	8³/₈
6	8³/₄
12	9

because of a steep, positively sloped yield curve,[2] which makes it significantly cheaper to borrow for the shorter period, as shown in Table 9.2.

Rate resets on most Eurodollar bank loans are normally done 2 business days before the maturity of the current loan period; this is also called doing the rate resets for "spot value" or the "spot date."

Some loan agreements will require a North American borrower to give 3 business days' notice for the interest period selection of Eurodollar loan rollovers, if the bank's notice address is in the United States. The bank may require the extra day to communicate the selected interest period to its London or European desk for the next morning, to arrange the "spot value" interest rate setting.

The swap trader asked the CFO what "interest period dates" had been drafted into the credit agreement. The section on interest rate selection included a very long paragraph about "end dates" and "business days," with the word "except" just before the middle. "Good, it's the *FRN or Eurodollar*

---

[2] The forward yield curve is a hypothetical yield curve generated by looking at forward interest rates at any point in time. In reality, it is a series of yield curves based on forward interest rates. Assume that an investor could invest funds for 1 month at 6.00 percent or 2 months at 6.0625 percent. A forward interest rate implies the following question.

At the maturity of a 1-month deposit, an investor will reinvest principal plus interest. What interest rate would the investor have to receive for a second 1-month time deposit in order to have the same yield as if he invested his original principal for 2 months? The formula below shows a simple example. Note that the interest rates used are the period interest rates, not the annual interest rates:

1-month rate: 0.5% = 6.00%/12 months
2-month rate: 1.0104% = 6.0625%/6 months

The 1-month rate 1 month forward (in the future) is

$$1.05079 = 1.010104/1.05$$

This formula takes into account implied compounding of interest at the end of each assumed rollover period. Annualized, the rate is 6.094527 percent.

By doing a series of such calculations, it is possible to generate a series of interest rates for each 1-month period 1 month forward. Plotted on a graph, these interest rates would be a forward yield curve 1 month forward. It is possible to generate a series of forward yield curves for any future point in time.

convention, and that's what we prefer for interest rate swaps," said the trader. The maturity date of the rollover period that the company selected would be the numerically same calendar day as the interest period just ended. If there was not a numerically corresponding day, then the interest period would mature on the next *business day*—unless the next business day was in the following calendar month, in which case the interest period would mature on the last business day in the preceding month and would continue thereafter to be the last business day of each month.

If the company's intent was to match perfectly the interest rate swap and the interest rate exposure under the proposed bank loan, then it needed to make certain that the interest period rate-setting dates on the loan and the interest rate swap were the same. It was not advisable to select either rate reset dates or maturities for the bank loan that were different from those of the interest rate swap. The company might decide that it preferred to incur some basis risk, however, in an attempt to minimize overall interest expense on the loan. For example, if the company thought floating interest rates would decline more sharply over the 6-month period than the 6-month rate available at the beginning of the interest period, the company might use 1-, 2-, or 3-month rollovers on the loan and try to obtain some incremental benefit. The business decision about whether to try profiting from basis risk between the two interest period rates should be based on careful calculations of the financial risks—and calendar dates—so that the swap and loan may eventually be resynchronized.

If an underlying credit agreement already in place has a date convention other than the FRN or Eurodollar convention or modified (following) business day convention, the provisions for the proposed interest rate swap agreement's dates should be closely negotiated to avoid date and rate setting problems. The borrower may find that the interest rate swap market prefers the above two conventions and may try to persuade the writing of a following business day convention agreement. Watching the calendar may get a better swap rate than trying to strong-arm a trader.

Before entering into a swap contract, the person responsible for rate settings and swap payments is well advised to obtain the ISDA Definitions (see Appendix B for the ISDA address), in order to understand fully the documentation on these alternatives.

Unwinding an Interest Rate Swap

If cash flow from the new locations became sufficiently high, the company might want to repay all or part of the loan before its 10-year maturity date. The company's president asked: "Can an interest rate swap be canceled before its maturity?" The swap trader answered "Yes" and explained the alternatives for "unwinding" an interest rate swap. ("Unwinding" is a colloquialism for "cash settlement.") Some method for computing the cash value of the interest rate swap prior to its termination date has to be agreed on, as part of the swap contract. If the ISDA contract is used, the "cash settlement amount" will be documented in the confirmation or as a schedule to the agreement. The cash settlement computation should be agreed on BEFORE the swap is contracted.

A swap is always "in the money" for either the fixed or floating rate side. Therefore, unwinding the swap involves some agreement on how much one party will pay the other. The ISDA Definitions suggest three alternatives,[3] broadly described as follows.

Alternative 1. This concept is to define a market value for the fixed or floating rate side of the swap for which termination is sought, or for both the floating and fixed sides, the entire swap. The swap agreement specifies reference financial institutions for the quotations. ISDA suggests that the highest and lowest quotations should be disregarded and a mean of the remaining bid and offer quotations should be used to determine the cash settlement to be paid by one party to the other.[4]

Alternative 2. The reference financial institutions are contacted to determine the floating rates that would apply for the company's or the bank's future payments to each other. These floating rates and the fixed payments are discounted to present value using a reference interest rate as specified in the swap contract. The bank or the company pays the cash settlement amount to terminate the swap. This is the present value of the payment streams based on market quotations for the floating rate periods.

Alternative 3. This alternative is the procedure defined under paragraph 6(e) of the ISDA Standard Agreement. This procedure is for computing a net settlement amount for terminated transactions arising because of default or because of other "termination events" such as illegality, indemnifiable tax, or merger or amalgamation. The settlement amount is based on market quotations for each transaction being terminated or, if market quotations are not available, the amount required to compensate for losses and costs as a result of early termination. Legal fees and out-of-pocket expenses are excluded. If the counterparty will benefit by the termination, the "loss" becomes a "gain"—for example, if market conditions are such that the counterparty is relieved of probable future payments under the swap. The ISDA agreement provides that amounts paid are preestimates of loss of protection and not a penalty.

Partial Drawdowns of the Bank Loan Facility

The interest rate examples provided thus far have all been computed on the full USD 50 million of the bank loan facility. On the closing date of the loan

---

[3] *1991 ISDA Definitions,* International Swap Dealers Association, Inc., New York, NY, v and vi.
[4] *Id.* at vi.

facility, the company would not need and hence would not draw down the full USD 50 million loan amount. In the first 2 to 3 years of the loan agreement, the company did not anticipate having the full USD 50 million utilized under the facility. Instead, the company anticipated drawing down different amounts on different dates as construction progressed on the new inns. If the company entered into the interest rate swap for the full USD 50 million at the same time that it closed the loan agreement, the notional principal amount of the interest rate swap would be larger than the principal amount of loan(s) outstanding under the credit facility. If Eurodollar rates remained below the fixed rate on the swap during the first 3 years of the loan and the notional amount of the swap was greater than the principal loan amount outstanding, then the company's actual interest expense would be substantially higher than the (approximate) 11.25 percent all-in rate estimated earlier. Because of the interest rate swap agreement, the company would be obligated to pay the difference to the bank.

When the company officers raised this concern, the swap trader replied that the problem could be resolved with *swaptions* (options to enter into interest rate swaps). Taking the company's projected drawdowns of USD 20 million in year 1 of the loan, USD 20 million in year 2, and USD 10 million in year 3, the company could take the following additional—but simple—steps to control interest rate risk.

On the closing date of the loan, Tryst could enter into an interest rate swap for USD 20 million for 10 years. The USD 20 million would correspond to the amount expected to be borrowed during the first year and outstanding for the full 10 years. Tryst would also purchase two swaptions: one for USD 20 million for 9 years, expiring 18 months thereafter, and a second option for USD 10 million for 8 years, expiring 36 months thereafter. The terms of the two swaps in the option agreements, the swaptions, would be identical to those in the original swap agreement. The amounts of the second and third swaps would be equal to the company's expected second- and third-year borrowings. The expiration dates of the two options would be midway between the expected second- and third-year drawdowns.

An important detail to remember is the matching of the swaption dates with the swap and loan payment dates. The swap trader gave a rough estimate of premiums for each swaption as 2 percent and 3 percent, respectively, of the notional amounts of the swaptions. The exact premiums would be determined by several factors at the time when the swaptions were done: the volatility of interest rates, the shape of the yield curve and the imputed forward yield curve—based on quotations, and the market's forecast of future interest rates.

(The Baby Bear business study later in the chapter discusses delayed start interest rate swaps and some other ideas for eliminating floating interest rate risk during progressive facility drawdowns.)

Doing the Deal

The company decided that the best course for financing its expansion was the bank loan coupled with the interest rate swap. The company based its decision on the CFO's calculations comparing the insurance company private placement (Table 9.3) to the lower present value of cash flows to service the bank loan with interest rate swap and swaptions (Table 9.4).

The bank loan's details had been negotiated, and one new provision had been added: drawdowns occurring after the initial drawdown would have the same interest rate reset dates as any existing amount outstanding on the loan. This provision assured the company that it could synchronize the maturity of any additional borrowings with the interest rate resets on the interest rate swaps. The loan documents were then executed.

After the loan was closed, the company wanted to enter into an interest rate swap and its CFO called the bank to arrange the deal. Because the swap trader who had explained the original transaction was unavailable, the company officer specified to another trader "on the desk" the desired transaction. The company wanted to enter into an interest rate swap in

Table 9.3   Insurance Company Private Placement Terms

Amount:	$50,000,000.00
Interest rate:	12.50%
Maturity:	5 years
Discount rate for present values:	9.00%

Year	Loan Fee	Annual Interest Expense	Present Value of Cash Flow
0	$500,000.00		$ 500,000.00
1		$6,250,000.00	6,047,405.55
2		6,250,000.00	5,786,990.95
3		6,250,000.00	5,537,790.39
4		6,250,000.00	5,299,320.94
5		6,250,000.00	5,071,120.52

Summary	Before Tax	After Tax
Total loan fees	$ 500,000.00	$ 310,000.00
Total interest expense	31,250,000.00	19,375,000.00
Total cash flows	$31,750,000.00	$19,685,000.00
Present value of all cash flows	$28,242,628.35	$17,510,429.58

Note: Assume semiannual interest payment.

Table 9.4   Bank Loan with Interest Rate Swap and Swaption

Amount, year 1:	$20,000,000.00
Amount, year 2:	$40,000,000.00
Amount, year 3:	$50,000,000.00
Interest rate:	11.00%
Maturity:	5 Years
Discount rate for present values:	9.00%

Year	Loan Fee	Swaption Premiums	Annual Interest Expense	Present Value of Cash Flow
0	$250,000.00	$700,000.00		$ 950,000.00
1	112,500.00		$2,200,000.00	2,128,686.75
2	37,500.00		4,400,550.00	3,284,529.34
3			4,950,000.00	4,609,256.10
4			5,500,000.00	4,663,402.43
5			5,500,000.00	4,462,586.06

Summary	Before Tax	After Tax
Total loan fees	$ 400,000.00	$ 248,000.00
Swaption premiums	700,000.00	434,000.00
Total interest expense	22,550,550.00	13,981,341.00
Total cash flows	$23,650,550.00	$14,663,341.00
Present value of all cash flows	$20,098,460.69	$12,461,045.63

Note: Assume semiannual interest payment and an interest rate swap with a fixed interest rate of 10 percent.

Drawdowns on the bank loan occur as follows:
$20,000,000 at the beginning of the loan;
$20,000,000 after 18 months;
$10,000,000 after 30 months.

Assume 38 percent federal tax rate and 0 percent state and local tax rate.

which (1) it would pay a fixed interest rate and receive 6-month LIBOR, and (2) the notional amount would be USD 20 million for 10 years, with the first rate set to occur on April 30—the last business day of the month—about a week after the expected drawdown of the first USD 20 million of the loan. The company would let the drawdown float at prime rate until April 30 and would then set the first LIBOR interest period under the loan facility. The swap's last 6-month floating rate setting and floating fixed cash settlement would occur 9½ years later, at the beginning of the last 6-month interest period of the swap.

The CFO also asked, during his telephone call, for quotes on swaptions, relying on the other swap trader's prior explanation, and specified all the details. He asked the bank's trader to quote the premiums for each swaption separately, both as to percentages and as to dollar amounts. First, however, they addressed the fixed rate on the interest rate swap. When the trader stated that the fixed rate would be "110 basis points over the 10 years," the CFO asked for clarification. The trader then amplified the answer, saying that the fixed rate would be "110 basis points or 1.10 percent higher than the 10-year Treasury."

The CFO still did not understand and asked the trader to state what the fixed rate would be. The trader replied that, because the current 10-year U.S. Treasury Note was yielding 8.95 percent, the fixed rate on the swap would be 10.05 percent for Tryst, assuming a semiannual coupon. The CFO agreed to the fixed rate and, to avoid any misunderstanding, summarized the transaction's terms. The company and the bank had closed an interest rate swap in which the company would pay a fixed rate of 10.05 percent and receive 6-month Eurodollar LIBOR. The first settlement date on the swap would be April 30. The last settlement date would be the last business day in October, 9½ years hence. The notional amount was USD 20 million. Interest amounts would be netted out on the interest reset dates at 6-month intervals, with one party paying to the other the dollar difference between the two interest calculations.

Next, the CFO and the bank trader discussed dealing the swaptions. Swaption 1 would be for a notional amount of USD 20 million and would have the same terms as the swap agreement. (Actual interest reset dates are not specified because they are determined at the future date when the swaption is exercised.) The swaption was to expire on October 31, 1991, 18 months hence. That expiration date would give Tryst flexibility to enter into the swap as the drawdown of the funds occurred. The underlying swap for Swaption 1 would be for 8 years because the company anticipated drawing down the additional USD 20 million by the middle of the following year. The company would also set the last reset date of the underlying swap to coincide with the last reset date of the loan, which it would hedge.

The CFO also asked what the premium would be on an identical swaption with a notional amount of USD 10 million to expire October 31, 1992, with underlying swap running for 7 years. The trader quoted the premiums as 2.15 percent or USD 570,000 for the first swaption and 2.91 percent or USD 291,000 for the second swaption. The CFO again carefully summarized all the details of each swaption before closing the transactions. Because his detailed summary of the swaptions had taken a few moments, the CFO then asked the trader if his premium quotes were still good. The trader confirmed they were the same, and the CFO closed the trades.

Comments

The company's management clearly identified its risk problem: how to control the overall borrowing cost that Tryst would incur. They asked many questions to make certain that they understood the transactions proposed by the bank. The company defined its primary goals for the financing of its expansion: to control the dollar cost of Tryst's borrowing, to maintain flexibility for its anticipated cash needs, and to incur no interest rate risk that could be avoided at a reasonable cost. The interest rate swap and swaptions enabled the company to control interest rate risk to a contracted rate. The goal of minimizing the interest expense was sacrificed to the surety of a known rate; the company gave up the downside opportunity to control upside risk.

BABY BEAR

The management of *interest rate swaps,* versus caps and *collars,* for a term loan is the topic in this study.

In the spring of 1988, a medium-size company, Baby Bear, decided to buy a much larger company, Papa Bear. The management personnel of Papa Bear, a subsidiary of a far larger company, were nearing retirement age. Two members of Papa Bear's board of directors were founding members of Baby Bear's board of directors and had for some years been close to its management. When Baby Bear contacted banks that had long-time relationships to Papa Bear, the bankers were receptive to arranging financing for 75 percent of the purchase price. The longer-range plan was to "take the company public" to the over-the-counter (OTC) market.

The immediate problem was how to structure the buy-out financing and ensure that there would be no default. The financial analyst, treasurer, and president quickly focused on the company's vulnerability to surges in interest rates. They were all confident of the forecasted range for net operating cash flow (gross revenues minus fixed costs and variable operating expenses). However, an overall increase in interest rates or surges to very high interest rates would jeopardize the company's ability to service the loan, especially during the first 3 years after the acquisition.

The company's president contacted some fixed rate lenders and received expressions of interest for 5-year, fixed rate, semiannual amortization loans. Indicative rates were 10.60 to 11 percent. The treasurer contacted the two banks that had provided term sheets for the financing; both banks were willing to include in the credit facilities provisions for securing payments the company might owe under interest rate swap or collar contracts. The treasurer also contacted a large bank not involved in the financing but known for its expertise in interest rate risk management products. The large bank doubted that it could contract a swap with the company because of the high leverage and first security interest that would be held by the lending bank. It did, however, express interest in working with the company to explore other alternatives for its interest rate risk management, particularly interest rate caps and, subject to its credit review, perhaps collars.

The banks and the company recognized that by swapping the floating rate interest payment obligations of a loan to a fixed rate—and if interest rates fell below the swap rate—the company would have to make swap payments to the bank counterparty. The interest rate cap required payment of the premium at the beginning of the contract. If at any cash settlement date under the cap contract the reference interest rate was higher than the cap rate, the bank would have to pay the company. Therefore, the bank writing the cap had no credit exposure to the company. The collar contract was different, although the treasurer argued that it had less credit risk than a swap. If, for example, the company entered into a 6 percent/8 percent collar, the company would pay the bank only if the reference interest rate at any settlement date was less than 6 percent. Conversely, the bank would pay the company if the reference rate was higher than 8 percent. Despite the limitations of obtaining credit, the treasurer was concerned about obtaining competitive quotations. He asked a large bank if it would quote, even if it would not contract with the company. The large bank replied that it did not quote "firm" on contracts that it was not prepared to write. The bank did agree to provide market range swap quotations along with its *indication* quotes for caps and collars.

The president and treasurer directed the financial analyst to assemble quotations for the purpose of comparing the interest rate risk management products. The president wanted to see the cost of 8.5 percent, 9 percent, and 9.5 percent caps for 2, 3, 4, and 5 years, for comparison to swaps rates for each year of the same time periods. The treasurer wanted also to see the swap rates for 6, 7, 8, 9, and 10 years. The financial analyst suggested that the company could use Eurodollar futures contracts to hedge at least the first year. The treasurer then wanted a quotation for a composite flat rate swap for 5 years, with a start date after the first year. The treasurer also wanted to see the cost of about a 1 percent collar around and a 2 percent collar below the general 2-year swap rate level. The treasurer observed, "We'll all have a different opinion on this one." The treasurer's financial analyst called the large bank and asked for indications on swaps, caps, and collars with a *notional amount* of USD 140 million. The bank's trader groaned and reminded the analyst that the trading desk would be busy until mid-afternoon. Trading desks doing a substantial amount of analytic or quotation work will expect to be part of any deal. Later that day, the trader faxed the quotations shown in Table 9.5.

The swap rates after the fifth year were as follows:

6 years, 8.93 percent;
7 years, 9.00 percent;
8 years, 9.05 percent;
9 years, 9.07 percent;
10 years, 9.09 percent.

Table 9.5 Swap, Cap, and Collar Quotations
(Dollars in Millions; Notional Amount: USD 140 Million)

Years	Swaps	8.5% Cap	9% Cap	9.5% Cap	7%/9% Collar	6%/8% Collar
2	8.19%	$1.46	$1.13	$ .89	$ .87	$1.91
3	8.42	2.94	2.40	2.12	1.97	3.52
4	8.65	4.30	3.60	3.30	2.95	4.97
5	8.80	5.59	4.76	4.07	3.93	6.36

The composite 5-year swap rate was 9.30 percent, "start in 1 year for 4 years." The 5-year fixed rates ranged from 10.60 percent to 11.00 percent.

The financial analyst then used a personal computer to prepare a spreadsheet comparison of the alternatives, using the 2- through 5-year quotations. The loan was assumed to be USD 125 million subject to semiannual amortization or 6-month LIBOR interest period rate settings. The notional amount of the swaps, caps, and collars was assumed to be the same as the loan amount assumption. The loan agreement was still being negotiated, but the worst-case margin seemed to be 1.75 percent over LIBOR and the amount of the loan was now assumed to be USD 125 million. The spreadsheets became long and unwieldy, but the president and treasurer could see everything they had requested.

The president was at first inclined to purchase a 5-year cap for around USD 4 million. The treasurer and financial analyst thought the company should hold on to its cash because its reserve for contingencies would be very small until at least a year after the merger. The treasurer reminded the financial analyst that the company might not have enough cash to survive maintenance margin if it hedged using Eurodollar futures contracts. The 6 percent/8 percent collar idea was abandoned because the collar did not fit prevailing rates; the 8 percent top of the collar was less than the swap rates. The company would be paying the counterparty to the collar from day 1; the large bank said it didn't write collars structured that way. The financial analyst pulled out historic data of interest rates and explored the probability of LIBOR rates being at various levels, hoping to determine whether a cap or collar—and at what level—was probably the best value for the company. The president and treasurer continued arguing about the cash flow forecast, contingencies, and the cost of caps and collars.

Meanwhile, interest rates started to go up. In 3 weeks, indicative swap rates had increased about 10 basis points ($^{1}/_{10}$ of a percent). The federal budget and the U.S. Treasury Bill and Note rates were becoming worrisome. The lending bank nagged at the president to find out what plan the company was adopting to protect the interest rate risk. The large bank decided that it could not extend credit for a swap; it was willing to consider a 2- or 3-year

Table 9.6 Updated Quotations, Caps, and Collars in Basis Points

Years	Swap	8.5% Cap	9% Cap	9.5% Cap	7%/9% Collar
2	8.34%	114bp	89bp	68bp	73bp
3	8.61	222	179	147	150
4	8.80	325	268	225	223
5	8.96	419	356	304	280

collar and would, of course, write caps. The financial analyst asked for updated quotations and mentioned that the notional amount was now USD 125 million instead of USD 140 million. The trader commented: "I'll let you compute this stuff yourself, in case they change the amount again." The trader sent a fax that looked different (see Table 9.6).

To compute the dollar cost in millions, the financial analyst had to multiply the basis points times the USD 125 million notional principal amount of the swap. For example, the 5-year 9.5 percent cap on a notional amount of USD 125 million was now 304 basis points or 3.04 percent (.0304) × 125 million or USD 3.800 million. The 5-year 9.5 percent cap cost 3 weeks earlier had been quoted as USD 4.070 million, but that had been computed on notional USD 140 million and was actually lower, 291 basis points (USD 4.070 million ÷ USD 140 million). Converting the dollar quotations in Table 9.5 to basis points for comparison to the updated quotations resulted in the data shown in Table 9.7.

As interest rates began to increase, the volatility factor in the premiums increased, as did the probability that the bank might have to make cash settlements to the company in the earlier periods of the contracts. The company decided against dedicating any cash to cap premiums. Also, the company decided to use swaps instead of a collar for the interest rate protection because, in the treasurer's opinion, the contracts could more easily be "unwound" than a collar.

Table 9.7 Comparison of Cap and Collar Basis Point Quotations

Year of Quotes	Swap Old/New	8.5% Cap Old/New	9% Cap Old/New	9.5% Cap Old/New	7%/9% Old/New
2	8.19/8.34	104/114	81/89	64/68	136/73
3	8.42/8.61	210/222	171/179	151/147	251/150
4	8.65/8.80	307/325	257/268	216/225	355/233
5	8.80/8.96	400/419	340/356	291/304	454/280

THE FUND FOR RICH COUNTRY

In the area of zero coupon interest rate swaps, the annals of financial engineering are replete with experiments. The following brief study describes the alternatives explored to allocate and invest sufficient funds for a future project's expenditures. A related problem was to eliminate the risk that interim investment interest income would be reinvested at lower rates than desired. Another variation of the zero coupon interest rate swap accelerates the payment of the fixed rate payments in order to increase operating income.

A capital markets specialist with a bank received an interesting request from the chief portfolio manager of an oil-producing country. The country had accumulated investable funds that were channeled through The Fund for Rich Country ("The Fund"). The Fund had many portfolios with a variety of objectives: long-term investments or for specific public purposes such as educational facilities, health care, social security, and infrastructure. Most of the country's receipts for sales of crude oil were in U.S. Dollars, and The Fund's portfolios were largely U.S. Dollar-denominated.

The portfolio manager informed the bank's specialist that The Fund needed to finance a project, tentatively scheduled about 8 years in the future, that would require about USD 35 million—the escalated future amount. The problem to be resolved: what amount should The Fund allocate today to investments, to ensure available funding for most of the project costs 8 years in the future? The Fund was conservative in its selection of investments. It hoped to invest less than USD 20 million in the project. The portfolio manager hoped to decrease the initial investment for the project's funding by an increase in the investment's interim 8 years' yield. A judicious increase in yield could reduce the initial principal amount dedicated for the project's funding.

Rather than buy fixed interest rate bonds to fund the obligation, the portfolio manager was considering a more complex transaction to earn a higher yield. The Fund could buy "at par" (1.00) a U.S. Dollar *Eurobond* with a 7-year maturity and an 8.10 percent interest coupon. The portfolio manager was concerned about a possible decline in U.S. interest rates during the life of the investment, with the resulting *reinvestment risk*. Although The Fund would continue to earn the 8.10 percent coupon over the life of the bond, the interest from the coupon payments might earn less than 8.10 percent if interest rates fell. Further, if the *yield curve* had a positive slope, the total yield on the invested funds would be less than the Fund's projected *yield to maturity*.

In a normal environment, shorter-term interest rates are lower than longer-term interest rates. To achieve the fund's indicated yield to maturity on the investment, the portfolio manager would need to be able to reinvest each interest coupon payment at the same 8.10 percent interest rates. Because shorter-term interest rates are lower in a normal environment, each coupon payment received would be reinvested at progressively lower rates. Therefore, the actual yield on the funds invested would be lower than the projected yield at the time of investment. The portfolio manager's opinion was that U.S. interest rates would indeed decline in coming months, and perhaps over the next 2 to 3 years, because the U.S. economy was increasingly stagnant.

The portfolio manager had considered another type of investment—a "spread over LIBOR"—that would mature in 8 years and pay 3-month LIBOR plus 1/2 percent. The risk of interest rates' declining also made this floating rate asset unappetizing to The Fund.

The bank's capital market specialist suggested that The Fund purchase a zero coupon issue with a maturity 8 years later. *Stripped* U.S. Treasury securities were the only paper that might be available with both sufficient quantity and credit quality to be acceptable to The Fund. The portfolio manager had already explored that alternative, but the only suitable issue available yielded 7.25 percent. Accepting this alternative would require The Fund's initial investment of nearly USD 20 million, more than The Fund was hoping to allocate for funding the particular project.

The capital markets specialists suggested that The Fund and bank explore an *interest rate swap*. The Fund would buy the floating rate Eurobond with the 1/2 percent spread over LIBOR. The Fund could then enter into an interest rate swap to pay the LIBOR and receive its desired fixed rate. The Fund would continue to receive the Euronotes' floating rate interest plus 1/2 percent spread. With these transactions, The Fund could increase its yield and still protect against the risk of interim declines in short-term interest rates during the 8 years. The portfolio manager rejected the proposed interest rate swap because The Fund would continue to have a reinvestment risk on the swap's fixed rate receipts. The portfolio manager was, however, willing to accept the reinvestment risk on the amount represented by the Euronotes' 1/2 percent spread over LIBOR.

The portfolio manager then asked whether the bank's capital markets specialist could arrange for The Fund to enter into a zero coupon interest rate swap. The objective was to eliminate the reinvestment risk of the floating rate receipts. The Fund would pay 3-month LIBOR. In the swap, The Fund would accrue the bank's obligation to pay, only at maturity, 8 percent interest on the initial notional amount of the swap. An 8.00 percent yield indicated that the notional amount of the swap would be equal to about USD 18.9 million, computed as follows:

$$USD\ 18,910,500 = USD\ 35,000,000 \times [1/(1.08^8)]$$
$$= 1/1.850930 = .5403\ (rounded)\ or$$
$$= USD\ 35,000,000 \times 0.5403.$$

The portfolio manager proposed that the bank would enter into an interest rate swap to receive quarterly from The Fund cash payments equal to 3-month LIBOR on the notional amount of USD 18.9 million. In exchange, The Fund would accrue interest at 8.00 percent for 8 years on the notional amount. At the end of 8 years, the bank would make a payment to The Fund of USD 16,082,580.97, computed as follows:

$$\text{USD } 16,082,580 = \text{USD } 18,900,000 \times [(1.08^8) - 1]$$

]The USD 16.083 million plus the maximum USD 18.910 million that The Fund would receive from the maturing Euronotes would about equal the USD 35 million needed in 8 years. The Fund would eliminate reinvestment risk on any interest payments except for the $1/2$ percent spread over LIBOR that the Fund would receive on the floating rate Euronotes.

The capital markets specialist proposed the zero coupon interest rate swap to the bank's swap trader, who had never done a zero coupon swap. The trader checked with the bank's in-house tax counsel, who advised that the proposed swap could entail some tax problems. Under the proposed deal, the bank would receive from The Fund a cash payment every quarter for 8 years. Against those payments, the bank would accrue interest expense that was payable only on the maturity of the swap. The tax counsel deemed it likely that the Internal Revenue Service (IRS) would rule that the fixed rate accrual could not be treated as expense for tax purposes until 8 years later, when the payment was actually made. The bank might have to pay income tax on the quarterly interest payments as received from The Fund, but might not receive any offsetting tax benefit for 8 years, until it actually made payment under the swap.

The tax counsel offered to ask the IRS for a ruling on the proposed swap but thought the IRS would take months to study such a problem and to issue a ruling. The bank could adjust downward the fixed rate side of the swap to compensate for a potential tax liability on the gross amount of its swap receipts. However, the lower fixed rate would significantly reduce the yield to The Fund and would make the transaction unattractive. Although the zero coupon interest rate swap seemed a clever form of financial engineering, one bank's view of the potential tax issue "nixed the deal."

APPENDIX

The formula used in the markets, for calculating interest yield on a fully hedged transaction, is as follows:

European terms

Foreign currency interest rate
$$I_{FX} = [(F/S) - 1] \times [(360/T) + I_{US}) + I_{US}$$

U.S. Dollar interest rate
$$I_{US} = [(S \times T \times I_{FX}) - (360 \times F) + I_{US}]/(F \times T)$$

American terms

Foreign currency interest rate
$$I_{FX} = [(S/F) - 1] \times [(360/T) + I_{US}] + I_{US}$$

U.S. Dollar interest rate
$$I_{US} = (F \times I_{FX}/S) - (360/T) + [(360 \times F)/(T \times S)]$$

where: I_{US} = U.S. Dollar interest rate
I_{FX} = foreign currency interest rate
S = spot foreign exchange rate
F = forward outright exchange rate
T = term or number of days.

Note that this formula assumes a 360-day year for interest rates. In the case of Sterling or domestic Canadian or domestic Australian instruments or any other currency or instrument that uses a 365-day formula, adjustments to both the interest rates used or calculated and/or the formula are needed. It is difficult to give a simple example because each situation may require a slightly different manipulation.

Compare the formula above for currencies quoted in American terms with the formula usually found in finance textbooks:

$$I_{US} = I_{FX} + \{[360 \times (F - S)]/(S \times T)\}$$

The formula used in the markets is more complex because it takes into account cash flows generated by interest rate differentials. The textbook formula is used only for illustrative purposes, to show the relationship in teaching situations.

These formulas in European and American terms can be used to calculate the interest yield on a fully hedged transaction or, if both interest rates are known, the forward points from a spot rate of exchange can be calculated. The following are examples of computations.

European terms

I^{US} = 4.25%, .0425
I^{DEM} = 9.50, .0950; this is the IFX in this example, Deutsche Marks

[Note that both the Eurodollar and Eurocurrency Interest rates are 360-day basis.]
S = DEM/USD 1.5975 Spot rate of exchange
F = Forward outright exchange rate to be computed
T = 182

$.0950 = (F/1.5975 - 1) \times (360/182 + .0425) + .0425$
$.0950 = (F/1.5975 - 1) \times (1.978022 + .0425) + .0425$
$.0950 = (F/1.5975 - 1) \times (2.020522) + .0425$
$.0950 = 2.020522F/1.5975 - 2.020522 + .0425$
$.0950 = 2.020522F/1.5975 - 1.978022$
$1.978022 + .0950 = 2.020522F/1.5975$
$2.073022 = 2.202522F/1.5975$
$3.311653 = 2.020522F$
$F = 1.639008$, the forward outright exchange rate

The forward points $(P) = F - S$, so
$1.639008 - 1.5975 = .041508$.
The forward points or "pips" are $+415$.

Please note that the forward points are positive.

American terms

[The numbers in this example are for the case of Jolly Jeans, in Chapter 8.]
$I^{US} = 8.00\%, .08$
$I^{DEM} = 14.50\%, .1450; .1450 \times 360/365 = .1430137$, rounded to $.143014$

[If the foreign currency interest rates are quoted on 365-day basis, the rate is converted to 360-day basis; for example, Pounds Sterling.]

$S = USD/GBP\ 1.7000$ spot rate of exchange
$F =$ Forward outright exchange rate to be computed
$T = 365$ days, one year
$.143014 = (1.7000/F - 1) \times (360/365 - .08) + .08$
$.143014 = (1.7000/F - 1) \times (.9863 + .08) + .08$
$.143014 = (1.7000/F - 1) \times (1.066300) + .08$
$.143014 = 1.81271/F - .9863$
$.9863 + .143014 = 1.81271/F$
$1.129314 = 1.81271/F$
$1.129314F = 1.81271$
$F = 1.605143$

The forward points $(P) = F - S$, so
$1.605143 - 1.7000 = -.094857$.
The forward points or "pips" are -949.

Please note that the forward points are negative.

10
Commodity Price Risk

In commodities, there's a big enough paddle for anyone.

Anonymous because no one will admit to saying it.

CONCEPTS, CONTRACTS, AND PRICES

The commodity derivatives market has much to thank Saddam Hussein for . . . . "Commodity price risk management is now a fact of life." . . . The war boosted the commodity derivatives market by triggering massive, highly visible volatility in the prices of crude oils and refined oil products.[1]

Producers of a commodity are in a natural long position—they are producing a commodity to sell. Processors or manufacturers using a commodity are in a natural short position—they need to buy a commodity. Because merchants commit to buy from producers and sell to consumers, they have no "natural" long or short position; their position is long, short, or balanced, depending on the status of their contracts. For example, if a merchant's purchase commitments, plus any inventory, total more of a commodity than the merchant has sold, the merchant is long. If the merchant has sold more of a commodity than the total of the merchant's purchase commitments, plus any inventory, the merchant is short. Producers, merchants, processors, and manufacturers try to transfer price risk to each other and to wholesalers and retail consumers. Their lending banks are confronted with the issue of their price risk management. A metropolitan rapid transit district recently joined the march to transfer commodity price risk by committing to a 1-year diesel fuel price swap to fix the fuel cost for buses.[2]

The first objective when contracting for physical delivery of commodities is to set the terms for purchase and physical delivery. Provisions for price risk management are not typically included. Processors and manufacturers often need to buy a commodity that has exact specifications and is to be delivered at a particular delivery location. Thus, many users of commodities need to tailor their physical delivery contracts in the cash or forward market with merchants or producers instead of taking delivery through the futures market or using an *exchange of future for physical (EFP)* or options. Merchants can offer both producers and consumers forward contracts and can transfer their own risk through either the futures market or the forward market. Merchants do not have to match almost simultaneously each purchase from a producer with a sale to a processor or manufacturer. The "planned" economies of Eastern Europe and the former Soviet Union offer a vivid comparison. Supplies and prices may sometimes lurch, but there are rarely long-term shortages in the United States.

All this seems straightforward, BUT a lot of things can complicate the business situation for commodities. Techniques for commodity price risk management cannot solve the physical production and delivery problems inherent to any commodity. Within each commodity sector, there are many variations of quality, grade, storage, and delivery points; the interbank currency market is tidy by comparison. Weather affects agriculture and livestock prices; livestock can get sick. Problems of underground geology can be a business risk to metals and petroleum companies. Bobbing and weaving because of the weather, the ups and downs of supply and demand, and the risks peculiar to each commodity, the producers, processors, manufacturers, and merchants in commodities include some of the more experienced financial engineers.

The purpose for a commodity contract that does not anticipate physical delivery can be speculation, *arbitrage,* or *hedging,* price risk management. This book is not about speculation, except to suggest that the absence of management of corporate financial risk is speculation. Arbitrage is sometimes confused with spread trading and hedging. The purpose of arbitrage is to obtain riskless profit (because of a difference in prices) by a simultaneous purchase and sale in different markets or time periods. Arbitrage is not financial risk management.

Comparing prices of a commodity usually discloses "basis" of all types. "Basis" or "differential" is usually defined as the cash market price minus the forward or futures price. In commodities, there is often a difference between

---

[2] "Case History: A Fuel Price Swap in the Public Interest," Banque Paribas advertisement, *The Economist* (London), May 4, 1991, p. 73.

the forward and futures price for the same delivery time because of differences between delivery locations and/or the quality or grade of the commodity. There is only one grade of Deutsche Mark, but there are many grades of oil, wheat, and other commodities.

A "price to be fixed" or "price fixation contract" or a "to be priced" contract is a forward contract for a commodity—with physical delivery—usually with the forward price referenced to a delivery month's futures contract price, sometimes with a premium or discount as appropriate. The contract may be arranged so that the seller/buyer of the commodity selects the price for all or a certain quantity under the forward contract on any day's trading of the relevant futures contract. The seller/buyer thus controls the price to be received. At the moment the seller/buyer selects a price, the buyer/seller knows its purchase price—the cost of its long or short forward position. The price risk has been transferred, and the price that may be subject to financial risk management is known.

The commodity price swap and *over-the-counter* (OTC) derivative contracts usually use an average of daily prices for the commodity as the floating *reference price*. To illustrate, let's compare the floating reference price of an interest rate swap with the floating "average price" for a *commodity price swap.* (Note that we are speaking of price swaps, not physical swaps.) An interest rate swap of fixed to 3-month LIBOR (see Chapter 9) references the 3-month LIBOR rate on the business day at the beginning of each 3-month interest period. On that day, the next interest period's rate for the *underlying* loan is established. By comparison, underlying commodity prices are usually subject to change every business day. The commodity price swap may, therefore, use an average of the daily prices for the underlying, thus swapping a fixed price, for example, to the average of daily prices over a 3-month period for quarterly cash settlement. The daily price may be referenced to cash or futures prices for the commodity. (The study in the next section gives a specific example using crude oil.) These swaps and OTC derivatives are sometimes called "average price" contracts: an *average price option (APO)* is an example of the term's application.

The swaps and OTC commodity derivative market grew throughout the 1980s.

> While West Texas Intermediate (WTI)—the benchmark crude oil price—continues to account for a large volume of transactions, the market has extended to other underlying commodities. Corporates can readily hedge several other fuel products such as natural gas, bunker fuel and jet fuel; a number of transactions have also been linked to precious metals, base metals, and soft commodities.[3]

---

[3] "Growing Pains of Commodity Swaps," *Corporate Finance* (London), no. 76 (March 1991): 9.

Crude oil, petroleum products, and natural gas are the most mature markets for commodity price swaps and OTC average price derivative contracts. Agriculture, by comparison, is the most mature market for physical swaps.

> The armoury of over-the-counter risk management exotica—caps, collars, floor, swaptions, structured options—is being turned by banks on the world's fragmented and highly volatile commodity markets.[4]

Derivative contracts can be arranged for margins. Oil refiners can arrange a contract guaranteeing the differential between crude oil and the refined products.[5]

As newcomers incur the risks of writing commodity price contracts, the merchants and securities houses in the spot, forward, and futures markets will be waiting for them when they try to hedge those risks. One quiet afternoon in 1991, the June 1993 crude oil futures contract was driven down 30 cents a barrel while other contracts traded unchanged. Someone seeking the perfect hedge kept selling the contract, and buyers waiting in the weeds kept knocking down the price. Trading in the New York Mercantile Exchange (NYMEX) longer dated crude oil futures contracts has "mushroomed" in the past two years.[6] The increased activity in longer dated commodity futures contracts is sometimes attributed to writers of swaps and commodity derivatives who are hedging their positions.[7]

As commodity price risk management becomes more frequently used by producers and consumers of companies that are publicly held, shareholders' performance expectations may become an issue. (This issue is detailed later in the chapter, in the discussion of gold loans.) If a company fixes or caps an important element of its income or expenses, the company's profits may not fluctuate as expected by equity investors who have seen the important commodity's price fluctuations.

Financial engineering for commodities would easily fill another book. This chapter's discussions present basic concepts and contracts and compare the structures with those presented in other business studies.

CRANKCASE CRUDE OIL COMPANY

Commodity price swaps, OTC derivatives, futures, and exchange-traded options are all covered in this study, which describes the process of a company

---

[4] "The Bandwagon Starts to Roll," *Euromoney* (May 1990): 87.
[5] S. Butler, "Oil Traders Devise Strategies for the 21st Century," Commodities and Agriculture, *Financial Times* (London), May 25, 1990, p. 38.
[6] *Id.*
[7] *Id.* at 92.

"gearing up" to define and administer a policy for commodity price risk management. The study also reviews some of the commodity price risk management alternatives for a producer, using crude oil as the commodity.

Business Risk Situation

Crankcase Crude Oil Co. ("Cranky Crude") has both domestic and Brent crude oil production. For discussion purposes, the quantities and production profiles have been simplified. The domestic production is constant at about 100,000 barrels per month, net of royalties and adjusted to WTI standard (see the previous section). The company is periodically allocated a crude oil cargo shipment from its interest in a North Sea crude oil field. It receives a cargo to sell every third month, except in winter when violent North Sea wind and weather slow ships' loading and may interrupt production.

The Brent crude oil had been sold under 1-year contract at floating reference price to a creditworthy counterparty. The domestic production is sold under *evergreen contracts* with 60 days' notice to terminate. Because Cranky's heavy, sour crude oil had a limited market to a few refiners, Cranky's production, marketing, and finance groups agreed that they did not want to break the "wet barrel" contracts. Some of the oil revenue was dedicated to a bank loan secured by the property's production. The issue was how to prevent the floating price's sinking to financially undesirable levels. The lending bank was concerned that the receipts be sufficient to cover interest on the loan and provide repayment of principal.

Cranky had never arranged a price protection contract for any of its crude oil. For many years, the company's management and board shared the view that, despite occasional price volatility, eventually crude oil prices would go and stay up, not go and stay down. In 1989, however, Cranky Crude's management was concerned that crude oil prices were peaking at about USD 16.00 per barrel for Brent crude oil and about USD 17.50 for West Texas Intermediate (WTI) sweet crude oil. OPEC was overproducing. Everyone at Cranky remembered when WTI was about USD 10.00 per barrel in the spring of 1986.

How Much Underlying Commodity to Hedge?

The finance and production group set about defining and forecasting Cranky's crude oil receipts by category and by month for the remainder of the calendar year.

The domestic sweet crude oil, WTI grade, production totaled about 85,000 barrels per month, or about 2,500 barrels per day, but was subject to a $16^{2}/_{3}$ percent royalty and severance tax. Cranky's net crude oil receipts were therefore equivalent to about 70,000 barrels per month. The finance group reminded production that there was no sense hedging the crude oil price for royalties or severance taxes. Cranky's financial risk was only on its net receipts.

The bank loan, secured by some of the properties producing light, sweet crude oil, was a small, old loan requiring service from about 20,000 barrels per month of Cranky's net 70,000 barrels per month of WTI equivalent crude oil. Cranky had to pay 70 percent of its net revenue from these properties to the bank; the receipts were first dedicated to payment of interest and the balance was applied to principal. If the present and forecasted prices of the crude oil were too low, Cranky would have to pay a higher percentage of crude oil sales receipts to the bank. For example, in 1986, Cranky had had to pay 100 percent of the net revenue to the bank because the forecasted loan value of the properties fell when crude oil prices "fell out of bed"—and worse, Cranky had had to make an additional prepayment of principal to prevent default.

After adjusting the heavy, sour crude oil to a price equivalent to that of the light, sweet crude oil, a factor of 60 percent was assigned. Each barrel of heavy, sour crude oil was only 60 percent equivalent in price to a light, sweet barrel of crude oil. For example, if WTI were selling for USD 18.00 per barrel, the heavy, sour crude sold for about USD 10.80 per barrel after being adjusted to gravity and grade, including sulphur content. Cranky's 30,000 barrels per month of heavy, sour crude oil was equivalent to 18,000 barrels per month of WTI crude oil.

The Brent crude oil production was light, sweet crude oil of a grade deliverable under the NYMEX WTI crude oil futures contract. This crude oil was not subject to royalties. The Brent/WTI differential varied, but Cranky figured that Brent usually sold about USD 1.00 to 1.50 less than WTI. The differential theoretically was attributable to transportation from the North Sea to the delivery location of the NYMEX WTI futures contract. Brokers had often contacted Cranky about trading on this differential, but Cranky had never participated in such transactions. Each cargo was about 350,000 barrels WTI equivalent. Cranky received a cargo about every third month from May through November, and one additional cargo sometime during the 5-month winter period, depending on the weather. The production management was very concerned that finance understand that the Brent oil could not be sold in the forward market because production could not guarantee delivery in any month or to any production and shipping forecast. The "wet barrels" of production had been sold through year-end. Because of production risks, any short- or long-term price risk management contracts had to be "dry barrel" (or "paper barrel") contracts.

Finance documented the monthly cargo shipping forecasts. Even in warm weather, the shipping schedule often slipped 20 to 30 days each month. For example, in May, Cranky was forecasted to receive a cargo in mid-July; by June, the forecast for the same cargo's receipt was early or even mid-August. The problem was worse in the winter, when subsea chains tended to break and other unforeseeable results of high waves and winds at sea occurred. Finance thought that splitting the cargo receipts between the month forecasted and the next month would cover the contingency of the production and shipping schedule's slippage. The vice president of production was convinced that the shipping schedule could be better controlled. The production staff and marketing pointed out that the weather and production difficulties, and therefore scheduling problems, would probably never change.

In summary, Cranky Crude's crude oil production to be hedged, in barrels per month (bbls/mo), looked like this:

Domestic: 70,000 bbls/mo light sweet

             18,000 bbls/mo WTI equivalent

             88,000 bbls/mo WTI to hedge

Note: 20,000 bbls/mo = collateral for bank loan.

Brent: 350,000 bbls WTI equivalent per cargo, subject to the shipping schedule.

In March, the production department forecasted quantities by month for the rest of the year. The finance group split the cargo quantities across 2 months, trying to allow for slippage in shipping.

The marketing department suggested that, because no one knew when Cranky's share of the Brent would be delivered, why not just spread it evenly across the months? Production and finance thought the simplistic approach of an equal number of barrels per month invited too much time basis risk, especially if the production were equally allocated to the worst winter months of January through March or early April. Cranky would be hedging price on too many barrels for the peak of winter and too few barrels in summer. Nonetheless, a third forecast, assuming four 350,000-bbl cargoes per year (about 117,000 bbls per month) was prepared. Table 10.1 compares the forecasts.

Pegging Cranky's cargoes into delivery pigeonholes was not promising of forecast reliability.

Alternatives

Cranky had been repeatedly contacted by companies selling crude oil price protection contracts—swaps, floors, and range forwards— to crude oil producers. One commodity trading company even invited Cranky's marketer to a black-tie party in New York, to meet participants in the oil swap and OTC derivatives markets. Cranky lived up to its nickname and did not attend. Cranky's finance group, concerned about the host company's financial strength, started a review of the business reputation and credit of companies writing OTC crude oil price contracts. NYMEX WTI crude oil futures or

Table 10.1 Comparative Forecasts of Crude Oil Deliveries,
in Thousands of Barrels per Month

	Domestic	Brent	Total
Production Department			
April	88	—	88
May	88	350	438
June	88	—	88
July	88	—	88
August	88	350	438
September	88	—	88
October	88	—	88
November	88	350	438
December	88	—	88
	792	1,050	1,842
Finance Department			
April	88	—	88
May	88	175	263
June	88	175	263
July	88	—	88
August	88	175	263
September	88	175	263
October	88	—	88
November	88	175	263
December	88	175	263
	792	1,050	1,842
Marketing Department			
April	88	117	205
May	88	117	205
June	88	116	204
July	88	117	205
August	88	117	205
September	88	116	204
October	88	117	205
November	88	117	205
December	88	116	204
	792	1,050	1,842

options contracts might offer liquidity and no counterparty credit risk. A group from production, the head marketer, and the finance group prepared for Cranky's executive committee a summary of the contracts and obtained some indication quotations for examples.

Forward contracts were dismissed both because of the existing sales contracts and, in general, because production convinced everyone that Cranky did not have enough cargoes or production to play in a market trading 600,000-barrel cargoes.

A commodity price swap or average price floor option, or a range forward or collar contract, could be compared as follows. Cash settlement could be made monthly, quarterly, semiannually, or at the end of the contract period. Cranky had not yet resolved the issues of what reference price and contract term to select. A writer of commodity price swaps and OTC derivative contracts offered to help with indicative quotations. The indicative quotations on a specific date assumed quarterly cash settlement and volumes not exceeding 1 million barrels in total; West Texas Intermediate crude oil was the reference commodity, but the writer was prepared to quote reference Brent crude oil, if Cranky so requested.

A commodity price swap would fix a price for the crude oil. If the average of the reference prices was less than the swap price, Cranky would be paid the difference by the counterparty. If the average of the reference prices was more than the swap price, Cranky would pay the difference to the counterparty. Cranky received indication quotations for WTI crude oil swaps of 3, 6, and 12 months for USD 17.50, USD 17.25, and USD 16.80 respectively. Suppose Cranky bought a 6-month price swap at 17.25 with a quarterly settlement. If the average price for the first 3 months was 17.00, at the end of the first 3 months the counterparty would pay Cranky USD .25 per barrel for the *notional* "dry/paper barrels" of the contract (USD 25,000 for a 100,000-barrel notional contract). If the average price for the second 3-month period was USD 17.35 per barrel, Cranky would pay the counterparty USD .10 per barrel on the 100,000 notional barrels, or USD 10,000. Cranky would continue to sell its "wet barrels" under its existing crude oil sales contracts.

An average price option (APO) would put a "floor" under Cranky's crude oil price. (The opposite contract for a purchaser instead of a producer of crude oil would be an APO "ceiling" or "cap" on the cost of crude oil.) Cranky would pay a premium to the writer of the average price floor option. If the average of the reference price for crude oil was less than the option's strike level, Cranky would receive payment from the option writer. If the average of the reference price for crude oil was more than the option's strike level, Cranky would not have to pay and would receive 100 percent of the price increase. Indication premiums for price floors were quoted as shown in Table 10.2.

Suppose Cranky purchased a 6-month USD 16.50/bbl option for 100,000 barrels. The cost would be USD 74,000. If the average price for the

Table 10.2 Quotations for Price Floors

Maturity	Strike Price (USD/bbl)			
(Months)	17.00	16.50	16.00	15.00
3	0.49	0.32	0.20	0.13
6	0.96	0.74	0.54	0.42
12	1.50	1.26	1.08	0.89

first 3 months was 16.25, at the end of the first 3 months the counterparty would pay Cranky USD .25 per barrel for the notional "dry/paper barrels" of the contract (USD 25,000 for a 100,000-barrel notional contract). If the average price for the second 3-month period was USD 16.95 per barrel, no cash settlement would occur because the average price was higher than the strike price of Cranky's floor. Cranky would continue to sell its "wet barrels" under its existing crude oil sales contracts.

A range forward or price collar would put a floor under and ceiling over Cranky's crude oil price. Cranky would be paid if the average price was less than the floor; Cranky would pay if the average price was more than the ceiling.

A "participating range forward" could be constructed to give Cranky some percentage of participation, if the average of reference prices was higher than the ceiling. Cranky would not give up all the upside, as happens in a swap or above the ceiling of the range forward. Cranky's premium would increase for increased upside participation. Quotations for range forwards with 2:1 floor ceiling ratios were as shown in Table 10.3.

For example, Cranky could buy a 6-month, 14.50/17.60, 2:1 range forward for 100,000 barrels at USD .32 per barrel, at a total cost of USD 32,000; if the average price for the first quarter was USD 14.25, at the end of

Table 10.3 Quotations for 2:1 Range Forwards (in USD/bbl)

Maturity (Months)	Floor	Ceiling	Premium
3	14.50	17.20	0.12
	14.00	17.60	0.09
6	14.50	17.60	0.32
	14.00	16.60	0.25
12	14.50	15.30	0.55
	14.00	15.75	0.45

the quarter Cranky would receive USD 25,000. If the average price for the second quarter was USD 18.00, Cranky would pay USD 20,000:

$$100,000 \text{ notional "dry/paper barrels"} \times \text{USD } 18.00 - \text{USD } 17.60$$
$$\text{ceiling} = \text{USD } 40,000 \div 2 = \text{USD } 20,000$$

Cranky would buy 100 percent protection below the floor and give up only 50 percent of the upside above the ceiling.

Exchange-traded futures contracts were another alternative for crude oil price protection. The crude oil price could be fixed by selling NYMEX futures contracts for each month to be price-protected. The gain or loss in the futures market would offset the loss or gain on Cranky's cash market sales of crude oil. The logic is that, if NYMEX crude oil traded above Cranky's futures sales price, the money Cranky lost on the futures contract would be offset by the money it made on the sale of the physical oil during the same period. If NYMEX crude oil traded below Cranky's futures sales price, Cranky could cover its short futures position at a profit that would offset the lower price on the sale of its physical oil. Futures contracts for Brent crude oil are traded on London's International Petroleum Exchange (IPE). Cranky could arrange deals on either the NYMEX or the IPE, or on both.

Cranky could purchase either NYMEX WTI or IPE Brent exchange-traded put option contracts, or both, for some or all of its future production. If crude oil traded below the put option strike price(s), Cranky could sell the option(s) at a profit. The exchange-traded option premium was similar to the premium for the OTC average price options—each premium bought price insurance.

Creating a "fence" from exchange-traded option contracts would limit Cranky's participation in a favorable price move but would reduce the cost of the premiums for protection against unfavorable price moves. A fence (writing call options and buying put options) is comparable to an OTC range forward contract. The NYMEX trades 12 months of crude oil options contracts. Arranging a longer-term fence would require contracting for an OTC range forward contract whether as a "bundled" contract or by buying an APO floor contract and writing an APO ceiling contract.

Another straightforward alternative was selling futures contracts and buying call options—a "synthetic put." If the price of crude oil futures went up instead of down, profit on the call options would protect against some of the loss on the short futures position. Suppose Cranky shorted one May contract at USD 18.00/bbl and purchased one May 19 call at .10 and held the option to its last trading day; these examples assume the option has zero *time value*. Cranky has a USD 1.00 difference between the futures sales price of 18.00 and the call strike of 19.00, plus USD .10 for the call premium, for a total of USD 1.10. If, on the last trading day of the option contract, May crude oil traded at USD 17.00 per barrel, Cranky could profit USD 1.00 on the futures contract minus .10 cost of the call option, which would have zero intrinsic and time value, for net .90/bbl times 1,000 bbls per contract. If May crude oil traded at USD 20.50 per barrel, Cranky could lose USD 2.50/bbl on the futures contract, minus 1.50/bbl intrinsic value on the May 19 call, plus the .10/bbl cost of the call, for a net loss of USD 1.10/bbl, but could gain 1.50 intrinsic value on the call option for a net profit of .40/bbl on the synthetic put.

For Cranky, there were complications to the simple concepts. Cranky did not have unlimited cash reserves; finance had not yet analyzed the cash margin requirements to maintain open futures contract positions. No one had yet discussed the credit requirements for an OTC swap or range forward contract. Cranky's finance manager did not want to begin the company's first crude oil price protection program by writing either OTC or exchange-traded options. Cranky's volume of oil changed each month, although the domestic production for the rest of the year was reasonably assumed to be constant. Cranky had both WTI and Brent crude oil. Which reference price should be used, WTI or Brent? Cranky's domestic production was too small for a separate swap or OTC option contract. A swap or OTC option could be written for up to 5 years. What period of time should Cranky select? Cranky was told that the OTC average price options could be written as either *European-style* or *American-style* options. Someone said the American-style options were called "NYMEX look-alikes." What were the advantages of an American-style? The European-style, which could be settled only at maturity, had a lower premium.

Cranky decided to "do something simple for a start."

Exchange-Traded Options

Cranky set an objective of protecting the price on the next 6 months' domestic crude oil production; the production was almost constant each month. The president and finance vice president did not think crude oil futures contracts were trading high enough to justify the risk of selling futures contracts. The president did not want to "give up the upside at these levels." The production vice president was nervous about futures contracts in general and about their administration. Why start off arguing about how the revenue budget would show money lost on futures being offset by gains in the cash market price? Decisions on longer-term price protection arrangements, counterparty credit risk, and the Brent crude oil price risk management could be postponed until finance had done more research.

The petroleum engineers turned to the question raised by the production vice president: "How much should we spend for the NYMEX put options?" For a small fee, a commodities broker provided option-pricing computer software. The engineers turned on their personal computers; 2 weeks later, they were still immersed in volatilities. The spot (cash market), forward, and futures prices of crude oil had moved up after Cranky first starting taking indicative quotations, but in the most recent 2 weeks, spot crude oil had again drifted down USD 1.00 per barrel. No one could decide what Cranky "should" spend for put options. "As little as possible" was not helpful. The analytic stalemate was defeating the objective of promptly obtaining some price protection.

Finance breached the impasse by suggesting that the put option premiums should be viewed like insurance premiums. The corporate financial risk from crude oil prices was analogous to the corporate risks being insured by the risk management group. Using NYMEX put options, the last 6 months of the year could be price-protected as follows:

Production month	May	Jun	Jul	Aug	Sep	Oct
NYMEX option month	Jun	Jul	Aug	Sep	Oct	Nov
Strike USD/bbl	20	19	18	18	18	18
NYMEX premium and fees	.25	.35	.40	.50	.55	.58

The premium and fees were based on current market quotations plus broker's commission and exchange fees.

Cranky would purchase 88 NYMEX put option contracts for each of the 6 months. Each put option contract was for 1,000 barrels; thus, Cranky's 88,000 barrels per month of domestic production would have price protection at the put options' strike prices. The total cost of the price protection, using the above estimates from then market prices, would be USD 231,400 or about USD .44/bbl for the 528,000 barrels. The weighted average strike price was USD 18.50/bbl; the current market price was about USD 21.00 per barrel; the put option "insurance" would cost about 2.38 percent of the prices.

Finance and marketing explained to production and the executive committee that the NYMEX options expired before the same contract month's future contract. The future contract expired before the beginning of the delivery month; its expiration coincided with the deadline set by the delivery location for nominating shipment of oil during the delivery month. Simply put, the price protection for July production would be the August futures contract, which expires in late July, and the option, which expires in mid-July.

The production vice president's next question was everyone's favorite: "How will we know when to sell the options?" The finance vice president growled, "Let's sell them all if we can make money." The production vice president retorted, "If they're insurance, I think we should hold them until the last day and then sell or let them expire." Crude oil futures prices stayed at or above the strike prices of the options. Cranky sold some options at a small loss and let other options expire. There was no big price drop to inflame the timing-of-sale argument between finance and production.

Commodity Price Swaps and OTC Derivatives

The finance group plodded through the brochures, sample contracts, and quotations provided by writers of commodity price swaps and OTC derivative contracts. Finally, Cranky Crude's executive committee decided it did not want to give up any opportunity to participate in favorable price moves: if crude oil went up, Cranky wanted 100 percent of the benefit. Cranky's refining affiliate had for the same reason avoided a commodity price swap; it wanted to participate in 100 percent of a favorable price move if crude oil went down in price. Cranky's finance group, therefore, proceeded to compare NYMEX, IPE, and OTC average price options for longer-term price protection of both the domestic and Brent crude oil.

Cranky's old loan on some of its domestic crude was, however, another matter. The loan related to 20,000 bbls per month of domestic WTI production or about 240,000 bbls per year. The production was forecasted to decrease about 15 percent per year. Finance telephoned around to see whether anyone would write a swap for a relatively small volume. Repayment for the loan was without recourse to Cranky Crude, and the company was reluctant to provide a corporate guarantee to secure its contingent payment obligations under a swap. The lending bank had provided all the domestic and international corporate and project financing that Cranky had needed for 15 years. The company did not want to jeopardize its long-term banking relationship by neglecting the problem loan, nor did it want to commit corporate funds to an option premium. The lending bank was willing to subordinate its right to repayment to contingent payment obligations under a swap or range forward contract that it approved. The lending bank was not involved in derivative or swap contracts for commodities, although it was active in these contracts for interest rates and currency exchange rates. By September 1990, events were heating up in the Middle East and crude oil prices were rising, but Cranky was having difficulty arranging credit. (See Chapter 12.) Swap counterparties wanted cash collateral marked-to-market daily, or a corporate guarantee, or a first security interest in the properties. Cranky is not big enough to satisfy such demands. Finally, the lending bank agreed to secure Cranky's contingent liability for payments under a commodity price swap with the bank's standby letter of credit, priced at a very low rate. A 3-year swap price of USD 22.80 per barrel substantially reduced the repayment risk on the loan. Cranky then contracted with the lending bank for a 3-year interest rate swap to minimize the risk of rising interest rates. In the fourth quarter of 1990's narrow time window of opportunity— with temporarily high crude oil prices and lower U.S. interest rates than had occurred in many years—the risk on the loan was substantially reduced and Cranky's favorable banking relationship was maintained. Starting the exercise on negotiating credit in late 1989 and early 1990 had enabled Cranky not to "miss the market."

When Cranky had closed the swaps, finance tried to relax for a day. Then the phone rang. A swaps and derivative dealer had a new product: Cranky could swap the risk of paying the bank's floating interest rates with the risk of floating the WTI oil price. The borrowing oil producer would receive a payment for the floating interest rate on the notional loan amount. But instead of paying a fixed interest rate (described in Chapter 9), the producer would pay the swap counterparty the WTI floating oil price. Finance thought the concept was quite interesting, but Cranky had already contracted hedges for the only loan it had that was suitable to the concept.

Meanwhile, by investigating swap and OTC derivative price risk management of crude oil, finance had accumulated an extensive array of comparative quotations. After its difficulties in arranging credit for the 3-year swap, options seemed Cranky's only choice. Cranky finally decided to request, from three writers of derivative commodity price contracts, simultaneous bids for average price options (APO) referenced to WTI for the constant volume of the next 6 months' 117,000 bbls per month of Brent production. Cranky's logic was that the APO premiums could be compared to the cost of purchasing NYMEX put options for the same production volumes and months. IPE put options were traded only for the next 3 months. Cranky was surprised at the spread in the "firm" dealing prices and went back to the drawing board.

Exchange-Traded Futures Contracts

The world and Cranky Crude watched crude oil prices moving up in the summer of 1990 as mobilization grew in the Middle East. By September 1990, the December 1990 and January 1991 NYMEX futures contracts were trading at over USD 36.00/bbl. The president told the production vice president to mind his own store—Cranky Crude wasn't going to miss selling oil at USD 36.00 per barrel! The finance vice president reminded the president that NYMEX margin requirements could turn the short futures position into a rich man's game if oil prices continued to increase another USD 10/bbl and war began. But Cranky had enough cash to sustain its planned futures positions even if oil went up another USD 15/bbl. The course was "full speed ahead."

In late September 1990, Cranky sold December 1990 crude oil NYMEX futures as follows:

	USD/bbl
Dec 90	36.75
Jan 91	36.25
Feb 91	34.00
Mar 91	32.50
Apr 91	31.50

The volumes covered the domestic production and a winter and spring cargo. The initial margin was USD 6,000 per contract. By November 30, 1990, the NYMEX margin for the "spot" month (January) had doubled to USD 12,000 per contract. The spot month's margin went up to USD 14,000 and the forward months' margins increased to USD 7,000. Meanwhile, the daily trading limit was continually increased. The exchange started with the concept that if the first-day limit of USD 1.00/bbl was reached, day 2's limit would be USD 1.50/bbl, day 3's limit, USD 2.00, and day 4's limit, USD 3.00. The crude oil market became more volatile. Before Iraq's invasion of Kuwait, the short-term volatility of crude oil prices was about 30 percent; it peaked at 200 percent. Some computerized option pricing models only worked with two-digit volatilities; thus, some option traders had a problem.[8] The exchange set the daily price range limit to USD 7.50/bbl for all months. Meanwhile, the threat of war posed a far more significant threat to European oil supplies than to those of the United States. The usual "basis" or differential between WTI and Brent crude oil reversed: WTI spot futures traded as much as USD 2.00/bbl below, instead of above, Brent spot crude oil. The price at which Cranky closed its futures contracts gave it an additional USD 2.00/bbl profit on the Brent crude oil cash market price it was hedging. No one heard much from companies that were long WTI futures at USD 36.00 per barrel.

The feeding frenzy was over. Advance planning for commodity price risk management—including credit requirements—had finally taken a front seat in many companies.

A company should maintain continuous, current market knowledge even if not always maintaining open hedge contracts.

METALS

Many of the alternatives for commodity producer price risk management were reviewed in the Cranky Crude Oil Company study. Selling futures, buying put options, or buying "synthetic puts" (short the futures and buy calls) are straightforward alternatives using exchange-traded contracts. Metals' producers also are being offered derivative products such as price swaps and average price forward/average price option contracts that *cash settle* rather than offer *settlement* by cash versus physical delivery. In addition to average price forward contracts, a "flexible forward" has been devised that enables the producer, for an additional premium, to give notice and then increase for any month or settlement period the notional amount for cash settle. These longer-term forward and option contracts are intended to fill a liquidity void on the London Metals Exchange (LME) beyond 12 to 18 months and to provide

[8] J. Lewis, *op. cit.* at 108.

average price contracts for price risk management. A synthetic put can also be constructed with OTC forward and call option contracts.

The world's first base metal index, the "MGMI," began trading on the LME in summer 1990. The index, named after its creator, Metallgesellschaft AG (nicknamed "MG"), is described as a "notional portfolio" of the six nonferrous metals traded on the LME: aluminum, copper, zinc, lead, nickel, and tin.

Recently, producers, merchants, and industrial consumers of base and precious metals have been reported in the financial press because of their use of swaps and OTC derivatives. However, the metals markets have long known both speculators and "financial engineers"; before that term was popular, they were called "hedgers." Activity in both the United States and London metals exchanges is regularly reported in the daily and weekly financial newspapers. A bit of litigation and some recent articles provide various examples.

A "price to be fixed" copper scrap contract that went awry was the subject of a 1979 decision by the federal district court of New York.[9] This case also provides the history of the word *contango*. Lissner was a company anxious to cause scrap dealers to sell it copper scrap during a period of low prices. Lissner "devised a new form of contract": delivery would be prompt against provisional payment, but the scrap dealer/seller could price the sale at an unspecified future date. The pricing terms of the contract read as follows:

(a) TERMS: 75% provisionally advanced upon receipt of material. Balance within 30 days after pricing.

(b) PRICE: The price is to be mutually agreed upon between buyer and seller, whenever seller wishes to price this contract.

(c) MATERIAL TO BE PRICED DURING COMEX TRADING HOURS.[10]

Lissner's contract did not state that the pricing had to occur within any stated number of days—for example, within 60 or 90 days after delivery. Lissner believed that copper prices were unreasonably low. Its strategy was to sell the scrap at fixed prices and to buy copper futures contracts for hedging the open, unpriced, "whenever" scrap purchase contracts. When a scrap seller priced a "whenever" contract, Lissner intended to close out the long futures contracts of the hedge. Things didn't work out quite right for Lissner. A scrap seller didn't price for about a year. The court held that the seller did not have to bear Lissner's contango costs. The case is good reading for those interested in "price to be fixed" commodity contracts.

An article entitled "The Stink in Zinc"[11] described the opportunity for any producer, merchant, or processor that was long zinc to profit in mid-April

---

[9] *Pepper's Steel & Alloys, Inc. v. Lissner Minerals & Metals,* 494 F. Supp. 487 (S.D.N.Y. 1979), *on damages* (1980).

[10] *Id.* at 490.

[11] J. Liscio, "The Stink in Zinc," Commodities Corner, *Barron's,* April 22, 1991, p. 62.

1991 on the LME. There is an old adage in financial markets: "The trend is your friend." The cash price of zinc had fallen 50 percent over 2 years. The writer observed: "A trend of those proportions attracts mindless shorts." It seems that the shorts were shorting on the LME at the same time a physical shortage was occurring in the cash market. The article pointed out that zinc is almost entirely a "trade market," the supply being controlled by producers. The naked shorts tried to roll over. Zinc for immediate delivery sold for USD 240 per ton more than the 3-month futures price on the prior Monday. Producers, merchants, and consumers with extra zinc sold the physical and bought the futures contract. The LME's physical stockpile hit a 7-year high. Those covering or rolling over shorts paid more than USD 100 per ton premium. The exchange did not repeat its December 1989 USD 20 per ton financing limit.

Black & Decker's treasury operation is active in commodity price, currency, and financial risk management. The company, concerned about managing the cost of the commodities it uses to manufacture motors and tools, hedges its copper purchases on the LME. A brief example illustrates the handling of a purchase 6 months hence. Black & Decker would buy one LME copper future at USD 2,310 per ton (contracts over 3 months are quoted in U.S. Dollars). If the 6-month forward exchange rate is USD/GBP 1.65, the Pounds Sterling price of the copper future is GBP 1,400. At this point, the company can choose to manage the foreign exchange risk by entering into a forward contract to sell Pounds Sterling and buy U.S. Dollars at USD/GBP 1.6500. At the end of the sixth month, it could purchase the physical copper and, assuming no change in the futures market, could sell the LME copper future at GBP 1,400. If the exchange rate is USD/GBP 1.6000, the USD sales price of the futures contract is USD 2,240 or a loss of USD 70.00, which may have been offset by the above described forward contract.[12]

Qualex is long silver because it is a large photoprocessor with a very seasonal business during holiday and vacation times. It is required to recycle silver from the film and photographic paper used to make prints. The recycled silver is sold as a by-product. Qualex arranged a 3-year price risk management program for the silver. The first contract was a commodity price swap to hedge about a third of the silver. The other two contracts were collars with the floor at the company's planned price, but the ceiling lets the company benefit from silver price increases up to 20 percent above the ceiling.[13]

---

[12] E. Sheridan, "Copper-Bottomed Hedging Strategy," Risk & Arbitrage, *Corporate Finance* (March 1990): 14–15.
[13] L. R. Quinn, "At Qualex, There's No Question About Hedging," *Corporate Risk Management* (March 1991): 10–12. Also reported in "Growing Pains of Commodity Swaps," *Corporate Finance* (March 1991): 11.

A much publicized copper price swap in 1989 was the bank syndicated USD 210 million facility led by Banque Paribas on behalf of Mexicano de Cobre (MdC). Banque Paribas is credited with structuring a syndicated deal giving MdC a 38-month loan and a creditworthy commodity customer, and then finding a commodity price swap counterparty to fix the price of the copper for the term of the loan. The lenders' objective was to prevent a decrease in copper prices that would cause the loan to default. The physical copper was sold at market prices and the proceeds were deposited in an escrow account controlled by the lender syndicate. The counterparty to the commodity price swap fixed its cost of copper. The price swap had semiannual settlement. If the swap's reference price of copper was less than the swap price, the counterparty made up the difference with payment into the escrow account. If the swap's reference price of copper was more than the swap price, Paribas paid the counterparty.[14] "The essence of this," said a Paribas spokesman, "is that we have exchanged financial risk for the banks for performance risk."[15]

GOLD MINE FINANCING

Much publicity about commodity price risk management has surrounded "gold loans." There are, however, more alternatives for the price risk management of a gold mining venture than "gold loans." The following excerpts provide some insight to at least the "tip of the iceberg." Some of the varieties of financial engineering discussed elsewhere in this book can be recognized between the lines of these quotations.

At about $420 an ounce the price was held back by the weight of selling, including forward sales by Australian and North American gold producers who rushed to lock in certain profits.[16]

One of the key issues is whether producers will "lower the ceiling they put over the market by bunching up forward sales" . . . this might happen because of a "collective shift in sentiment among mining company executives."[17]

. . . [T]he important influence on the gold price, however, was the net new hedging business last year. . . . "The more mines hedge, the more their cumulative

---

[14] J. Goff, "Paribas's Commodity Swap Shop," *Corporate Finance* (September 1989): 32; P. B. Spraos, "The Anatomy of a Copper Swap," *Corporate Risk Management* (January/February 1990): 8.

[15] John Grobstein of Banque Paribas, as quoted in "Mexicano de Cobre Borrows $210m," *Financial Times* (London), July 27, 1989, International Capital Markets.

[16] K. Gooding, "How Gold Is Losing Its Lustre," *Financial Times* (London), June 13, 1990.

[17] K. Gooding, "Forward Selling by Producers 'Putting Cap on Gold Price,'" *Financial Times* (London), January 24, 1991.

activity caps the gold price and therefore the more they need to hedge to protect their profitability. Hedging has become self-fulfilling."[18]

Gold producers were accused yesterday of killing the investment market for the precious metal and destroying the attraction of gold mining company share by their hedging activities.[19] [The debate heated; one of the more aggressive companies in hedging put all its efforts into] . . . minimizing the risks involved in a fall in the gold price and at the same time permitted at least 70 percent of the upside price potential to remain; . . . the new financial instruments made it possible for producers to enhance revenue while investors received some gain; . . . too many gold market participants were reluctant to use options and other financial derivatives, probably because of a shortage of suitably experience[d] people.[20]

A conservative estimate . . . talks of $5 billion of gold loans between 1987 and 1989. . . . Their peculiarity was that the companies borrowed gold (not money) from the commercial banks; and that the commercial banks had in turn usually borrowed the gold from central banks. . . . As the bullion pays no interest—unlike currencies—this gold sits idly around the central banks' vaults. Offers of annual interest rates of 1–2% delighted the central banks. They gladly lent some of their gold to commercial banks, who then lent it to developing gold mines as a supposedly cheap source of financing . . . these mines sold the gold they had borrowed . . . and spent the money on developing their mines.[21]

While the banks seem to have the most to lose, they have insisted that [name of company] future production be sold forward to lock in enough cash flow to cover operating costs this year and next.[22]

The size of Barrick's [American Barrick Resources] gold reserves has enabled the company to enter into the most comprehensive price hedging programme in the industry and thus guarantee at least a minimum level of profits and effectively insulate itself against falling gold prices. . . . Barrick has about 4m ounces of gold hedged through gold loans, forward sales, options, and spot deferred contracts . . . earnings would be higher with a gold price of $300 an ounce than with a price of $400 because of the protection given by the hedging programme and because the company would pay lower royalties.[23]

---

[18] K. Gooding, "Producer Hedging Keeps Price Low," quoting J. Jacks, *Financial Times* (London), June 25, 1991.
[19] K. Gooding, "Gold Hedgers 'Killing' Investment," *Financial Times* (London), June 26, 1991, p. 27.
[20] *Id.*
[21] "Gold Loans, Wagging the Dog," *The Economist,* February 3, 1990, p. 88.
[22] "High-Cost Gold Mining in Canada's Frozen Wastes," *Financial Times* (London), September 6, 1990, p. 26.
[23] K. Gooding, "American Barrick Finds Profit Behind the Hedge," *Financial Times* (London), April 9, 1991.

Three of the more common types of financing for gold mining companies involve techniques of financial risk management. Bankers that make cash loans often require that the borrower provide price protection "by forward selling or by some form of floor price scheme."[24] Assuming that the production is achieved, the bankers seek some comfort that the production revenue will be sufficient to cover principal and interest on the loan. These arrangements are sometimes called a "synthetic gold loan." The proceeds from the forward sales are synchronized to loan repayment obligations.

A "gold loan" is a transaction whereby a bullion bank provides gold in exchange for future deliveries of gold from the mine. The loan typically has a low interest rate. Commodity price and currency risks are eliminated because the gold borrowed is replaced with gold mined. A "gold loan" can provide for the borrower's drawing down in gold or currency and can permit switching. A variation is the deferred forward sale: the gold mining company sells gold forward to the financier, receives cash, and has a deferred obligation to deliver gold.

A third approach is gold price linked securities. A gold bond has a fixed coupon rate and the option in the future to be repaid in gold—a bond with gold warrants, or just gold warrants. The gold bonds have a relatively low rate of interest because the security provides a bonus to gold "bulls."

The arrangements for gold mine financings and producer price risk management cannot always be successfully retrofitted to base metals and other commodities. Gold's status as a precious metal confers some different options on its final engineers.

AGRICULTURE—BASIS AND THE HEDGER

Forward contracts in agricultural commodities can be traced back to the 16th-century grain trade in the Antwerp Bourse. Futures contracts were developed in Chicago during the Civil War.[25] Generations of producers, "middlemen," and merchants for agricultural products have fine-tuned basis trading and hedging. (See the discussion of commodity prices in Chapter 2.)

This brief discussion presents a schematic of basis for the hedger. It is intended as a convenient reference map for basis beginners and people who do not deal with "basis" or "differentials" every day. There is truly enough material for another book, where basis or differential trading and hedging

---

[24] P. J. Doyle, "Gold-Denominated Financing—Legal and Practical Aspects and Project Finance Applications," in *Gold Mine Financing*, Mineral Law Series, The Rocky Mountain Mineral Law Foundation (1988), 3–3 and 3–4.
[25] ICC Publishing S.A., *Futures + Options Trading in Commodity Markets*, publ. no. 426 (1986), p. 10.

and the many commercial applications are concerned. Basis is babbled about: "long the basis and short hedged" or "short the basis and long hedged." For a hedger, the favorable price move of basis is often not intuitively obvious.

The cash price comes first in the formula: basis or differential is the cash price minus the futures or forward price. In the following examples, bu is the abbreviation for bushel.

Why Commodity Basis or Differential Strengthens

- The cash price rises and the futures/forward price declines.

  Example: Cash wheat USD 4.50/bu, spot future basis Kansas City USD 4.35/bu, difference is USD + .15/bu; cash wheat rises to USD 4.75/bu, spot future basis Kansas City drops to USD 4.30/bu, difference is USD + .45/bu; the basis or differential increases USD .30/bu from + .15/bu to + .45/bu.

- The cash price declines less than the futures price declines.

  Example: Cash wheat USD 4.50/bu, spot future basis Kansas City USD 4.35/bu, difference is USD + .15/bu; cash wheat declines to USD 4.30/bu, spot future basis Kansas City declines to USD 4.00/bu, difference is USD + .30/bu; the basis or differential increases USD .15/bu from + .15/bu to + .30/bu.

- The cash price rises more than the futures price rises.

  Example: Cash wheat USD 4.50/bu, spot future basis Kansas City USD 4.35/bu, difference is USD + .15/bu; cash wheat rises to USD 4.75/bu, spot future basis Kansas City rises to USD 4.40/bu, difference is USD + .35/bu; the basis or differential increases USD + .20/bu from + .15/bu to + .35/bu.

Why Commodity Basis or Differential Weakens

- The cash price declines and the futures/forward price increases.

  Example: Cash wheat USD 4.35/bu, spot future basis Kansas City USD 4.50/bu, difference is USD − .15/bu; cash wheat declines to USD 4.30/bu, spot future basis Kansas City rises to USD 4.55/bu, difference is USD − .25/bu; the basis or differential decreases USD − .10/bu from − .15/bu to − .25/bu.

- The cash price rises less than the futures price rises.

  Example: Cash wheat USD 4.35/bu, spot future basis Kansas City USD 4.50/bu, difference is USD − .15/bu; cash wheat rises to USD 4.40/bu, spot future basis Kansas City rises to USD 4.75/bu, difference is USD – .35/bu; the basis or differential decreases USD – .20/bu from – .15/bu to – .35/bu.

- The cash price declines more than the futures price declines.

  Example: Cash wheat USD 4.35/bu, spot future basis Kansas City USD 4.50/bu, difference is USD – .15/bu; cash wheat drops to USD 4.15/bu, spot future basis Kansas City drops to USD 4.45/bu, difference is USD – .35/bu; the basis or differential decreases USD – .20/bu from – .15/bu to – .35/bu.

The following rules are ironclad on commodities:

- The short hedger is trying to protect against decline in commodity prices.

  Example: A farmer would sell wheat futures contracts or enter into forward sale contracts to price-protect at the level sold. The short hedger is long the *underlying* and, not surprisingly, is therefore long the basis. For that short hedger—protecting against price decline and long the basis—a strengthening basis produces a profit and a weakening basis produces a loss.

- The long hedger is trying to protect against rising commodity prices.

  Example: A food processing company (*e.g.,* a baked goods producer) will buy wheat futures or enter into forward purchase contracts to price-protect at the level purchased. The long hedger is short the *underlying* and, not surprisingly, is therefore short the basis. For that long hedger—protecting against price increase and short the basis—a weakening basis produces a profit and a strengthening basis produces a loss.

CATTLE LOANS: TRIPARTITE AGREEMENT TO FINANCE EXCHANGE-TRADED FUTURES

Commodity price swaps and other OTC derivatives have recently been widely publicized for the petroleum industry and, to a somewhat lesser extent, the mining industry. These contracts are marketed to offer price protection over time periods for which futures contracts are also available. As noted early in the chapter, one reason for longer dated futures contracts' being created may be to meet the needs of writers of longer dated swaps and OTC derivative contracts. These same types of contracts are offered for longer-term pricing arrangements—periods of time beyond available futures contracts. One of the advantages sometimes cited for the shorter-term swaps and OTC derivatives is that daily cash margin maintenance is not required as it is for futures contracts.

The agriculture industry offers an interesting alternative. In this discussion, we use an example from livestock. Bankers arrange financing for the cash margin required for a rancher's futures contract hedging transactions. The bank holds a security interest over both the hedging account and the livestock. Starting with one 700-pound steer purchased at USD 560 (USD 60 cash and a USD 500 loan), suppose the rancher spends 35 cents per pound to add 400 pounds to the steer (a total of USD 140). The rancher then has an 1,100-pound animal with an all-in cost of 64 cents per pound (USD 700/1,100 pounds). The bank also provides the financing for hedging the price. Suppose the animal's sales price can be hedged at 76 cents per pound. The rancher and the bank still have a profitable deal.

The security agreement over a hedging account is a tripartite agreement among the borrower, the brokerage firm, and the lending bank. Typically, the agreement will anticipate both futures and exchange-traded options contracts. The company confirms the bank's security interest in the physical commodity being price-hedged. A segregated account is established with the brokerage firm, which is directed to make any and all payment to the bank upon demand. The bank has the authority to liquidate open contracts. This type of tripartite agreement is, at this writing, starting to appear in commodity business sectors other than agriculture, specifically crude oil.

It may be worth investigating with a banker the use of exchange-traded contracts for short-term price risk management.

PART THREE
MAKING THE DECISION

11
Hedging: The Decision, Dealing, and Credit

Betwixt ourselves, let us decide it then.

Shakespeare, I Henry VI, *act 4, scene 1*

Always on the watch.

Motto of Frederick the Great (c. 1740)

THE HEDGING DECISION

In considering different tools and strategies of financial engineering, some common faults should be avoided:

- Failure to consider the ramifications of the hedge;
- Oversimplification of the hedging tool;
- An attitude of "That is the way the company's hedging decisions have always been made";
- Failure to consider the cost, tax, or cash flow of the proposed hedge.

The purpose of this chapter is to address in general terms some of the main considerations in deciding whether to hedge an exposure. The chapter's goal is to "open doors" by raising questions, not necessarily to provide answers. Usually, each hedging decision is a separate determination; the proper hedge for one situation is not necessarily the correct hedge for any other. Only the basic procedure for making a decision is essentially similar for all strategies. Much of what follows may seem simplistic, but too many financial executives assume that they understand the issues and consequently embark on a wrong course of action.

DEFINING THE EXPOSURE

The first step in any hedging decision is to exactly define and then approximately measure the risk. In some cases, that step can be easy; for example:

- An importer who has ordered goods from a European producer has an exposure: the purchase price of the goods will be converted from the currency of the purchase agreement, letter of credit, or other document into U.S. Dollars.
- An oil refiner who needs to purchase crude oil for its refinery has obvious exposures: it must buy crude oil, with the risk that crude oil's price will rise or that its refined product may decline in price after the price of the crude oil is locked-in.
- A portfolio manager faces reinvestment risk for investment income: if interest rates fall between the time of the initial investment and the time when the final obligation comes due, then the funds invested will not generate the funds projected or needed to meet the obligation.

Each of these three examples has a cash flow implication. If certain market events take place, the result will be a negative impact on cash flow. If the U.S. Dollar depreciates, the cost of the importer's goods will go up. If the price of oil rises, the refiner may not be able to raise the price of the refined product enough to make a profit. If interest rates fall, the portfolio manager may not be able to meet the obligations that the manager wants to fund.

Defining precisely what is at risk is far more difficult in situations that require valuation of accounting statements or of investment portfolios. For example, a German subsidiary, wholly owned by a U.S. corporation, obtains all its raw materials in Germany; its other expenses are all denominated in Deutsche Marks (DEM). It sells all of its products to German customers. The subsidiary's revenues and its balance sheet are denominated only in DEM, and it has no non-DEM assets or liabilities. Because the subsidiary is very profitable, the parent permits it to reinvest its profits in its own business. The parent is receiving no dividends from the subsidiary and does not plan to sell it.

Defining the risk in this example is somewhat complicated. Is it the U.S. Dollar value of the balance sheet, net income, net cash flows, shareholders' equity, current assets minus current liabilities, or some other amount? Would it be the value of the subsidiary if the parent decided to liquidate it or sell it?

The "strategic hedge" is another problem of risk definition related to foreign exchange. Heatherstone China, studied in Chapter 5, competed with Japanese producers, but the company's management decided that it had no foreign exchange exposure because it did no international business. Whenever the Japanese Yen weakened against the U.S. Dollar, however, Japanese producers would have a cost advantage relative to Heatherstone. Thus, Heatherstone had a significant foreign exchange exposure even though it did no international business. The "strategic hedge" risk is not easy to define; one author has pointed out: "Only the most sophisticated risk management departments both understand and can quantify their competitive, or economic exposures. Such exposures arise from the competitive environment of the firm."[1]

Defining and measuring an exposure is always a complex task, and often no one, final, correct answer is possible. The decision may depend partially on the philosophy of management; when it does, subjective values enter into the decision process, and risk profiles change. A chain of situations is likely under certain circumstances, especially when trying to hedge projected budgets for foreign subsidiaries, or when trying to hedge budgeted dividend payments. Dividends depend on profits. Profits depend on costs of raw materials and labor, interest expense, taxes, exchange rates applied to the cost of imported components, and the generation of sufficient sales to yield the cash flows needed to support the dividend. With this list of variables, one correct answer to risk exposure is not realistic.

DEFINING RISK PARAMETERS AND EXPOSURES

The next step after defining and measuring the exposure is to answer the question "What is our 'appetite' for risk?" Many financial risk managers answer this question by stating that they are not in the business of speculating in financial markets and want no financial risk. Instead, their policy is to hedge every exposure, regardless of the hedging cost. This is an expensive approach to solving the problem of risk exposure. Hedging any financial risk is essentially an insurance problem. Although insurance is available to protect against almost any risk at a price, that price may be prohibitively high, and self-insurance may be a more economically prudent course.

In considering the level of risk it is willing to incur, a company should take into account whether the risk offers potential reward in the form of either profit or significantly reduced expenses. Many commodity companies have found that it can indeed be profitable to assume risk by setting up trading operations to manage exposures arising from the production or

---

[1] C. Heston and G. Greiff, MA, Risk and Arbitrage, "*Defining the Risk Profile,*" 69 *Corporate Finance* (August 1990): 10.

consumption of large quantities of grain, oil, other commodities, or metals. Financial risk can often be considered another business risk. A company may shy away from foreign exchange risk, yet it may incur substantial risk by investing heavily to develop and bring to market new products, with no assurance that they will be successful.

A prospective hedger needs to consider both the potential risk and reward. This should be an ongoing process as the business grows, develops, and changes. One major computer corporation makes an annual, formal review of its foreign exchange and interest rate exposure position. It then appraises that position by asking these questions: What is the risk? What is the staff trying to do with these positions taken? How much risk should the firm incur? How should it be measured? What is the best method for controlling or exploiting the risk? Has the company achieved its goals with the procedures used in the past? Is it measuring itself correctly? Are the previous year's assumptions still valid? The moral: defining the degree of risk on a regular basis that a company is willing to incur is an essential part of any hedging decision.[2]

SELECTING THE PROPER INSTRUMENT OR TOOL

The morass of the savings and loan scandal includes the tale of a small New Jersey savings and loan ("the S&L"), whose management wanted to lock-in the cost of funding its mortgage loan portfolio. Management sold GNMA ("Ginnie Mae": Government National Mortgage Association) futures contracts as the means for achieving its goal of a 10.5 percent average cost of funds on its deposits. Management reasoned that: (1) if interest rates rose, the value of the futures contracts sold would decline, offsetting the increased interest cost of certificates of deposits issued; (2) if interest rates fell, the loss incurred on the futures contracts would be offset by the decrease in the interest cost for customer deposits.

Interest rates did fall. The S&L's management made two mistakes in its calculations. The value of the GNMA futures contracts it was short increased sharply because the futures contracts represented the present value of approximately 30 years' worth of cash flows. As discussed in Chapter 2, as interest rates fell, the price of the GNMAs went up. The cost of interest on deposits fell slowly because the interest rates on certificates outstanding did not change. To compound the problem, borrowers refinanced their mortgages at the new lower interest rates. Hence, the S&L could not take advantage of a wider spread between its cost of funds and its loans outstanding.

---

[2] J.C. Chan and C.S. Smithson, *Reading Between the Lines (III)*, 2 *Corporate Risk Management* (January/February 1990): 32.

As a result, the S&L incurred a net loss of USD 3 million because of the hedge. The S&L had not taken the step of ascertaining exactly what it needed to hedge. In one sense, the hedge did what it was supposed to do: it locked-in a funding cost over the long term. Management did not realize, however, that the interest expense of its deposits would drop more slowly than the futures market would rise in value. In short, management failed to consider what actions its customers might take to exploit the drop in interest rates, and it locked-in a funding mismatch. It chose an instrument that, in one sense, substituted basis risk for interest rate risk.

The example of the German subsidiary of the U.S. corporation, described earlier, is also applicable here. Assume that management of the parent had elected to hedge its equity in the subsidiary by selling Deutsche Marks 1 year forward at a rate of USD/DEM 1.7000, to lock-in the U.S. dollar value of the equity. This decision ensures potential negative impacts, for the following reason.

If the Deutsche Mark appreciated in value against the U.S. Dollar to DEM 1.6000, the parent company would have to purchase DEM at a worse exchange rate than the rate at which it had sold the DEM. The DEM purchased would be more expensive than those sold. In liquidating the forward foreign exchange contract, the parent would incur a net cash outflow of USD 37,000 for each DEM 1 million that had been sold forward. This negative cash flow would only be offset by the change in U.S. Dollar value of the DEM amount of shareholder equity.

The conclusion to be drawn is that a forward contract is not the proper tool to select for hedging a balance sheet or other translation exposure of a stand-alone subsidiary, as in this case. An appreciation of the value of the U.S. Dollar against the Deutsche Mark would make the forward contract profitable. It would also probably result in an income tax charge for the U.S. Dollar value of the profit on the contract; hence, part of the amount of the gain on the forward contract would be lost, and the contract would not cover the full amount of the depreciation of the U.S. Dollar value of the shareholders' equity in the subsidiary.

Practical Advice

When choosing a hedging vehicle, choose the one that is least likely to have unexpected, negative implications that may be more severe than the original problem. If cash flows are to be protected, choose an instrument whose cash flows will most nearly match those of the underlying exposure. If balance sheets are to be hedged, the instrument should be one that will appreciate or depreciate in value against opposite changes in value on the accounting statements.

Become acquainted with risk management or hedging software systems: one of the many now available may be adaptable to unique corporate risk needs. Appropriate software will save time, enable more accurate selection of the proper hedging instrument, and facilitate monitoring of hedging positions taken.[3]

THE COST OF THE HEDGE

A key issue is how much a firm is willing to spend in order to hedge a perceived risk. Again, if price is not a factor, it is possible to purchase insurance against any risk. Similarly, if the firm is willing to spend the required money, it can hedge 100 percent of its market exposure for any given set of financial circumstances. As a practical matter, such a strategy makes little sense. In the case of an option, for example, in order to receive $1.00 of protection for each $1.00 change in the price of the underlying, a hedger must spend more money than if a 50-cent benefit for each $1.00 change in the price of an underlying is acceptable.

The key is the sensitivity of the corporate financial risk management situation to market changes. There are a series of trade-offs. Increased flexibility raises the cost of the hedge. Increased price protection will raise the cost of the hedge, reduce the flexibility of management, or both. If reducing hedging costs is a key goal, then some degree of price protection or flexibility in hedge management must be foregone.

The cost of a hedging tool can, in some cases, be explicitly measured. For example, purchasing a currency forward that has a lower interest rate than the U.S. Dollar will make that forward purchase more expensive relative to the spot exchange rate. That is a cost of hedging a foreign exchange exposure. Purchasing a commodity forward will, in a normal market environment, entail an expense because of the interest expense and the seller's storage expense for holding the commodity until the delivery date. These are the usual basis risks.

Some instruments may result in an unexpected income tax expense, if a gain on the hedge cannot be offset by a decline in value of the *underlying* being hedged. (This was outlined in the preceding section.) Another factor in the cost of the hedge is the accounting controls and market monitoring that may be necessary; if they entail additional payments, they may also involve a cost. A hedging tool that requires the payment of cash, such as an option premium, must be funded. The more complex the hedging tool or tools, the greater the possibility that a costly mistake will be made.

Some hedging strategies involve the use of brokers on different exchanges. Brokerage fees can be substantial for a hedge that must be actively managed.

[3] W.D. Falloon, "Who's Winning with Corporates," 3 *Corporate Risk Management* (January 1991): 30; X.X. Stein, "A Software Comparison," 2 *Corporate Risk Management* (March/April 1990): 41; J. Stein, "Let the Software Show Begin," 2 *Corporate Risk Management* (January/February 1990): 27.

The active management of one or more exposures may require that highly paid financial professionals be hired or consulted.

THE COMPLEXITY OF THE TOOL

An old adage applies to hedging tools: "Other things being equal, simple is better." Many of the financial engineering strategies being sold in today's financial markets are combinations of various futures, options, and swaps. Many financial executives have found that, when they dissect complex strategies recommended by brokers or bankers, they can themselves devise simpler, cheaper, and nearly as effective strategies. In general, the more complex the tool being offered, the greater the risk of doing something wrong. A basic rule of business courtesy applies, however: if a hedger requests that a broker or banker do a significant amount of work preparing alternative hedging strategies, the hedger should, at the very least, give that broker or banker the opportunity to do the business. Brokers and bankers will happily do an enormous amount of work for a hedger if they will have the opportunity to do the deals required to fulfill a hedging strategy. Asking someone to study a problem morally obligates the hedger to reciprocate.

NATURAL HEDGES

One of the best places to look for a hedge is at home. A company may often have a situation in which an existing exposure can be used to offset another exposure elsewhere in the company. This was the situation for the elevator company bidding for the contract in the Côte d'Ivoire (see Chapter 6). The parent company was able to use excess Canadian funds in one division to offset a Canadian payable elsewhere in the company.

Natural offsets may provide other opportunities to solve many apparently unrelated problems in different divisions of the company. One of the more imaginative uses of offsetting exposures was exemplified by Cornucopia Company, studied in Chapter 7. Two unrelated problems, one in Germany and one in the United States, allowed the company to reduce its borrowing costs very significantly, and to hedge a major foreign exchange exposure.

TIMING OF THE HEDGE TRANSACTION

Timing a hedging transaction so as to achieve the lowest possible cost and lock-in the largest possible gain is every financial risk manager's dream transaction. Every market participant wants to sell at the top of a market trend and buy at the bottom, but this does not happen unless a market participant is extraordinarily lucky. Most traders in any market will quickly confess that it is much easier to buy at the top and sell at the bottom than it is to do it the right way around.

Trying to play a market is difficult even for trading professionals. In selecting the timing, a few rules of thumb will help. The first is: "The trend is your friend." In a market where prices are rising, it is not a good idea to be short. For a hedger who is worried about short-term exposure to rising prices, it is not a good idea to delay buying in order to achieve a lower price. Generally, the strategy will cost money over the long haul.

The corollary to this concept is: Avoid picking turns or reversals in market trends. Elaborate technical models purport to show turning points in markets on a monthly, weekly, daily, and even hourly basis. For someone who does not use these models regularly and understand their strengths and weaknesses, their use can be a dangerous and costly strategy. Even traders that use them frequently lose money because of false "buy signals" and false "sell signals." One trader calls this "picking the point where the freight train stops—picking a market turn is like standing in the middle of the railroad tracks and saying that the train barreling down a half mile away will stop right here." The odds of being right are small; the cost of being wrong can be devastating.

The timing of a hedging transaction depends on many considerations and factors that are more important than the exact level of a market at any given point in time. Some of those factors are outlined in this chapter.

UNWINDING A HEDGE

An important consideration in selecting a hedge is how easily the hedge transaction can be unwound if necessary or desirable. Some transactions and tools can be liquidated easily: options can be sold; foreign exchange contracts can be netted—a strategy of Biped Shoes, in Chapter 5. Others are more difficult to liquidate. Cornucopia Company, studied in Chapter 7 issued Euronotes. When the company decided to hedge the possible depreciation of the U.S. Dollar against the Deutsche Mark and the Swiss Franc, it could not simply retire the bonds. It had to add yet another hedge transaction to its books. Interest rate and currency swaps can also be difficult and costly transactions to unwind.

For complex hedging strategies, the "unwinding" rule is this: Any strategy that involves multiple instruments will be more difficult to unwind. Custom hedges may be difficult or impossible to unwind. Consider Tau Tire and Chi Computer, studied in Chapter 8. The bank devised a unique hedging strategy particular to the needs of the two companies. If either company's situation had changed, it is highly unlikely that either company would have been able to walk away from the transaction. The unwinding would have been very costly or perhaps impossible.

SUMMARY

Many other factors require consideration in making a hedging decision: accounting, documentation, taxation, credit risk, and legal issues. Each issue can be critical to the successful hedging of an exposure. Each key factor should be carefully addressed before entering into a hedging contract.[4]

DEALING

DEALING WITH BANKERS AND BROKERS

The basic rule in dealing with banks and brokers is to be explicit and fair. Most traders and brokers want to be fair to their clients. In the long run, a relationship built on trust and respect will serve a company better than one based on "milking" a trader for the last cent on a deal.

Before calling a banker or broker for prices on a trade, the hedger should have clearly defined what needs to be done. The details of the proposed trade should be in a written outline that can be read to the banker or broker when calling for an indication on the proposed transaction. Generally, slang or market jargon that either has multiple meanings or can be misunderstood should be avoided. If jargon is used, the underlying transaction should be detailed. For example, if a hedger wants to enter into a range forward or a tunnel against the Deutsche Mark, the hedger should state the details of the proposed trade: "I want to purchase a German Mark call and write the Mark put." The details of each option should be plainly stated before discussing pricing.

Many instruments are complex, and the markets are volatile. A trader or a broker has a right to expect the client who calls for a price to know precisely what trade(s) is wanted. The costs, aggravation, and bad feeling generated by making a mistake are not worth the few minutes saved by assuming that a counterparty understands vague instructions. (Issues relating to correcting mistakes are covered in a later section.)

PRICING

When dealing with over-the-counter instruments and trades, competitive pricing may be attractive to ensure that a hedger receives the best price

---

[4] D.J. Schaffer, "Managing Interest Rate Risk," 2 *Corporate Risk Management* (March/April 1990): 46; S. London, "How Returns Are Protected," *Financial Times* (London) March 13, 1991, p. 30.

possible. Again, it is necessary to be explicit about the details of a trade. Generally, for commonly traded instruments such as foreign exchange contracts, calling more than two or three banks for a price is not cost-effective.

When possible, it is preferable to request a price from each bank or broker at the same time. Each competing institution can then quote the price at the same time under identical circumstances. Calling one counterparty, obtaining a price, and then putting him or her on hold or calling a second time, is a time-consuming strategy that can be counterproductive. Markets may move against the hedger during the second telephone call. The first institution cannot and should not be expected to honor a price quoted if it has been put on hold and the market has moved.

Two final comments on competitive pricing are in order. First, some hedgers have concluded that competitive pricing of transactions is no longer warranted, given the amount of information available on the various electronic services. Where there are close relationships and a high degree of trust, some firms are willing to forego the last cent in any given transaction, in exchange for a very high level of service from bankers and brokers.

Second, for proprietary products or strategies, competitive pricing may not be available. Some strategies are particular to one firm or one individual. A hedger who chooses to use those strategies must be willing to deal on that banker's or broker's price.

Fairness

If a prospective hedger presents a problem to a bank or a broker for its advice, the bank or broker reasonably expects to be compensated for the time it spends advising a client or designing a hedging strategy. In the case of Tau Tire and Chi Computer (see Chapter 7), the bank earned a large profit on the transaction. The traders had spend several weeks, however, in designing the strategy and tailoring it to the two companies' particular situations. They had then made detailed presentations to each company and reasonably expected to be compensated for their work. How much the bank should have made is open to discussion.

A prospective hedger who spends a lot of time consulting with traders and brokers and then does not do business with the people consulted is wasting everyone's time.

Avoiding Mistakes

By being precise in planning and executing trades, the hedger can avoid or correct most trading mistakes before they become costly. Unfortunately, no matter how careful two parties to a transaction try to be, there can be misunderstandings or simple errors at any step along the way.

At the time a trade is executed, the details should be clearly stated. After the trade is closed, each counterparty should repeat the important details— the amount or amounts involved, the price or rate applied to the trade, the settlement dates, and, if timely, the payment instructions by each party.

If one party to a trade believes that the other has made an error in pricing a transaction, that possibility should be addressed before closing the trade. Knowingly doing a trade on a price that is either obviously or possibly "off market" is unprofessional. This is known as "stuffing a trader" and will probably lead to trouble later—either when attempting to unwind the trade or in future relationships between the two parties. The person who did the stuffing will acquire a bad reputation in the market.

If a hedger calls the attention of a trader or a broker to a trader's possible mispricing and the trader repeats that the price is correct, then it is proper to close a trade at that price. A hedger should, however, make a reasonable effort to ensure that the price quoted is the correct one.

ERROR DISCLOSED AFTER THE TRADE

An error may occasionally be discovered in the confirmation process, which usually occurs several hours or days after a trade is done. Some errors are not discovered until several months after a trade has been executed. The longer the time between the trade and the discovery of the error, the greater the likelihood that one or both parties will incur a significant loss. An effective and prompt confirmation procedure—preferably by someone knowledgeable and other than the persons who actually closed the trade—is crucial.

When an error in a trade is discovered long after a trade has been executed or confirmed, the problem should be addressed immediately. Typically, one side or the other may discover that a trade ticket was not properly written or not written at all. Or, one party will realize that he or she has done a deal the wrong way around: the party may have bought an instrument, contract, or currency, when a sale was intended. These situations are the nightmares of every market participant. When such an error is discovered, it should be brought to the attention of the area supervisor or senior officer. As soon as the error has been discovered and confirmed, it should be corrected. If a corporation wanted to sell Deutsche Marks to hedge a dividend payment and bought them instead, it should immediately sell the Deutsche Marks back to the bank or broker, liquidating the position and the additional exposure. There will be plenty of time later to investigate the cause of the error. Riding an open position that was created by a mistake has the potential to compound the cost of the mistake.

As soon as the error is discovered, the counterparty to the trade should be informed of the error. After a trade has been closed and confirmed, the trade is a valid and binding transaction. The general rule is that both parties, regardless of the cause and the outcome of the error, are bound by the terms of the trade. It may be possible to negotiate a settlement of the problem, but the party making the mistake should be prepared to honor the trade as done.

A Final Note

The world of financial engineering continues to develop new ideas every day. Financial salespeople constantly present these new strategies as unique opportunities. Many may be productive, useful ideas—if not perfect—for many situations. If an idea seems attractive, it should be studied seriously. A hedger should not be afraid to experiment on a small scale with some of these new ideas. Similarly, a firm should encourage its hedging staff to develop strategies in-house and to experiment with them.

Mistakes in hedging strategies or implementation will be made, and the strategies implemented will not always work as planned. Learning from these situations is an important process in developing and implementing future strategies. Management should include in any hedging policy a provision for implementing and learning from new ideas, even when they do not work exactly as planned.

CREDIT

Counterparty credit risk too often receives insufficient consideration in the hedging decision.[5] A well-conceived and well-implemented strategy will founder if the counterparty to any hedging contract is not financially able to meet its commitments under that contract. A related consideration when recently developed instruments are used is that scant legal precedent yet exists as to how such instruments should be treated in insolvency proceedings.[6] The purpose of this section is to give the reader a basic knowledge of how to evaluate credit risk.[7]

CREDIT RISK DEFINED

This book has concentrated on the cash flow impacts of the different hedging strategies and their related instruments. Credit risk is defined here as the

---

[5]Counterparty credit risk, credit risk, and counterparty risk are used as synonyms in this chapter.
[6]See Chapter 13 for a discussion of the legal issues surrounding the instruments and strategies.
[7]G. Bousbib, "Measuring Counterparty Credit Risk," 3 *Corporate Risk Management* (June 1991): 24.

negative cash impact that will be incurred by the failure of a counterparty to honor the terms of a financial obligation. From a practical point of view, the counterparty risk will usually be recognized only when a counterparty becomes insolvent.

MEASURING CREDIT RISK: IN GENERAL

The first rule in measuring credit risk is to understand the cash flows required for each hedging contract. If a hedger does not understand the cash flows that a hedging contract generates, the hedger cannot measure the risk that the financial failure of a counterparty will have on his or her own position. The hedger must understand the details of each leg of a complex transaction and how each interacts with the whole strategy.

The complexity of most new hedging contracts makes it difficult to understand the cash flows involved. For many of the new types of contracts, however, the counterparty credit risk is much smaller than the *notional* amount of the contract.

For each instrument addressed in the following sections, the cash flow is defined, the potential risks if the counterparty becomes insolvent are explained, and a rule of thumb for measuring the amount of credit risk is stated.

The risk measure applied to each instrument assumes that the hedger has a portfolio of the instruments, which would diversify the credit risk over a variety of contracts and counterparties. If a hedger uses only one contract at a time or only a few counterparties, the degree of credit risk could be greater. The degree of increased risk would depend on the type of contract, the financial strength of the counterparty, and the underlying volatility of the cash market for the underlying.

SPOT FOREIGN EXCHANGE CONTRACTS

The cash flow risk for a spot foreign exchange contract arises from the time zone differences around the world. If AAA Corporation sold Deutsche Marks to Broke & Co. against U.S. Dollars, AAA Corporation would be obligated to pay the Deutsche Marks in Germany during normal banking hours. During most of the year, because of the time difference between the United States and Germany, 6 hours would elapse before Broke & Co. would pay the U.S. Dollar equivalent to AAA Corporation's Bank in the United States. If AAA received its dollar payments at a bank on the West Coast, the time difference could be as long as 9 hours. The location of the counterparties does not control the location of the banking payments, which are controlled by the currencies involved.

For example, suppose that AAA sold DEM 18 million to Broke & Co. and had purchased USD 10 million. AAA might pay out the DEM 18 million and never receive the U.S. Dollar equivalent. This possibility became reality in 1971, when Germany's Herstatt Bank failed. Without advance warning, Herstatt simply closed its doors one day. Counterparties that had sold currencies to Herstatt paid those currencies into Herstatt's respective bank accounts. Herstatt, however, failed to make any payments at all that day. Herstatt's counterparties lost 100 percent of the amounts they had paid to Herstatt.

In summary, a spot foreign exchange contract has 100 percent credit risk of the amount of the contract.

If a hedger becomes concerned about a deterioration in the credit quality of a counterparty, several alternatives are available. The hedger can enter into an offsetting contract with the same counterparty. Consider again the example of the contract between AAA Corporation and Broke & Co. If AAA became concerned about Broke's financial situation, it might ask Broke to sell back to AAA the Deutsche Mark amount and net out the U.S. Dollar difference. Table 11.1 shows the effects of this strategy.

By compensating the original contract, AAA could reduce its credit risk to the U.S. Dollar difference in the value of the two contracts. AAA had originally sold Deutsche Marks to Broke & Co. By purchasing them back at an exchange rate greater than DEM 1.8000, AAA could reduce its original credit risk. Thus, if AAA repurchased the DEM at an exchange rate of DEM 1.9000 per dollar, AAA would reduce its settlement risk from approximately USD 10 million to approximately USD 526,000. If the exchange rate fell below DEM 1.8000, AAA would eliminate the settlement altogether because AAA would then owe the USD 588,000 difference to Broke & Co.

A second possible alternative for partially alleviating the credit risk with a financially shaky counterparty is a mirror image of the first alternative. Assume that AAA Corporation had purchased Deutsche Marks from Broke & Co. and was required to pay U.S. Dollars to Broke & Co. If the cash management controls of AAA were effective and if it had a good relationship with its Deutsche Mark clearing bank, then AAA could do the following: obtain confirmation from its German bank that AAA's account had been credited with the Deutsche Mark amount before it paid out the U.S. Dollars to Broke's U.S.

Table 11.1 Offsetting Contract: Effect on Cash Flow

DEM/USD Exchange Rate	USD Equivalent	USD Cash Flow to AAA Corporation
1.8000	$10,000,000.00	
1.7000	$10,588,235.29	−$588,235.29
1.9000	$ 9,473,684.21	+$526,315.79

bank. This process is cumbersome and time-consuming; it should not be used routinely on payments and it absolutely should not be used as a substitute for credit judgment.

A third possibility is to request or, if possible, require presettlement. In the example, AAA Corporation might require that Broke & Co. pay its side of the foreign exchange contract one day before the agreed-on settlement date. In this way, AAA could ensure that it would receive the counter value expected. AAA might agree to pay Broke interest for one day on the amount paid—a cheap expense for corporate peace of mind when the counterparty may have become "flaky" or has not had time to establish credit. By receiving its countervalue one day early, AAA could then earn interest on that amount in the local currency money market.

FORWARD FOREIGN EXCHANGE CONTRACTS

The counterparty credit risk in a forward foreign exchange contract is substantially different from that of a spot foreign exchange contract. At its maturity, every forward foreign exchange contract becomes a spot transaction, subject to settlement risk. Until the contract matures, the credit risk is different from and much less than that of a spot foreign exchange contract. The principal concern with a forward contract is that of marking the contract to market.

For example, suppose that on October 1, 1990, a company bought DEM 5 million from Broke & Co. for delivery 1 year forward on October 3, 1991, at an exchange rate of DEM 2.00 per U.S. Dollar. On January 2, 1991, Broke & Co. informed all its counterparties to all trades that it would not honor any outstanding forward foreign exchange contracts. AAA needed to know the extent of its financial risk exposure to Broke & Co.

During the preceding 3 months, the U.S. Dollar had weakened against the Deutsche Mark, falling from DEM 2.00 to DEM 1.75 per USD at the end of 1990. After Broke & Co. announced it would no longer honor any existing forward foreign exchange contracts, AAA had to replace the DEM 5 million that it had purchased at DEM 2.00 with another contract representing the current exchange rate of DEM 1.75 per USD. This replacement would cost AAA more than USD 350,000, as follows:

Cost of the Original Contract

DEM 5,000,000/DEM 2.00 = USD 2,500,000.00

Cost of the Replacement Contract

DEM 5,000,000/DEM 1.75 = USD 2,857,142.86

Net Cost to the Company

USD 2,857,142.86 – USD 2,500,000 = USD 357,142.86

The counterparty credit risk of a forward foreign exchange contract is less than the face amount of the contract. It is the difference between the cost of the original contract and the cost of the replacement contract. In this example, the cost was USD 357,000 or approximately 14.3 percent of the original USD value of the contract:

14.286% = USD 357,142.86/USD 2,500,000

From a practical point of view, one cannot contrive a perfect way to measure the exact credit exposure of every contract at all future points in time. At any single point in time, it is possible to revalue all contracts outstanding and determine whether there is a net gain or a net loss. The amount of credit risk at that point in time is the sum of the unrealized gains from all contracts that have appreciated in value.

A SAMPLE PORTFOLIO OF FORWARD CONTRACTS

An example of a forward book—a portfolio of forward foreign exchange contracts—may help to clarify the issue. Figure 11.1 illustrates a sample portfolio that a company has acquired over a period of time. Currency purchases and sales, contract exchange rates and U.S. Dollar equivalents, a revaluation or mark-to-market rate, and the current market value of the outstanding contracts are included. The right-hand column shows whether there is a U.S. Dollar gain or loss on each individual contract.

Following the detail by contract is a summary of the portfolio: a sum of the Deutsche Mark and U.S. Dollar amounts of all contracts outstanding, both purchases and sales, as well as the net positions after adding purchases and subtracting sales. To the right of the sums and the net positions appears the profit and loss number, based on the exchange rates used to revalue the position.

Below the "net USD long/(short)" number is a number labeled "deemed credit risk." This number is 10 percent of the "total USD contracts outstanding." Many participants assume that the credit risk of any forward foreign exchange contract outstanding is 10 percent of the amount of the contract. According to this assumption, a portfolio of forward contracts with contract values equal to USD 15.99 million would have a deemed credit risk of USD 1.599 million.

This assumption is based largely on statistical exercises. These indicate that, on average, the potential loss on replacing any particular forward foreign

DEM Contract Amount	Our DEM Buy or Sale	Contract Exchange Rate	U.S. Dollar Cash Flow	Revaluation Rate	New U.S. Dollar Value	Net Gain (Loss)
5,000,000	B	2.0000	($2,500,000.00)	1.7500	$2,857,142.86	$357,142.86
(3,000,000)	S	1.8800	$1,595,744.68	1.7500	($1,714,285.71)	($118,541.03)
(2,500,000)	S	1.6500	$1,515,151.52	1.7500	($1,428,571.43)	$86,580.09
8,000,000	B	1.7400	($4,597,701.15)	1.7500	$4,571,428.57	($26,272.58)
(10,000,000)	S	1.7300	$5,780,346.82	1.7500	($5,714,285.71)	$66,061.11

Total DEM Contracts Outstanding

28,500,000

Net DEM Long/(Short)

(2,500,000.00)

	Average Rate
	1.39389

Portfolio Summary

Total USD Contracts Outstanding

$15,988,944.17

Net USD Long/(Short)

$1,793,541.87

Deemed Credit Risk

$1,598,894.42

Total Credit Risk for All Contracts That Are Profitable

$509,784.05

Total Portfolio Profit Profit/(Loss)

$364,970.44

FIGURE 11.1 Revaluation of a portfolio of forward foreign exchange contracts.

exchange contract from a large portfolio of forward contracts with another is equal to 10 percent of the value of the contract. This 10 percent has become the industry standard for estimating the credit risk of any particular forward contract.

The actual credit risk for any particular forward contract may be substantially more than 10 percent. The earlier example of the contract between AAA and Broke & Co. is a case in point. The total risk in a portfolio of forward contracts may well be much less than 10 percent.

In the portfolio shown in Figure 11.1, 10 percent of the value of all contracts outstanding is USD 1.599 million. A somewhat more sophisticated approach would reduce that amount of credit risk even further. That approach is based on the assumption that all counterparties to the contracts go into bankruptcy proceedings or for some other reason decide not to honor any contracts outstanding that result in a loss to the counterparty. In short, the assumption is that any profitable contracts in the portfolio will not be honored by the counterparty. Hence, the company would have to replace all the profitable contracts with new ones at the current market rate. The company would then lose about USD 510,000[8] in profits by replacing the three profitable contracts. Stated differently, it would incur an additional USD 510,000 in expense in replacing the three contracts.

In the worst-case scenario, the company would also have to honor the two contracts that are not profitable. This would result in the company's incurring losses of USD 145,000 as well as giving up USD 510,000 from the profitable contracts. Based on this reasoning, the credit risk in the forward book is approximately USD 655,000, and not the deemed risk of 10 percent of the value of all the contracts outstanding (USD 1.599 million). Stated as a percentage, the credit risk at this point in time is slightly more than 4 percent of the portfolio. As the exchange rate used to revalue the portfolio changes, the 4 percent credit risk might also change.

As the profitability of a portfolio of forward contracts increases, the credit risk associated with the portfolio will increase. As the profitability of a portfolio of forward contracts decreases, credit risk will also decrease.

By comparison, for a forward foreign exchange contract, the actual credit risk as opposed to deemed credit risk is the cost of replacing the contract with another at the current market forward foreign exchange rate at any point in time.

Recommended Policy. For prudent and conservative management of credit risk, the 10 percent deemed credit risk is more than acceptable. Settlement risk should also be taken into account. There should be a limit on both the total amount of forward contracts outstanding and the U.S.

---

[8] This amount is the "total credit risk for all contracts that are profitable," which appears at the bottom of Figure 11.1.

Dollar amount of contracts that mature on a single date. The U.S. Dollar amount of settlement risk for spot and forward foreign exchange contracts for any counterparty should increase as the creditworthiness of the counterparty improves, but decrease as creditworthiness deteriorates.

FOREIGN EXCHANGE OPTIONS

Foreign exchange options have two sides to their credit risk. The credit risk is substantially different, depending on whether one is buying or writing options.

Purchasing Options

The credit risk for purchasing options is identical to that of a forward exchange contract. If it becomes profitable to exercise an option, two issues arise: (1) replacing a profitable option with a new one at the current market premium; and (2) managing settlement risk on the settlement dates of the payments underlying the option.

If a company owns an option, will the counterparty that has written the option be able to honor its financial obligations as contracted for in the option agreement?

Recommended Policy. Use the 10 percent deemed credit risk and 100 percent settlement risk policies recommended in the preceding sections.

Writing Options

Writing options has significantly less credit exposure than purchasing options. Before expiration, the only significant risk is whether the purchaser will be able to pay the premium as agreed. If the purchaser does not pay the premium, then the option contract can be voided. The purchaser is the party who decides whether to exercise the option—the option party who incurs the credit risk equivalent to that of a forward foreign exchange contract. Once the option writer receives the premium from the purchaser, the writer incurs no further credit risk until expiration.

At expiration, the question of settlement risk arises, as discussed earlier.

Recommended Policy. Count 100 percent of settlement risk.

Complex Option Strategies

The credit risk for complex strategies that involve a combination of writing and purchasing options—for example, *range forwards*—is more difficult to measure.

Recommended Policy. To determine the credit risk for a complex option, the hedger should count 10 percent of the value of the options that are purchased and 100 percent of the settlement risk.

To measure the credit risk of new types of option strategies, the option user must understand the mechanics of the strategy proposed. Will the option user be writing or purchasing options and, if so, in what ratio of writes to purchases?

Interest Rate Options

The credit risk to the purchaser of an interest rate cap or floor is virtually identical. For the purpose of this discussion, only caps are discussed.

Assume that ABC Corporation has purchased an interest rate cap for USD 25 million for 3 years against 6-month LIBOR with a strike of 8 percent. The notional amount of the cap is USD 25 million. So long as LIBOR is below 8 percent on any of the payment dates, ABC will not receive anything from the seller. ABC will receive a payment from the seller only on payment dates when 6-month LIBOR is greater than 8 percent. Hence, if on the first payment date, 6-month LIBOR is $7\frac{7}{8}$ percent or less, ABC will receive nothing. If 6-month LIBOR is $8\frac{1}{4}$ on the payment date, ABC will receive USD 31,250.00. The computation is:[9]

$1,000,000.00 = $25,000,000 \times 8.00\% \times (180/360)$
$1,031,250.00 = $25,000,000 \times 8.25\% \times (180/360)$
$31,250.00 = $1,031,250.00 - $1,000,000.00$

The credit risk on this payment date would be $31,250, the amount due to ABC from the seller of the cap. The U.S. Dollar amount of the risk is small relative to the notional amount. If Eurodollar rates rose from 8 percent to 12 percent immediately after ABC purchased the cap, ABC's credit risk would be 4 percent per year for the life of the cap.

Credit Risk for an Interest Rate Cap

The credit risk is the cash flow expected to be generated over the life of the cap. That cash flow is equal to the difference in interest amounts, at each payment date, between the strike and the current market interest rate.

Recommended Policy. The credit risk policy recommended is that used by many portfolio managers: measure the credit risk of a cap or floor as 5 percent per year of the notional amount of the interest rate option. For

---

[9] The interest calculation is simplified by reducing the number of days from the actual for the interest period to 180 days.

example, in the case of ABC's cap, the deemed credit risk would be 15 percent of the notional amount, USD 3,750,000.

$3,750,000 = $25,000,000 \times 5\%/\text{year} \times 3 \text{ years}$

At the end of 1 year, the deemed risk would be reduced to 10 percent of the notional amount, or USD 2,500,000, because the cap would have only 2 years to run at that time. At the end of 2 years, the deemed credit risk would be only 5 percent of the notional amount, or USD 1,250,000, because the cap would have only 1 year to run.

For most interest rate hedging tools, credit risk decreases as time passes, because of the decreasing tenor of the instrument. In the example given here, the writer of the option incurs no credit risk. The writer's obligation to pay the purchaser is expressed in the interest rate option. The purchaser has no expressed or contingent liability to the writer.

FORWARD RATE AGREEMENTS

The credit risk for a *forward rate agreement* (FRA) is based on the same principle as that applicable to an interest rate cap or floor. Deemed credit risk is assumed to be 5 percent of the notional amount. For a 3×9 FRA having a notional value of USD 25 million with a strike of 8 percent, the deemed credit risk is USD 1.25 million. In practice, the probable credit risk is substantially smaller.

SWAP CREDIT RISK

The credit risk for swaps can be quantified by estimating the cost of replacement if a counterparty defaults. This concept is relevant to physical swaps, price swaps, and derivative contracts. Regardless of the type of contract, specifying the computations to be used in the event of default or early termination is always good business practice. The parties may otherwise disagree—perhaps all the way to litigation—about reference price assumptions and calculations.

The basic concept in this context is to enable computation of the difference between the present value of the existing swap and the presently available replacement. An interest rate swap is used here as a simple example. The first step would be to determine the difference between the existing swap's fixed interest rate and the contract's defined default rate or the currently available reinvestment opportunity rate with the same maturity date. Suppose the interest rate swap's fixed rate is 12 percent with semiannual cash settlement and the remaining term is 5 years when early termination occurs. (Note that all or part of a periodic payment may be due if a multi-period swap cash settles in arrears instead of in advance.) If the existing swap interest rate of 12 percent were higher than a currently available 8 percent rate to the same maturity date, then a fixed rate recipient would be concerned about the present value of the 4 percent difference for the remaining period of the swap, computed on the notional principal amount(s). If the existing swap interest rate of 12 percent were lower than a currently available 14 percent rate to the same maturity date, then the converse would apply—the defaulting party might be owed money.

The ISDA contract in Appendix C is a useful, self-explanatory reference for standard provisions for this problem. Particular attention should be given to Section 5, Events of Default and Termination Events, and Section 6, Early Termination, especially Section 6(e), Payments on Early Termination.

EXCHANGE-TRADED CONTRACTS

Because the exchange is the counterparty to all contracts, the counterparty credit issue is, as a practical matter, eliminated. Exchange-traded futures and written option contracts are subject to revaluation and margin. Failure to comply can result in the exchange's closing the position(s).

The exchange also limits the total number of contracts that an individual investor may hold. This limitation assists maintaining a diversity of other investors and restricts opportunities to "corner the market." Although special situations arise under conditions of war or other crises, the exchanges have generally weathered the storm to provide market liquidity and fair dealing. The exchanges' function is not to eliminate volatility.

For the typical corporate financial risk management situation, the exchanges provide minimal credit risk. The scenarios for margin requirements to maintain a hedge should, however, be planned.

HEDGING ADMINISTRATION—A CHECKLIST

Hedging administration, its importance and its methods, is an integral part of much of this book. Listed here, in capsulated form, are 10 essential components of effective hedging administration:

1. Identify specifically the risk exposure: its amount, nature, and timing. Determine the objective of a hedge.
2. Prepare a written plan documenting the risk, the assumptions made, and the alternatives for managing the financial risk.
3. Document the *underlying,* including identification of any *basis* risk.

4. Obtain required approvals of management and/or board of directors for the proposed financial risk management policy and procedures.
5. Make the hedging decision, taking into consideration the factors discussed in the early sections of this chapter.
6. Perform a thorough analysis of the proposed hedging transaction. Review credit and cash requirements, and terms and conditions of contracts.
7. Outline specifically the proposed hedging transaction before telephoning a bank or broker to obtain an indication.
8. Obtain indications from several banks or brokers for competitive pricing, if competitive pricing is appropriate.
9. When the trade(s) is executed, verify the terms on the confirmation immediately upon receipt.
10. Maintain a separate record of all open positions on hedge transactions, and monitor those positions.

12
Financial Reporting and Tax Highlights

> There is great variety of intelligibles in the world . . . and every several object is full of subdivided multiplicity and complicatedness.
>
> *Sir Matthew Hale,* The Primitive Organization of Mankind (1677)

The financial engineering techniques discussed in this book involve important accounting and tax considerations. The caution given at the outset of Chapter 4 bears repetition here: no specific legal, accounting, or tax advice is given or intended to be given. Such advice would be improper for the authors and unsafe for readers because this type of advice should be given—and applied—only with respect to a particular factual situation. Reliance on generic legal, accounting, or tax advice is risky for corporate financial engineers.

This book would render a disservice, however, if it did not remind readers that each transaction discussed requires careful attention—*before* entering into the transaction—to its accounting and tax consequences. This chapter is divided between financial reporting highlights and tax highlights, and is designed to provide a sample taste of some "flavors" of those consequences.[1] A final caution before embarking on this chapter: *forwards, futures, options,* and *swaps* all have different tax and accounting impacts on the corporation.

---

[1] The sample here provided is necessarily small; a thorough treatise is A. Kramer, *Financial Products—Taxation, Regulation, and Design* (2 vols., 1991), comprised of almost 1,500 pages.

FINANCIAL REPORTING HIGHLIGHTS

FINANCIAL REPORTING REQUIREMENTS: IN GENERAL

Financial reporting requirements for U.S. corporations differ substantially from the requirements for corporations in other countries. "In fact, increasing controversy surrounds the methods accounting communities of different countries use to arrive at numbers. Issues being raised include what it costs business both directly and indirectly to comply and whether U.S. companies in particular are at a disadvantage to European and Asian competitors."[2] This general statement may be accurately considered to include hedge accounting. In the United States, the Financial Accounting Standards Board (FASB), a private organization, prescribes the "official" accounting standards. The Securities and Exchange Commission has historically recognized FASB Statements as the standards for the domestic accounting community, but in 1990 it expressed concern about whether the standards were creating a disadvantage in international competition.

To be meaningful for corporate management, financial reporting of hedging gains and losses may require keeping three sets of records: records conforming to FASB accounting standards; records complying with the tax requirements of governmental authorities; and records providing pertinent information to management. The records for management's information are designed to enable control of the hedging risks and include allocation of hedging gains and losses to appropriate divisions within the company. They report the cost of designing, implementing, and monitoring each hedge transaction. Under present generally accepted accounting principles (GAAP), futures and forwards are not balance sheet items.

This part of the chapter is confined to stating, in brief and simplified terms, the key provisions pertinent to hedge accounting, as presented in the following FASB Statements:

- FASB Statement No. 52, "Foreign Currency Translation" (January 1982);
- FASB Statement No. 80, "Accounting for Futures Contracts" (August 1984);
- FASB Statement No. 95, "Statement of Cash Flows" (effective July 1988);
- FASB Statement No. 105, "Disclosure of Information about Financial Instruments with Off-Balance-Sheet Risk and Financial Instruments with Concentrations of Credit Risk" (March 1990).

[2] L. Keslar, "U.S. Accounting: Creating An Uneven Playing Field?," 3 *Corporate Risk Management* (February 1991): 20.

FASB Statement No. 105 (FASB 105) has a broad scope, covering all financial instruments that have a risk of accounting loss. In its definition of financial instruments, FASB 105 includes options, swaps, and other notional instruments, but excludes commodity contracts that can be settled by delivery.

FASB STATEMENT NO. 52, "FOREIGN CURRENCY TRANSLATION"

The Translation Process

The purpose of FASB 52 is to state the accounting and financial statement reporting requirements applicable to the reporting entity for translation of foreign currency transactions into the reporting currency. Under FASB 52, translation of foreign currency transactions has two objectives: (1) to provide information generally compatible with the expected economic effects of a currency rate change on the reporting entity's cash flows and equity; and (2) to reflect in the reporting entity's consolidated financial statements the financial results and relationships of each unit in the entity, measured in its functional currency, in accordance with U.S. generally accepted accounting principles (GAAP). FASB 52 emphasizes "functional currency"—the currency of the primary economic environment in which the business entity operates and generates cash. The concept of functional currency in hedge transactions is important not only in financial reporting, but also in tax considerations, as discussed later in the chapter.

The translation of foreign currency transactions is a three-step process. First, the functional currency must be identified. The reporting entity's management needs to identify the functional currency for the entity and for each of the entity's components. The functional currency decision is not necessarily based on legal entity; a foreign entity may have separable operations with different functional currencies. FASB 52 lists in its Appendix A six economic factors that can guide management in determining the functional currency applicable to the foreign currency transaction to be reported: cash flow, sales price, sales market, expenses, financing, and intercompany transactions and arrangements. For each of these factors, the appendix briefly describes two situations: in one, the functional currency is the foreign currency; in the other, the functional currency is the currency of the reporting parent entity. Corporate management should document, with reference to the economic factors relied on, the basis for its decision regarding the functional currency for the currency translation.

The second step in the foreign currency translation process is remeasurement of the foreign currency transaction. Remeasurement means measuring in the applicable functional currency the amounts that are stated in another currency. The third step, which is distinct from remeasurement, is translation adjustment. When the functional currency is the reporting currency, for example, the U.S. Dollar, the translation adjustment is made to current income. When the functional currency is a foreign currency, it is translated into the U.S. Dollar at the current exchange rate and the adjustment is not made to current income. FASB 52 superseded FASB 8,[3] which had been criticized, especially for its recognition of all translation gains and losses on the income statement. FASB 52 provides instead for a deferral of translation gains and losses in a foreign functional currency and for their accumulation in a separate component of shareholders' equity, pursuant to designated criteria. Appendix B of FASB 52 is a useful guide to remeasurement.

Hedge Accounting Under FASB 52

FASB 52 prescribes special standards for hedging transactions, including a forward exchange contract, and it expands application of the standards to agreements that are in substance similar to forward contracts. "Currency swaps" are specifically cited as an example of such an agreement. FASB 52 allows hedging in different currencies if not feasible to hedge in the same currency, but the hedging currency should be one for which the exchange rate usually moves in tandem with the currency being hedged. FASB 52 does not require the dates of the hedging commitment to match with the dates of the hedged commitment.

FASB 52 states the accounting standards for forward contracts and their ilk, with respect to exchange adjustments, as well as for reporting premium or discount on such contracts. FASB 52 requires amortization of discount or premium on foreign exchange contracts. The accounting required for exchange adjustments depends on the intent of management when it entered into the hedge transaction. Depending on the intent, the gain or loss on a hedging contract will be either deferred or reported in current income. Intent when entering into the transaction is classified in two categories: (1) to make a firm foreign currency commitment or a net investment in a foreign entity with a foreign functional currency, or (2) to enter into hedges other than those designated in (1). If the contract hedges a firm foreign currency commitment, the gain or loss is deferred and is part of the basis of the related foreign exchange transaction when recorded. If the contract hedges a net investment in a foreign entity, the translation adjustment (the gain or loss) is shown in a separate component of shareholders' equity. The discount or premium for either the foreign currency commitment or for the net investment in a foreign entity may be either (1) reported the same as the gain or loss on the contract, or (2) amortized over the life of the contract.

---

[3] FASB Statement No. 8, "Accounting for the Translation of Foreign Currency Transactions and Foreign Currency Financial Statements" (October 1975).

If, however, the hedging contract is other than a firm foreign currency commitment or a net investment in a foreign entity, then the gain or loss is included in current income. The discount or premium for either type of "nonfirm" hedging contract must be amortized over the life of the contract. Finally, if the contract is deemed to be a "speculation" rather than a hedge, the gain or loss is included in current income.

FASB STATEMENT NO. 80, "ACCOUNTING FOR FUTURES CONTRACTS"

In 1984, FASB Statement No. 80 (FASB 80) established standards of financial accounting and reporting for futures contracts, except for foreign currency futures, which remain governed by FASB 52. Forward contracts are not included in the standard. The FASB stated as a reason for excluding forward contracts from FASB 80 the fact that forwards usually result in delivery, whereas futures are hedging or investment contracts. FASB 80 defines a "futures contract" in its Appendix A; the definition reads in part:

> A legal agreement between a buyer or seller and the clearinghouse of a futures exchange. The futures contracts covered by this Statement include those traded on regulated futures exchanges in the United States and contracts having similar characteristics that are traded on exchanges in other countries.

The most noteworthy feature of FASB 80 is that it establishes mark-to-market procedure for a futures contract that does not meet the Statement's hedge criteria. Paragraph 3 of FASB 80 is express recognition of mark-to-market: "A change in the market value of a futures contract shall be recognized as a gain or loss in the period of the change unless the contract meets the criteria specified in this Statement to qualify as a hedge of an exposure to price or interest rate risk." The footnote to this sentence states that, under FASB 80, "the change in the market value of a futures contract equals the change in the contract's quoted market price multiplied by the contract size." The footnote provides the example of a $100,000 U.S. Treasury Bond futures contract whose price moves from 80-00 to 78-00, with resulting change in market value of $2,000. FASB 80's mark-to-market recognition for nonhedging futures "represents a significant departure from the concept of accounting for assets at historical cost."[4]

Paragraph 3 of FASB 80 also prescribes the accounting for a futures contract that meets the hedge criteria of paragraph 4. Two criteria are used: (1) the item to be hedged exposes the enterprise to price (or interest

---

[4] A. M. Stanger, "Accounting Developments—Accounting for Futures Contracts—to Hedge or Not to Hedge," 8 *Corporate Law Review* (Spring 1985): 173.

rate) risk, and (2) the futures contract reduces that exposure and is designated as a hedge. To meet the "risk" criterion, FASB 80 requires that the item(s) to be hedged contribute to the price or interest rate risk of the enterprise. To determine whether the item(s) to be hedged do so contribute, the enterprise must consider whether other assets, liabilities, firm commitments, and anticipated transactions already offset the exposure. The assessment of risk should be based on the total enterprise. If the enterprise cannot make this overall determination, however, because its risk management activities are not centralized, then the condition can be met if the intended hedge item exposes to risk the particular business unit entering into the hedging contract.

The second criterion—that the futures contract both reduces the exposure and is designated as a hedge—requires a "high correlation" between the market value of the futures contract and that of the hedged item. Stated otherwise, high correlation means that changes in the futures contract's market price move in the same direction and to the same degree as the hedged item's market price. The purpose of this "high correlation" requirement is to ensure that the futures contract(s) "will substantially offset the effects of price or interest rate changes on the exposed item(s)."[5]

If the transaction meets the hedge criteria, then "the accounting for the futures contract shall be related to the accounting for the hedged item so that changes in the market value of the futures contract are recognized in income when the effects of related changes in the price or interest rate of the hedged item are recognized."

Note these differences between FASB 52 and FASB 80:

- FASB 52, which relates to foreign exchange, requires amortization of discount or premium, and does not allow hedging future events;
- FASB 80, which relates to futures, does not allow amortization of discount or premium, and does allow hedging of future events.

Because no Financial Accounting Statement yet addresses accounting for swaps, FASB 80 is a useful guide, by analogy, for swap accounting.

FASB 80, a 6-page document comprised of 14 paragraphs, confines itself to broad guidelines and has three appendixes that are useful for applying the guidelines. Its Appendix A is a glossary that defines three terms used in the Statement: financial instrument, firm commitment, and futures contract. Its Appendix B provides four detailed examples of application of FASB 80. Its Appendix C, entitled "Background Information and Basis for Conclusions," offers a table of contents for ready reference and is recommended reading for

---

[5] FASB 80, par. 170, 4, a. and b.; the footnotes to par. 4 provide examples for application of both criteria.

the financial risk professional seeking needed familiarity with FASB 80. For corporate financial risk managers, a special recommendation is appropriate here: document the "judgment calls" that will be necessary to fulfill the hedge accounting requirements of FASB 80.

FASB STATEMENT NO. 95, "STATEMENT OF CASH FLOWS"

This Statement (FASB 95), adopted in 1987 and effective for fiscal years ending after July 15, 1988, was the culmination of a cash flow information project begun in 1981. The ensuing 6 years of work on the project included several exposure drafts, each followed by hundreds of comment letters; the 1984 FASB Concepts Statement No. 5; a Task Force on Cash Flow Reporting; and an Advisory Group on Cash Flow Reporting by Financial Institutions. FASB 95 was adopted by a 4-to-3 vote of the FASB. This brief background of FASB 95, derived from its Appendix A, manifests the importance, complexity, and controversial nature of cash flow reporting standards.

Appendix B to FASB 95, "Basis for Conclusions," begins with setting forth the need for cash flow information. After recognizing that financial reporting about an entity requires several financial statements, Appendix B quotes from FASB Concepts Statement No. 1, "Objectives of Financial Reporting by Business Enterprises," and from FASB Concepts Statement No. 5, "Recognition and Measurement in Financial Statements of Business Enterprises," concerning the need for cash flow information in financial statements. The following excerpt from paragraph 52 of FASB Concepts Statement No. 5 describes the role of information in the statement of cash flows:

> It provides useful information about an entity's activities in generating cash through operations to repay debt, distribute dividends, or reinvest to maintain or expand operating capacity; about its financing activities, both debt and equity; and about its investing or spending of cash. Important uses of information about an entity's current cash receipts and payments include helping to assess factors such as the entity's liquidity, financial flexibility, profitability, and risk.

The review here of FASB 95 is limited to paragraph 25, "Foreign Currency Cash Flows." The standard adopted is that a statement of cash flows by an enterprise with foreign currency transactions or foreign operations shall "report the reporting currency equivalent of foreign currency cash flows using the exchange rates in effect at the time of the cash flow." The standard allows, however, the alternative translation of "an appropriately weighted average exchange rate for the period . . . if the result is substantially the same as if the rates at the dates of the cash flows were used." FASB

95 notes that this alternative is consistent with paragraph 12 of FASB 52, which also permits an appropriately weighted average exchange rate for translation. The rationale for the alternative is the impracticality of translating receipts, expenses, gains, and losses at the exchange rates on the dates when they are recognized.

The standard for foreign currency cash flows concludes by requiring the effect of exchange rate changes on cash held in foreign currencies to be reported as a separate part of the reconciliation of the change in cash and cash equivalents during the reporting period. Paragraph 101 of Appendix B explains the reason for this requirement: because exchange rate changes do not themselves give rise to cash flows, the only effect of those changes on the reporting currency equivalent of cash held in foreign currencies is to affect the change in the enterprise's cash balance during the reporting period.

Appendix C to FASB 95 provides illustrations for preparing statements of cash flows. Example 2 (paragraphs 136 through 146 of Appendix C) illustrates a statement of cash flows under the direct method for a manufacturing company with foreign operations. In Example 2, a multinational U.S. corporation has two wholly owned foreign subsidiaries: (1) Subsidiary A, for which the local currency is the functional currency, and (2) Subsidiary B, for which the U.S. Dollar is the functional currency because the subsidiary is operating in a highly inflationary economy. The parent company's year-end Consolidating Statement of Cash Flows[6] lists "Effect of exchange rate changes on cash" as a separate item and shows the amounts attributable to each of the two subsidiaries. The year-end Consolidating Statement of Financial Position[7] notes the U.S. Dollar equivalents of one unit of local currency applicable to Subsidiary A and to Subsidiary B. The notes to the year-end Statements of Incomes[8] provide a detailed illustration of reporting the U.S. Dollar equivalent of the local currency amount for Subsidiary A and Subsidiary B respectively: for both subsidiaries, the U.S. Dollar equivalent is based on the exchange rate at the date of each transaction, except that, as to B, "For convenience, all purchases of inventory were based on the weighted-average exchange rate for the year."

Also included in Example 2 of Appendix C is a "Computation of Effect of Exchange Rate Changes on Cash,"[9] a helpful reference for ascertaining how a proposed hedging transaction will be reflected in the company's cash flow reporting.

---

[6] FASB 95, Appendix C, par. 136.
[7] *Id.*, par. 137.
[8] *Id.*, par. 142.
[9] *Id.*, par. 146.

FASB STATEMENT NO. 105, "DISCLOSURE OF INFORMATION ABOUT FINANCIAL INSTRUMENTS WITH OFF-BALANCE-SHEET RISK AND FINANCIAL INSTRUMENTS WITH CONCENTRATIONS OF CREDIT RISK"

Statement No. 105 (FASB 105), adopted March 1990 and effective for fiscal years ending after June 15, 1990, is a comprehensive accounting standard requiring all entities to disclose information about financial instruments with off-balance-sheet risk of accounting loss. "Financial instruments" are broadly defined and include:

1. Contracts imposing on one entity an obligation to deliver cash or another financial instrument and granting to a second entity a right to receive the cash or other financial instrument;
2. Contracts imposing on one entity an obligation to exchange financial instruments on potentially unfavorable terms;
3. Contracts granting a second entity a right to exchange other financial instruments on potentially favorable terms.

FASB 105's definition of "financial instruments" includes, therefore, instruments such as options and swaps.

"Risk of accounting loss" is a key concept in FASB 105 and relates only to losses from credit and market risks. When is a risk of accounting loss deemed to exist? Whenever adverse change may result because of recognizing an accounting loss that exceeds the amount shown in the balance sheet as attributable to a financial instrument contract.

What disclosure does FASB 105 require the reporting entity to make for a financial instrument with off-balance-sheet credit or market risk? The four basic requirements, simply stated, are as follows:

1. The face, contract, or *notional* principal amount;
2. The type and terms of the instrument, with (a) a description of its credit and market risk, and (b) pertinent accounting policies;
3. The entity's potential accounting loss (a) if any party to the financial instrument defaulted in performance under the contract, and (b) if any collateral securing the amount due proved to be valueless to the entity;
4. With respect to collateral or other security, (a) the entity's policy for requiring collateral, and (b) a short description of the collateral presently held, including its accessibility.

FASB 105 requires the entity to make a separate evaluation of each financial instrument or class of such instruments, to decide whether an off-balance-sheet risk exists. How to make this decision for the type of financial instruments discussed in this book is illustrated by the following:

> For example, a company that has written a call option on a security it holds in its portfolio has effectively offset any exposure resulting from changes in the value of the option and security. This type of option is referred to as a "covered call." Nonetheless, the call exposes the writer to off-balance-sheet risk because the option must be evaluated independently of the method of settlement.[10]

Although FASB 105 requires disclosure of financial instruments with "concentrations of credit risk," the Statement does not expressly define that term and does not indicate "how much" equals a reportable concentration. Instead, FASB 105 leaves that decision to the reporting entity. As part of sound corporate financial risk management, a policy should be developed stating the criteria for determining when a disclosable "concentration of credit risk" has occurred. See Chapter 11.

NO CONCLUSION—BUT SOME CONCLUSIONS

The accounting highlights included in this chapter are the warning tip of a large iceberg of accounting considerations for the continually increasing variety of corporate financial risk management contracts. Sound financial engineering obviously requires expert and "custom-tailored" accounting advice, but the highlights presented are intended to help the financial risk professional ask the right questions. Excellent treatises are available for further study, as are current articles in periodicals such as *Corporate Finance* and *Corporate Risk Management.*

Some questions do not yet have authoritative answers, and the accounting adviser can only make credible recommendations. Two of many examples have been selected. First, what is the proper accounting treatment for a *swaption?* In response to this question involving a corporation that issued fixed-rate debt at face for cash and simultaneously sold a swap option for the same notional amount to a third party for a premium, one expert opinion deemed that this would require mark-to-market accounting treatment.[11] The reason: the swaption hedges an anticipated transaction, that is, issuance of floating rate debt to refund the fixed rate term debt. The same opinion states that, to obtain deferral accounting, the swaption "should be linked to the future issuance of floating rate debt" and meet FASB 80's hedge criteria, or be linked to an effective fixed rate debt issuance.

---

[10] Ernst & Young, *Financial Reporting and Accounting 1990 Update* (November 1990), 19.
[11] "Taxation and Accounting—How To Treat Term Notes," 2 *Corporate Risk Management* (March/April 1990): 16.

Second, what is the accounting treatment for a "synthetic security"? A "synthetic security" has been defined, for accounting purposes, as "using one financial instrument to modify the terms of another. Modifications to a debt issue, for example, could include adjustments to interest payment streams, maturity dates or the currency denomination of cash flows."[12] An expert, after an analysis of current FASB regulations concerning options, concluded that no authoritative regulation for swaptions yet exists and recommended:

> [S]ynthetic security accounting should be applied in all cases where the precise accounting definition of a synthetic security is met. Basically, any cap, swaption, swap, call or put linked to the underlying basic financial instrument (e.g., debt) that is carried at historical cost should be accounted for as if it were imbedded in that basic financial instrument.[13]

What is the present status of accounting standards for strategic hedging and what is the prognosis? To answer this question adequately would require a long chapter, but some brief comments can be made. Some U.S. multinationals are concerned that their strategic hedging programs are in jeopardy because domestic accounting guidelines are a "source of confusion and contradiction," a situation that places the companies at a competitive disadvantage internationally.[14] For example, many foreign companies hedge their future earnings risk on foreign currency cash flows.

Both FASB 52 and FASB 80 provide for hedge accounting. "Both are designed to achieve some symmetry between accounting for the hedging instrument—forwards, futures, options and swaps—and the assets, liabilities or transactions being hedged. But the rules get inconsistent when transactions do not meet their specific criteria."[15]

FASB 52 and FASB 80, the two hedge accounting standards, have been criticized not only for their content but also for their omissions. No accounting guidance is provided by either standard for interest rate forwards or for interest rate and commodity swaps, and what is included in the standards suffers from inconsistencies.[16] A positive event merits mention: Neither FASB 52 nor FASB 80 addressed option contracts. In 1984, the Accounting Standards Executive Committee of the American Institute of Certified Public Accountants (AICPA) established a committee and task force which, 2 years later, reported the AICPA Options Issues Paper to provide guidance

---

[12] "Taxation and Accounting—FASB's Synthetic Fault Line," 2 *Corporate Risk Management* (January/February 1990): 12.

[13] *Id.* at 14.

[14] "Hedging Handicap," *Corporate Finance* (April 1990): 19. This 2-page article summarizes the position of risk managers at 50 Fortune 500 companies.

[15] Keslar, *op. cit.,* 20, 24.

[16] "FASB: Animal, Mineral or Hedge?," 3 *Corporate Risk Management* (February 1991): 25.

in reporting options transactions. A recent article reports: "The Emerging Issues Task Force (EITF) of the Financial Accounting Standards Board (FASB) has recently clarified some ambiguity regarding the use of foreign currency options contracts to hedge foreign currency exposure."[17] The international financial community does not have uniform standards, and a persuasive argument can be made for a global conference to develop uniform hedge accounting standards that would be applicable also in the United States.

In 1986, the Bank for International Settlements recognized the need for international guidelines for hedge accounting and suggested a sensible approach to hedge accounting problems:

> The accounting problems arising from these new instruments [innovative financial instruments] are best examined from two points of view. The first concerns the most appropriate manner in which specific instruments should be reported in financial statements and how they should be related to other positions, most importantly those existing on the balance sheet . . . .
>
> The second way in which accounting questions can be examined is from the point of view of the users. On the one hand, for management and supervisors these innovations affect their appraisal of organizational control systems of performance, since the monitoring of exposures is rendered more complex. On the other hand, for external users of accounts—shareholders and creditors, and the tax authorities—inadequate accounting hampers the evaluation of risk and return relationships.[18]

TAX HIGHLIGHTS

The American author O. Henry changed the familiar "Fools rush in . . ." maxim to "A kind of mixture of fools and angels—they rush in and fear to tread at the same time."[19] The authors of this book are ineligible for the category of angels. They hope to be also ineligible for the category of fools, even after undertaking to discuss, in a very few pages, the highlights of tax considerations for financial risk engineering. Nonetheless, with a light tread, entry is made into the maze of the tax laws and regulations applicable to the contracts involved in corporate financial risk management. The limited purposes for including "tax" are these: to provide key statutory and regulatory references and to assist the financial risk professional in asking a qualified tax adviser the right questions at the right time. Readers are

[17] M. S. Joseph, "Hedge Accounting Puzzle Clarified," 3 *Corporate Risk Management* (March 1991): 8.
[18] Bank for International Settlements, *Recent Innovations in International Banking* (1986), 227.
[19] *The Moment of Victory* (1909).

warned that the U.S. and foreign tax laws relating to the contracts needed for financial engineering are not an area in which tax advice should be obtained by obliging a relative or friend who is "trying to get started" as a tax expert.

CODE SECTION 1221: WHEN IS A "HEDGING" TRANSACTION A CAPITAL ASSET?

Section 1221 of the Internal Revenue Code ("the Code") defines "capital asset" broadly: "property held by the taxpayer (whether or not connected with his trade or business)." Seven specific classes of property are excluded from capital-asset status; of the seven, the inventory exception is relevant here.

In 1955, the United States Supreme Court decided *Corn Products Refining Co. v. Commissioner.*[20] The taxpayer was a company that converted corn into starches, sugars, and other products. The taxpayer had contended that its sales of corn futures resulted in capital gains and losses, because hedging is not within Code Section 1221's exclusions. The Court rejected that contention and held that the taxpayer's dealings in corn futures resulted in ordinary income or loss.

In 1988, the United States Supreme Court decided *Arkansas Best Corp. v. Commissioner.*[21] The taxpayer relied on the *Corn Products* decision to support its position that it was entitled to take an ordinary loss for additional bank stock purchased to infuse more capital into a problem bank in which it had acquired a controlling interest. The taxpayer argued that the Court in *Corn Products* intended to create a general exemption from capital-asset status for assets acquired for business purposes, that is, an asset's status as "property" turns on the motivation for its acquisition. The Court rejected the taxpayer's contention and held that the loss resulting from sale of the stock was a capital loss. The Court acknowledged that the motive test for determining an asset's status "finds much support in the academic literature and in the courts." Nonetheless, the Court held that the motive test directly conflicts with Code Section 1221 and that a business connection is relevant only to determine the applicability of the statutory exceptions. *Corn Products* was then distinguished on the ground that it involved application of Code Section 1221's inventory exception. The Court declared: "We conclude that *Corn Products* is properly interpreted as standing for the narrow proposition that hedging transactions that are an integral part of a business's inventory-purchase system fall within the inventory exclusion of § 1221."

[20] 350 U.S. 46 (1955).
[21] 485 U.S. 212, 108 S. Ct. 971 (1988).

Arkansas Best has been the subject of much comment and criticism, well-summarized by the following:

> "*Arkansas Best* created a world of uncertainty," says Daniel Breen of the Office of Chief Counsel at the U.S. Internal Revenue Service (IRS).
>
> Worse, the 1988 Supreme Court decision "has left open the potential for serious tax whipsaws for both taxpayers and the IRS," according to several attorneys familiar with the court case often cited in connection with attempts to define "hedging."[22]

CODE SECTION 1256: "CONTRACTS MARKED-TO-MARKET"—NOT APPLICABLE TO HEDGING TRANSACTIONS

Code Section 1256 provides when a gain from a Code Section 1256 contract is to be treated as a capital asset, unless the taxpayer elects to claim that the contract is exempt as a "hedging transaction" under Code Section 1256(e). Code Section 1256(e)(4) imposes certain limitations on losses from hedging transactions. Code Section 1256 will apply unless "the taxpayer clearly identifies such transaction as being a hedging transaction" before the close of the day on which the transaction is entered into—or at an earlier time, if prescribed by regulation. A Code Section 1256 contract is defined to mean any regulated futures contract, any foreign currency contract, any nonequity option, and any dealer equity option. The statute defines each of these contracts, in Code Section 1256(g):

- A regulated futures contract means a contract:

   (A) with respect to which the amount to be deposited, and the amount which may be withdrawn depends on a system of marking to market, and
   (B) which is traded on or subject to the rules of a qualified board of exchange.

- A foreign currency contract means a contract:

   (i) which requires delivery of, or the settlement of which depends on the value of, a foreign currency which is a currency in which positions are also traded through regulated futures contracts,
   (ii) which is traded in the interbank market, and
   (iii) which is entered into at arm's length at a price determined by reference to the price in the interbank market.

---

[22] K. Schap, "For U.S. Grain 'Hedgers,' Options Can Prove Taxing," 20 *Futures* (May 1991): 42.

- A nonequity option means any listed option that is not an equity option.
- A dealer equity option means any listed option which:

    (A) is an equity option,

    (B) is purchased or granted by such options dealer in the normal course of his activity of dealing in options, and

    (C) is listed on the qualified board or exchange on which such options dealer is registered.

An option with respect to a group of stocks or stock index is excepted from the statute's application if the Commodities Futures Trading Commission has in effect a designation, approved by the Treasury, of a contract market for a contract based on that group or index.

The taxpayer may also elect to have Code Section 1256 not apply to all Code Section 1256 contracts that are part of a "mixed straddle," as "straddle" is defined in Code Section 1092(c). In order to have Code Section 1256 not apply, one, but not all, of the positions of the straddle may be Code Section 1256 contracts; the taxpayer must clearly identify each position forming part of the straddle before the close of the day on which the Code Section 1256 contract is entered into, unless the Treasury prescribes an earlier time.

The Congressional Committee Reports on Code Section 1256[23] are recommended reading for a better understanding of the provisions of the statute and the intended effect. A fair comment is that Code Section 1256 has not clarified the tax situation for risk management. A recent survey of the views of "advisors, bankers, hedging specialists, journalists and tax and accounting specialists (but hardly [constituting] a valid statistical sample)" is a striking illustration that determining the tax and accounting treatment for a risk management tactic is at best a credible guess.[24] The survey, which related to grain hedging, included six risk management tactics for declining prices and four for rising prices; their respective economic consequences; and tax and accounting treatment. Diverse responses were made to the question asked for each tactic: "Is it a hedge?" A reliable answer to this question awaits further, and improved, Congressional action with respect to hedging status under the tax laws. Until legislation eases the uncertainty, let the risk manager be aware and beware.

---

[23] Committee Reports on Pub. L. No. 99-514, 98-369, 97-44, and 97-34. A reference source for these Reports is Stand. Fed. Tax. Rep. (CCH), par. 32,700.

[24] Chart, attributed to Tony Freeland, a grain market analyst and hedger for Demeter, Inc. and Continental Bank tax and accounting specialists, 20 *Futures* (May 1991): 44.

FOREIGN CURRENCY-DENOMINATED TRANSACTIONS UNDER THE CODE

Code Sections 985 through 989, added by the Tax Reform Act of 1986, comprise the extensive rules governing taxation by the United States of transactions denominated in a foreign currency—a currency that is not the taxpayer's functional currency.

Code Section 985 defines functional currency and generally requires all federal income tax determinations to be made in a taxpayer's functional currency. The concept of a functional currency, according to a Senate Committee Report, "presupposes a long-term commitment to a specific economic environment." Gain or loss on a foreign currency transaction is governed by Code Section 988 and almost 50 pages (in small print) of Temporary Regulations. Code Section 989 defines a "qualified business unit" (QBU) and the criteria for identifying its functional currency.

Code Section 985: "Functional Currency"

Code Section 985(a) provides that all tax determinations made regarding foreign currency transactions shall be made in the taxpayer's functional currency "unless otherwise provided in regulations." Code Section 985(b)(1)(A) provides that the functional currency is the U.S. Dollar, except as provided in subparagraph (B), which states that the functional currency for a QBU means "the currency of the economic environment in which a significant part of each unit's activities are conducted and which is used by such unit in keeping its books and records." Code Section 985(b)(2) provides that the functional currency of any QBU "shall be the dollar if activities of such unit are primarily conducted in dollars." Code Section 985(b)(3) allows the taxpayer to elect, if very limited prescribed conditions are met, to use the U.S. Dollar as the functional currency for a QBU. Code Section 985 is important because federal income tax treatment of foreign currency-denominated transactions depends on the "identity" of the taxpayer's functional currency.

The Treasury Department, through the Internal Revenue Service, has promulgated Treasury Regulations, both temporary and permanent, with respect to Code Section 985.[25] These Regulations merit the financial risk manager's reading, to become acquainted with the scope and general nature of the functional currency provision. For example, the Regulations address: functional currency for a non-QBU taxpayer and a QBU;[26] factors determining the QBU's economic environment, which in turn determines the QBU's

---

[25] Treas. Reg. §§ 1.985.1–1.985-6T.
[26] Treas. Reg. §§ 1.985-1(b)(1) and 1.985-1(c). *See also* Treas. Reg. §§ 1.989-1(a) and 1.989-1(b)(2)(i) and (ii).

functional currency;[27] the QBU's functional currency under GAAP usually acceptable for tax purposes;[28] the determination and effect of the QBU's residence; election of the U.S. Dollar as the functional currency;[29] and the concomitant of the election, computing income using the U.S. Dollar approximate separate transactions method (DASTM).[30]

Code Section 988

This provision prescribes the rules for treatment of exchange gain or loss on transactions in a currency that is *not* the taxpayer's functional currency. *Subject to certain exclusions and election provisions, foreign currency gain or loss on a Code Section 988 transaction is computed separately and treated as ordinary income or loss.* In 1988, the Technical and Miscellaneous Revenue Act (TAMRA)[31] amended Code Section 988 in several respects that are important to hedging contracts. These included:

- The term "Section 988 transaction" was redefined to include "entering into or acquiring any forward contract, futures contract, option or similar financial instrument."[32] TAMRA omitted from the end of this definition the 1986 language: "unless such instrument would be marked to market under Section 1256 if held on the last day of the taxable year." This amendment clarified that taxpayers acquiring Code Section 1256 contracts cannot elect, by disposing of the contracts before the last day of the taxable year, to have Code Section 988 rules apply.
- Any regulated futures contract or nonequity option remains subject to "marked to market under Section 1256 if held on the last day of the taxable year" and thereby also subject to gain or loss under Code Section 1256, with two exceptions. The contract or option is not subject to "marked-to-market" rules or to gain and loss treatment if it is part of a hedging transaction under Code Section 1256(e), or it is subject to an "election out" under Code Section 988. The election-out provision allows a taxpayer to consent to have certain regulated futures and options treated as Code Section 988 transactions, and hence ordinary income or loss provisions will apply.
- Code Section 988(a)(3) provides rules for sourcing of gains, and merits careful attention. Sourcing is important for a foreign tax credit.

[27] Treas. Reg. § 1.985-1(c)(2).
[28] Treas. Reg. § 1.985-1(f).
[29] Treas. Reg. §§ 1.985-2 and 1.985-3.
[30] Treas. Reg. §§ 1.985-2(d) and 1.985-3(b), (c), and (d).
[31] Pub. L. No. 100-647, 102 Stat. 3342 (1986).
[32] I.R.C. § 988(c)(1)(B)(iii).

The Temporary Regulations for Code Section 988 are lengthy, exhaustive, and have numerous detailed examples that aid in understanding the Regulations' intricate provisions. An attempt to describe, even generally, the content of the Temporary Regulations relating to Code Section 988 would cause both the reader and the authors to disobey the childhood precept: "Don't be like little Johnny Possum, full of tales half-heard and very badly told." Instead, reference is made to an excellent and readable analysis of the Temporary Regulations.[33]

INTERNAL REVENUE SERVICE NOTICE 89-21

Notice 89-21[34] provides "guidance concerning federal income tax treatment of lump-sum payments received in connection with interest rate and currency swap contracts, interest rate cap contracts, and similar financial products ('notional principal contracts')." The Notice announces that regulations will be issued providing specific rules regarding the method that a taxpayer must use to take into account, over the life of a notional principal contract, payments made or received under that contract. For notional principal contracts entered into before the regulations become effective, a method of accounting will "generally" be treated as clearly reflecting income if it takes the payments into account "over the life of the contract under a reasonable amortization method."

TREASURY REGULATION § 1.863-7 (1991)

On January 11, 1991, the Internal Revenue Service published final Treasury Regulation § 1.863-7. This Regulation sets forth the rules for determining the source of income attributable to notional principal contracts. The income source for income from a notional principal contract is generally determined by the residence of the party receiving the payment. Thus, if a foreign counterparty, resident outside the United States, receives payment from a U.S. counterparty under a notional principal contract, the payment is treated as foreign source income not subject to U.S. income tax withholding. If the income under the notional principal contract is derived from conduct of a U.S. business, then the income is treated as "effectively connected" to the conduct of a U.S. business. For a U.S. resident, the source of income from the notional principal contract is determined by the residence of a "qualified business unit" if applicable conditions are met.

---

[33] A.B.A. Section on Taxation, Committee on Foreign Activities of U.S. Taxpayers, "Comments on Regulations Dealing with Foreign Currency Transactions," 44 *Tax Lawyer* (Fall 1990): 71.
[34] 1989-1 C.B. 651.

An important reminder with respect to withholding tax on income from the risk-hedging contracts that are the subject of this book: the withholding tax requirements vary from country to country; hence, when doing a deal with a foreign counterparty, the withholding tax requirement of the counterparty's country should be ascertained—and factored into the financial appraisal of the proposed transaction.

CONCLUSION

About 25 B.C., Quintius Horatius Flaccus, a/k/a Horace, wrote: "He has half the deed done, who makes a beginning." This chapter's brief recounting of financial reporting and tax highlights pertinent to financial engineering has served its purpose if "half the deed" is done.

13
Selected Developments in the Legal Arena

Make use now, and provide for thine own future safety.

Shakespeare, Henry VIII

The contents of this chapter are constrained by both the allowable length for this book and the fact that this is not a law book. This is not stated as an apology but as an explanation for omissions and for the brief coverage given to each subject. The intention here is to whet the reader's appetite to pursue further information. The selections made are attributable only to arbitrary choice. Nonetheless, the chapter serves as a reminder that the law is far from static in the area of corporate financial risk transactions. Corporate financial risk professionals are urged, therefore, to keep informed of the major changes and potential trends in the laws affecting the transactions discussed in this book. Each topic selected is prefaced by a scrap from Shakespeare as a descriptive aid.

THE HAMMERSMITH AND FULHAM DEBACLE

Behold the great impact of authority.

The whole Hammersmith and Fulham affair is a dramatic illustration of the necessity for banks to assess the legal risk—*the authority*—as well as the credit risk, of its counterparties in swap transactions. If the counterparty is a foreign country, the political risk should also be considered. The cliché that "hard facts make bad law" takes on renewed truth when applied to the *Hammersmith* case, which has become a byword in the law applicable to swaps. Nearly 80 international banks face mark-to-market losses of approximately GBP 600 million, arising out of interest rate swap agreements with 130 British local councils and other local authorities.[1]

The local authorities had entered into interest rate swaps, in which they exchanged fixed interest rate payments for floating rate payments on the same notional debt. After 2 years in the courts, the highest court in Great Britain, the House of Lords, ruled on January 24, 1991, that all swap contracts entered into by local authorities are illegal and void. The ruling by the Law Lords came in a case involving the Hammersmith and Fulham Council, which is the London borough's local council. The Council had undertaken, in numerous separate contracts, to accept the interest rate risk on a large amount of floating rate debt—with the faulty anticipation that interest rates would fall. Instead, interest rates went up. The Council engaged in interest rate swaps, worth hundreds of millions of Pounds Sterling, with 55 banks; incurred huge losses; owed the banks about GBP 300 million; and, at one stage, the Council's swap dealings accounted for 1/2 percent of the entire worldwide swap market.[2] When the Council suspended payments for its losses, a group of the banks brought the suit that ended in the swap contracts' being declared void.

Beyond dispute is the fact that the Hammersmith and Fulham Council engaged in a speculative binge.[3] The Council had only about GBP 385 million of outstanding debt, but in a 2-year period entered into swaps totaling a notional principal amount of over GBP 6 billion. The banks credibly claimed that they were unaware of the speculation because the Council had dealt with so many banks. Nonetheless, the hard fact of "speculation" was before the Law Lords, with the result that all swap contracts entered into by all the local authorities were declared void. In May 1991, the central government decided not to intervene and hence not to seek to alter existing legal obligations.

The final *Hammersmith* chapter has not yet been written: the banks will be instituting suits against the local authorities, seeking restitution; some of the local councils did well with their interest rate swaps and are displeased with the decision; and the impact on the City of London's reputation is still being debated. The *Financial Times,* in commenting on *Hammersmith,* stated a warning with international application: "More generally, the swaps affair has vividly demonstrated the speed with which financial innovation can overtake the law."[4]

---

[1] "Cleaning Up the Town Hall Mess," *Euromoney* (April 1991): 31.
[2] *Id.*
[3] *Financial Times* (London), January 25, 1991.
[4] *Financial Times* (London), May 25, 1991.

The crux of the *Hammersmith* debacle was that the local councils did not have the legal capacity, that is, the authority, to enter into interest rate hedging contracts. The banks had sought advice from lawyers and governmental agencies concerning the authority of local councils to enter into swap dealings. Although the Council officers had authorized the swap transactions under client agreements, the authorizations were *ultra vires*—outside the legal powers that Parliament has granted to councils. Hindsight suggests that both parties should have given further attention to the authority of the councils to enter into the interest rate swaps.

The ISDA Agreement (see Chapter 4 and Appendix C) is structured so that if the counterparty is a financial institution holding itself out as having the capacity to transact in the swaps market by having authorized its dealers, prompt confirmation of that authority is feasible. If, however, the counterparty is a sovereign state, local governmental entity, or quasi-governmental body, corporation, or partnership, the ISDA Agreement has relevant schedules for documenting the counterparty's authority to enter into a swap transaction.

As yet, no legal debacle involving swaps in the dimensions of *Hammersmith* has yet occurred in the United States. Nonetheless, the famous public bond default in the State of Washington, "WHOOPS,"[5] is legally analogous to the *Hammersmith* debacle. The court viewed the huge bond issue as *ultra vires* and hence void. *Hammersmith* and WHOOPS combined provide the potential for U.S. courts to invalidate swap transactions entered into by a governmental entity.

THE ARBITRATION ALTERNATIVE

A good note: that keeps you from the blow of the law.

Alternative dispute resolution, often abbreviated as ADR, is increasingly used as a more economical, expert, and expeditious means of resolving civil disputes than resort to the courts. Although arbitration has been used for

[5] WHOOPS refers to the substantial litigation arising from the public sale of over $2 billion of revenue bonds by the Washington Public Power Supply System (WPPSS), a municipal corporation with several cities and public utility districts as members. The purpose of the bonds was to fund construction of two nuclear power plants, which were never completed. WPPSS entered into a Participants' Agreement with 88 public utilities, under which the utilities agreed to pay WPPSS for the nuclear projects whether or not they were ever completed or operable. In Chemical Bank v. Washington Public Power Supply System, 99 Wash. 772, 666 P.2d 329 (1983), *aff'd on reh'g,* 102 Wash. 2d 874, 691 P.2d 524 (1984), *cert. denied,* 471 U.S. 1075 (1985), the Washington Supreme Court held that none of the participating public utilities had legal authority to enter into the elaborate financing arrangement to guarantee bond payments. With the bonds in default, private class action litigation was instituted by the bondholders; citations to the opinions in those actions are omitted here. Ultimately, a settlement of $274,600,000 was approved for 10,000 bondholders. 20 Securities Regulation & Law Report (BNA) 1720 (1988).

many years, its use has greatly increased in recent years, as evidenced by the following:

1. Court-annexed arbitration and mediation,[6] authorized by statute or rule and either mandatory or voluntary, are becoming prevalent;
2. Private organizations providing arbitration and mediation services have proliferated;
3. The American Arbitration Association reported that in 1990 its filings had grown to over 60,000 cases.

The federal government has long fostered arbitration. The Federal Arbitration Act (FAA), originally enacted in 1925, was amended in 1988 to provide that the "act of state" doctrine—the acts of a foreign government are not subject to review by a United States court—is inapplicable.[7] The FAA had been amended in 1970 to declare the enforceability of the Convention on the Recognition and Enforcement of Foreign Arbitral Awards, and was amended again in 1990 to declare the enforceability of the Inter-American Convention of International Commercial Arbitration.[8]

Federal policy, as exemplified by statute and court decisions, strongly favors arbitration as an alternative dispute resolution process. For example, in *Necchi S.p.A. v. Necchi Sewing Machine Sales Corp.,*[9] the court stated that federal arbitration policy requires that "any doubts concerning the

---

[6] Mediation is different from arbitration: it is less formal; the mediator is not empowered to render a binding decision; and no evidentiary hearings are held. Mediation is a procedure by which the disputants voluntarily submit their dispute to a neutral mediator, who need not be a lawyer and who works with them to reach a settlement of the dispute. The mediator may meet separately and jointly with the disputants. Mediation can occur before or after a lawsuit is filed or arbitration is undertaken, without causing a delay in either process. Mediation probes the facts, explores alternatives for solutions to the dispute, and seeks to structure a settlement.

[7] The act of state doctrine, which is judicially created, has undergone evolution over the years. The doctrine is a consequence of the separation of powers under the United States Constitution, reflecting "the strong sense of the Judicial Branch that its engagement in the task of passing on the validity of foreign acts of state may hinder" the conduct of foreign affairs. Banco Nacional de Cuba v. Sabbatino, 376 U.S. 398, 423, 84 S.Ct. 923, 937, 11 L.Ed.2d 804 (1964).

The United States Supreme Court recently redefined the doctrine in W.S. Kirkpatrick v. Environmental Tectonics Corp., _____ U.S. _____, 110 S.Ct. 701, 107 L.Ed.2d 816 (1990):

> The act of state doctrine does not establish an exception for cases and controversies that may embarrass foreign governments, but merely requires that, in the process of deciding, the acts of foreign sovereigns taken within their own jurisdictions shall be deemed valid. 110 S.Ct. at 707.

[8] The United States Arbitration Act is found in 9 U.S.C. §§ 1–14; first enacted February 12, 1925, 43 Stat. 883; codified July 30, 1947, 61 Stat. 770; amended September 3, 1954, 68 Stat. 1233; Chapter 2 added July 31, 1970, 84 Stat. 692; inapplicability of act of state doctrine added November 16, 1988, 102 Stat. 3969; Chapter 3 added August 15, 1990, 104 Stat. 449.

[9] 348 F.2d 693 (2d Cir. 1965), *cert. denied,* 383 U.S. 909, 86 S.Ct. 892, 15 L.Ed.2d 664 (1966).

scope of arbitrable issues should be resolved in favor of arbitration." A 1991 application of this policy is provided by *David L. Threlkeld & Co. v. Metallgesellschaft Ltd.*[10] Threlkeld is a Vermont corporation engaged in trading forward contracts for metals. To purchase and sell forward contracts on the London Metals Exchange (LME) (which also trades futures), a licensed "ring-dealing" member must execute the transaction as principal. Metallgesellschaft (MG) is a ring-dealing member with whom Threlkeld entered into a collateral agreement for evaluation of Threlkeld's outstanding forward contracts. The LME Rules require arbitration of all disputes "arising out of or in relation to" a particular contract. Although the collateral agreement between Threlkeld and MG did not contain an arbitration provision, it did incorporate the LME Rules.

Threlkeld sued MG for breach of the collateral agreement, claiming that the LME Rules mandating arbitration did not apply to that agreement, and that Vermont law voids any arbitration agreement lacking a specific acknowledgment of arbitration signed by both parties. The trial court agreed and granted summary judgment in favor of Threlkeld. The Second Circuit Court of Appeals reversed, and certain grounds for its reversal are pertinent here.

1. The international business transactions involved were governed by federal arbitration law, which preempted the Vermont arbitration statute.[11]

2. "The policy in favor of arbitration is even stronger in the context of international business transactions." The court cited two United States Supreme Court decisions in support of this statement, *Mitsubishi Motors Corp. v. Soler Chrysler-Plymouth,*[12] and *Scherk v. Alberto-Culver Co.*[13]

3. Because the metals contracts were contracts for the purchase and sale of commodities futures in London, England, by a Vermont-based corporation, they "certainly involved international commerce." The

---

[10] 923 F.2d 245 (2d Cir. 1991), *cert. docketed,* No. 91-19 (U.S. Sup. Ct. June 27, 1991).

[11] *Cf.* Volt Information Sciences v. Board of Trustees of Leland Stanford Junior University, 489 U.S. 468, 109 S.Ct. 1248, 103 L.Ed.2d 488 (1989), in which the court affirmed a California court's stay of arbitration in a matter involving interstate commerce. The contract had a broad arbitration clause and the choice of law clause provided that the contract was "governed by the law of the place where the Project is located," which was California. California law allows stays of arbitration, but the FAA does not. The Supreme Court held that the FAA did not conflict with the California law, because the federal act permits arbitration by state rule, including a rule to stay arbitration. The decision has engendered controversy as to whether it reflects a shift from the view that the federal arbitration act preempts state arbitration statutes. *See* J.D. Becker, "Choice of Law and the Federal Arbitration Act: the Shock of Volt," *Arbitration & the Law, 1989–90,* AAA General Counsel's Annual Report (American Arbitration Association), 31.

[12] 473 U.S. 614, 629–31, 105 S.Ct. 3346, 3355–56, 87 L.Ed.2d 444 (1985).

[13] 417 U.S. 506, 516–18, 94 S.Ct. 2249, 2455–57, 41 L.Ed.2d 270 (1974).

collateral valuation agreement was "inextricably tied" to those international trading contracts and hence was a contract "involving commerce" within the meaning of the FAA.

4. The court expressly resolved all doubts as to enforceability of the arbitration clause in favor of arbitration, in accordance with federal policy. The court then broadly construed the LME Rules on arbitration to cover the dispute between Threlkeld and MG.

The states are also supportive of arbitration as a means of resolving civil disputes and relieving the courts of their burden. Thirty-four states and the District of Columbia have adopted the Uniform Arbitration Act and most of the nonadopting states—New York, for example—have some form of state-sanctioned arbitration. Thus, at both the federal and state level, alternative dispute resolution enjoys a favorable climate.

Alternative dispute resolution offers a procedure that financial risk management professionals are encouraged to consider favorably. Disputes between the parties to hedging contracts may be ill-suited for satisfactory resolution by trial by jury or to a court. As this basic book illustrates: modern contracts for corporate financial risk management are varied, inherently complex, and written in their own technical vocabulary. Alternative dispute resolution appears to offer a practical means for resolving disputes between the parties to these hedging contracts: ADR is less costly and more expeditious than the court system; time-consuming and hence expensive discovery is limited, with depositions a rarity; and the disputing parties can submit the dispute to a third-party neutral, either lawyer or nonlawyer, who has experience with the type of contract on which the dispute is based.

RISK-BASED CAPITAL ADEQUACY RULES

Measure for measure must be answered.

In 1989, the three United States banking agencies, the Board of Governors of the Federal Reserve System (FRB), the Office of the Comptroller of the Currency (OCC), and the Federal Deposit Insurance Corporation (FDIC), issued final risk-based capital guidelines. A caution and recommendation are appropriate: only a cursory mention of the risk-based capital guidelines is suitable in this book; the financial risk professional should, however, maintain awareness of the applicable guidelines.

The guidelines of all three agencies include a definition of capital and a framework for calculating weighted risk assets by assigning assets and off-balance-sheet items to broad risk categories. Off-balance-sheet items include special provisions for interest rate and foreign exchange rate instruments.

Although the risk-based capital guidelines make no express reference to commodity price swaps, a reasonable inference is that they would be subject to the same capital adequacy requirements applicable to interest rate and currency swap contracts. The inference is supported by two OCC Staff No-Objection Letters, No. 87-5[14] and No. 90-1.[15] In Staff No-Objection Letter No. 87-5, which antedated adoption of the OCC guidelines, the OCC took the position of no objection to a bank's acting as principal in matched commodity price index swaps and stated:

> Finally, it should be noted that the Office has proposed risk based capital guidelines on interest rate swaps and foreign currency swaps which are consistent with this no objection position. . . . The risk associated with commodity price index swaps is not different from that posed by these types of swaps and can be prudently managed and covered by capital requirements.

In 1990, the OCC in its No-Objection Letter No. 90-1, after adoption of the guidelines, took the position of no objection to a bank acting as principal in unmatched commodity price index swaps. The OCC acknowledged that banks acted as principals in matched and unmatched interest rate and currency swaps, as well as in matched commodity price index swaps. The OCC found that, by entering into an unmatched commodity price swap contract, a bank does not undertake any qualitatively different risk, but suggested: "In determining appropriate exposure limits, the Bank may wish to take into consideration the principles for netting multiple interest rate and currency swap contracts with a single counterparty set forth in Section 3(b)J(5) of OCC's Risk-Based Capital Guidelines."

JURISDICTIONAL DISPUTES: *CFTC V. SEC; STATE BUCKET SHOP LAWS V. FEDERAL LAWS*

In these nice sharp quillets of the law . . . .

Jurisdiction of a court means its authority, granted by constitution or statute, to hear and decide cases. Jurisdiction of an administrative agency is its authority, prescribed by statute, to regulate and to make administrative decisions.

CFTC v. SEC

The jurisdictional dispute between the Commodity Futures Trading Commission (CFTC) and the Securities and Exchange Commission (SEC), more

---

[14] July 20, 1987; reprinted in Fed. Banking L. Rep. (CCH), ¶84,034.

[15] February 16, 1990); reprinted in Fed. Banking L. Rep. (CCH), ¶ 83,095.

often but less politely called the "turf war," is still ongoing. The corporate financial risk professional, as a noncombatant, can best avoid the war zone by keeping informed of the respective positions of the CFTC and the SEC.

The roots of the dispute help to identify current developments and are here briefly described.[16] In 1922, Congress enacted the Commodity Exchange Act (CEA); in 1974, it amended the CEA to establish the Commodity Futures Trading Commission (CFTC). The 1974 amendments to Section 2 of the Act granted the CFTC exclusive jurisdiction over commodity futures contracts and options, and added the so-called Treasury Amendment.[17] The Treasury Amendment provides:

> Nothing in this chapter shall be deemed to govern or in any way be applicable to transactions in foreign currency, security warrants, security rights, resale of installment loan contracts, repurchase options, government securities, or mortgages and mortgage purchase commitments unless such transactions involve the sale thereof for future delivery conducted on a board of trade.

The courts have not applied a uniform standard in determining the scope of the Treasury Amendment's exclusion of cash forward contracts.[18] In 1975, the CFTC granted the Chicago Board of Trade's application to designate and trade futures contracts on Government National Mortgage Association (GNMA) certificates.[19] The SEC deemed these contracts to be securities subject to SEC jurisdiction and responded by urging Congress in 1978 to grant the SEC jurisdiction over hybrid hedging instruments. Although the SEC's effort was unsuccessful, Congress did amend the CEA in 1978 to require the CFTC to "maintain communications" with the Department of the Treasury, the Federal Reserve's Board of Governors, and the SEC; to keep those agencies informed of relevant CFTC activities; to seek their views; and to consider the relationships between commodity

---

[16] J.W. Markham, "Regulation of Hybrid Instruments under the Commodity Exchange Act: A Call for Alternatives," 1 *Columbia Business Law Review* (1990): 1 is recommended reading, for its excellent historical review of regulation of hybrid instruments and its wealth of references. Also see P. Johnson and T. Hazen, *Commodities Regulation* (2d Ed.), 1990 Supp. at 81 *et seq.* (reprint of article by the former chairman of the CFTC, Philip Johnson, "Reflections on CFTC/SEC Jurisdiction." Another good recent source is J.V. Jordan, R.S. Mackay, and E. Moriarty, "The New Regulation of Hybrid Debt Instruments," 2 *Journal of Applied Corporate Finance* (Winter 1990): 72, which discusses the effects of regulatory criteria on hybrid instrument design.

[17] 7 U.S.C. § 2 (1988).

[18] CFTC v. CoPetro Marketing Group 680 F.2d 573 (9th Cir. 1982) (contracts were futures contracts because "speculative ventures . . . marketed to those for whom delivery was not an expectation"); Abrams v. Oppenheimer Government Securities, 737 F.2d 582 (7th Cir. 1984) (the court relied mainly on the Treasury Amendment: the contracts were forward contracts, although similar to futures contracts, because not traded on contract markets.)

[19] These GNMA contracts were not the same over-the-counter contracts involved in Abrams v. Oppenheimer Government Securities, cited in note 17.

contracts for future delivery and securities and financial instruments under those agencies' jurisdiction.

After the 1978 amendment, the SEC granted the Chicago Board Options Exchange, which is subject to SEC regulation, the right to trade options on GNMA certificates. The Chicago Board of Trade successfully sued the SEC to enjoin the Options Exchange from trading the options: the Seventh Circuit Court of Appeals held that the CFTC had exclusive jurisdiction to authorize trading of the GNMA options.[20] The decision was vacated as moot, however, because in 1982 the CFTC and the SEC entered into a jurisdictional accord.

The 1982 CFTC–SEC accord has subsequently proved a source of discord between the two agencies, especially as new forms of hybrid hedging instruments have been developed. For example, when the SEC granted permission in 1988 for index participation contracts to be traded on the Chicago Board Options Exchange, a lawsuit disputing that permission promptly ensued. In *Chicago Mercantile Exchange v. SEC,*[21] the Seventh Circuit held that the CFTC, instead of the SEC, had jurisdiction over index participation. The opinion is recommended reading for the court's analytical discussion of the CFTC–SEC jurisdictional dispute. The court aptly describes the problem:

> The CFTC regulates futures and options on futures; the SEC regulates securities and options on securities; jurisdiction never overlaps. Problem: The statute does not define either "contracts . . . for future delivery" or "option"—although it says that "future delivery" . . . shall not include any sale of any cash commodity for deferred shipment or delivery. . . . [citation omitted] Each of these terms has a paradigm, but newfangled instruments may have aspects of each of the prototypes.[22]

The court pointed out that Congress enacted almost verbatim the jurisdictional agreement between the CFTC and the SEC, with explicit reference to provisions in Section 3(a)(10) of the 1934 Securities Exchange Act and the SEC savings clause in Section 2(a)(i) of the CEA. Nonetheless, this enactment did not resolve the jurisdictional discord because, as the Seventh Circuit recognized:

> Like many an agreement resolving a spat, the Accord addressed a symptom rather than the problem. Options are only one among many instruments that can have attributes of futures contracts as well as securities. . . . Exchanges and professional investors therefore continually devise financial products to fill unoccupied niches. . . . Which means that the dispute of 1980–82 about options will be played out—is being played out—about each new instrument.[23]

[20] Chicago Board of Trade v. SEC, 677 F.2d 1137 (7th Cir. 1982), *vacated as moot,* 459 U.S. 1026 (1982).
[21] 883 F.2d 537 (7th Cir. 1989), *cert. denied,* _____ U.S. _____, 110 S.Ct. 3214 (19_____).
[22] *Id.* at 539.
[23] *Id.* at 544.

The 508-point stock market break of October 19, 1987 refueled the CFTC/SEC jurisdictional dispute. The Presidential Task Force, appointed to investigate that market break, included in its report a recommendation for coordination of CFTC and SEC regulation of financial and stock index options and futures. In 1990, the Treasury Department submitted to Congress a legislative proposal that would: change the CFTC's exclusive jurisdiction under the CEA to end "pointless litigation and remove barriers"; shift to the SEC jurisdiction over stock index futures; and grant the SEC oversight authority over setting of margins.[24] The CFTC, by its Commissioner, viewed the proposed jurisdictional shift as "disastrous" for the agricultural markets.[25]

In April 1991, the U.S. Senate passed the Futures Trading Practices Act of 1991.[26] Title III of the Act is a jurisdictional compromise worked out by the Senate Agriculture Committee, the CFTC, the Federal Reserve, and the Treasury Department; it represents generally the views of swap dealers, as well as of the futures and securities industries. Title III includes provisions that:

1. Grant the CFTC authority to exempt from the CEA any contract or transaction where the exemption is consistent with the public interest;
2. Clarify that the CEA does not apply to swaps entered into for hedging or business-related risk management and where the parties expect to make specified payments under the agreement;
3. Codify a new "functional" test for resolving jurisdiction questions involving hybrid instruments.

Also in 1991, the House of Representatives had passed the Commodity Futures Improvements Act of 1991.[27] The House-passed bill, HR 707, is the renumbered version of the Senate's bill, S.207, but does not contain any jurisdiction provisions. As of the time this book went to press: "The status of the Senate and House versions [of the CFTC bill] is in limbo as the industry waits for the House to determine the conference members who will work with Senate members to nail out a merged bill."[28] What will happen to this legislation cannot be foretold, but the outcome merits watching.

---

[24] 22 Securities Regulations & Law Report (BNA) 859 (June 8, 1990); 22 Securities Regulations & Law Report (BNA) 731 (May 11, 1990).
[25] 22 Securities Regulations & Law Report (BNA) 748 (May 11, 1990).
[26] Commodity Futures Law Reports (CCH), No. 401 (March 22, 1991), comprised of the text of Senate Report No. 102-22 and S. 207 (the Senate Report is recommended reading); 23 Securities Regulations & Law Report (BNA) 606 (April 26, 1991).
[27] Commodity Futures Law Reports (CCH), No. 400 (March 11, 1991), comprised of the texts of both House Report No. 102-6 and H.R. 707.
[28] "Global roundup," 20 *Futures* (September 1991): 42; see also 23 Securities Regulations & Law Report (BNA) 697 (May 3, 1991).

The need for resolution of the CFTC–SEC jurisdictional dispute is obvious. The market for derivatives of traditional hedging instruments now approximates USD 3 trillion,[29] and the International Association of Swap Dealers recently estimated that more than USD 3 billion in swap transactions are currently outstanding, mostly involving exposure in interest rates and currencies.[30] An excerpt from a recent article in *The Wall Street Journal* about the derivatives market is an apt summary on the CFTC–SEC jurisdictional dispute:

> Meet the market that's outgrown its regulators . . . any newcomer[s] to the arcane world of customized securities will soon find themselves asking: Who's in charge here?[31]

State Bucket Shop Laws v. Federal Laws

For the more youthful reader, "A bucket shop operator 'buckets', i.e., discards, an order for the fictitious purchase or sale of a commodity rather than executing it on a futures exchange or arranging for actual delivery."[32] In the earlier years of the 20th century, bucket shops became so prevalent that many states enacted laws prohibiting bucket shop practices. The statutory prohibitions are found in various types of statutes, for example, gambling, nuisance, or commercial statutes. The law is not settled as to whether these state laws are preempted by federal laws regulating hedging contracts. The Futures Trading Practices Act of 1991, to date passed only by the Senate, does not provide for federal preemption.

People v. Gardner[33] is a well-known case in which the defendants were charged with nine counts of "bucketing," in violation of California's Corporations Code. The defendants sold "double options" to purchase future delivery contracts for purchase and sale of sugar and silver. The lower court dismissed the bucketing counts, but the appellate court reversed the dismissal. The appellate court held that the evidence was sufficient for a trier of fact to find that the defendants did not intend delivery of the future delivery contracts called for in the options: "At no time did defendants ever own, or have arrangements to acquire, *any* future delivery contracts." [Emphasis by court.]

---

[29] *The Wall Street Journal,* July 24, 1991, P. Cl.
[30] Senate Report No. 102–22, 102nd Cong., 1st Sess. (1991) at 9.
[31] *Id.,* n. 27.
[32] B.W. Taylor, "Swaps: Commodities Laws in Transition: Advanced Swaps and Derivative Financial Products," Practising Law Institute, *Corporate Law and Practice,* No. 746 (1991), 99, n. 29. An excellent article.
[33] 72 Cal. App. 3d 641, 140 Cal. Rptr. 238 (1977).

The *Gardner* court held that federal law did not preempt the state bucket shop law prosecution, because the transactions involved occurred before applicable federal law had become effective.

INSOLVENT PARTY TO THE HEDGE: THE *FRANKLIN* SAGA; BANKRUPTCY CODE VIS-À-VIS FIRREA

The thicket is beset.

The Franklin Saga

The two court opinions that comprise the Franklin saga are included because it has attracted the widespread attention of both hedgers and accountants. The method of hedge accounting was a primary factor in determining whether a federal conservator should have been appointed for the Franklin Savings Association (Franklin), a state-chartered thrift.

The Trial Court's Decision for Franklin. In *Franklin Savings Association v. Director of the Office of Thrift Supervision,*[34] the United States District Court for the District of Kansas held in favor of Franklin, which had sued to attack the legality of the appointment by federal regulators of a conservator for Franklin and seeking the conservator's removal. The Office of Thrift Supervision (OTS; the regulator) made the decision to appoint the Resolution Trust Corporation (RTC) as conservator for Franklin, based on its findings that Franklin was in an unsafe and unsound condition for several reasons, including allegedly having insufficient capital. The court held an 18-day nonjury trial to the court, during which substantial testimony, including experts for both sides, and voluminous documents were received into evidence.

The district court's 39-page opinion has 209 findings of fact, of which Findings 89–135 relate to Franklin's hedge accounting practice. Briefly, Franklin sent notice to the OTS that: (1) Franklin had available means to meet regulatory capital requirements, even if the OTS's hedge accounting and credit enhancement write-downs were valid; and (2) the RTC was preparing a public announcement of Franklin's solvency. On the day after receiving this notice, OTS imposed two additional write-downs, including a USD 61.9 million (later corrected to USD 51.9 million) "safety and soundness" hedge accounting write-down. The court found that "this second wave of adjustments . . . was arbitrary and capricious and lacked any reasonable basis."

[34] 742 F. Supp. 1089 (D. Kan. 1990).

The hedge accounting issue was whether Franklin's policy and proce-dures for determining the existence of high correlation and substantial offset in past periods on an ongoing basis were appropriate application of the guidelines of FASB 80 (see Chapter 12), in accordance with GAAP. The findings review in detail the hedge correlation policy used and include tables comparing the dollar offset method with the absolute value method. The court found that Franklin's use of the absolute value method was a reliable method for testing correlation, which "accurately measures high correlation and substantial offset as required by [FASB 80]." Based on expert testimony, the court found that Franklin's use of nonparallel shifts in the treasury yield curve constituted "unusual events" in the institution's correlation policy and was "a reasonable application of [FASB 80] and accords with GAAP." The court further found that Franklin's hedging pro-gram had not caused any economic losses to the institution.

The Appellate Court's Reversal in Favor of OTC.   The OTC appealed from the adverse decision to the Tenth Circuit Court of Appeals, which reversed the trial court in *Franklin Savings Association v. Director, Office of Thrift Super-vision.*[35] The ground for reversal was that the district court had used an im-proper standard of judicial review of an administrative decision. A summary of the Tenth Circuit's opinion follows:

- The trial court's review should have been limited to the administrative record; instead, the trial court heard the live testimony of 25 witnesses and received over 650 exhibits.
- Although Franklin had argued the agency record was one-sided and incomplete, the agency record had "ample evidence" to establish a high level of high-risk assets.
- "The reviewing court, particularly when reviewing such technical de-terminations and predictive judgments, must apply a deferential stand-ard of review," and the reviewing court should begin its review "by acknowledging that a presumption of procedural and substantial regu-larity attaches" to the administrative decision.[36] The trial court failed to give appropriate deference to the OTC's standards.
- The OTC's decision to appoint a conservator, when based on technical matters such as those in this case, including accounting standards, "should not be set aside by the reviewing court unless the findings transgress the bounds of reason."

---

[35] 934 F.2d 1127 (10th Cir. 1991).
[36] *Id.* at 1147.

Neither space nor occasion makes appropriate an analysis and evaluation of the *Franklin* saga's outcome in the Tenth Circuit Court of Appeals. Instead, the words of Hamlet serve as closing comment: "A hit, a very palpable hit."

Bankruptcy Code vis-à-vis FIRREA

If a counterparty to a hedging contract becomes insolvent, the insolvency law that applies is determined by the insolvent party's status. The federal Bankruptcy Code applies to an insolvent corporate counterparty. The Financial Institutions Reform, Recovery, and Enforcement Act of 1989 (FIRREA) applies to an insolvent bank or thrift counterparty. The insolvency law of a foreign country will need checking if a foreign counterparty becomes insolvent. In certain situations, the state insurance laws for insolvent insurance companies may become applicable. Here, discussion is limited to a brief look at the distinctions between the Bankruptcy Code and FIRREA that affect hedging contracts.

On June 25, 1990, Congress enacted thirteen amendments to the Bankruptcy Code that clarify and improve the status of the solvent party to a hedging contract, when the counterparty is in insolvency proceedings under the Bankruptcy Code. The amendments were in House Report No. 4612 ("H.R. 4612") and House Report No. 101-484. The House Report that accompanied the bill stated in part: "The purpose of H.R. 4612 is to ensure that the swap and forward contract financial markets are not destabilized by uncertainties regarding the treatment of their financial instruments under the Bankruptcy Code."

The thirteen amendments were enacted[37] and have been codified in Title 11 (the Bankruptcy Code) of the United States Code. Each is briefly addressed below, in the numerical order of the sections.

Section 101. Definitions

> . . . "forward contract" means a contract (other than a commodity contract) for the purchase, sale, or transfer of a commodity, *as defined in section 761(8) of this title, or any similar good, article, service, right, or interest which is presently or in the future becomes the subject of dealing in the forward contract trade,* product or byproduct thereof, with a maturity date more than two days after the date the contract is entered into, *including but not limited to a repurchase transaction, reverse repurchase transaction, consignment, lease, swap, hedge transaction, deposit, loan, option allocated transaction, unallocated transaction, or any combination thereof or option thereon* [italics in original].

---

[37] Pub. L. No. 101-311, 104 Stat. 267 (1990).

The amendment to the definition of "forward contract merchant" is the same as the italicized portion at the end of the "forward contract" definition.

Comment.   The italicized passages in the "forward contract" definition are the 1990 amendment, which broadened the definition of "commodity." The House Report stated:

> This amendment is intended to clarify that these exemptions in the Bankruptcy Code apply to genuine forward contracts regarding a commodity not currently listed in the Commodity Exchange Act, but that the exemptions do not apply to ordinary supply-of-goods contracts, which are not essentially financial in character.

"Margin payment" and "settlement payment" were added as new definitions. They include the types of margin and settlement payments commonly used in the forward contract market.

A new "swap agreement" definition added in 1990 reads:

> "[S]wap agreement" means—
>   (A) an agreement (including terms and conditions incorporated by reference therein) which is a rate swap agreement, basis swap, forward rate agreement, commodity swap, interest rate option, forward foreign exchange agreement, rate cap agreement, rate floor agreement, rate collar agreement, currency swap agreement, cross-currency rate swap agreement, currency option, any other similar agreement (including any option to enter into any of the foregoing);
>   B. any combination of the foregoing; or
>   C. a master agreement for any of the foregoing together with all supplements.

"Swap participant" means an entity that, at any time before the filing of the petition, has an outstanding swap agreement with the debtor.

Comment.   These definitions serve to modify the treatment given swap agreements under the Bankruptcy Code. Note that a swap participant is defined to include any entity that had an outstanding swap agreement with the bankruptcy debtor during the 90-day period before the bankruptcy petition was filed.

Section 362. Automatic Stay.   The Bankruptcy Code grants an automatic stay against any debtor who is the subject of a voluntary or involuntary petition in bankruptcy. This automatic stay not only applies to any pending actions, but also bars actions against the debtor's property.

The 1990 amendments added two important exemptions from the automatic stay provisions. Section 362(b)(6) is amended to broaden the types of margin payments and settlement payments for which setoff is exempt from the automatic stay provision. Section 362(b)(14) is a new paragraph providing that a setoff pursuant to a swap agreement between two parties is *not* subject to automatic stay upon the filing of a bankruptcy petition by one of the parties.

Comment. The House Report stated that Section 362(b)'s new paragraph 14 "permits the swap participant to make a final accounting of the net amount due from or owed to the bankruptcy debtor under a swap agreement, by offsetting any amounts due against any amounts owed." The House Report pointed out: "The setoff process, which is at the center of the swap agreement, may be skewed if one of the parties has filed for bankruptcy." This new provision ensures that: (1) the filing of bankruptcy by one party to a swap will not automatically stay setoff of a swap agreement; and (2) the trustee in bankruptcy cannot refuse setoff and unfairly "cherry pick" the part of the swap advantageous to the debtor and reject the part unfavorable to the debtor. The new paragraph does not authorize any setoff that would otherwise be unlawful under any law other than the Bankruptcy Code.

Section 546. Limitations on Avoiding Powers. Two important changes were enacted that broadened the exemption from the bankruptcy trustee's power to avoid certain transfers and obligations incurred by the debtor. Section 546(e) was amended to broaden the types of margin payments and settlement payments, made by the debtor before filing bankruptcy, that the trustee is prohibited from avoiding. A new provision, Section 546(g), prohibits a bankruptcy trustee from avoiding a transfer under a swap agreement entered into before the bankruptcy petition was filed. This exemption from avoidance is subject to an exception for any swap agreement that the debtor has entered into with the intent to hinder, delay, or defraud a creditor—in such instance, the trustee may avoid the agreement.

Section 548. Fraudulent Transfers and Obligations. Section 548(d)(2) was amended to provide that "a swap participant that receives a transfer in connection with a swap agreement takes for value to the extent of such transfer." The House Report stated: "This provision exempts swap agreement setoffs from scrutiny by the trustee and the bankruptcy court as to whether the setoff was actually fair value for the amount owed." Section 548(d)(2)(B) was amended to broaden the types of margin payments and settlement payments that a forward contract merchant may accept which will be deemed taken "for value to the extent of such payment."

Section 553. Setoff. Section 553(b)(1) authorizes the trustee to readjust any setoff involving the debtor that occurred on or within 90 days before the bankruptcy petition was filed, under specified circumstances. This section had previously exempted from adjustment setoffs involving securities contracts, commodities contracts, forward contracts, and repurchase agreements. According to the House Report, the 1990 amendment added swap agreements to the exempted contracts "because of the routine nature of swap agreement setoffs."

Section 556. Contractual Right to Liquidate a Commodities Contract or Forward Contract. This amendment expanded the types of contractual rights to liquidate a forward contract, if the counterparty files in bankruptcy, to add "a right, whether or not evidenced in writing, arising under common law, under law merchant or by reason of normal business practice."

Section 560. Contractual Right to Terminate a Swap Agreement. The last of the "baker's dozen" amendments described here is the new provision that expressly allows a swap participant to exercise any contractual right to terminate a swap agreement and to offset any amounts owed to it, if the counterparty files in bankruptcy—despite the automatic stay and trustee avoidance provisions of the Bankruptcy Code. The House Report stated: "The intent of this provision is to permit either the non-debtor swap participant or the trustee to terminate a swap agreement, so that a swap agreement may continue after the bankruptcy petition is filed only by mutual consent of both the non-debtor swap participant and the trustee."

Admittedly, the foregoing description of the thirteen 1990 amendments to the Bankruptcy Code is not engrossing reading. Nonetheless, these amendments are important for the corporate financial risk professional: they improve the stability of the swap and forward contract markets by imparting some certainty to the treatment of hedging instruments under the Bankruptcy Code. Insufficient time has elapsed since their enactment for any judicial or administrative interpretation of the amendments, but the reader is urged to keep apprised of interpretation as it occurs.

FIRREA

The Financial Institutions Reform, Recovery, and Enforcement Act of 1989 (FIRREA),[38] which was signed into law on August 9, 1989, made major changes in the law governing financial institutions.[39] The changes included extending the powers of the Federal Deposit Insurance Corporation (FDIC), as the conservator or receiver of a financial institution, to almost all domestic banks and savings institutions. FIRREA distinguishes between the FDIC as a conservator and as a receiver. As a conservator, the FDIC may take necessary action to put the institution into a sound condition and carry on

---

[38] Pub. L. No. 101-73, 103 Stat. 183 (1989).
[39] D.P. Cunningham and W.P. Rogers, "Netting is the Law," in Cunningham, *Advanced Swaps and Derivative Financial Products,* Practising Law Institute (1991). A good summary of the provisions in FIRREA and the Bankruptcy Code that are applicable to swaps.

its business.[40] As a receiver, the FDIC may place the institution in liquidation and realize on its assets.[41] As conservator or receiver, the FDIC may take over the assets of and operate the institution, as well as collect all obligations due the institution.[42]

As either conservator or receiver, the FDIC has authority to repudiate any contract, with certain exceptions. The pertinent exception here is a qualified financial contract (QFC), which FIRREA defines to mean "any securities contract, commodity contract, forward contract, repurchase agreement, swap agreement, and any similar agreement" that the FDIC by regulation determines to be a QFC.[43] Each of the specified QFCs is defined; and FIRREA adopts by statutory reference the Bankruptcy Code's definitions of commodity contract and forward contract. The definition of "swap agreement" is quoted verbatim because of its comprehensive list of agreements:

> The term "swap agreement"—
> (I) means any agreement, including the terms and conditions incorporated by reference in any such agreement, which is a rate swap agreement, basis swap, commodity swap, forward rate agreement, interest rate future, interest rate option purchased, forward foreign exchange agreement, rate cap agreement, rate floor agreement, rate collar agreement, currency swap agreement, currency future, or currency option purchased or any other similar agreement, and
> (II) includes any combination of such agreements.[44]

FIRREA also provides that a master swap agreement, together with all its supplements, "shall be treated as 1 swap agreement."[45]

FIRREA provides that, in the case of conservatorship (as opposed to receivership) and subject to certain limitations, the party to a QFC shall not be stayed or prohibited from exercising: (1) any right to terminate, liquidate, or accelerate any QFC with a depository institution in conservatorship based on default enforceable under noninsolvency law; and (2) any right to offset or to net out the QFC—a key "netting" provision that protects the parties to a QFC.[46] On December 12, 1989, the FDIC issued a Policy Statement regarding QFCs that was also adopted by the RTC.[47] The Policy Statement was issued to clarify and to provide guidance concerning two aspects of FIRREA that had caused considerable concern to the financial markets. First, the Policy Statement declared that the "written agreement" requirements of the statute for

[40] 12 U.S.C. § 1821(d)(2)(D).
[41] 12 U.S.C. § 1821(d)(2)(E).
[42] 12 U.S.C. § 1821(d)(2)(B).
[43] 12 U.S.C. § 1821(8)(D).
[44] 12 U.S.C. § 1821(e)(8)(D)(vi).
[45] 12 U.S.C. § 1821(e)(88)(D)(vii).
[46] 12 U.S.C. § 1821(e)(8)(E).
[47] Federal Banking Law Report, ¶ 47,351 (1990).

QFCs and Fed Funds transactions would be met by a writing evidencing that: the transaction would be enforceable under noninsolvency law; proper authority existed for the transaction; and proper records had been maintained. Second, the Policy enumerated three sentences "inadvertently deleted from the statute. The sentences clarify the receiver's absolute right to transfer [QFCs]. Absent the clarification, the statute is unworkable." Clarification includes the procedures for the receiver's notifications to the noninsolvent counterparty.

In addition to the "netting" provision, FIRREA protects the noninsolvent QFC party by its "cherry-picking" prohibition: the conservator or receiver is not allowed to "cherry-pick" among QFCs between the insolvent financial institution and any particular counterparty.[48]

FIRREA is a major, complex, and lengthy (50 pages) overhaul of statutes regulating financial institutions. The provisions selected here exemplify FIRREA's importance to the hedging contract market and show the need to keep apprised of developments in FIRREA regulations and judicial interpretations.

CONCLUSION

A fitting summary to this chapter on the law pertaining to the contracts now being used and developed for financial engineering is the wise language from over a century ago written by the great American lawyer, Joseph P. Story:

> The law must forever be in a state of progress, or change, to adapt itself to the exigencies and changes of society; . . . even when old foundations remain firm, the shifting channels of business must often leave their wonted beds deserted, and require new and broader substructures to accommodate and support new interests.

---

[48] 12 U.S.C. § 1821(e)(9).

Appendix A
Functional Glossary

To ease your trip into the glossary and your bad days, the authors offer:

"OBITER DICTUM"

Many terms are used in describing the USD/DEM (U.S. Dollar to/from Deutsche Mark) market; here are some useful definitions . . .

Chart Target. Where you thought it was going when you sold it.

Consolidation. What happens when everyone has a short position.

Technical Move. One that you had not anticipated.

Correction. When the price rises and you're still short.

Underlying Bearishness. When everyone else is still short.

Short Covering. What your friends claim to have done yesterday.

Resistance Level. Where you hope they will start selling again.

Support. When your boss agrees that you're right to still be short.

> —*David Deakin, The Nikko Bank (UK) PLC,*
> *London; reprinted with permission.*

This Functional Glossary is comprised of more than definitions. Some of the terms used in corporate financial risk management are readily defined; others require definition plus explanation; still others require definition, explanation, and example. Our objective has been to make this glossary as useful as possible.

Note: Any CAPITALIZED TERM within a definition of the glossary is separately defined in its alphabetical location.

Many of the terms in this Functional Glossary are nearly or exactly synonymous because the inventors of the many new derivative contracts for corporate financial risk management also have developed their own marketing terms. Repeating the warning of Chapter 3, readers should be certain to understand the detailed terms and conditions for a specific contract, particularly as to the computation for payments.

Actual   A COMMODITY ready or almost immediately available for delivery. "Actual" price is the price for such delivery terms. See also CASH and cross-references at PHYSICAL.

Alternate delivery procedure (ADP)   If a seller and buyer of futures contracts have been matched by the exchange to take and make delivery (see EXCHANGE OF FUTURE FOR PHYSICAL), the parties may agree to different terms and conditions. Notice of such arrangement, the "alternate delivery notice," is provided to the exchange by the clearing members, thus releasing them of obligation to the exchange.

American-style option   An option that can be exercised on any date between the option's purchase SETTLEMENT DATE up to and including its EXPIRATION DATE.

American terms   Quoting a currency in terms of U.S. Dollars per unit of foreign currency. Examples are U.S. Dollar 1.75 per Pound Sterling or 90 cents U.S. to one Canadian Dollar. See also EUROPEAN TERMS. See Chapter 2 for discussion.

Arbitrage   1. Using the difference in prices in different markets for the same assets, or their equivalent substitutes, intending to obtain a profit without market risk. The abbreviated verb form is "to arb," and the doers are "arbitrageurs." 2. The simultaneous sale and purchase of commodities, currencies, or financial instruments to make a profit from discrepancies in prices in different markets. For example, see INTEREST RATE ARBITRAGE. An arbitrage for time is to purchase in one time period and sell in another, calculating that because the "cost of carry" (see Chapter 2) is less than the price difference, a profit might be made. An arbitrage for space is buying in one market and selling in another, again calculating that the cost of carry is less than the price difference.

Asian option   An option for which the STRIKE PRICE is computed as an average of the option's REFERENCE prices. A form of AVERAGE PRICE OPTION.

Assignment   1. Notice to the WRITER of a traded OPTION that an option has been exercised by the option HOLDER. 2. In foreign exchange contracts, when one bank transfers its rights and obligations under a FORWARD FOREIGN EXCHANGE CONTRACT with a counterparty to a second bank. Usually, a three-party contract, with both banks and the counterparty customer signing the assignment agreement.

At best order Customer's authorization to bank or broker to buy or sell on a customer's behalf at the best execution price available at the time of the order.

At the money An option STRIKE PRICE that equals or almost equals the current cash market price.

At the money forward A foreign currency option with a STRIKE PRICE equal to the FORWARD RATE for the option's EXPIRATION DATE.

At the money option An option with a STRIKE PRICE equal to the cash market's price for the UNDERLYING.

At the money spot An option with a STRIKE PRICE equal to the current SPOT rate for currencies or commodities.

Average price options (APOs) Contracts DERIVATIVE of OVER-THE-COUNTER (OTC) options for which the STRIKE PRICE is an average of prices of the UNDERLYING for certain periods, as defined by the specific contract. See also CEILING, COLLAR, FLOOR.

Backwardation A relationship of prices whereby CASH or SPOT market prices are higher than FORWARD or FUTURES prices.

Balance sheet hedge Hedge of a MARK-TO-MARKET valuation of an asset, liability, or equity account on a balance sheet. The UNDERLYING item being hedged may or may not result in a cash flow in less than 1 year. If the hedge is not chosen carefully, it may result in an adverse cash flow impact.

Basis Usually, the cash/spot market price minus the forward or futures price for the same or most nearly comparable UNDERLYING. The price differential for the same or nearly comparable underlying(s) because of time, locations, or quality.

Basis point $1/100$th of one percentage point (.01%); used in quoting spreads between interest rates. Also known as a "tick." Not the same as PIP.

Bookout, bookout contracts Separate contracts entered into by the parties to the original contracts whereby they settle their respective obligations under the original contracts by payment to each other of the difference between the contract price and the agreed-on reference price.

Breakage The cost of breaking a financial commitment with a fixed expiration date; for example, early termination of a time deposit.

Bullet The entire principal of a loan scheduled for repayment only at maturity.

Business day convention(s) If a calendar day is not a business day, the method of determining the applicable business day. "Following" and "Preceding" business day conventions are obvious. "Modified following" provides that the next business day will not be in the next calendar month. See also FRN CONVENTION (EURODOLLAR CONVENTION).

Buyer The purchaser of an option; the holder of the option's rights. See also HOLDER, SELLER, and WRITER.

Cable The currency exchange rate between U.S. Dollars and U.K. Pounds Sterling. The term probably arose from the practice of using telex (or "cable") to request exchange rates between the U.S. Dollar and Pounds Sterling—the cable price for sterling.

Call option An option contract that gives the option holder or purchaser the right, but not the obligation, to enter into a contract with the option WRITER for the HOLDER to purchase the UNDERLYING currency, financial instrument, or commodity at a specified price, on or before a specified date if an AMERICAN-STYLE OPTION or on a specified date if a EUROPEAN-STYLE OPTION. See also PUT OPTION.

Cap See CEILING, FLOOR, INTEREST RATE CAP.

Capital market The market for issuing or trading MEDIUM-TERM or LONG-TERM instruments of debt.

Cash (market) 1. For any UNDERLYING, the market for same day or soonest usual settlement. 2. For indexes, the numeric value of an index (for example, S&P 500) computed from current cash prices. 3. For commodities, the price for immediate or very early delivery. Also, ACTUAL or PHYSICAL or SPOT.

Cash flow swap See SWAPS.

Cash settle SETTLEMENT by payments of cash without physical delivery, usually because the UNDERLYING is impossible to deliver—for example, an index value or reference price in a price SWAP.

Ceiling A DERIVATIVE contract with a NOTIONAL AMOUNT in which the WRITER of the ceiling contract agrees to pay the BUYER, who has a "call" on the writer, (a) if, at contractually set interim dates or at maturity, the price of the UNDERLYING is higher than the "ceiling" price or (b) if, for interim periods or the option contract duration, the average price of the underlying has been higher than the "ceiling" price or rate. See also INTEREST RATE CAP.

Class (of traded options) All CALL OPTIONS or PUT OPTIONS on the same UNDERLYING. Examples would be all call options for IBM stock or all put options on the International Monetary Market (IMM) June Deutsche Mark futures contract.

Close out (closed) Liquidation of a contract or position. Liquidation does not usually involve delivery of the UNDERLYING. Rather, "closing out" involves cash settlement by one counterparty to the other. Examples: an option holder selling an option back to the writer rather than exercising; or, selling a long futures contract rather than taking physical delivery. See also SETTLEMENT.

Collar A DERIVATIVE contract involving the purchase of an out of the money CALL OPTION and the writing of an out of the money PUT OPTION with a different, usually lower STRIKE PRICE. The purpose is to lock-in a range of prices, exchange rates, or interest rates while reducing or eliminating any option premium. Some synonyms are CORRIDOR, CYLINDER, RANGE FORWARD, TUNNEL. A "fence" is a collar using exchange-traded contracts. As an example of an interest rate collar, the borrower will buy the CAP and, at the same time, will sell the FLOOR. The borrower accomplishes two objectives by entering into a collar: (a) the cap fixes the maximum borrowing cost for the period specified in the agreement; (b) the floor fixes the minimum borrowing cost. A collar agreement reduces or eliminates the premium that a cap would require because, by selling the floor, the borrower sacrifices part of the gain otherwise obtainable if interest rates fall. The premium may be zero by adjusting the collar size—namely, the range between the cap and the floor.

Combination An option position created by buying or WRITING both a put and a call on the same UNDERLYING. It can also involve buying and writing combinations of puts and calls, combinations of puts or combinations of calls with all terms being equal except one feature, such as different STRIKE PRICES or EXPIRATION DATES.

Commodity, commodities In this book, raw materials, semimanufactured goods, and physical products in primary form.

Commodity swap See SWAP. A commodity swap is not the same as a commodity price swap.

Compensating forward foreign exchange contract Entering into an offsetting forward foreign exchange contract to close out an existing forward foreign exchange contract. From the point of view of a U.S. Dollar-based client, it usually involves the offsetting purchase or sale of a foreign currency amount to eliminate the non-U.S. Dollar cash flows that would have resulted from settling an outstanding foreign exchange contract on maturity. The compensation process will result in a net U.S. Dollar cash flow from one counterparty to the other. The cash SETTLEMENT will be made on the VALUE DATE of the two forward contracts. See also NETTING.

Contango A word of Cockney origin referring to the PREMIUM a seller may demand of a buyer for delay in delivery for FORWARD SETTLEMENT. A price curve increasing over time is said to "contango." See also BACKWARDATION.

Contract period The period of time or duration between the contract's effective date and its termination. In foreign exchange and for the computation of interest on money market instruments, it is the time between the SETTLEMENT DATE (the purchase payment date or effective date for starting computations) and the MATURITY DATE of the contract. In any contract involving the periodic computation of average prices over specified periods of time, such as SWAPS, the contract period begins on the starting date for the first computation and ends on the last cash settlement date.

Counterparty The opposite party to a purchase and sale or exchange contract.

Cover Protection for a currency exchange rate, interest rate, or commodity price risk.

Covered call See COVERED WRITE.

Covered put See COVERED WRITE.

Covered write Writing a PUT or CALL OPTION against an offsetting UNDERLYING position. Thus, with a LONG position, one would write a CALL OPTION. With a SHORT position, one would write a PUT OPTION. See also NAKED WRITE.

Cross rate 1. An exchange rate between two currencies that does not involve quoting against the U.S. Dollar. Normally, all currency exchange rates are quoted in terms of an exchange rate against the U.S. Dollar. Examples of important cross rates are DEM/JPY, DEM/CHF, and AUD/JPY. 2. Less commonly, quoting a foreign exchange rate in AMERICAN TERMS when it is usually quoted in EUROPEAN TERMS. An example would be: quoting the Deutsche Mark at 50 cents U.S. when the same rate, in European terms, would be quoted as DEM 2.00 per U.S. Dollar. 3. Some references define cross rate as the relationship between two currencies that are foreign to the place of the foreign exchange transaction. For example, CHF/DM is the Swiss Francs to Deutsche Mark exchange rate.

Currency, currencies The notes and coin that are the medium of exchange in a country. In this book, the European Currency Unit (ECU) is considered a currency.

Currency option The WRITER of the option is obligated, according to the terms of the option, to sell (writing a call) or to buy (writing a put) the UNDERLYING, if the option is exercised. Market practice is to purchase or write options against foreign currencies rather than U.S. Dollars. For example, a Deutsche Mark put is the same as a dollar call against Deutsche Marks. It is also practice to write options against CROSS RATES.

Currency swap See SWAP.

Cylinder options See COLLAR.

Daylight limit 1. The credit limit for the total of transactions to be settled during any given business day, particularly in the foreign exchange market. See also SETTLEMENT. 2. Alternately called "daylight overdraft." For clearing payments through a bank account, the maximum amount of overdrafts created by making payments early in the business day, before incoming funds are received. Most banks and corporations send electronic payment instructions early in the morning on the day payments are to be made. The paying bank debits the client's account and makes the payment. Covering funds for these payments are often not received and credited to the client's account until later in the business day. This results in an overdraft condition in the account during the business day until covering funds are received. Many banks now limit the size of a client's "daylight overdrafts" that can occur. (3). From the view of a trader or speculator, the dollar value of all open positions that a trader is allowed to maintain during the business day, after summing all purchases and sales that have occurred during that day for the particular commodity, currency, or financial instrument that the dealer trades.

Deemed credit risk An estimate of the credit risk for a financial obligation. Any transaction creates a risk that the counterparty may not be able to meet its financial obligations. For transactions involving contracts for financial risk management, the amount at risk may be less than the NOTIONAL AMOUNT of the contract because the SETTLEMENT amount is less than the contract amount. The amount of the settlement, as estimated from time to time, is the amount at deemed credit risk.

Delta The amount that an option's PREMIUM changes in relation to a corresponding change in the UNDERLYING CASH MARKET price. The unit change in option premium value is divided by the unit change in the value of the UNDERLYING.

Delta hedging A type of hedging based on the concept that the computed DELTA determines the amount of option(s) suitable to hedge the UNDERLYING exposure. For example, delta has a value of .50 for an AT THE MONEY OPTION; therefore, if the option writer is hedging a SHORT (delivery) obligation by writing at the money options, the face amount of the options should be twice the underlying obligation. As the market conditions change, the option writer would increase or decrease the options outstanding relative to the underlying exposure. The face amount of the options written would equal the amount of the underlying only as delta approaches the value of one. In all other cases, the face amount of the options written would be greater than the amount of the underlying exposure.

Managing delta hedging may require constant market monitoring and trading capabilities. The strategy may not, therefore, be suitable to managing corporate financial risk with a limited number and amount of underlying exposure(s) and limited dedication of managerial resources of time and money.

Derivative   In the context of finance, the types of contracts for financial risk management "derived" from combinations and modifications of the basic cash, spot, forward, and futures contracts. Examples include options, CAPITAL MARKET swaps, and FORWARD RATE AGREEMENTS, among others.

"Diff" contracts   Eurorate differential futures contracts, which began trading on the Chicago Mercantile Exchange in 1989. The three Diff contracts relate U.S. Dollar interest rates against U.K. Pounds Sterling interest rates (Dollar-Sterling Diff), against Deutsche Mark rates (Dollar-Mark Diff), and against Japanese Yen rates (Dollar-Yen Diff). Relatively new, somewhat complex, and, to date, thinly traded contracts, they may be useful to hedgers; information with examples is available from the Chicago Mercantile Exchange.

Discount   The meaning of this term depends entirely on the context in which it is used. Any single definition is too broad to be useful. An understanding of how the term is being used in a specific situation is critical.

Disintermediation   Refers to the large-scale withdrawal of funds from one or a group of financial institutions. Examples are consumers' withdrawal of savings from banks, to support or increase a level of consumption. Another is investors' withdrawal of funds from financial institutions, to invest in higher-yielding investments. For example, in the early 1980s, savers moved funds from savings accounts into money market mutual funds.

Duration   The weighted average life of all cash flows received from a fixed income security. See Chapter 2.

Dutch auction   One of two auction processes: (a) The price is lowered until the entire lot is sold; this is the opposite of the traditional auction process of raising the price. (b) Bids are solicited; the lowest bid that allows the entire lot to be sold is the price or interest rate.

ECU (European Currency Unit)   A European monetary unit that is the composite of currencies of member countries in the European Community. The value of the ECU trades in exchange with non-ECU currencies—for example, in exchange with the U.S. Dollar. The ECU is used for loans, bonds, and MONEY MARKET instruments. See Chapter 7 for discussion.

Eurobond   A medium-term debt instrument that is issued in a currency other than that of the country in which it is issued. Most Eurobonds are bearer bonds, usually issued by governments, international organizations, and creditworthy, well-known multinational corporations.

Eurocurrency The "generic" term for currency deposited in a bank or branch bank outside the country of that currency. For example, Euromarks are Deutsche Marks deposited outside Germany, Euroyen are Japanese Yen deposited outside Japan; Deutsche Marks, Japanese Yen, or U.S. Dollars might be deposited in the London, Zurich, or Singapore branch of a bank.

Eurodollar A unit of U.S. Dollars deposited outside the United States in either a foreign branch of a United States bank or in a foreign bank.

Eurodollar convention See BUSINESS DAY CONVENTION and FRN CONVENTION.

Euronote See EUROBOND.

European-style option An option that can be EXERCISED only on its expiration date.

European terms Quoting a currency in terms of foreign currency per unit of U.S. Dollars. See also AMERICAN TERMS. See Chapter 2 for discussion.

Evergreen contract A contract clause providing that the contract's term will be extended for some specified period beginning with the date of the expiration of the primary term. Thus, the contract would remain in effect until action by one of the parties giving the required notice.

Exchange of future for physical (EFP) A simultaneous swap of cash market and futures market positions. The EFP enables the parties to choose their trading partners between the cash market and futures market. Descriptive brochures are available from relevant exchanges.

Exercise (of option) An option contract provides the right to enter into a purchase or sale contract with the WRITER of the option by EXERCISE of the option according to its terms. Exercising a CALL OPTION is entering into a contract to purchase the UNDERLYING currency, financial instrument, or commodity according to the terms of the option. Exercising a PUT OPTION is entering into a contract to sell the underlying according to the terms of the option. The option will control whether, upon exercise, the contract entered into is a CASH, FORWARD, FUTURES, or SPOT contract.

Exercise price See STRIKE PRICE.

Expiration date The date on which the rights under an option contract expire. After a predetermined time of day on that date, the option writer has no further obligation to the option holder. Options should be calendared carefully for administration. An option's expiration date may not be the same as the cash SETTLEMENT DATE of a CASH or SPOT contract pursuant to that option. The customary expiration date for an option on a spot foreign exchange contract is 2 business days before the settlement date. U.S. exchange-traded commodity options may expire in the month prior to the month designated in the name of the contract. For example, a "December" NYMEX crude oil option expires in November. Remember to check the option and futures contract expiration dates in comparison to relevant cash, forward, or futures market contract dates or months.

Far date   In a foreign exchange SWAP, the VALUE DATE for the leg of the transaction that occurs further in the future. See also NEAR DATE.

Fed funds   In the United States, the excess cash balances that banks may loan overnight to other banks so those banks can meet their Federal Reserve System Requirements.

Fills   One or more completed FUTURES contract transactions to fill an order. For example, an order to sell 100 futures at "25.00 or better" could be filled with multiple transactions at varying prices and volumes per transaction.

Financial instruments   Debt and equity instruments. See also COMMODITY and INDEX.

First notice day   For exchange-traded futures contracts, the first day a LONG can receive a delivery notice. Longs not wishing to receive a delivery notice should offset positions prior to first notice day.

First trading day   For exchange-traded futures contracts, the day trading is opened for each contract.

Fixed (rate debt) or (price)   Debt for which the interest rate is fixed for the term; a contract for which the price is fixed for the term.

Flat   Arranging for each LONG or SHORT position to be offset or closed by entering into an offsetting contract, thus becoming "flat" or "no position." See also SQUARING THE POSITION.

Floating (rate debt) or (price)   Debt for which the interest rate "floats" by periodically being reset against a previously agreed REFERENCE RATE in a specific market and at a time of day, for example, 3-month LIBOR at 11:00 A.M. London time. A contract for which the price(s) "floats" by periodically being reset or computed against a previously agreed reference price in a specific market and, often, a time or event in that market's business day, for example, a commodity price SWAP referenced to the 3-month average of closing prices for the NYMEX crude oil futures contract, second month traded.

Floor   1. A DERIVATIVE of a PUT OPTION contract with a NOTIONAL AMOUNT, in which the WRITER of the floor agrees to pay the BUYER at contractually set interim dates if the average REFERENCE PRICE of the UNDERLYING is lower than the floor's rate or price. See also CEILING. 2. An interest rate agreement in which the option writer agrees to pay the buyer, usually an investor, if interest rates decline below a certain rate (the floor) over a specified period. The floor could be defined as an interest rate or "discounted" financial instrument price, for example, Treasury Bill price.

Foreign exchange The purchase or sale of one currency against another.

Foreign exchange rate agreement (FERA) An agreement between two parties in which each agrees to guarantee an exchange rate between two currencies at some future date. This agreement is settled when one party makes to the other a cash payment equal to the difference in value between the two currencies, according to the terms of the agreement. See Chapter 8.

Foreign exchange swap See SWAP.

Forward A one-time contract between a BUYER and SELLER for delivery of a certain amount of a COMMODITY or CURRENCY or financial instrument at a specified future date, at a fixed price or rate of exchange. Also called a "cash forward." See also FUTURE.

Forward date The SETTLEMENT date of a FORWARD contract. Always some date in the future after the CASH or SPOT DATE.

Forward foreign exchange contract A foreign exchange contract for the purchase or sale of one currency against another at some future date after the SPOT DATE.

Forward forward A foreign exchange SWAP in which both contracts mature after the SPOT DATE. An example would be buying Deutsche Marks against U.S. Dollars 1 month forward and selling the Deutsche Marks 2 months forward.

Forward outright contract A foreign exchange contract for the purchase or sale of one currency against another at some future date after the SPOT DATE.

Forward outright exchange rate The exchange rate for delivery of a foreign currency against a FORWARD FOREIGN EXCHANGE CONTRACT on some VALUE DATE after the SPOT DATE. See also FORWARD OUTRIGHT CONTRACT.

Forward range agreement A foreign exchange COLLAR for which the REFERENCE RATE is the SPOT exchange rate at MATURITY versus an average price computation.

Forward rate Foreign exchange rate for the purchase or sale of one currency against another for delivery at a certain future date. See also FORWARD OUTRIGHT EXCHANGE RATE and FORWARD RATE AGREEMENT. The term FORWARD RATE AGREEMENT is sometimes applied to currency forward rate, which causes confusion.

Forward rate agreement (FRA) An agreement for a certain interest rate starting and ending during a FORWARD period for a certain loan or deposit NOTIONAL AMOUNT, for a specified time, and at a referenced interest rate. An FRA usually relates only to interest rates; but see FORWARD RATE. When the FRA's FORWARD period begins, the reference interest rate is the then current CASH market interest rate for the FRA time period.

FRN convention   The FRN (Floating Rate Note) or EURODOLLAR convention defines swap or period end dates during the term of the floating interest rate transaction. These provisions are usually stated for Eurodollar loan interest periods. As a simple example, if the next succeeding business day to a 3-month interest period from March 31 is July 1, the new interest period will end on the last business day of June. Consult the 1991 ISDA Definitions.

Future(s)   A standardized contract, traded on a regulated exchange, for the purchase or sale, for one or more periods of future delivery, of commodities and financial instruments, including currencies. A "futures price" is the price of a "futures contract" determined by open outcry on the exchange floor.

Gilts   United Kingdom bonds issued and guaranteed by the government.

Good indication   See INDICATED PRICE.

Good till canceled (order)   Orders are assumed to be valid for the trading day and, at the end of the trading day, are canceled if not filled ("day order"). To keep an order open until filled, it must be specified as "good till canceled."

Hedge, hedging   1. The purchase or sale of one or more types of CASH, COMBINATION, DERIVATIVE, FORWARD, FUTURES, or SWAP contracts intended to provide protection against adverse price or rate change. 2. Entering into any financial transaction with the purpose of offsetting a perceived financial risk. An example would be a U.S. company's borrowing Swiss Francs in order to hedge a Swiss Franc receivable.

Historical rate rollover   A foreign exchange SWAP to offset a maturing forward contract. The exchange rate used is the same as the exchange rate on the maturing contract, even if that rate does not reflect the current SPOT market exchange rate. The purpose of this transaction is to defer marking a position to market. In 1990, the Internal Revenue Service gave this definition: ". . . an extension of the maturity date of a forward contract where the new forward rate is adjusted on the rollover date to reflect the taxpayer's gain or loss on the contract as of the rollover date plus the time value of such gain or loss through the maturity date." Temp. Treas. Reg. § 1.988-5T(b)(2)(iii)(C) (1990); 55 Fed. Reg. 3792.

Holder   The holder of an option contract. See also BUYER.

Implied volatility   The imputed or estimated VOLATILITY of an option's UNDERLYING, often calculated via a computer model (Black–Scholes) using the current market price of an option with a STRIKE PRICE at or near the current CASH market price. A serious issue for hedgers because it affects the option premium to be paid or received.

In the money   An option contract that has INTRINSIC VALUE. An in the money CALL OPTION (right to buy) has a STRIKE PRICE less than the current CASH MARKET price. An in the money PUT OPTION (right to sell) has a strike price higher than the current cash market price.

Index A computed average based on a specific group of prices using measurements, often expressed as a percentage of base period index of 100. Forward and futures contracts can be defined using indexes as UNDERLYING. See Chapter 2 for discussion.

Indicated price A quotation of approximate market price, used for information but not as a "dealing" price. Requesting and receiving an "indication" means that the requestor does not intend to do a trade on the indication; there is no commitment by either the requestor or quoter to trade at the price indicated. The indicated price is only a general level of the current market price or rate for a currency, financial instrument, or commodity.

Indication (quotation) See INDICATED PRICE.

Initial margin The MARGIN required by the exchange and brokerage firm when opening a FUTURE contract or writing an exchange traded option.

Interbank market The market in which banks lend money among themselves. The loans may be to manage the banks' own liquidity or further onlending.

Interest rate arbitrage Sometimes referred to as "covered interest arbitrage." Purchasing one currency in the SPOT FOREIGN EXCHANGE market against a second currency, investing the proceeds in the MONEY MARKET of the first currency, and selling the principal plus interest against the second currency FORWARD to the MATURITY date of the investment. The purpose of the exercise is to obtain a higher yield without incurring more foreign exchange risk than would have resulted from simply investing in the second currency.

Interest rate cap A DERIVATIVE contract to set the maximum interest rate for a specified period of time with one or more SETTLEMENT DATES. The NOTIONAL AMOUNT of principal may be constant, amortizing, or structured to match the forecasted outstanding principal balance of the actual floating rate loan.

Interest rate differentials The difference in interest rates between two currencies for similar financial instruments and maturities.

Interest rate differentials swap See SWAP.

Interest rate swap See SWAP.

Intrinsic value An option that has intrinsic value is IN THE MONEY. In another view, the amount that could be realized if the option were currently EXERCISED. For example, an investor has a CALL OPTION on 100 shares of XYZ Corp. at a STRIKE PRICE of $95 per share. If the current market price for XYZ Corp. is $100 per share, the call option has an intrinsic value of $5.00 per share.

Knight Ridder A computerized information service with financial news headlines and stories, prices, foreign exchange quotations, and interest rate information for various financial markets. QUOTRON, REUTERS, and TELERATE are competing services.

Last trading day   For exchange-traded futures contracts, the last day for LONGS and SHORTS to offset positions before being obligated to make or take delivery.

LIBID (London Interbank Bid Rate)   The interest rate at which a bank bids for funds from other banks in the London INTERBANK MARKET or depositors, generally for amount of USD 5 million or the equivalent in other currencies, in the EURODOLLAR or EUROCURRENCY market.

LIBOR (London Interbank Offered Rate)   The interest rate at which a bank will loan funds to another bank in the London INTERBANK MARKET for a certain period. The currency can be any EUROCURRENCY traded in London, including EURODOLLARS. The most common appearance is for 3- and 6-month Eurodollars for the large volume of LIBOR-based U.S. Dollar customer loans. Loan agreements will usually reference LIBOR at 11.00 A.M. London time. Some of the U.S. financial press and market services will show the London Eurodollar offered quotations at 11:00 A.M. as "LIBOR" and the market's close as "late Eurodollars." LIBOR, however, can refer to other Eurocurrencies, such as Sterling LIBOR.

Lifting charges   In foreign exchange, service charges deducted by banks from payments they process. Typically, European and Japanese banks deduct a small percentage from payment amounts which they pay to another bank for credit to a third party's bank account at the receiving bank. For example, if XYZ Corp. instructed German Bank One to pay German Bank Two DEM 1 million for credit to the account of its customer ABC Corp., German Bank One might deduct 15 mils (DEM 1,500) from the payment as a "commission."

Limit (order)   Sets a price level "or better" for an order to be executed. A buy order is to be filled at or less than the limit; a sell order is to be filled at or more than the limit.

Liquidity   1. Having sufficient cash or liquid assets on hand to meet payment obligations. 2. In financial markets, a market that has many participants who quote prices in both small and very large transactions. Executing a purchase or sale in a liquid market can be done quickly at a very small or negligible transaction cost. Examples are the major world stock markets, U.S. Treasury Bills, note and bond markets, major money markets, foreign exchange markets, and most futures markets. Examples of less liquid or illiquid markets include real estate markets, developing-country stock markets, and foreign exchange markets for many minor or exotic currencies.

London Interbank Bid Rate   see LIBID.

London Interbank Offered Rate   See LIBOR.

Long (position)   Owning a currency, financial instrument, security, or commodity, or having the obligation to take delivery at a future date.

Long-term   In the international capital markets, debt securities with maturities of 3 years or more. See also MEDIUM-TERM and SHORT-TERM.

Lookback (price)   A contract pricing arrangement that "looks back" to a prior period's reference prices or rates to determine final price after interim contract payments. A contract may provide for interim payments at a fixed currency exchange rate, with adjustments to an average exchange rate for a prior period; a commodity contract may look back to a prior period's average FUTURES or CASH prices. Sometimes called a "contract exposure band."

Margin   1. For borrowers, the interest rate the bank charges in addition to the REFERENCE RATE; for example, LIBOR plus margin plus RESERVES; see also SPREAD. 2. For securities purchased on margin, futures contracts bought and sold, and options transactions written, the deposit and maintenance of sufficient cash or acceptable collateral (Treasury Bills, in the United States) as partial security for the contract; the amount of margin will vary as the open positions are MARKED-TO-MARKET; see VARIATION MARGIN. 3. The difference between purchase and sale price, thus "positive margin" or "negative margin." 4. Any profit spread added by a market maker or trader onto a transaction with a client, in order to enhance the trade's profitability.

Margin call   A call for cash or acceptable collateral as INITIAL MARGIN or negative VARIATION MARGIN.

Mark-to-market   Valuation of LONG and SHORT positions of CURRENCIES, COMMODITIES, FINANCIAL INSTRUMENTS, Securities, SWAPS, or DERIVATIVE contracts based on current market quotations.

Market (order)   For exchange-traded FUTURES contracts, an order to the broker to execute upon receipt at the prevailing market price. A market order will be filled unless futures contracts are locked-in at the daily limit or the order is received at the end of the trading day.

Market if touched (order) (MIT order)   A LIMIT ORDER that becomes a MARKET ORDER if the limit price is reached. For comparison, a limit order is to be filled at the limit price or better. If the market trades at the MIT limit, the order becomes a market order and may be filled at, above, or below the MIT limit.

Maturity date   The date when the CONTRACT PERIOD ends and the obligations under the contract must be fulfilled.

Maximum daily limit   The maximum amount by which an exchange-traded FUTURES contract price can change from the previous trading day's SETTLED PRICE. Each futures contract will have a date—"spot contracts limits removed on"—when the maximum daily limit is removed, usually by the

FIRST NOTICE DAY but sometimes during the last trading month. A futures broker can provide specific guidance through the logistics.

Medium-term In the international capital markets, debt securities with maturities from about 1½ years to 10 years. See also LONG-TERM and SHORT-TERM.

Money market The market for issuing or trading SHORT-TERM instruments of debt, for example, commercial paper, banker's acceptances, and government bills. As a rule of thumb, in this market the financial instruments have an original maturity of 1 day to 1 year. In recent years, however, some money market instruments such as bank certificates of deposit have been issued with maturities as long as 5 years. See also CAPITAL MARKETS.

Naked write Writing or selling an option with no offsetting UNDERLYING position. Also called "uncovered writing." See also COVERED WRITE.

Near date In a foreign exchange SWAP, the earlier VALUE DATE of the transaction. See also FAR DATE.

Netting (in foreign exchange) The SETTLEMENT of FORWARD foreign exchange contracts by entering into an offsetting contract and netting out the cash flow differences. Often, netting is distinguished from "compensating contracts," in which netting involves calculating the difference in cash flows resulting from the offsetting transactions, discounting to present value the future value of those cash flows, and paying them immediately.

Netting system 1. A cash management system frequently used by large multinational corporations to manage frequent, multicurrency cash flows generated by different overseas operating divisions. A multinational corporation might have a number of marketing, manufacturing, and product groups in different countries, and each may receive and pay different amounts of different currencies at various points in time. A netting system allows the multinational parent to centralize cash flows for its subsidiaries in one location using one set of bank accounts. In this manner, currency payments by one entity will be netted against currency receipts by another subsidiary. Currency purchases and sales, and bank transaction fees, can thus be minimized. 2. The administrative system to identify and manage the net LONG and SHORT commodity, currency, or financial instrument position for one or more time periods. The netting system would identify amounts of long/short gaps, funding or hedging requirements, and credit risk (also called credit exposures). An example is netting of amounts receivable and payable by month, in one or more currencies, with customers and vendors. Another example is netting amounts of a commodity receivable and payable by month, at various delivery locations, and the respective credit exposures.

Notional amount The specific amount or quantity of the UNDERLYING on which calculations of payments are made; not a "make believe" or hypothetical amount. The notional amount of the commodity or financial instrument is, however, not physically delivered or paid; it is usually the amount of the underlying that is intended to be HEDGED. The term arises from the definition of "notion" as "in the mind only." Exact "notional" amounts are required for the many types of financial risk management contracts providing for exchange of payments based on changes in valuation for specific, notional quantities of underlyings. The term is critical to understanding the operation of many DERIVATIVE contracts such as the volume for commodity price or the principal amount for interest rate caps, floors, FRAs, swaps, options, and collars. See Chapter 3 for discussion.

One cancels other (order) ("OCO order")   Results in one order's being canceled if the other order is executed. An example is entering a LIMIT ORDER with a STOP. This type of order is not accepted by some exchanges.

Open contract   A contract for the delivery of a commodity or payment of money for which the due date has not yet arrived.

Open interest   For exchange-traded futures, the number of contracts carried overnight. "Volume" in this context is the number of contracts traded during the day.

Opportunity cost   Profit opportunity not realized.

Option   See CALL OPTION and PUT OPTION.

Out of the money   An option that would be unprofitable to exercise and, therefore, has no INTRINSIC VALUE. In the case of a CALL OPTION, it is an option with a STRIKE PRICE higher than the current cash market price for the UNDERLYING. In the case of a PUT OPTION, it is an option whose strike price is less than the current cash market price. See also IN THE MONEY and TIME VALUE.

Over-the-counter (OTC)   Generally and historically, the market at the "counter" (desk) of a financial institution or outside the regulated commodity and securities exchanges. All contract terms are subject to individual negotiation. The term is often used to refer to "over-the-counter options." In the United States, the OTC market for equities dealers registered with the National Association of Securities Dealers and their electronic dealing system, NASDAQ.

Over spot   See SPOT.

Participating forward   An options strategy combining the purchase and writing of call and put contracts to buy or sell a certain NOTIONAL AMOUNT of an UNDERLYING at a specified future date. A "participating forward contract" provides the customer with a guaranteed maximum or minimum rate or price for the deal, with a reduced (or no) up-front option premium, in exchange for allowing the counterparty to participate in a portion or percentage of favorable price moves or changes.

Participation A DERIVATIVE, average price, CAP, or FLOOR contract with the right to "participate" in favorable moves at a certain percentage. Compared with PARTICIPATING FORWARD, the difference is that the forward is not an average price contract. This term is also used to describe one type of securitization of bank loans, but that process is not related to the subject of this book.

Physical See ACTUAL, CASH, and SPOT.

Pips The smallest, usually quoted, unit of price change in a foreign exchange rate. The difference between JPY 137.80 and JPY 137.90 would be 10 pips. The difference between DEM/USD 1.6780 and 1.67805 would be one-half of one pip. Pips should not be confused with TICKS.

Premium For an option, the total market value or cost of the option, the sum of any INTRINSIC VALUE plus any TIME VALUE. See also DISCOUNT.

Prime rate In the United States, a SHORT-TERM interest rate posted by commercial banks from day to day. Traditionally defined as the interest rate at which a bank lends to its most creditworthy customers—a less relevant rate now because most large, creditworthy borrowers can raise short-term funds more cheaply in the MONEY MARKETS than by borrowing "at prime" from banks. The bank prime rate is still used for many small and mid-size business loans in the United States, typically with a "markup" over prime, for example, "prime plus 2 percent." The bank prime rate or another day-to-day reference interest rate is still included in most credit facilities to provide a REFERENCE RATE flexibility for the borrower's debt administration.

Put option An option contract that gives the option holder or purchaser the right, but not the obligation, to enter into a contract with the option WRITER for the HOLDER to sell the UNDERLYING currency, financial instrument, or commodity at a specified price on or before a specified date if an AMERICAN-STYLE OPTION, or on a specified date if a EUROPEAN-STYLE OPTION. See also CALL OPTION.

Quotron A computerized information service specializing in stock quotations. KNIGHT RIDDER, REUTERS, and TELERATE are competing services.

Range forward Usually, a COMMODITY price COLLAR. See also COLLAR.

Reference (rate) or (price) The CASH, FORWARD, or FUTURES contract's interest rate, currency exchange rate, posting, publication, or commodity price used for computing a contract's payment amount. Examples are LIBOR, or a certain bank's quoted interest rate or currency exchange rate, or a cash or futures market commodity price.

Reinvestment risk The risk that invested funds or interim interest payments will be reinvestable at the expected or planned interest rate or terms, when the payments are received at future payment dates.

Reserves The Federal Reserve requires banks to maintain a minimum percentage of deposits at a local Federal Reserve Bank in a demand deposit account called a reserve account. The purpose of this account, in theory, is to provide banks with a minimum amount of liquidity. Reserve accounts are one of the main tools that the Federal Reserve uses to control the amount of bank credit available to the U.S. economy. In December 1990, the Federal Reserve eliminated the reserve on all time deposits in the name of corporations with maturities exceeding 7 days. Currently, banks must post reserves only on demand deposit accounts (checking accounts), individual accounts, and time deposits with original maturities less than 7 days. Certain types of loans are priced against certain bank instruments that require banks to post reserves to their reserve account at the Federal Reserve. Banks pass those charges along to their loan customers as a percentage rate; in loan agreements, these charges are called "reserves." In other countries, similar charges are passed through to borrowers.

Reuters A computerized information service providing foreign exchange quotes, commodities price quotes, money market and bond market rates, and news stories. KNIGHT RIDDER, QUOTRON, and TELERATE are competing services.

Reuters Direct Dealing System ("Reuters Dealing") A computerized, real-time interbank dealing system for foreign exchange and money market transactions.

Roll (rolling and rollover) 1. For value on a MATURITY DATE, establishing a new contract, usually without full cash SETTLEMENT. For example, arranging to "roll over" a bank time deposit's principal plus interest on its maturity date without wire transfer from and to the bank of the prior time deposit's maturing funds. 2. For a maturing FORWARD FOREIGN EXCHANGE CONTRACT, roll means entering into an offsetting contract and a new forward contract on the maturity date. There may be a full settlement of both the original and offsetting contract; or, the two currency amounts may be netted against one another and only the net difference paid from one counterparty to another.

Seller (of option) The SELLER is either the WRITER initiating a new option contract or a HOLDER or BUYER closing out an option position. Caution: some terminologies do not distinguish between "writer" and "seller."

Settled price In FUTURES, the average of a contract's prices for the last 90 seconds if not the last trading day, or the last 30 minutes of the last trading day.

Settlement Payment or settlement by physical delivery or by other means of satisfying a contractual obligation. Settlement may be by ROLLOVER. See also CASH SETTLE.

Settlement date The date when the SETTLEMENT amount is due. A SPOT foreign exchange contract normally settles 2 business days after the transaction; an options contract settles on the next business day.

Settlement risk The risk that one party to a contract will settle without being able to know that the counterparty has effected SETTLEMENT. The risk very commonly arises in foreign exchange transactions if payments are "settling" in widely different time zones. For example, when Japanese Yen are paid in Tokyo before receiving U.S. Dollars in New York, the party paying the Yen in Tokyo will pay hours before it can determine that it has received in New York the U.S. Dollars due.

Short (position) The obligation to deliver a currency, financial instrument, security, or commodity that the obligor does not own. According to one humorist, "A transaction of expediency for physical action until a later date."

Short-term In the international money market, debt securities with maturities from overnight to about $1\frac{1}{2}$ years. See also LONG-TERM and MEDIUM-TERM.

Spot 1. The price of an asset for immediate delivery or, for foreign currencies, 2 business days later. Except for foreign currencies, synonymous with ACTUAL, CASH, and PHYSICAL. In the United States and Canada, spot for USD to/from CAD is usually 1 business day. 2. For FUTURES contracts, the first contract month being traded is the "spot month."

Spot date The SETTLEMENT DATE for SPOT contracts.

Spot rate See SPOT.

Spot trade Usually refers to a FOREIGN EXCHANGE transaction done at a SPOT for SETTLEMENT on the SPOT DATE.

Spread 1. In requesting a "two-way" (bid and offer) price for a commodity in foreign exchange, or for a financial instrument, the numerical difference between the dealer's bid and offer price. For example, a dealer normally is willing to purchase a commodity and sell it on the offer. The difference or "spread" is the theoretical gross profit potential on a given trade. 2. For loans, see MARGIN. 3. For traded options, a position of both LONG and SHORT options of the same UNDERLYING class. 4. For FUTURES, being long/short the same commodity in different months is a "calendar spread"; being long/short different commodities is an intercommodity spread.

Squaring the position (square) In FOREIGN EXCHANGE, offsetting each LONG or SHORT contractual position.

Stop-loss order A "stop buy" or "stop sell" order is executed if the market reaches the stop order price level, usually in order to limit losses on an open position. For example, in the case of a stop-loss sell order, if the market trades at or below the stop order price level, the stop order becomes a MARKET ORDER. The market may move through the stop price before the order can be executed. If that occurs, the order will be executed at the current market price or rate, which may be substantially worse than the price level of the order.

Stop-limit (order) A combination of STOP and LIMIT orders. The stop-limit places a limit on the execution price, once the market trades past the stop. Similar to a STOP-LOSS ORDER, with the exception that the order can be executed only at the price or rate at which the order was placed. In the preceding example of a stop-loss sell order, the sell order will not be executed if the market price falls below the level of the order before the order can be executed.

Straddle A combination of exchange-traded CALL or PUT OPTIONS, of otherwise identical options, with the same STRIKE PRICE and EXPIRATION DATE.

Strike price For a CALL OPTION, the price at which the option holder may purchase the UNDERLYING from the writer under the terms of the option. For a PUT OPTION, the price at which the option holder may sell the underlying to the writer under the terms of the option. The price or exchange rate at which the option holder can exercise its rights under the terms of the option. This definition also applies to the strike prices or rates of AVERAGE PRICE OPTIONS.

Strip, stripped 1. A FUTURES strategy in which futures contracts for a particular interest rate instrument but with different maturities are purchased to create a HEDGE similar to an UNDERLYING cash position. The CASH position normally will have a different maturity or cash flow cycle from the available futures contracts. The hedger, therefore, will combine identical positions in a contract over several maturities in a proportion that would approximate the cash generated by the underlying position. 2. The practice of stripping U.S. government notes and bonds. Simplistically, a stripper purchases a quantity of U.S. Treasury Bonds and establishes a trust fund with the securities. The semiannual interest payments on the notes and bonds are sold to investors seeking regular cash flow. The present value of the face amount of the note or bond is also sold to investors who seek a specified amount of cash at a certain future date. These are usually investors who are not seeking interim cash flow or who want to avoid REINVESTMENT RISK.

Style (of option) In the context of options, whether an option is an AMERICAN-STYLE OPTION or a EUROPEAN-STYLE OPTION. ASIAN OPTIONS refer to the method for calculating the STRIKE PRICE, not the terms for EXERCISE.

Swap An exchange of two things of value. There are two categories of swaps: physical swaps and derivative swaps. Physical swaps involve the physical exchange of underlying commodities, foreign exchange between two currencies, or financial instruments. Derivative swaps involve the exchange of a "feature"—but not the UNDERLYING(S)—of commodities, foreign currencies, or financial instruments.

Basis swap Sometimes used to describe a derivative swap of BASIS for the same UNDERLYING. For example, if the underlying is defined as LIBOR, a swap of 3-month with 6-month LIBOR would be considered a "basis swap." Another description of this swap could be "a LIBOR interest period swap."

Cash flow swap A DERIVATIVE swap that is a form of INTEREST RATE SWAP, custom-tailored for multiple cash flow profiles over a period of time. For example, a cash flow swap can be used to hedge the interest rates on amortizing debt payments or variable debt levels on a revolving loan facility or for levels of debt increasing during the precompletion phase of project financing.

Commodity price swap A DERIVATIVE of a physical commodity swap. A contract to exchange periodic payments or payment at the contract's maturity, the payment(s) being computed by using a notional volume of the UNDERLYING commodity and based on the exchange of FLOATING and FIXED or different types of floating REFERENCE PRICES. Two other terms used are "commodity price index swap" and "commodity swap"—the latter term may be either a physical swap or a price swap, so clarification is required. A simply stated example using crude oil may clarify the derivative concept. A producer enters into a 1-year crude oil price swap with SETTLEMENT each calendar quarter-end for a NOTIONAL AMOUNT of 1,000 barrels per day. The fixed price is USD 20.00 per barrel; the floating reference price is the average for each calendar quarter of the closing price on the NYMEX for the second month traded crude oil futures contract. If at the end of each calendar quarter, the average of the NYMEX prices is less than USD 20.00, the producer receives a payment for the difference between such average and USD 20.00; if the average is more than USD 20.00 per barrel, the producer pays the difference to the price swap counterparty. The producer has swapped the price feature of the crude oil—a floating price for the physical oil sales for a fixed USD 20.00 per barrel.

Commodity swap An agreement for the exchange of physical commodity deliveries in the cash or forward markets. With two different UNDERLYINGS, this swap is "barter."

Cross-currency swap See CURRENCY SWAP, discussion of interest differential swap.

Currency swap An agreement between two parties to buy from each other fixed amounts of two different currencies, usually at SPOT currency exchange rate, and to sell the same amount of the respective currencies back to each other on one or more specified future date(s). The important criteria for a currency swap are (a) the purchase and sale of the same currency are simultaneous; (b) the delivery dates are not the same; (c) the amounts purchased and sold in at least one of the two currencies are the same; and (d) the term is for a period of three or more years. A currency swap should not be confused with a FOREIGN EXCHANGE SWAP. A currency swap is a CAPITAL MARKET agreement. The equivalent U.S. Dollar volume of outstanding currency swaps at the end of 1989 was estimated to be USD 436 billion.[1]

There are two general types of currency swaps: "interest differential currency swaps" and "outright forward swaps." An interest differential swap is a currency swap with the spot and FORWARD transactions both at the spot exchange rate. Another name is "par forward swap." During the term of the currency swap contract, the parties make payments to each other for interest on the respective currencies. The interest can be agreed to be FIXED RATE interest or FLOATING RATE interest, or one interest rate can be fixed and the other can be floating. A "cross currency swap" is a form of interest differential currency swap in which the interest is floating rate interest to fixed rate interest.

Some terminologies distinguish a cross currency swap from an interest differential swap by characterizing the interest differential swap as having only fixed rate interest to fixed rate interest. If the amounts of the respective currencies are periodically MARKED-TO-MARKET, the interest differential currency swap may be called a "parallel loan." A derivative of the interest differential currency swap in which the NOTIONAL AMOUNTS are not exchanged is also called a currency swap or a "dual-currency interest rate swap." Warning: examine the contract's provisions or ask for a written explanation to determine the proposed interest rate terms; do not rely on terminology titles. 2. The term outright forward swap is usually used to describe a currency swap with different, instead of the same, spot and forward outright exchange rates. The difference in exchange rates results from the different interest rates for each currency having been built into the forward outright exchange rate. Payments based on the different currencies' interest rates are not involved. The payments under this currency swap involve only the exchange of payments of the two currencies.

Foreign exchange swap   An arrangement involving two separate SPOT and FORWARD foreign exchange contracts. A currency is purchased or sold at spot with a simultaneous, offsetting forward transaction. The foreign exchange swap is considered a MONEY MARKET transaction because its term typically does not exceed 18 months. The foreign exchange swap is a convenient money management tool for accelerating or deferring the actual delivery or receipt of foreign currency cash flows. A foreign exchange swap can also be handy to hedge fully any

---

[1] "International Swaps Growth Moderates," *Financial Times* (London), May 24, 1990.

foreign exchange rate change for an investment or borrowing in another currency.

Interest rate swap   This swap could more fully be named a "single currency interest rate swap." It is a DERIVATIVE contract, an agreement between two parties making payments computed on a NOTIONAL AMOUNT of money, the principal, to exchange periodic payments, with one party making payments based on a fixed interest rate and the second party making payments based on a referenced floating interest rate, such as LIBOR, a Treasury Bill rate, or a commercial paper reference rate. The fixed and floating payment amounts are usually netted for cash settlement on the payment due dates. The floating rate is typically referenced to either a published source such as the LIBOR page of Reuters Monitor Money Rates Service or the weekly Federal Reserve Statistical Release, or a counterparty bank's quoted rate. An interest rate swap contract term ranges from 1 to 12 years. Most of the swaps are referenced to U.S. Dollar notional amounts. Single-currency interest rate swaps can be arranged in currencies other than U.S. Dollars, but most are in other EUROCURRENCIES.

The interest rate swap market is huge, particularly for notional amounts in U.S. Dollars. The estimate of outstanding interest rate swaps at the end of 1989 was USD 1.9 trillion.[2] Swaps are used by borrowers and CAPITAL MARKET investors. Dealers are also customizing interest rate swaps for the portfolios of fixed income money managers.[3]

Swaption (swap option)   An option agreement for which the UNDERLYING is a derivative SWAP. For example, a borrower can purchase an option to enter into an interest rate swap. A "puttable" swap is a swap with an option to cancel by "putting" the swap back to the writer. An "extendable" swap is a swap that has an option for it to be extended in time according to the terms of the original swap contract.

SWIFT (Society for Worldwide Interbank Financial Telecommunications)   A computerized message and funds transfer system owned by hundreds of banks around the world. It is the most important electronic funds transfer (EFT) system in the world.

Synthetics   In financial engineering, a position replicating another position but built from different contracts.

Telerate   A computerized information service that provides "live" information regarding prices in various financial markets, including foreign exchange, bonds, money markets, and futures markets. News headlines and market commentaries are also available. KNIGHT RIDDER, QUOTRON, and REUTERS provide competing services.

[2] *Id.*
[3] "Son of Swaps," *Institutional Investor* (February 1991): 89.

Tenor   The time to maturity of a financial instrument or contract.

Time decay   The decrease in the value of an option solely because of the passage of time. Options with a longer time to expiration have a greater TIME VALUE than options with a shorter time to expiration. The time decay curve drops quickly near the option's expiration.

Time value   The amount by which an option's total PREMIUM exceeds its INTRINSIC VALUE. If the option has no intrinsic value, it may still have time value; hope springs in an option trader's heart to the moment of expiration. An option with no intrinsic value will still have some time value, unless it is deep OUT OF THE MONEY and very close to its EXPIRATION DATE. See also TIME DECAY.

Timing "option"   Watch out: this is not a true option. The contract is also called an "option date forward contract." The holder may select any date to exercise—and here's why it is NOT a true option—but the "option" must be exercised on or before its maturity date. Stated otherwise, fulfilling the contract's stated obligation is required, not "optional."

Tranche   From the French word meaning "slice," as of cake or pie, this term refers to a predetermined segment or installment of a financial transaction, contract, or credit facility.

Transaction exposure   The corporate financial risk arising from changes in currency exchange rates, interest rates, or commodity prices on specific transactions, contracts, or physicals. In foreign exchange, the risk of an unfavorable exchange rate move on a particular transaction. An example would be the appreciation of the Pound Sterling against the U.S. Dollar if a U.S. importer had contracted to purchase goods in the United Kingdom.

Translation exposure   Sometimes referred to as accounting or balance sheet exposure, this exposure arises when the balance sheet and income statements include items denominated in a foreign currency, not the company's functional currency for accounting purposes. These items require periodic revaluation into the accounting functional currency, which is reflected in noncash adjustments showing nonrealized gains or losses.

Transparency   The visibility of transaction prices and volumes to market participants. For example, regulated markets for currencies and interest rates are more "transparent" than the OTC interbank market.

Type (of option)   Whether an option is a PUT OPTION or a CALL OPTION. See also STYLE (OF OPTION).

Underlying   The COMMODITY, CURRENCY, FINANCIAL INSTRUMENT, or INDEX—or feature thereof—against which an option, swap, or derivative contract is written.

Value date   The SETTLEMENT date. The term is most commonly used with FOREIGN EXCHANGE or foreign currency deposit transactions.

Variation margin   For open FUTURES contracts and writers of exchange traded options, the margin computation resulting from daily MARK-TO-MARKET. Positive variation margin can be repaid in cash by the brokerage firm and negative variation margin must be paid in cash to the brokerage firm. See also INITIAL MARGIN and MARGIN.

Volatility   The probability of changes in price of the UNDERLYING. The more likely the underlying is to fluctuate in price, the more volatile it is. A measure of the extent to which the value of an underlying is expected to fluctuate.

Warehousing   Storing an OTC contract that is not yet offset. In 1991, a phrase to describe having written a DERIVATIVE or SWAP contract without having yet established an offsetting contract(s) or position. The capacity to "warehouse" may eliminate delay for the counterparty while the writer of the contract arranges an offset.

Wash   Opening and closing a transaction with neither a profit nor a loss; a "wash sale."

Wire transfer   The transfer of funds through electronic banking networks. In the United States, such transfer provides immediately available funds to the recipient. International wire transfers and funds transfers in foreign countries are subject to the value date systems of their banking regulations, with allowances for time zone differences. Intended recipients of transfers should consult with the international department of a bank for recommended banking procedures and particulars. See also SWIFT.

Writer   The party to an option contract who incurs an obligation by selling contractual rights to the option holder; also called an option SELLER. The writer sells the option contract when writing the option contract.

Writing (an option)   Most option transactions are two-stage transactions: (a) an opening transaction, and (b) a closing transaction. Writing refers to an opening transaction in which the writer sells an option short to a counterparty. To close the position, the writer must repurchase the option from the original or subsequent counterparty, the HOLDER. See also BUYER and SELLER.

Yield curve   The graphic relationship between the yields and current maturities of debt financial instruments with equal credit ratings. If longer maturities have higher interest rates than shorter maturities, the curve is called a "positive yield curve." If longer maturities have lower interest rates than shorter maturities, the curve is called a "negative yield curve."

Yield to Maturity (YTM)   The percentage rate of return on a debt financial instrument, including both the interest payments and the capital gain or loss. Synonymous with "internal rate of return." See most calculator instructions and any finance text.

Appendix B
References

This Appendix provides a noncomprehensive, selected bibliography of books; recommended periodicals, with addresses; newspapers; and major exchanges, and regulatory and supervisory bodies, also with addresses.

BOOKS

Bannock, G., and W. Manser, 1989. *International Dictionary of Finance.* London, England: The Economist Books, Hutchinson Business Books.

Bishop, P., and D. Dixon, 1992. *Foreign Exchange Handbook.* New York: McGraw-Hill.

Eckl, S., J. Robinson, and D. Thomas, 1991. *Financial Engineering.* Cambridge, MA: Basil Blackwell, Inc.

Koziol, J., 1990. *Hedging,* New York: John Wiley & Sons.

Kramer, A., 1991. *Financial Products — Taxation, Regulation, and Design,* rev. ed., 2 vols. New York: John Wiley & Sons.

Logue, D., 1984 and update. *Handbook of Modern Finance.* Boston, MA: Warren, Gorham & Lamont.

Loosigian, A., 1981. *Foreign Exchange Futures.* New York: Dow Jones-Irwin.

———. 1980 New York: Dow Jones-Irwin. *Interest Rate Futures.*

McGraw-Hill Handbook of Commodities and Futures, The, 1985. M. Pring, ed. New York: McGraw-Hill.

McMillan, L., 1986. *Options as a Stragegic Investment,* 2d ed. New York: New York Institute of Finance.

Riehl, H., and R. Rodriguez, 1983. *Foreign Exchange and Money Markets.* New York: McGraw-Hill.

Schwager, J., 1984. *A Complete Guide to the Futures Markets.* New York: John Wiley & Sons.

Schwarz, E., 1979. *How to Use Interest Rate Futures Contracts.*

Stigum, M., 1990. *The Money Market,* rev. ed. New York: Dow Jones-Irwin.

PERIODICALS

Corporate Cash Flow, Communications Channels, Inc., 6255 Barfield Rd., Atlanta, GA 30328 (Tel: 404-256-9800).

Corporate Finance, Reed Business Publishing (USA), 205 East 42nd Street, New York, NY 10017 (Tel: 212-867-2080); or, Quadrant Subscription S Oakfield House, Perrymount Road, Haywards Heath RH16 3DH England (Tel: 011 (44)-444-440421).

Corporate Risk Management, Oster Communications, Inc., 219 Parkade, Cedar Falls, IA 50613. (Tel: 319-277-1271). Magazine discontinued in 1992.

Euromoney, Euromoney Publications PLC, Nestor House Playhouse Yard, London EC4V 5EX England (Tel: 011 (44)-071-236-3288).

Futures—The magazine of commodities and options, 219 Parkade, Cedar Falls, IA 50613 (Tel: 319-277-6341); 250 South Wacker Drive, Suite 1150, Chicago, IL 60606 (Tel: 312-977-0999); 1 Marble Quay, St. Katharine's Way, London E19UL England.

Global Finance, 55 John Street, New York, NY 10038 (Tel: 212-766-8014).

Treasury and Risk Management, CFO Publishing Corporation, 253 Summer Street, Boston, MA 02210 (Tel: 617-345-9700). New Publication in March 1992.

NEWSPAPERS

Barron's (a weekly)

The Wall Street Journal (daily)

Financial Times (daily from London, distributed in U.S.)

UNITED STATES

Exchanges

Note: Each exchange has its own separate clearing corporation.

Chicago Board of Trade (CBOT)
La Salle at Jackson
Chicago, IL 60604
Tel: 312-435-3500; Telex: 253-223

Chicago Mercantile Exchange (CME)
International Monetary Market (IMM)
444 West Jackson Boulevard
Chicago, IL 60606
Tel: 312-648-1000

Mid-America Commodity Exchange
(The Market Place of Minicontract)
175 West Jackson Boulevard
Chicago, IL 60604
Tel: 312-435-0606

New York Cotton Exchange
4 World Trade Center
New York, NY 10048
Tel: 212-938-2900

FINEX, A Division of the New York Cotton Exchange
4 World Trade Center
New York, NY 10048
Tel: 212-938-2634

New York Coffee, Cocoa and Sugar Exchange
4 World Trade Center
New York, NY 10048
Tel: 212-938-2900

Commodity Exchange, Inc. (COMEX)
4 World Trade Center
New York, NY 10048
Tel: 212-938-2900

The Board of Trade of Kansas City, Missouri, Inc. (KCBT)
4800 Main Street, Suite 274
Kansas City, MO 64112
Tel: 816-753-7500
Minneapolis Grain Exchange
4th Ave. and 4th St. S., Room 150
Minneapolis, MN 55415
Tel: 612-338-6212

New York Futures Exchange (NYFE)
20 Broad Street
New York, NY 10005
Tel: 212-623-4968

Regulatory and Supervisory Bodies

Commodity Futures Trading Commission
2033 K Street, N.W.
Washington, DC 20581
Tel: 202-254-6287

National Futures Association
200 West Madison Street
Chicago, IL 60606

UNITED KINGDOM

Exchanges

London Commodity Exchange:
    London Cocoa Terminal Market Association Ltd.
    Coffee Terminal Market Association of London Ltd.
    United Terminal Sugar Market Association Ltd.
    International Petroleum Exchange of London Ltd.
Cereal House, 58 Mark Lane
London EC3R 7NE England
Tel: 011 (44)-071-481-2080

Baltic Exchange:
   Gafta Soyabean Meal Futures Association Ltd.
   Gafta EEC Wheat, Barley, and Potatoes Futures Market
Baltic International Freight Futures Exchange Ltd.
Baltic Exchange Chambers, 24/28 St. Mary Ace
London EC3A 8EP England
Tel: 011 (44)-071-283-5146
London Metals Exchange
Plantation House, 'E' Section
Fenchurch Street
London EC3M 3AP England
Tel: 011 (44)-071-626-3311

Clearing Houses

International Commodities Clearing House, Ltd.
Roman Wall House, 1-2 Crutched Friars
London EC3N 2AN England
Tel: 011 (44)-071-488-3200

Professional Associations

The Federation of Commodity Associations
Plantation House, Mincing Lane
London EC3M 3HT England
Tel: 011 (44)-071-626-1745

CANADA

Agricultural Commodities

Winnipeg Commodity Exchange
500 Commodity Exchange Tower
360 Main Street
Winnipeg, Manitoba R3L 32A2 Canada

Appendix C

ISDA Interest Rate and Currency Exchange Agreement (1987)

International Swap Dealers Association, Inc.

INTEREST RATE
AND
CURRENCY EXCHANGE AGREEMENT

Dated as of...

.... and ....

have entered and/or anticipate entering into one or more transactions (each a "Swap Transaction"). The parties agree that each Swap Transaction will be governed by the terms and conditions set forth in this document (which includes the schedule (the "Schedule")) and in the documents (each a "Confirmation") exchanged between the parties confirming such Swap Transactions. Each Confirmation constitutes a supplement to and forms part of this document and will be read and construed as one with this document, so that this document and all the Confirmations constitute a single agreement between the parties (collectively referred to as this "Agreement"). The parties acknowledge that all Swap Transactions are entered into in reliance on the fact that this document and all Confirmations will form a single agreement between the parties, it being understood that the parties would not otherwise enter into any Swap Transactions.

Accordingly, the parties agree as follows:–

1.   Interpretation

(a)   *Definitions.* The terms defined in Section 14 and in the Schedule will have the meanings therein specified for the purpose of this Agreement.

(b)   *Inconsistency.* In the event of any inconsistency between the provisions of any Confirmation and this document, such Confirmation will prevail for the purpose of the relevant Swap Transaction.

2.   Payments

(a)   *Obligations and Conditions.*

(i)   Each party will make each payment specified in each Confirmation as being payable by it.

(ii)   Payments under this Agreement will be made not later than the due date for value on that date in the place of the account specified in the relevant Confirmation or otherwise pursuant to this Agreement, in freely transferable funds and in the manner customary for payments in the required currency.

(iii)   Each obligation of each party to pay any amount due under Section 2(a)(i) is subject to (1) the condition precedent that no Event of Default or Potential Event of Default with respect to the other party has occurred and is continuing and (2) each other applicable condition precedent specified in this Agreement.

(b)   *Change of Account.* Either party may change its account by giving notice to the other party at least five days prior to the due date for payment for which such change applies.

(c)   *Netting.* If on any date amounts would otherwise be payable:–

    (i)   in the same currency; and

    (ii) in respect of the same Swap Transaction,

by each party to the other, then, on such date, each party's obligation to make payment of any such amount will be automatically satisfied and discharged and, if the aggregate amount that would otherwise have been payable by one party exceeds the aggregate amount that would otherwise have been payable by the other party, replaced by an obligation upon the party by whom the larger aggregate amount would have been payable to pay to the other party the excess of the larger aggregate amount over the smaller aggregate amount.

If the parties specify "Net Payments — Corresponding Payment Dates" in a Confirmation or otherwise in this Agreement, sub-paragraph (ii) above will cease to apply to all Swap Transactions with effect from the date so specified (so that a net amount will be determined in respect of all amounts due on the same date in the same currency, regardless of whether such amounts are payable in respect of the same Swap Transaction); *provided that,* in such case, this Section 2(c) will apply separately to each Office through which a party makes and receives payments as set forth in Section 10.

(d)   *Deduction or Withholding for Tax.*

    (i)   *Gross-Up.* All payments under this Agreement will be made without any deduction or withholding for or on account of any Tax unless such deduction or withholding is required by any applicable law, as modified by the practice of any relevant governmental revenue authority, then in effect. If a party is so required to deduct or withhold, then that party ("X") will:–

        (1)   promptly notify the other party ("Y") of such requirement;

        (2)   pay to the relevant authorities the full amount required to be deducted or withheld (including the full amount required to be deducted or withheld from any additional amount paid by X to Y under this Section 2(d)) promptly upon the earlier of determining that such deduction or withholding is required or receiving notice that such amount has been assessed against Y;

        (3)   promptly forward to Y an official receipt (or a certified copy), or other documentation reasonably acceptable to Y, evidencing such payment to such authorities; and

        (4)   if such Tax is an Indemnifiable Tax, pay to Y, in addition to the payment to which Y is otherwise entitled under this Agreement, such additional amount as is necessary to ensure that the net amount actually received by Y (free and clear of Indemnifiable Taxes, whether assessed against X or Y) will equal the full amount Y would have received had no such deduction or withholding been required. However, X will not be required to pay any additional amount to Y to the extent that it would not be required to be paid but for:–

            (A)   the failure by Y to comply with or perform any agreement contained in Section 4(a)(i) or 4(d); or

            (B)   the failure of a representation made by Y pursuant to Section 3(f) to be accurate and true unless such failure would not have occurred but for a Change in Tax Law.

    (ii) *Liability.* If:–

        (1)   X is required by any applicable law, as modified by the practice of any relevant governmental revenue authority, to make any deduction or withholding in respect of which X would not be required to pay an additional amount to Y under Section 2(d)(i)(4);

        (2)   X does not so deduct or withhold; and

        (3)   a liability resulting from such Tax is assessed directly against X,

then, except to the extent Y has satisfied or then satisfies the liability resulting from such Tax, Y will promptly pay to X the amount of such liability (including any related liability for interest, but including any related liability for penalties only if Y has failed to comply with or perform any agreement contained in Section 4(a)(i) or (d)).

(e)   *Default Interest.* A party that defaults in the payment of any amount due will, to the extent permitted by law, be required to pay interest (before as well as after judgment) on such amount to the other party on demand in the same currency as the overdue amount, for the period from (and including) the original due date for payment to (but excluding) the date of actual payment, at the Default Rate. Such interest will be calculated on the basis of daily compounding and the actual number of days elapsed.

3. Representations

Each party represents to the other party (which representations will be deemed to be repeated by each party on each date on which a Swap Transaction is entered into and, in the case of the representations in Section 3(f), at all times until the termination of this Agreement) that:–

(a)   *Basic Representations.*

(i)   *Status.*   It is duly organised and validly existing under the laws of the jurisdiction of its organisation or incorporation and, if relevant under such laws, in good standing;

(ii)   *Powers.*   It has the power to execute and deliver this Agreement and any other documentation relating to this Agreement that it is required by this Agreement to deliver and to perform its obligations under this Agreement and any obligations it has under any Credit Support Document to which it is a party and has taken all necessary action to authorise such execution, delivery and performance;

(iii)   *No Violation or Conflict.*   Such execution, delivery and performance do not violate or conflict with any law applicable to it, any provision of its constitutional documents, any order or judgment of any court or other agency of government applicable to it or any of its assets or any contractual restriction binding on or affecting it or any of its assets;

(iv)   *Consents.*   All governmental and other consents that are required to have been obtained by it with respect to this Agreement or any Credit Support Document to which it is a party have been obtained and are in full force and effect and all conditions of any such consents have been complied with; and

(v)   *Obligations Binding.*   Its obligations under this Agreement and any Credit Support Document to which it is a party constitute its legal, valid and binding obligations, enforceable in accordance with their respective terms (subject to applicable bankruptcy, reorganisation, insolvency, moratorium or similar laws affecting creditors' rights generally and subject, as to enforceability, to equitable principles of general application (regardless of whether enforcement is sought in a proceeding in equity or at law)).

(b)   *Absence of Certain Events.*   No Event of Default or Potential Event of Default or, to its knowledge, Termination Event with respect to it has occurred and is continuing and no such event or circumstance would occur as a result of its entering into or performing its obligations under this Agreement or any Credit Support Document to which it is a party.

(c)   *Absence of Litigation.*   There is not pending or, to its knowledge, threatened against it or any of its Affiliates any action, suit or proceeding at law or in equity or before any court, tribunal, governmental body, agency or official or any arbitrator that purports to draw into question, or is likely to affect, the legality, validity or enforceability against it of this Agreement or any Credit Support Document to which it is a party or its ability to perform its obligations under this Agreement or such Credit Support Document.

(d)   *Accuracy of Specified Information.*   All applicable information that is furnished in writing by or on behalf of it to the other party and is identified for the purpose of this Section 3(d) in paragraph 2 of Part 3 of the Schedule is, as of the date of the information, true, accurate and complete in every material respect.

(e)   *Payer Tax Representation.*   Each representation specified in Part 2 of the Schedule as being made by it for the purpose of this Section 3(e) is accurate and true.

(f)   *Payee Tax Representations.*   Each representation specified in Part 2 of the Schedule as being made by it for the purpose of this Section 3(f) is accurate and true.

4. Agreements

Each party agrees with the other that, so long as it has or may have any obligation under this Agreement or under any Credit Support Document to which it is a party:–

3

(a)   *Furnish Specified Information.* It will deliver to the other party:–

(i)   any forms, documents or certificates relating to taxation specified in Part 3 of the Schedule or any Confirmation; and

(ii)   any other documents specified in Part 3 of the Schedule or any Confirmation,

by the date specified in Part 3 of the Schedule or such Confirmation or, if none is specified, as soon as practicable.

(b)   *Maintain Authorisations.* It will use all reasonable efforts to maintain in full force and effect all consents of any governmental or other authority that are required to be obtained by it with respect to this Agreement or any Credit Support Document to which it is a party and will use all reasonable efforts to obtain any that may become necessary in the future.

(c)   *Comply with Laws.* It will comply in all material respects with all applicable laws and orders to which it may be subject if failure so to comply would materially impair its ability to perform its obligations under this Agreement or any Credit Support Document to which it is a party.

(d)   *Tax Agreement.* It will give notice of any failure of a representation made by it under Section 3(f) to be accurate and true promptly upon learning of such failure.

(e)   *Payment of Stamp Tax.* It will pay any Stamp Tax levied or imposed upon it or in respect of its execution or performance of this Agreement by a jurisdiction in which it is incorporated, organised, managed and controlled, or considered to have its seat, or in which a branch or office through which it is acting for the purpose of this Agreement is located ("Stamp Tax Jurisdiction") and will indemnify the other party against any Stamp Tax levied or imposed upon the other party or in respect of the other party's execution or performance of this Agreement by any such Stamp Tax Jurisdiction which is not also a Stamp Tax Jurisdiction with respect to the other party.

5.   Events of Default and Termination Events

(a)   *Events of Default.* The occurrence at any time with respect to a party or, if applicable, any Specified Entity of such party, of any of the following events constitutes an event of default (an "Event of Default") with respect to such party:–

(i)   *Failure to Pay.* Failure by the party to pay, when due, any amount required to be paid by it under this Agreement if such failure is not remedied on or before the third Business Day after notice of such failure to pay is given to the party;

(ii)   *Breach of Agreement.* Failure by the party to comply with or perform any agreement or obligation (other than an obligation to pay any amount required to be paid by it under this Agreement or to give notice of a Termination Event or any agreement or obligation under Section 4(a)(i) or 4(d)) to be complied with or performed by the party in accordance with this Agreement if such failure is not remedied on or before the thirtieth day after notice of such failure is given to the party;

(iii)   *Credit Support Default.*

(1)   Failure by the party or any applicable Specified Entity to comply with or perform any agreement or obligation to be complied with or performed by the party or such Specified Entity in accordance with any Credit Support Document if such failure is continuing after any applicable grace period has elapsed;

(2)   the expiration or termination of such Credit Support Document, or the ceasing of such Credit Support Document to be in full force and effect, prior to the final Scheduled Payment Date of each Swap Transaction to which such Credit Support Document relates without the written consent of the other party; or

(3)   the party or such Specified Entity repudiates, or challenges the validity of, such Credit Support Document;

(iv)   *Misrepresentation.* A representation (other than a representation under Section 3(e) or (f)) made or repeated or deemed to have been made or repeated by the party or any applicable Specified Entity in this Agreement or any Credit Support Document relating to this Agreement proves to have been incorrect or misleading in any material respect when made or repeated or deemed to have been made or repeated;

(v)   *Default under Specified Swaps.* The occurrence of an event of default in respect of the party or any applicable Specified Entity under a Specified Swap which, following the giving of any applicable notice or the lapse of any applicable grace period, has resulted in the designation or occurrence of an early termination date in respect of such Specified Swap;

(vi) *Cross Default.* If "Cross Default" is specified in Part 1 of the Schedule as applying to the party, (1) the occurrence or existence of an event or condition in respect of such party or any applicable Specified Entity under one or more agreements or instruments relating to Specified Indebtedness of such party or any such Specified Entity in an aggregate amount of not less than the Threshold Amount (as specified in Part 1 of the Schedule) which has resulted in such Specified Indebtedness becoming, or becoming capable at such time of being declared, due and payable under such agreements or instruments, before it would otherwise have been due and payable or (2) the failure by such party or any such Specified Entity to make one or more payments at maturity in an aggregate amount of not less than the Threshold Amount under such agreements or instruments (after giving effect to any applicable grace period);

(vii) *Bankruptcy.* The party or any applicable Specified Entity:–

(1) is dissolved; (2) becomes insolvent or fails or is unable or admits in writing its inability generally to pay its debts as they become due; (3) makes a general assignment, arrangement or composition with or for the benefit of its creditors; (4) institutes or has instituted against it a proceeding seeking a judgment of insolvency or bankruptcy or any other relief under any bankruptcy or insolvency law or other similar law affecting creditors' rights, or a petition is presented for the winding-up or liquidation of the party or any such Specified Entity, and, in the case of any such proceeding or petition instituted or presented against it, such proceeding or petition (A) results in a judgment of insolvency or bankruptcy or the entry of an order for relief or the making of an order for the winding-up or liquidation of the party or such Specified Entity or (B) is not dismissed, discharged, stayed or restrained in each case within 30 days of the institution or presentation thereof; (5) has a resolution passed for its winding-up or liquidation; (6) seeks or becomes subject to the appointment of an administrator, receiver, trustee, custodian or other similar official for it or for all or substantially all its assets (regardless of how brief such appointment may be, or whether any obligations are promptly assumed by another entity or whether any other event described in this clause (6) has occurred and is continuing); (7) any event occurs with respect to the party or any such Specified Entity which, under the applicable laws of any jurisdiction, has an analogous effect to any of the events specified in clauses (1) to (6) (inclusive); or (8) takes any action in furtherance of, or indicating its consent to, approval of, or acquiescence in, any of the foregoing acts;

other than in the case of clause (1) or (5) or, to the extent it relates to those clauses, clause (8), for the purpose of a consolidation, amalgamation or merger which would not constitute an event described in (viii) below; or

(viii) *Merger Without Assumption.* The party consolidates or amalgamates with, or merges into, or transfers all or substantially all its assets to, another entity and, at the time of such consolidation, amalgamation, merger or transfer:–

(1) the resulting, surviving or transferee entity fails to assume all the obligations of such party under this Agreement by operation of law or pursuant to an agreement reasonably satisfactory to the other party to this Agreement; or

(2) the benefits of any Credit Support Document relating to this Agreement fail to extend (without the consent of the other party) to the performance by such resulting, surviving or transferee entity of its obligations under this Agreement.

(b) *Termination Events.* The occurrence at any time with respect to a party or, if applicable, any Specified Entity of such party of any event specified below constitutes an Illegality if the event is specified in (i) below, a Tax Event if the event is specified in (ii) below, a Tax Event Upon Merger if the event is specified in (iii) below or a Credit Event Upon Merger if the event is specified in (iv) below:–

(i) *Illegality.* Due to the adoption of, or any change in, any applicable law after the date on which such Swap Transaction is entered into, or due to the promulgation of, or any change in, the interpretation by any court, tribunal or regulatory authority with competent jurisdiction of any applicable law after such date, it becomes unlawful (other than as a result of a breach by the party of Section 4(b)) for such party (which will be the Affected Party):–

5

(1)   to perform any absolute or contingent obligation to make a payment or to receive a payment in respect of such Swap Transaction or to comply with any other material provision of this Agreement relating to such Swap Transaction; or

(2)   to perform, or for any applicable Specified Entity to perform, any contingent or other obligation which the party (or such Specified Entity) has under any Credit Support Document relating to such Swap Transaction;

(ii)   **Tax Event.**

(1)   The party (which will be the Affected Party) will be required on the next succeeding Scheduled Payment Date to pay to the other party an additional amount in respect of an Indemnifiable Tax under Section 2(d)(i)(4) (except in respect of interest under Section 2 (e)) as a result of a Change in Tax Law; or

(2)   there is a substantial likelihood that the party (which will be the Affected Party) will be required on the next succeeding Scheduled Payment Date to pay to the other party an additional amount in respect of an Indemnifiable Tax under Section 2(d)(i)(4) (except in respect of interest under Section 2(e)) and such substantial likelihood results from an action taken by a taxing authority, or brought in a court of competent jurisdiction, on or after the date on which such Swap Transaction was entered into (regardless of whether such action was taken or brought with respect to a party to this Agreement);

(iii)   **Tax Event Upon Merger.** The party (the "Burdened Party") on the next succeeding Scheduled Payment Date will either (1) be required to pay an additional amount in respect of an Indemnifiable Tax under Section 2(d)(i)(4) (except in respect of interest under Section 2(e)) or (2) receive a payment from which an amount has been deducted or withheld for or on account of any Indemnifiable Tax in respect of which the other party is not required to pay an additional amount, in either case as a result of a party consolidating or amalgamating with, or merging into, or transferring all or substantially all its assets to, another entity (which will be the Affected Party) where such action does not constitute an event described in Section 5(a)(viii); or

(iv)   **Credit Event Upon Merger.** If "Credit Event Upon Merger" is specified in Part 1 of the Schedule as applying to the party, such party ("X") consolidates or amalgamates with, or merges into, or transfers all or substantially all its assets to, another entity and such action does not constitute an event described in Section 5(a)(viii) but the creditworthiness of the resulting, surviving or transferee entity (which will be the Affected Party) is materially weaker than that of X immediately prior to such action.

(c)   **Event of Default and Illegality.** If an event or circumstance which would otherwise constitute or give rise to an Event of Default also constitutes an Illegality, it will be treated as an Illegality and will not constitute an Event of Default.

6.   Early Termination

(a)   **Right to Terminate Following Event of Default.** If at any time an Event of Default with respect to a party (the "Defaulting Party") has occurred and is then continuing, the other party may, by not more than 20 days notice to the Defaulting Party specifying the relevant Event of Default, designate a day not earlier than the day such notice is effective as an Early Termination Date in respect of all outstanding Swap Transactions. However, an Early Termination Date will be deemed to have occurred in respect of all Swap Transactions immediately upon the occurrence of any Event of Default specified in Section 5(a)(vii)(1), (2), (3), (5), (6), (7) or (8) and as of the time immediately preceding the institution of the relevant proceeding or the presentation of the relevant petition upon the occurrence of any Event of Default specified in Section 5(a)(vii)(4).

(b)   **Right to Terminate Following Termination Event.**

(i)   **Notice.** Upon the occurrence of a Termination Event, an Affected Party will, promptly upon becoming aware of the same, notify the other party thereof, specifying the nature of such Termination Event and the Affected Transactions relating thereto. The Affected Party will also give such other information to the other party with regard to such Termination Event as the other party may reasonably require.

(ii)   **Transfer to Avoid Termination Event.** If either an Illegality under Section 5(b)(i)(1) or a Tax Event occurs and there is only one Affected Party, or if a Tax Event Upon Merger occurs and the Burdened Party is the Affected Party, the Affected Party will as a condition to its right to designate an Early Termination Date under Section 6(b)(iv) use all reasonable efforts (which will not require such party to incur a loss, excluding immaterial, incidental expenses) to transfer within 20 days after it gives notice under Section 6(b)(i) all its rights and obligations under this Agreement in respect of the Affected Transactions to another of its offices, branches or Affiliates so that such Termination Event ceases to exist.

If the Affected Party is not able to make such a transfer it will give notice to the other party to that effect within such 20 day period, whereupon the other party may effect such a transfer within 30 days after the notice is given under Section 6(b)(i).

Any such transfer by a party under this Section 6(b)(ii) will be subject to and conditional upon the prior written consent of the other party, which consent will not be withheld if such other party's policies in effect at such time would permit it to enter into swap transactions with the transferee on the terms proposed.

(iii) *Two Affected Parties.* If an Illegality under Section 5(b)(i)(1) or a Tax Event occurs and there are two Affected Parties, each party will use all reasonable efforts to reach agreement within 30 days after notice thereof is given under Section 6(b)(i) on action that would cause such Termination Event to cease to exist.

(iv) *Right to Terminate.* If:–

(1) a transfer under Section 6(b)(ii) or an agreement under Section 6(b)(iii), as the case may be, has not been effected with respect to all Affected Transactions within 30 days after an Affected Party gives notice under Section 6(b)(i); or

(2) an Illegality under Section 5(b)(i)(2) or a Credit Event Upon Merger occurs, or a Tax Event Upon Merger occurs and the Burdened Party is not the Affected Party,

either party in the case of an Illegality, the Burdened Party in the case of a Tax Event Upon Merger, any Affected Party in the case of a Tax Event, or the party which is not the Affected Party in the case of a Credit Event Upon Merger, may, by not more than 20 days notice to the other party and provided that the relevant Termination Event is then continuing, designate a day not earlier than the day such notice is effective as an Early Termination Date in respect of all Affected Transactions.

(c) *Effect of Designation.*

(i) If notice designating an Early Termination Date is given under Section 6(a) or (b), the Early Termination Date will occur on the date so designated, whether or not the relevant Event of Default or Termination Event is continuing on the relevant Early Termination Date.

(ii) Upon the effectiveness of notice designating an Early Termination Date (or the deemed occurrence of an Early Termination Date), the obligations of the parties to make any further payments under Section 2(a)(i) in respect of the Terminated Transactions will terminate, but without prejudice to the other provisions of this Agreement.

(d) *Calculations.*

(i) *Statement.* Following the occurrence of an Early Termination Date, each party will make the calculations (including calculation of applicable interest rates) on its part contemplated by Section 6(e) and will provide to the other party a statement (1) showing, in reasonable detail, such calculations (including all relevant quotations) and (2) giving details of the relevant account to which any payment due to it under Section 6(e) is to be made. In the absence of written confirmation of a quotation obtained in determining a Market Quotation from the source providing such quotation, the records of the party obtaining such quotation will be conclusive evidence of the existence and accuracy of such quotation.

(ii) *Due Date.* The amount calculated as being payable under Section 6(e) will be due on the day that notice of the amount payable is effective (in the case of an Early Termination Date which is designated or deemed to occur as a result of an Event of Default) and not later than the day which is two Business Days after the day on which notice of the amount payable is effective (in the case of an Early Termination Date which is designated as a result of a Termination Event). Such amount will be paid together with (to the extent permitted under applicable law) interest thereon in the Termination Currency from (and including) the relevant Early Termination Date to (but excluding) the relevant due date, calculated as follows:–

(1) if notice is given designating an Early Termination Date or if an Early Termination Date is deemed to occur, in either case as a result of an Event of Default, at the Default Rate; or

(2) if notice is given designating an Early Termination Date as a result of a Termination Event, at the Default Rate minus 1% per annum.

Such interest will be calculated on the basis of daily compounding and the actual number of days elapsed.

(e) **Payments on Early Termination.**

(i) **Defaulting Party or One Affected Party.** If notice is given designating an Early Termination Date or if an Early Termination Date is deemed to occur and there is a Defaulting Party or only one Affected Party, the other party will determine the Settlement Amount in respect of the Terminated Transactions and:–

(1) if there is a Defaulting Party, the Defaulting Party will pay to the other party the excess, if a positive number, of (A) the sum of such Settlement Amount and the Termination Currency Equivalent of the Unpaid Amounts owing to the other party over (B) the Termination Currency Equivalent of the Unpaid Amounts owing to the Defaulting Party; and

(2) if there is an Affected Party, the payment to be made will be equal to (A) the sum of such Settlement Amount and the Termination Currency Equivalent of the Unpaid Amounts owing to the party determining the Settlement Amount (''X'') less (B) the Termination Currency Equivalent of the Unpaid Amounts owing to the party not determining the Settlement Amount (''Y'').

(ii) **Two Affected Parties.** If notice is given of an Early Termination Date and there are two Affected Parties, each party will determine a Settlement Amount in respect of the Terminated Transactions and the payment to be made will be equal to (1) the sum of (A) one-half of the difference between the Settlement Amount of the party with the higher Settlement Amount (''X'') and the Settlement Amount of the party with the lower Settlement Amount (''Y'') and (B) the Termination Currency Equivalent of the Unpaid Amounts owing to X less (2) the Termination Currency Equivalent of the Unpaid Amounts owing to Y.

(iii) **Party Owing.** If the amount calculated under Section 6(e)(i)(2) or (ii) is a positive number, Y will pay such amount to X; if such amount is a negative number, X will pay the absolute value of such amount to Y.

(iv) **Adjustment for Bankruptcy.** In circumstances where an Early Termination Date is deemed to occur, the amount determined under Section 6(e)(i) will be subject to such adjustments as are appropriate and permitted by law to reflect any payments made by one party to the other under this Agreement (and retained by such other party) during the period from the relevant Early Termination Date to the date for payment determined under Section 6(d)(ii).

(v) **Pre-Estimate of Loss.** The parties agree that the amounts recoverable under this Section 6(e) are a reasonable pre-estimate of loss and not a penalty. Such amounts are payable for the loss of bargain and the loss of protection against future risks and except as otherwise provided in this Agreement neither party will be entitled to recover any additional damages as a consequence of such losses.

7. Transfer

Subject to Section 6(b) and to any exception provided in the Schedule, neither this Agreement nor any interest or obligation in or under this Agreement may be transferred by either party without the prior written consent of the other party (other than pursuant to a consolidation or amalgamation with, or merger into, or transfer of all or substantially all its assets to, another entity) and any purported transfer without such consent will be void.

8. Contractual Currency

(a) **Payment in the Contractual Currency.** Each payment under this Agreement will be made in the relevant currency specified in this Agreement for that payment (the ''Contractual Currency''). To the extent permitted by applicable law, any obligation to make payments under this Agreement in the Contractual Currency will not be discharged or satisfied by any tender in any currency other than the Contractual Currency, except to the extent such tender results in the actual receipt by the party to which payment is owed, acting in a reasonable manner and in good faith in converting the currency so tendered into the Contractual Currency, of the full amount in the Contractual Currency of all amounts due in respect of this Agreement. If for any reason the amount in the Contractual Currency so received falls short of the amount in the Contractual Currency due in respect of this Agreement, the party required to make the payment will, to the extent permitted by applicable law, immediately pay such additional amount in the Contractual Currency as may be necessary to compensate for the shortfall. If for any reason the amount in the Contractual Currency so received exceeds the amount in the Contractual Currency due in respect of this Agreement, the party receiving the payment will refund promptly the amount of such excess.

(b)   *Judgments.* To the extent permitted by applicable law, if any judgment or order expressed in a currency other than the Contractual Currency is rendered (i) for the payment of any amount owing in respect of this Agreement, (ii) for the payment of any amount relating to any early termination in respect of this Agreement or (iii) in respect of a judgment or order of another court for the payment of any amount described in (i) or (ii) above, the party seeking recovery, after recovery in full of the aggregate amount to which such party is entitled pursuant to the judgment or order, will be entitled to receive immediately from the other party the amount of any shortfall of the Contractual Currency received by such party as a consequence of sums paid in such other currency and will refund promptly to the other party any excess of the Contractual Currency received by such party as a consequence of sums paid in such other currency if such shortfall or such excess arises or results from any variation between the rate of exchange at which the Contractual Currency is converted into the currency of the judgment or order for the purposes of such judgment or order and the rate of exchange at which such party is able, acting in a reasonable manner and in good faith in converting the currency received into the Contractual Currency, to purchase the Contractual Currency with the amount of the currency of the judgment or order actually received by such party. The term ''rate of exchange'' includes, without limitation, any premiums and costs of exchange payable in connection with the purchase of or conversion into the Contractual Currency.

(c)   *Separate Indemnities.* To the extent permitted by applicable law, these indemnities constitute separate and independent obligations from the other obligations in this Agreement, will be enforceable as separate and independent causes of action, will apply notwithstanding any indulgence granted by the party to which any payment is owed and will not be affected by judgment being obtained or claim or proof being made for any other sums due in respect of this Agreement.

(d)   *Evidence of Loss.* For the purpose of this Section 8, it will be sufficient for a party to demonstrate that it would have suffered a loss had an actual exchange or purchase been made.

9.   Miscellaneous

(a)   *Entire Agreement.* This Agreement constitutes the entire agreement and understanding of the parties with respect to its subject matter and supersedes all oral communication and prior writings with respect thereto.

(b)   *Amendments.* No amendment, modification or waiver in respect of this Agreement will be effective unless in writing and executed by each of the parties or confirmed by an exchange of telexes.

(c)   *Survival of Obligations.* Except as provided in Section 6(c)(ii), the obligations of the parties under this Agreement will survive the termination of any Swap Transaction.

(d)   *Remedies Cumulative.* Except as provided in this Agreement, the rights, powers, remedies and privileges provided in this Agreement are cumulative and not exclusive of any rights, powers, remedies and privileges provided by law.

(e)   *Counterparts and Confirmations.*

    (i)   This Agreement may be executed in counterparts, each of which will be deemed an original.

    (ii)   A Confirmation may be executed in counterparts or be created by an exchange of telexes, which in either case will be sufficient for all purposes to evidence a binding supplement to this Agreement. Any such counterpart or telex will specify that it constitutes a Confirmation.

(f)   *No Waiver of Rights.* A failure or delay in exercising any right, power or privilege in respect of this Agreement will not be presumed to operate as a waiver, and a single or partial exercise of any right, power or privilege will not be presumed to preclude any subsequent or further exercise of that right, power or privilege or the exercise of any other right, power or privilege.

(g)   *Headings.* The headings used in this Agreement are for convenience of reference only and are not to affect the construction of or to be taken into consideration in interpreting this Agreement.

10. Multibranch Parties

If a party is specified as a Multibranch Party in Part 4 of the Schedule, such Multibranch Party may make and receive payments under any Swap Transaction through any of its branches or offices listed in the Schedule (each an "Office"). The Office through which it so makes and receives payments for the purpose of any Swap Transaction will be specified in the relevant Confirmation and any change of Office for such purpose requires the prior written consent of the other party. Each Multibranch Party represents to the other party that, notwithstanding the place of payment, the obligations of each Office are for all purposes under this Agreement the obligations of such Multibranch Party. This representation will be deemed to be repeated by such Multibranch Party on each date on which a Swap Transaction is entered into.

11. Expenses

A Defaulting Party will, on demand, indemnify and hold harmless the other party for and against all reasonable out-of-pocket expenses, including legal fees and Stamp Tax, incurred by such other party by reason of the enforcement and protection of its rights under this Agreement or by reason of the early termination of any Swap Transaction, including, but not limited to, costs of collection.

12. Notices

(a) *Effectiveness.* Any notice or communication in respect of this Agreement will be sufficiently given to a party if in writing and delivered in person, sent by certified or registered mail (airmail, if overseas) or the equivalent (with return receipt requested) or by overnight courier or given by telex (with answerback received) at the address or telex number specified in Part 4 of the Schedule. A notice or communication will be effective:–

    (i)   if delivered by hand or sent by overnight courier, on the day it is delivered (or if that day is not a day on which commercial banks are open for business in the city specified in the address for notice provided by the recipient (a "Local Banking Day"), or if delivered after the close of business on a Local Banking Day, on the first following day that is a Local Banking Day);

    (ii)   if sent by telex, on the day the recipient's answerback is received (or if that day is not a Local Banking Day, or if after the close of business on a Local Banking Day, on the first following day that is a Local Banking Day); or

    (iii)   if sent by certified or registered mail (airmail, if overseas) or the equivalent (return receipt requested), three Local Banking Days after despatch if the recipient's address for notice is in the same country as the place of despatch and otherwise seven Local Banking Days after despatch.

(b) *Change of Addresses.* Either party may by notice to the other change the address or telex number at which notices or communications are to be given to it.

13. Governing Law and Jurisdiction

(a) *Governing Law.* This Agreement will be governed by and construed in accordance with the law specified in Part 4 of the Schedule.

(b) *Jurisdiction.* With respect to any suit, action or proceedings relating to this Agreement ("Proceedings"), each party irrevocably:–

    (i)   submits to the jurisdiction of the English courts, if this Agreement is expressed to be governed by English law, or to the non-exclusive jurisdiction of the courts of the State of New York and the United States District Court located in the Borough of Manhattan in New York City, if this Agreement is expressed to be governed by the laws of the State of New York; and

    (ii)   waives any objection which it may have at any time to the laying of venue of any Proceedings brought in any such court, waives any claim that such Proceedings have been brought in an inconvenient forum and further waives the right to object, with respect to such Proceedings, that such court does not have jurisdiction over such party.

Nothing in this Agreement precludes either party from bringing Proceedings in any other jurisdiction (outside, if this Agreement is expressed to be governed by English law, the Contracting States, as defined in Section 1(3) of the Civil Jurisdiction and Judgments Act 1982 or any modification, extension or re-enactment thereof for the time being in force) nor will the bringing of Proceedings in any one or more jurisdictions preclude the bringing of Proceedings in any other jurisdiction.

(c) *Service of Process.* Each party irrevocably appoints the Process Agent (if any) specified opposite its name in Part 4 of the Schedule to receive, for it and on its behalf, service of process in any Proceedings. If for any reason any party's Process Agent is unable to act as such, such party will promptly notify the other party and within 30 days appoint a substitute process agent acceptable to the other party. The parties irrevocably consent to service of process given in the manner provided for notices in Section 12. Nothing in this Agreement will affect the right of either party to serve process in any other manner permitted by law.

(d) **Waiver of Immunities.** Each party irrevocably waives, to the fullest extent permitted by applicable law, with respect to itself and its revenues and assets (irrespective of their use or intended use), all immunity on the grounds of sovereignty or other similiar grounds from (i) suit, (ii) jurisdiction of any court, (iii) relief by way of injunction, order for specific performance or for recovery of property, (iv) attachment of its assets (whether before or after judgment) and (v) execution or enforcement of any judgment to which it or its revenues or assets might otherwise be entitled in any Proceedings in the courts of any jurisdiction and irrevocably agrees, to the extent permitted by applicable law, that it will not claim any such immunity in any Proceedings.

14. Definitions

As used in this Agreement:–

"Affected Party" has the meaning specified in Section 5(b).

"Affected Transactions" means (a) with respect to any Termination Event consisting of an Illegality, Tax Event or Tax Event Upon Merger, all Swap Transactions affected by the occurrence of such Termination Event and (b) with respect to any other Termination Event, all Swap Transactions.

"Affiliate" means, subject to Part 4 of the Schedule, in relation to any person, any entity controlled, directly or indirectly, by the person, any entity that controls, directly or indirectly, the person or any entity under common control with the person. For this purpose, "control" of any entity or person means ownership of a majority of the voting power of the entity or person.

"Burdened Party" has the meaning specified in Section 5(b).

"Business Day" means (a) in relation to any payment due under Section 2(a)(i), a day on which commercial banks and foreign exchange markets are open for business in the place(s) specified in the relevant Confirmation and (b) in relation to any other payment, a day on which commercial banks and foreign exchange markets are open for business in the place where the relevant account is located and, if different, in the principal financial centre of the currency of such payment.

"Change in Tax Law" means the enactment, promulgation, execution or ratification of, or any change in or amendment to, any law (or in the application or official interpretation of any law) that occurs on or after the date on which the relevant Swap Transaction is entered into.

"consent" includes a consent, approval, action, authorisation, exemption, notice, filing, registration or exchange control consent.

"Credit Event Upon Merger" has the meaning specified in Section 5(b).

"Credit Support Document" means any agreement or instrument which is specified as such in this Agreement.

"Default Rate" means a rate per annum equal to the cost (without proof or evidence of any actual cost) to the relevant payee (as certified by it) of funding the relevant amount plus 1% per annum.

"Defaulting Party" has the meaning specified in Section 6(a).

"Early Termination Date" means the date specified as such in a notice given under Section 6(a) or 6(b)(iv).

"Event of Default" has the meaning specified in Section 5(a).

"Illegality" has the meaning specified in Section 5(b).

"Indemnifiable Tax" means any Tax other than a Tax that would not be imposed in respect of a payment under this Agreement but for a present or former connection between the jurisdiction of the government or taxation authority imposing such Tax and the recipient of such payment or a person related to such recipient (including, without limitation, a connection arising from such recipient or related person being or having been a citizen or resident of such jurisdiction, or being or having been organised, present or engaged in a trade or business in such jurisdiction, or having or having had a permanent establishment or fixed place of business in such jurisdiction, but excluding a connection arising solely from such recipient or related person having executed, delivered, performed its obligations or received a payment

under, or enforced, this Agreement or a Credit Support Document).

"law" includes any treaty, law, rule or regulation (as modified, in the case of tax matters, by the practice of any relevant governmental revenue authority) and *"lawful"* and *"unlawful"* will be construed accordingly.

"Loss" means, with respect to a Terminated Transaction and a party, an amount equal to the total amount (expressed as a positive amount) required, as determined as of the relevant Early Termination Date (or, if an Early Termination Date is deemed to occur, as of a time as soon thereafter as practicable) by the party in good faith, to compensate it for any losses and costs (including loss of bargain and costs of funding but excluding legal fees and other out-of-pocket expenses) that it may incur as a result of the early termination of the obligations of the parties in respect of such Terminated Transaction. If a party determines that it would gain or benefit from such early termination, such party's Loss will be an amount (expressed as a negative amount) equal to the amount of the gain or benefit as determined by such party.

"Market Quotation" means, with respect to a Terminated Transaction and a party to such Terminated Transaction making the determination, an amount (which may be negative) determined on the basis of quotations from Reference Market-makers for the amount that would be or would have been payable on the relevant Early Termination Date, either by the party to the Terminated Transaction making the determination (to be expressed as a positive amount) or to such party (to be expressed as a negative amount), in consideration of an agreement between such party and the quoting Reference Market-maker and subject to such documentation as they may in good faith agree, with the relevant Early Termination Date as the date of commencement of such agreement (or, if later, the date specified as the effective date of such Terminated Transaction in the relevant Confirmation), that would have the effect of preserving for such party the economic equivalent of the payment obligations of the parties under Section 2(a)(i) in respect of such Terminated Transaction that would, but for the occurrence of the relevant Early Termination Date, fall due after such Early Termination Date (excluding any Unpaid Amounts in respect of such Terminated Transaction but including, without limitation, any amounts that would, but for the occurrence of the relevant Early Termination Date, have been payable (assuming each applicable condition precedent had been satisfied) after such Early Termination Date by reference to any period in which such Early Termination Date occurs). The party making the determination (or its agent) will request each Reference Market-maker to provide its quotation to the extent practicable as of the same time (without regard to different time zones) on the relevant Early Termination Date (or, if an Early Termination Date is deemed to occur, as of a time as soon thereafter as practicable). The time as of which such quotations are to be obtained will, if only one party is obliged to make a determination under Section 6(e), be selected in good faith by that party and otherwise will be agreed by the parties. If more than three such quotations are provided, the Market Quotation will be the arithmetic mean of the Termination Currency Equivalent of the quotations, without regard to the quotations having the highest and lowest values. If exactly three such quotations are provided, the Market Quotation will be the quotation remaining after disregarding the quotations having the highest and lowest values. If fewer than three quotations are provided, it will be deemed that the Market Quotation in respect of such Terminated Transaction cannot be determined.

"Office" has the meaning specified in Section 10.

"Potential Event of Default" means any event which, with the giving of notice or the lapse of time or both, would constitute an Event of Default.

"Reference Market-makers" means four leading dealers in the relevant swap market selected by the party determining a Market Quotation in good faith (a) from among dealers of the highest credit standing which satisfy all the criteria that such party applies generally at the time in deciding whether to offer or to make an extension of credit and (b) to the extent practicable, from among such dealers having an office in the same city.

"Relevant Jurisdiction" means, with respect to a party, the jurisdictions (a) in which the party is incorporated, organised, managed and controlled or considered to have its seat, (b) where a branch or office through which the party is acting for purposes of this Agreement is located, (c) in which the party executes this Agreement and (d) in relation to any payment, from or through which such payment is made.

"Scheduled Payment Date" means a date on which a payment is due under Section 2(a)(i) with respect to a Swap Transaction.

ISDA 1987

"Settlement Amount" means, with respect to a party and any Early Termination Date, the sum of:–

(a)   the Termination Currency Equivalent of the Market Quotations (whether positive or negative) for each Terminated Transaction for which a Market Quotation is determined; and

(b)   for each Terminated Transaction for which a Market Quotation is not, or cannot be, determined, the Termination Currency Equivalent of such party's Loss (whether positive or negative);

provided that if the parties agree that an amount may be payable under Section 6(e) to a Defaulting Party by the other party, no account shall be taken of a Settlement Amount expressed as a negative number.

"Specified Entity" has the meaning specified in Part 1 of the Schedule.

"Specified Indebtedness" means, subject to Part 1 of the Schedule, any obligation (whether present or future, contingent or otherwise, as principal or surety or otherwise) in respect of borrowed money.

"Specified Swap" means, subject to Part 1 of the Schedule, any rate swap or currency exchange transaction now existing or hereafter entered into between one party to this Agreement (or any applicable Specified Entity) and the other party to this Agreement (or any applicable Specified Entity).

"Stamp Tax" means any stamp, registration, documentation or similar tax.

"Tax" means any present or future tax, levy, impost, duty, charge, assessment or fee of any nature (including interest, penalties and additions thereto) that is imposed by any government or other taxing authority in respect of any payment under this Agreement other than a stamp, registration, documentation or similar tax.

"Tax Event" has the meaning specified in Section 5(b).

"Tax Event Upon Merger" has the meaning specified in Section 5(b).

"Terminated Transactions" means (a) with respect to any Early Termination Date occurring as a result of a Termination Event, all Affected Transactions and (b) with respect to any Early Termination Date occurring as a result of an Event of Default, all Swap Transactions, which in either case are in effect as of the time immediately preceding the effectiveness of the notice designating such Early Termination Date (or, in the case of an Event of Default specified in Section 5(a)(vii), in effect as of the time immediately preceding such Early Termination Date).

"Termination Currency" has the meaning specified in Part 1 of the Schedule.

"Termination Currency Equivalent" means, in respect of any amount denominated in the Termination Currency, such Termination Currency amount and, in respect of any amount denominated in a currency other than the Termination Currency (the "Other Currency"), the amount in the Termination Currency determined by the party making the relevant determination as being required to purchase such amount of such Other Currency as at the relevant Early Termination Date with the Termination Currency at the rate equal to the spot exchange rate of the foreign exchange agent (selected as provided below) for the purchase of such Other Currency with the Termination Currency at or about 11.00 a.m. (in the city in which such foreign exchange agent is located) on such date as would be customary for the determination of such a rate for the purchase of such Other Currency for value the relevant Early Termination Date. The foreign exchange agent will, if only one party is obliged to make a determination under Section 6(e), be selected in good faith by that party and otherwise will be agreed by the parties.

"Termination Event" means an Illegality, a Tax Event, a Tax Event Upon Merger or a Credit Event Upon Merger.

"Unpaid Amounts" owing to any party means, with respect to any Early Termination Date, the aggregate of the amounts that became due and payable (or that would have become due and payable but for Section 2(a)(iii) or the designation or occurrence of such Early Termination Date) to such party under Section 2(a)(i) in respect of all Terminated Transactions by reference to all periods ended on or prior to such Early Termination Date and which remain unpaid as at such Early Termination Date, together with (to the extent permitted under applicable law and in lieu of any interest calculated under Section 2(e)) interest thereon, in the currency of such amounts, from (and including) the date such amounts became due and payable or would have become due and payable to (but excluding) such Early Termination Date, calculated as follows:–

(a)   in the case of notice of an Early Termination Date given as a result of an Event of Default:–

(i) interest on such amounts due and payable by a Defaulting Party will be calculated at the Default Rate; and

(ii) interest on such amounts due and payable by the other party will be calculated at a rate per annum equal to the cost to such other party (as certified by it) if it were to fund such amounts (without proof or evidence of any actual cost); and

(b) in the case of notice of an Early Termination Date given as a result of a Termination Event, interest on such amounts due and payable by either party will be calculated at a rate per annum equal to the arithmetic mean of the cost (without proof or evidence of any actual cost) to each party (as certified by such party and regardless of whether due and payable by such party) if it were to fund or of funding such amounts.

Such amounts of interest will be calculated on the basis of daily compounding and the actual number of days elapsed.

IN WITNESS WHEREOF the parties have executed this document as of the date specified on the first page of this document.

....
(Name of party)

....
(Name of party)

By: ....

By: ....

Name:

Name:

Title:

Title:

SCHEDULE
to the
Interest Rate and Currency Exchange Agreement

dated as of ....

between .... and ....

("Party A")   ("Party B")

Part 1
Termination Provisions

In this Agreement:–

(1)   *"Specified Entity"* means in relation to Party A for the purpose of:–

Section 5(a)(iii) and (iv) and Section 5(b)(i). ....

Section 5(a)(v). ....

Section 5(a)(vi). ....

Section 5(a)(vii). ....

in relation to Party B for the purpose of:–

Section 5(a)(iii) and (iv) and Section 5(b)(i). ....

Section 5(a)(v). ....

Section 5(a)(vi). ....

Section 5(a)(vii). ....

(2)   *"Specified Swap"* will have the meaning specified in Section 14 unless another meaning is specified here..

....

....

(3)   The *"Cross Default"* provisions of Section 5(a)(vi) will/will not* apply to Party A

will/will not* apply to Party B

If such provisions apply:–

"Specified Indebtedness" will have the meaning specified in Section 14 unless another meaning is specified here...

....

"Threshold Amount" means ....

....

(4)   *"Termination Currency"* means .... , if such currency is specified and freely available, and otherwise United States Dollars.

(5)   The *"Credit Event Upon Merger"* provisions of Section 5(b)(iv) will/will not* apply to Party A

will/will not* apply to Party B

*Delete as applicable   15   ISDA 1987

334

Part 2

Tax Representations

Representations of Party A

(1) *Payer Tax Representation.* For the purpose of Section 3(e), Party A will/will not* make the following representation:–

It is not required by any applicable law, as modified by the practice of any relevant governmental revenue authority, of any Relevant Jurisdiction to make any deduction or withholding for or on account of any Tax from any payment (other than interest under Section 2 (e)) to be made by it to the other party under this Agreement. In making this representation, it may rely on:–

(i) the accuracy of any representation made by the other party pursuant to Section 3(f);

(ii) the satisfaction of the agreement of the other party contained in Section 4(a)(i) and the accuracy and effectiveness of any document provided by the other party pursuant to Section 4(a)(i); and

(iii) the satisfaction of the agreement of the other party contained in Section 4(d).

(2) *Payee Tax Representations.* For the purpose of Section 3(f), Party A makes the representation(s) specified below:–

(a) The following representation will/will not* apply:–

It is fully eligible for the benefits of the ''Business Profits'' or ''Industrial and Commercial Profits'' provision, as the case may be, the ''Interest'' provision or the ''Other Income'' provision (if any) of the Specified Treaty with respect to any payment described in such provisions and received or to be received by it in connection with this Agreement and no such payment is attributable to a trade or business carried on by it through a permanent establishment in the Specified Jurisdiction.

If such representation applies, then:–

"Specified Treaty" means ....

"Specified Jurisdiction" means ....

(b) The following representation will/will not* apply:–

Each payment received or to be received by it in connection with this Agreement relates to the regular business operations of the party (and not to an investment of the party).

(c) The following representation will/will not* apply:–

Each payment received or to be received by it in connection with this Agreement will be effectively connected with its conduct of a trade or business in the Specified Jurisdiction.

If such representation applies, then *"Specified Jurisdiction"* means ....

(d) The following representation will/will not* apply:–

It is a bank recognised by the United Kingdom Inland Revenue as carrying on a bona fide banking business in the United Kingdom, is entering into this Agreement in the ordinary course of such business and will bring into account payments made and received under this Agreement in computing its income for United Kingdom tax purposes.

(e) Other representations:– ....

....

....

....

N.B. The above representations may need modification if either party is a Multibranch Party.

*Delete as applicable   16   ISDA 1987

Representations of Party B

(1) *Payer Tax Representation.* For the purpose of Section 3(e), Party B will/will not* make the following representation:–

It is not required by any applicable law, as modified by the practice of any relevant governmental revenue authority, of any Relevant Jurisdiction to make any deduction or withholding for or on account of any Tax from any payment (other than interest under Section 2 (e)) to be made by it to the other party under this Agreement. In making this representation, it may rely on:–

(i) the accuracy of any representation made by the other party pursuant to Section 3(f);

(ii) the satisfaction of the agreement of the other party contained in Section 4(a)(i) and the accuracy and effectiveness of any document provided by the other party pursuant to Section 4(a)(i); and

(iii) the satisfaction of the agreement of the other party contained in Section 4(d).

(2) *Payee Tax Representations.* For the purpose of Section 3(f), Party B makes the representation(s) specified below:–

(a) The following representation will/will not* apply:–

It is fully eligible for the benefits of the "Business Profits" or "Industrial and Commercial Profits" provision, as the case may be, the "Interest" provision or the "Other Income" provision (if any) of the Specified Treaty with respect to any payment described in such provisions and received or to be received by it in connection with this Agreement and no such payment is attributable to a trade or business carried on by it through a permanent establishment in the Specified Jurisdiction.

If such representation applies, then:–

"Specified Treaty" means ....

"Specified Jurisdiction" means ....

(b) The following representation will/will not* apply:–

Each payment received or to be received by it in connection with this Agreement relates to the regular business operations of the party (and not to an investment of the party).

(c) The following representation will/will not* apply:–

Each payment received or to be received by it in connection with this Agreement will be effectively connected with its conduct of a trade or business in the Specified Jurisdiction.

If such representation applies, then *"Specified Jurisdiction"* means ....

(d) The following representation will/will not* apply:–

It is a bank recognised by the United Kingdom Inland Revenue as carrying on a bona fide banking business in the United Kingdom, is entering into this Agreement in the ordinary course of such business and will bring into account payments made and received under this Agreement in computing its income for United Kingdom tax purposes.

(e) Other representations:– ....

....

....

....

N.B. The above representations may need modification if either party is a Multibranch Party.

Part 3
Documents to be delivered

For the purpose of Section 4(a):–

(1) Tax forms, documents or certificates to be delivered are:–

Party required to deliver document	Form/Document/ Certificate	Date by which to be delivered
....	....	....
....	....	....
....	....	....
....	....	....
....	....	....

(2) Other documents to be delivered are:–

Party required to deliver document	Form/Document/ Certificate	Date by which to be delivered	Covered by Section 3(d) Representation
....	....	....	Yes/No*
....	....	....	Yes/No*
....	....	....	Yes/No*
....	....	....	Yes/No*
....	....	....	Yes/No*

Part 4

Miscellaneous

(1) *Governing Law.* This Agreement will be governed by and construed in accordance with English law/the laws of the State of New York without reference to choice of law doctrine*.

(2) *Process Agent.* For the purpose of Section 13(c):–

Party A appoints as its Process Agent ....

....

....

Party B appoints as its Process Agent ....

....

....

(3) *"Affiliate"* will have the meaning specified in Section 14 unless another meaning is specified here

....

....

* Delete as applicable   18   ISDA 1987

(4) *Multibranch Party*. For the purpose of Section 10:–

Party A is/is not* a Multibranch Party and, if so, may act through the following Offices:–

| .... | .... | .... |
| .... | .... | .... |

Party B is/is not* a Multibranch Party and, if so, may act through the following Offices:–

| .... | .... | .... |
| .... | .... | .... |

(5) *Addresses for Notices*. For the purpose of Section 12(a):–

Address for notices or communications to Party A:–

Address: ....

Attention: ....

Telex No: .... Answerback: ....

(For all purposes/only with respect to Swap Transactions through that Office*.)

Address for notices or communications to Party B:–

Address: ....

Attention: ....

Telex No: .... Answerback: ....

(For all purposes/only with respect to Swap Transactions through that Office*.)

(6) *Credit Support Document*. Details of any Credit Support Document:–

....

....

....

....

(7) *Netting of Payments*. If indicated here, ''Net Payments – Corresponding Payment Dates'' will apply for the purpose of Section 2(c) with effect from the date of this Agreement:– _____**

Part 5

Other Provisions

Printed by Financial Print & Communications Ltd **FPC**   6083

ISDA 1987

339

Index